"Here, There and Everywhere"

Salzburg Seminar books
address global
contemporary issues
in the arts, education,
business, law,
government, and science.

"Here, There and Everywhere"

The Foreign Politics of American Popular Culture

Reinhold Wagnleitner
and
Elaine Tyler May, editors

University Press of New England
Hanover and London

Salzburg Seminar

Published by University Press of New England, Hanover, NH 03755

Library of Congress Cataloging-in-Publication Data

"Here, there and everywhere" : the foreign politics of American popular culture / Reinhold Wagnleitner and Elaine Tyler May editors.
      p.   cm.
Includes bibliographical references.
ISBN 1–58465–034–6 (cl : alk. paper) — ISBN 1–58465–035–4 (pa: alk. paper)
   1. Americanization—Congresses. 2. Civilization, Modern—American influences—Congresses. 3. Popular culture—United States—Congresses. 4. Arts, American—Foreign countries—Congresses. 5. Arts, Modern—20th century—United States—Congresses. I. Wagnleitner, Reinhold, 1949–   II. May, Elaine Tyler.
E169.12 H495 2000
303.48'273—dc21   99–58012

For Elisabeth and Lary

Contents

Acknowledgments   xi

Reinhold Wagnleitner and Elaine Tyler May
Here, There, and Everywhere: Introduction   1

PART I   Background

John G. Blair
First Steps toward Globalization: Nineteenth-Century Exports of
American Entertainment Forms   17

James T. Campbell
The Americanization of South Africa   34

Oliver Schmidt
No Innocents Abroad: The Salzburg Impetus and American
Studies in Europe   64

PART II   The World of Hollywood

Theodore A. Wilson
Selling America via the Silver Screen? Efforts to Manage the
Projection of American Culture Abroad, 1942–1947   83

Aurora Bosch and M. Fernanda del Rincón
Dreams in a Dictatorship: Hollywood and Franco's Spain,
1939–1956   100

Giuliana Muscio
Invasion and Counterattack: Italian and American Film Relations
in the Postwar Period   116

Nosa Owens-Ibie
Programmed for Domination: U.S. Television Broadcasting and
Its Effects on Nigerian Culture   132

PART III Rock, Rap, and All That Jazz

Elizabeth Vihlen
Jammin' on the Champs-Elysées: Jazz, France, and the 1950s   149

Penny M. Von Eschen
"Satchmo Blows Up the World": Jazz, Race, and Empire during
the Cold War   163

Michael May
Swingin' under Stalin: Russian Jazz during the Cold War and
Beyond   179

Thomas Fuchs
Rock 'n' Roll in the German Democratic Republic, 1949–1961   192

Christoph Ribbat
How Hip Hop Hit Heidelberg: German Rappers, Rhymes,
and Rhythms   207

PART IV The Empire Strikes Back

Masako Notoji
Cultural Transformation of John Philip Sousa and Disneyland
in Japan   219

Myles Dungan and David Gray
Consumption of American Pop Culture in Ireland and England   227

Gülriz Büken
Backlash: An Argument against the Spread of American Popular
Culture in Turkey   242

Michael Ermarth
German Unification as Self-Inflicted Americanization: Critical
Views on the Course of Contemporary German Development   251

PART V Contemporary Issues

Rob Kroes
Advertising: The Commodification of American Icons of Freedom   273

J. Michael Jaffe and Gabriel Weimann
New Lords of the Global Village? Theories of Media Domination
in the Internet Era   288

Reinhold Wagnleitner
Encartafication or Emancipation: The Internet as the New
American Frontier?   309

Contributors   329

Index   333

Acknowledgments

We would like to thank the Salzburg Seminar for supporting this project from beginning to end. We also want to express our gratitude to Phil Pochoda, our editor at the University Press of New England, for all his enthusiasm and help along the way; and his assistant, April Ossmann, for all her efforts and good work. We are especially grateful to David Gray and Mary Strunk for their outstanding editorial assistance, to Dave Morice, and to the staff of the University Press of New England. Lastly, thanks to Elisabeth Wagnleitner and Lary May for sharing in our work, our discussions, our many visits, and for being with us here, there, and everywhere.

Reinhold Wagnleitner and Elaine Tyler May

Here, There, and Everywhere

Introduction

To almost any casual observer, it looks as though the popular culture of the United States of America has spread all over the world: here, there, and everywhere. From Argentina to Zaire, India to Nigeria, kids wear Levi's (and are even *called* "kids" in dozens of tongues); radios blare rap songs; television stations broadcast American programs dubbed in scores of languages; Hollywood movies dominate the world's screens; and McDonald's restaurants dot the landscape.[1] It could easily be argued that the products, icons, and myths of American popular culture represent the single most unifying and centripetal cultural force for the global triumph of the American Century. On the other hand, in many areas of the world, American cultural products are potentially among the most disruptive and centrifugal cultural forces of the twentieth century.[2]

Why, then, would the title of a book about American popular culture be drawn from the words of a song by the Beatles, a British group whose popularity spanned the globe as powerfully as any American cultural icon? The answer is clear: without the global diffusion of American popular culture, there would have been no Beatles. Influenced by American rhythm & blues and rock 'n' roll, four guys from Liverpool put together one of the most popular music groups of all time. Indeed, the fact that Liverpool was to become the capital of the pop universe in the early 1960s is quite revealing in itself. The Liverpudlians were exposed to such a large number of American sailors and soldiers—many of them African American—and their music precisely because of the global extension of the American empire as a result of the Second World War. And that cultural encounter also represented an ironic (and historically rather sad) form of poetic justice: after all, the port on the river Mersey had been one of the major centers of the slave trade. One could argue, therefore, that the blues only returned back home to one of its *original* sites. Clearly, the

1

Beatles are no exception to the power of American popular culture across the world; they are the proof. But one might ask, as this volume does, how *American*—at least in the apple pie sense—is American popular culture if many of those who created its most popular forms were the underdogs and outsiders in America? And what makes these forms of popular culture *American* if those who consumed and reproduced them in other countries could make them their own?

The idea for this book emerged at the Salzburg Seminar, during a session entitled "The Globalization of American Popular Culture."[3] It was a fitting setting to take on such a topic. A lively group of people from all over the world, and from all walks of life, gathered in the splendid halls of the Schloss Leopoldskron, a dazzling castle perched by a lake in Salzburg, Austria. The history of the Salzburg Seminar itself touches somewhat on the theme of this book. In 1947, a small group of Harvard academics, graduate students and faculty decided to launch an experiment in intellectual exchange out of the rubble of war-torn Europe. The idea was to bring together people from the formerly warring parties to expose them to American intellectual and artistic developments from which they had been cut off for more than a decade, transcending the bitter experiences of the recent past. The setting was ideal: a castle that had once belonged to the Salzburg Prince-Archbishops was purchased by the Austro-German-Jewish theater wizard, entrepreneur and co-founder of the Salzburg Festival, Max Reinhardt, who was married to the theater star Helene Thimig. During the interwar period, the Schloss and its picturesque park became the natural setting for some of Reinhardt's most beautiful productions. When the German army invaded Austria in 1938, the couple fled to the United States. The Nazis transformed Schloss Leopoldskron into a recreation center for army and SS officers during the Second World War.

After the war, the widowed actress—Reinhardt had died in exile in the United States—opened the castle to idealistic young scholars, and seminars gathering together intellectuals from all over the world have taken place there ever since. As part of its colorful history, the Schloss became a central icon of American popular culture when it was used as the setting for the film version of the musical *The Sound of Music*, a Hollywood movie about the Von Trapp family's escape from encroaching Nazism. One might argue, then (as Oliver Schmidt does in his essay in this collection), that the Salzburg Seminar itself represents one example of the globalization of American culture. After all, it had been named the Salzburg Seminar in American Studies, and the entrenchment of American Studies as an important new academic discipline was one of the priorities of the cultural Cold War.

But in the gilded halls of the Schloss, participants at our Seminar immediately began to question the entire idea of the "globalization of

American popular culture." Did the title of the seminar imply some deliberate scheme on the part of American culture brokers to colonize the world with American political ideas and material goods? Did people in the countries where these cultural products arrived simply roll over and play dead in the face of the massive power of American mass media? Alternatively, did the audiences and consumers in the importing countries accept American movies, music, consumer goods, television programs, clothes, and fast food because they matched and fit local trends and desires? Did receiving communities transform these products to fit their own needs, to the point where they were no longer "American" but in fact became indigenous? And who was in charge of all of this, anyway? Was it Wall Street, Madison Avenue, the Pentagon, the CIA, or Hollywood? Or was it, at least partly, local economic and political elites in the receiving countries? Was it the World Trade Organization (WTO)? Or was it simply "the people," nationalities be damned?

In a lively week, these issues were debated in impassioned arguments during full days of workshops, and long into the night in the *Bierstube*, over pints of Austrian beer, guitars strumming popular American and European songs, drunken sing-alongs in a multitude of languages, and dances to all sorts of music from waltzes to rock 'n' roll. In the end, there was no consensus. Globalization could mean many different things, and what was American about global popular culture was still open to debate. Meanwhile, new friendships were forged across national boundaries, even though some of the participants from former Soviet republics still believed that the whole enterprise was secretly funded by the CIA.

Participants at the Salzburg Seminar were not all scholars and academics. In fact, most were not. The group included political leaders, artists and writers, journalists, teachers, students, diplomats, civil servants, and entrepreneurs. They brought to the discussion their experiences, their knowledge, and their passions. In this volume we have tried to preserve as much of the spirit of the gathering as possible, including a wide range of essays, from broad theoretical overviews to particular case studies. The collection contains an eclectic mix of articles about the impact of American cultural products on particular localities. Some express the attitudes and passions of the writers themselves and are not meant to be examples of scholarly objectivity. But they reflect the strong impressions and emotions that can be evoked by the presence of American popular culture abroad; and they convey some of the flavor of the discussions and debates at the seminar itself.

The co-editors bring very different perspectives to this project as well. Reinhold Wagnleitner is an Austrian historian who has studied extensively the influence of American popular culture in Europe. As a longtime bass guitarist in rock 'n' roll and jazz bands, he is both a scholar and practitioner of American popular culture. Elaine Tyler May is an American historian whose work is primarily concerned with the internal workings of American culture, and how the nation's international entanglements have influenced the development of its domestic culture. Both have been Fulbright lecturers: May as a carrier of American culture from the United States to Ireland; Wagnleitner as a carrier of American culture from Austria to the United States. That fact alone speaks to the complex patterns of call and response embedded in the American cultural presence around the world.

Our collaboration on this project has included many heated discussions, reflecting and continuing the debates at the Seminar. We have argued over Big Macs and beer (!) at a McDonald's drive-in in Salzburg (fully decorated with pictures of violins), conferred in an Irish pub in Warsaw, brainstormed over fish and chips in Dublin, hollered over country and western ballads at a Tex-Mex joint at the Mall of America in Minnesota, and deliberated over Greek cuisine in New Orleans. Our travels and travails have proven to us that cultural exports flow in many directions.

This collection is part of a growing literature on the influence of American culture abroad. In recent years the topic has captured the attention of scholars in fields ranging from diplomatic history to cultural studies.[4] Many books have been published on the topic, and many more are in progress. One of the recent titles perfectly illustrates the extreme political and ideological scope of the debate: *Americanisation and the Transformation of World Cultures: Melting Pot or Cultural Chernobyl?*[5]

For more than a century, the increasing impact of American popular cultural products at home and abroad sparked heated debates. On one side were those who defended the presumed virtues of "traditional culture" against the corruptions of "modern civilization." On the other side were those who promoted American popular culture as the expression of freedom, democracy, and liberation in the face of worn-out conventions, hierarchies, and artificial boundaries between groups and classes. In this vein, historian Frank Ninkovich argues that American cultural relations with foreign countries are not only antitraditional but also anticultural.[6]

In the late nineteenth century, English critics set the tone for the debate by predicting the eventual demise of high culture that had been inseparably bound to the domination of the aristocracy and grand bourgeoisie. These critics predicted the replacement of fine art and authentic folk culture by tasteless industrialized artifacts produced on a mass scale in order to satisfy the lowest common denominator. Mass culture, in their opinion, represented the cultural equivalent of the politics of mob rule, of democracy run amok.[7]

World War I served to heighten the debate. Millions of Americans came to Europe as soldiers, businessmen, investors, artists, missionaries, and cultural brokers of various sorts.[8] The political, social, economic, and cultural implications of the Great War amounted to a watershed in the relations between the old world and the new. Europe's major powers, which had colonized much of the world and exposed ancient societies to European cultural hegemony, were now experiencing an equally dramatic loss of power and tradition. Europe, once the center, was now pushed to the periphery by its former colony, the United States. No matter how isolationist U.S. foreign policy appeared during the years between the wars, isolationism hardly existed in the realm of economics and was completely absent in regard to culture.[9] American music and film, stars and crazes, heroes and villains captured the attention of European audiences and conquered the consciousness of much of the youth.[10]

The massive wave of American cultural products flooding Europe brought tremendous opposition in its wake. Many experienced it as a cultural invasion of unprecedented proportions. Along with the traditional objections to the United States as a cultural upstart, the most vociferous complaints now came from the far right as well as the far left of the political spectrum. Few commentators doubted that the American experience represented the essence of modernity, the model for the future. The question remained whether it augured the dream of plenty or the nightmare of conformity.[11]

For the political right, American popular culture was the epitome of the inauthentic, the impure, the artificial, and the degenerate. Since African-Americans produced much of popular music, and Jewish immigrants created the movies, their cultural products were associated with decadence and racial mixing. European conservatives and fascists portrayed Americans as mindless and inferior slaves of conformity who had lost the essence of Anglo-Saxon racial purity and the culture of *the folk*. Presumably, a small ruling class of plutocrats was able to exploit the American masses who worked and consumed in tune with the cacophony of the machine age and squandered their leisure time dancing to "jungle" rhythms.[12] Needless to say, these notions were carried to the extreme by the German Nazis in their hatred of anything black or Jewish.

On the left, the United States had long been associated with progress. Yet the power of its gigantic corporations and financial empires, the problematic treatment of labor and minorities, the huge dislocation and impoverishment of large groups of the population, as well as the general disillusionment with capitalism as a result of the Great Depression, all contributed to the identification of America with the brutal exploitation of workers and the excesses of uncontrolled capitalism. In short, for the European right wing, American popular culture suggested *"racial impurity,"* and for the left it evoked *class exploitation.*

World War II, which for many European and Japanese fascists was not only a military struggle but also a crusade against degenerate Western culture, moved this fight for cultural supremacy onto the global arena.[13] The Allied military victory was not paralleled by an Allied cultural victory. Neither Britain nor France had the economic resources to compete in the modern culture wars. While communist economics and politics held their attractions for considerable minorities in countries around the world, communist popular culture was a losing proposition. Under those circumstances, American popular culture reigned supreme.

During and after the war, the United States government established bridgeheads for American popular culture in those areas where it had been cut off by the advances of the German and Japanese armies since the thirties. The Cold War intensified the political meanings and economic implications of the spread of American popular culture. Arts, music, and movies were among the most important exports that linked American capitalism to freedom of expression, consumerism, and the good life.[14] But the hegemony of American popular culture remained contested throughout the years of the Cold War because critics in countries around the world saw it as propaganda used to promote American cultural imperialism, political interests, and the expansion of corporate capitalism.[15] After the official end of the Cold War, the last barriers against the global extension of markets for American cultural and material products came down. It remains to be seen whether the enduring resistance to American popular culture will eventually evaporate, or whether it will take on new life as other cultural forms vie for hegemony in the new global marketplace.[16]

This volume extends the debate over American cultural hegemony by providing a unique collection of essays written by observers from many different countries. It thus reflects the concerns that emerged at the Salzburg Seminar. The contributors included here also represent the general demographic makeup of the seminar participants. Most were from Europe; a few were from Asia, Africa, and the Middle East. Most were men, but there was a strong representation of women. Most were teachers and professionals, but many were students. We have tried to include as many of these voices in this collection as possible. Many of the contributors were present at the seminar itself; all of the essays engage and express the issues debated and discussed there.

We have divided the volume into five parts. Part I, Background, contains essays that cover historical and theoretical issues. John Blair examines the nineteenth and early-twentieth century export of American popular culture, particularly blackface minstrel and Wild West shows. His essay illustrates how these early forms of popular culture established the centrality of race in American cultural exports. Blair demonstrates that these shows, created by whites, carried powerful racial stereotypes. The essay also shows how audiences brought their own readings and interpretations to these productions. Even in this early phase of the spreading of American popular culture, the empire of race became encoded in entertainment. James T. Campbell, looking specifically at South Africa, traces the long-term impact of the United States there. While the Dutch and English established formal colonial structures of power, the Americans provided an informal economic and cultural colonial overlay that extended from the late nineteenth century to the present. Oliver Schmidt provides an analysis of the Salzburg Seminar itself, as an example of the complex relationship between culture and politics during the early Cold War.[17]

Part II, The World of Hollywood, focuses on the impact of Hollywood, the prime educational institution of the twentieth century on a global scale, through movies, television, videos, and the Internet.[18] The essays in this section show the complex ways in which American propaganda efforts during World War II and the Cold War fit uneasily with the cultural politics emerging in other countries. Theodore A. Wilson explores film censorship and propaganda in the policies of the U.S. Office of War Information during the war. Following the example of the Creel Commission in the final years of World War I, the struggle against the axis powers prompted an intimate collaboration between Washington and Hollywood that was to continue, albeit on a more informal basis, throughout the Cold War.[19] Aurora Bosch and M. Fernanda del Rincón look at the reception of American movies in post–Civil War Spain. "Decadent" American films (especially in their depiction of independent, glamorous, and scantily clad women) competed successfully against the Spanish film industry, which produced "authentic" and "virtuous" local films, even when the Spanish offerings were scripted by dictator Generalissimo Franco himself. As in the United States, the portrayal of women, in terms of sexuality and gender relations, sparked heated debates.[20] Giuliana Muscio looks at the impact of the American cinema in postwar Italy.[21] The Italian fascists took Hollywood very seriously and countered it by founding their own cinema city, Cinecittà. Ironically, Cinecittà became a safe haven immediately after the war for quite a different brand of cinema artists: American leftist actors, writers, and producers who had been branded as un-American by anticommunist government investigators.[22] These blacklisted artists found political refuge in this former fascist cinema factory, and thereby transformed it into the most important economic outpost of Hollywood in Europe. At the same time, the Italian film industry was able to revitalize itself in the face of American competition. Nosa Owens-Ibie brings the discussion into the realm of television, examining the economic and cultural power of American programming in Nigeria.

Part III, Rock, Rap, and All That Jazz, focuses on popular music. Elizabeth Vihlen examines the cultural politics of jazz in postwar France. Vihlen points out that French intellectuals and artists (most of them on the left) were the main enthusiasts and theoreticians of jazz and other American cultural products in Europe in the first half of the twentieth century. At the same time, they were also the avant-garde of European criticism of American capitalism as the prime root of modern alienation. They were drawn to jazz not only aesthetically but also politically, because of its origins among outsiders to American capitalism, and because it represented an anticolonial artistic expression. Although African American artists welcomed the support of the French leftists against American racism and exploitation, Vihlen demonstrates that many French jazz enthusiasts harbored their own brand of racial essentializing. Penny M. von Eschen takes us back to Africa in the company of some of the most important African American jazz musicians.[23] The State Department sponsored jazz tours in order to further American Cold War aims. Ironically, the artists showcased abroad often had to enter concert halls in the United States through the back doors. Nevertheless, these tours helped promote the message that American race relations at home, if not perfect, were improving. Michael May examines Russian jazz, a hybrid of American and Russian influences that was sometimes celebrated, and sometimes repressed, in the Soviet Union.[24] His interviews with a number of jazz artists suggest that the story of jazz in Russia during the Cold War and beyond is open to a wide range of interpretations.

Thomas Fuchs analyzes another cultural paradox of the Cold War, manifest not only in Germany but also in many other societies, including the United States.[25] The capitalist and conservative West German elites had little in common with the communist leaders of East Germany, their deep division finally taking shape in the Berlin Wall. Yet one common enemy remained: American rock 'n' roll. This music attracted the rebellious young not only because of its intrinsic excitement, but also because it offended adults on the right, who called it "the devil's music," as well as those on the left, who denounced it as a sonic weapon of capitalist subversion.[26] Christoph Ribbat follows this analysis with an exploration of the cultural and political implications of multiethnic rap in unified Germany during the 1990s. As in American ghettos, hip hop in Germany provides newscasts from the underside. In the German case we hear the shouts of dissent uttered by representatives of millions of German-born children of foreign workers, mostly, but not exclusively, from Turkey and former Yugoslavia.[27]

Part IV, The Empire Strikes Back, includes observations and personal expressions of authors with very different opinions about the impact and reception of American cultural products in their countries. Masako Notoji remarks on the unique ways in which Japan takes American originals, such as John Philip Sousa's music and Disneyland, and makes them its own. Myles Dungan and David Gray discuss the enthusiasm—as well as the disdain—for American pop culture in their respective countries, Ireland and England. Gülriz Büken expresses her passionate dislike of American culture and what she sees as its devastating influence on the traditional values of Turkey. Michael Ermarth provides an in-depth look at Germany, where the political and philosophical debates over American influence (Amerikanismus) have raged since the end of the nineteenth century and, in particular, since reunification. While the German right has established itself as the vanguard of racist European anti-Americanism, the German left as well has resisted the cultural influence of the United States.[28]

Part V, Contemporary Issues, illuminates a number of current concerns about the global power of American cultural products. Rob Kroes illustrates how the idea of American freedom, embodied in product images, becomes something different in the cultural context of the Netherlands. He shows that what America sells best is America itself, although what is sold is not necessarily American at all.[29] J. Michael Jaffe and Gabriel Weimann examine the global powers of the new media lords, some of them, but by no means all, American. They offer a forward-looking analysis of the question of globalization as media domination, from Hollywood to the Internet. Finally, Reinhold Wagnleitner looks back to the future of the Internet with his examination of the potential of cyberspace to transcend national boundaries and cultures. He argues that the struggle for power over the Web, like the contest over the control of popular culture, is characterized by the conflict between public space and private corporate control.

According to the German cultural anthropologists Joana Breidenbach and Ina Zukrigl, the *global* in global culture has to be understood as a global system of references.[30] And the Internet has become the medium that allows a worldwide dialogue. But "globalization" will not necessarily lead to a global cultural meltdown. Anthropological research has shown that, while many communication structures have become global, they are filled with different meanings in different situations. To understand the contours and limits of a global culture, we must also recognize resistance to hegemonic influences, as well as the appropriation or localization of imported ideas, goods, and institutions. The cultural mélange created by *creolization* or hybridization rests on "structures of common difference."[31]

New cultural forms may constitute something quite original and become more than simply the sum of tradition plus foreign influence.[32] The new global hegemony will be one of structure, not of content. It remains to be seen whether cultural flow will lead to an increase or a decrease of cultural fundamentalism, and whether the growth of a comparative consciousness will strengthen *globocentrism* or *ethnocentrism*.[33]

The essays in this collection confront the intriguing question of why the popular culture of one country has spread so rapidly and captured the imagination of peoples around the world. For better or for worse, this reality cannot be denied. One explanation for the power of American popular culture is the very diversity of American society. Another is the might of American capitalism. Whatever the engine of this diffusion, it is clear that American cultural products change their meanings whenever they cross international borders. Many of the contributors to this volume provide concrete examples from their own countries where American cultural products have taken hold. They offer both empirical data and personal perspectives that anchor the global theoretical debates in local case studies. We do not expect this volume to resolve all debates; but we hope that it will raise some new questions and provide a bit more than just some fast food for thought.

Notes

1. Reinhold Wagnleitner, "The Empire of the Fun, or Talkin' Soviet Union Blues: The Sound of Freedom and U.S. Cultural Hegemony in Europe" in *Diplomatic History* 23, no. 3 (Summer 1999): 499–524.

2. George Ritzer, *The McDonaldization of Society: An Investigation into the Changing Character of Contemporary Social Life* (Newbury Park, Calif., 1995); Simon Frith, *Sound Effects. Youth, Leisure and the Politics of Rock 'n' Roll* (New York, 1978).

3. *http://www.salsem.ac.at/*

4. See most recently Edward Said, *Culture and Imperialism* (New York, 1994); Arjun Apadurai, *Modernity at Large: Cultural Dimensions of Globalization* (Minneapolis, 1996); Frederic Jameson and Masao Miyoshi (eds), *The Cultures of Globalization* (Durham, N.C., London, 1998); Saskia Sassen and Kwame Anthony Appiah, *Globalization and Its Discontents* (New York, 1998); Anthony D. King, ed., *Culture, Globalization and the World-System: Contemporary Conditions for the Representation of Identity* (Minneapolis, 1997); Ann Cvetkovich and Douglas Kellner, *Articulating the Global and the Local: Globalization and Cultural Studies* (Boulder, Colo., 1997); Akira Iriye, *Cultural Internationalism*

and World Order (Albert Shaw Memorial Lectures) (Baltimore, Md., 1997); John Tomlinson, *Cultural Imperialism* (Baltimore, 1991); *Globalization/Localization: Paradoxes of Cultural Identity. Special issue focaal. Tijdschrift voor antropologie* 30–31 (1997); Pierre Bourdieu, *Acts of Resistance: Against the Tyranny of the Market* (New York, 1999); Don Kalb, et al., *The Ends of Globalization: Bringing Society Back In* (Boulder, London, 1999); John Tomlinson, *Globalization and Culture* (Chicago, London, 1999).

5. Edwin Mellen Press, 1996 edited by Philip H. Melling and Jon Roper.

6. Frank Ninkovich, "The Trajectory of Cultural Internationalism," in Joyce K. Kallgren and Dennis Fred Simon, eds., *Educational Exchanges: Essays on the Sino-American Experience* (Berkeley, Calif., 1987).

7. Matthew Arnold, *Civilization in the United States* (London, 1888); Rob Kroes, *If You've Seen One, You've Seen the Mall: Europeans and American Mass Culture* (Chicago, 1997); C. Vann Woodward, *The Old World's New World* (New York, 1991); Richard Ruland, *America in Modern European Literature: From Image to Metaphor* (New York, 1976); John Martin Evans, *America: The View from Europe* (New York, 1976).

8. Emily S. Rosenberg, *Financial Missionaries to the World: The Politics and Culture of Dollar Diplomacy, 1900–1930* (Cambridge, Mass., 1999); Emily S. Rosenberg, *Spreading the American Dream: American Economic and Cultural Expansion, 1890–1945* (New York, 1982); Frank Costigliola, *Awkward Dominion: American Political, Economic, and Cultural Relations with Europe, 1919–1933* (Ithaca, N.Y., 1984)

9. Richard Maltby, *Passing Parade: A History of Popular Culture in the Twentieth Century* (Oxford, New York, 1989); Akira Iriye, *The Globalizing of America, 1913–1945* (Cambridge, Mass., 1995).

10. Victoria deGrazia, "Mass Culture and Sovereignty. The American Challenge to European Cinemas, 1920–1960," *Journal of Modern History* 61 (1989): 53–87.

11. Reinhold Wagnleitner, *Coca-Colonization and the Cold War: The Cultural Mission of the United States in Austria after the Second World War* (Chapel Hill, N.C., London, 1994).

12. Adolf Halfeld, *Amerika und der Amerikanismus* (Jena, 1928).

13. Frank Ninkovich, *The Diplomacy of Ideas: U.S. Foreign Policy and Cultural Relations, 1938–1950* (Cambridge, Mass., 1981); Allan M. Winkler, *The Politics of Propaganda: The Office of War Information, 1942–1945* (New Haven, Conn., 1978); Morrell Heald and Lawrence S. Kaplan, *Culture and Diplomacy: The American Experience* (Westport, Conn., 1977); Akira Iriye, *Power and Culture* (Cambridge, Mass., 1982).

14. Lary May, "Made for Export: Hollywood and the Creation of Cold War Americanism, 1940–1958," in John G. Blair and Reinhold Wagnleitner, eds., *Empire: American Studies* (Tuebingen, 1997): 91–121.

15. Wagnleitner, *Coca-Colonization and The Cold War*; Kyoko Hirano, *Mr Smith Goes to Tokyo. Japanese Cinema Under the American Occupation, 1945–1952* (Washington, D.C., 1992); Richard Kuisel, *Seducing the French. The Dilemma of Americanization* (Berkeley, Calif., 1993); Ralph Willett, *The Americanization of Germany, 1945–1949* (London, 1989); Roger Rollin, ed., *The Americanization of the Global Village: Essays in Comparative Popular Culture* (Bowling Green, 1989); Timothy Ryback, *Rock Around the Bloc: A History of Rock Music in Eastern Europe and the Soviet Union* (New York, 1990); Steven

F. White, *Progressive Renaissance: America and the Reconstruction of Italian Education, 1943–1962* (New York, 1991); Nicholas Haiducek, *Japanese Education: Made in the U.S.A.* (New York, 1991); Rob Kroes, Robert W. Rydell, and Doeko F. J. Bosscher, eds., *Cultural Transmissions and Receptions: American Mass Culture in Europe* (Amsterdam, 1993); Richard P. Horwitz, ed., *Exporting America: Essays on American Studies Abroad* (New York, 1993); David H. Flaherty and Frank E. Manning, eds., *The Beaver Bites Back? American Popular Culture in Canada* (Montreal, 1993); Mel van Elteren, *Imagining America. Dutch Youth and Its Sense of Place* (Tilburg, 1994); Scott Shane, *Dismantling the Iron Curtain: How Information Ended the Soviet Union* (Chicago, 1994); Edward Larkey, *Pungent Sounds. Constructing Identity with Popular Music in Austria* (New York, 1993); Peter Duignan and Lewis H. Gann, *The Rebirth of the West: The Americanization of the Democratic World, 1945–1958* (Lanham, Md., 1996); Walter L. Hixson, *Parting the Curtain: Propaganda, Culture, and the Cold War, 1954–1961* (New York, 1997); Richard F. Pells, *Not Like US: How Europeans Loved, Hated and Transformed American Culture Since World War II* (New York, 1997); Mike-Frank G. Epitropoulos and Victor Roudometof, eds., *American Culture in Europe* (Westport, Conn., 1998); Gilbert M. Joseph, Catherine C. Legrand, and Ricardo D. Salvatore, eds., *Close Encounters of Empire: Writing the Cultural History of U.S.–Latin American Relations* (Durham, N.C., London, 1998); Gerd Gemunden, *Framed Visions: Popular Culture, Americanization, and the Contemporary German and Austrian Imagination* (Ann Arbor, Mich., 1999); David F. Good and Ruth Wodak, eds., *From World War to Waldheim: Culture and Politics in Austria and the United States* (New York, Oxford, 1999).

16. Annemoon van Hemel, Hans Mommaas, and Cas Smithuijsen, eds., *Trading Culture: GATT, European Cultural Policies and the Transatlantic Market* (Amsterdam, 1996).

17. Thomas H. Eliot and Lois J. Eliot, *Salzburg Seminar: First Forty Years* (Ipswich, 1987); F. O. Matthiessen, *From the Heart of Europe* (New York, 1948), *http://www.salsem.ac.at/csacl/hist/FIVE.HTM.*

18. David Puttnam, *The Undeclared War: The Struggle for Control of the World's Film Industry* (London, 1997); David F. Ellwood and Rob Kroes, eds., *Hollywood in Europe: Experiences of a Cultural Hegemony* (Amsterdam, 1994).

19. Gore Vidal, *Hollywood: A Novel of America in the 1920s* (New York, 1999).

20. International relations and gender relations are still a fairly novel field. See Cynthia Enloe, *Bananas, Beaches, and Bases. Making Feminist Sense of International Politics* (Berkeley, Calif., 1990); Sherma B. Gluck, *Rosie the Riveter Revisited. Woman, the War, and Social Change* (Boston, 1987); Marc Hillel, *Die Invasion der Be-Freier* [The Invasion of Liberators and Suitors] (Bergisch Gladbach, 1983); Elaine Tyler May, *Homeward Bound: American Families in the Cold War Era* (New York, 1988); Sibylle Meyer and Eva Schulze, *Von Liebe sprach damals keiner: Familienalltag in der Nachkriegszeit* [Nobody Spoke About Love Then: Everyday Life of Families in the Postwar Period] (Munich, 1985), and *Perlonzeit: Wie Frauen ihr Wirtschaftswunder erlebten* [Plastic Time: How Women Experienced the Economic Miracle] (Berlin, 1986); Heike Sander and Barbara Johr, eds., *BeFreier und Befreite. Krieg, Vergewaltigungen, Kinder* [Liberators, Rapists and Liberated: War, Rape, Children] (Munich, 1992); Elisabeth Wilson, *Only Halfway to Paradise. Women in Postwar Britain, 1945–1948* (London, 1980); Ingrid Bauer, "'Austria's Prestige Dragged Into the Dirt?' The GI-Brides and

Postwar Austrian Society (1945–1955)," *Contemporary Austrian Studies* 6 (1998): 41–55; Ingrid Bauer, ed., *Welcome Ami Go Home: Die amerikanische Besatzung in Salzburg 1945–1955* (Salzburg, 1998); Ingrid Bauer, "The GI-Bride—On the (De)Construction of an Austrian Postwar Stereotype," in Irene Bandhauer-Schöffmann and Claire Duchen, eds., *When the War Was Over: Women, War and Peace in Europe 1944–1950* (London, forthcoming); Emily S. Rosenberg, "Consuming Women: Images of Americanization in the American Century," *Diplomatic History* 23, no. 3 (Summer 1999): 479–97.

21. David W. Ellwood, *Italy, 1943–1945 (Politics of Liberation)* (London, 1985); David W. Ellwood, *Rebuilding Europe: Western Europe, America and Postwar Reconstruction* (London, 1992); Christopher Duggan and Christopher Wagstaff, eds., *Italy in the Cold War: Politics, Culture and Society, 1948–1958* (Oxford, Washington, D.C., 1995).

22. Patrick McGilligan, Paul Buhle, Alison Morley (photographer), and Willi Winburn, *Tender Comrades: A Backstory of the Hollywood Blacklist* (New York, 1997).

23. Penny M. Von Eschen, *Race Against Empire: Black Americans and Anti-colonialism, 1937–1957* (Ithaca, N.Y., 1997).

24. S. Frederick Starr, *Red and Hot: The Fate of Jazz in the Soviet Union, 1917–1980* (New York, 1983); Elliot Bratton, "The Sound of Freedom: Jazz and the Cold War. Part One: The Trick Bag," *Crisis* (February/March 1998): 14–19.

25. Tony Bennett, Simon Frith, and Lawrence Grossberg, *Rock and Popular Music: Politics, Policies, Institutions* (New York and London, 1993).

26. Peter Wicke, *Rock Music: Culture, Aesthetics, and Sociology* (Cambridge, U.K., 1990); Peter Wicke and Lothar Müller, *Rockmusik und Politik* (Berlin, 1995).

27. David Toop, *Rap Attack 2: African Rap to Global Hip Hop* (London and New York, 1992).

28. Dieter Dettke, ed., *The Challenge of Globalization for Germany's Social Democracy: A Policy Agenda for the Twenty-First Century* (New York, Oxford, 1998).

29. See also Rob Kroes, "American Empire and Cultural Imperialism," in *Diplomatic History* 23, no. 3 (Summer 1999): 463–77.

30. Joana Breidenbach and Ina Zukrigl, *Tanz der Kulturen. Kulturelle Identität in einer globalisierten Welt* (München, 1998).

31. Richard R. Wilk, *Economies and Cultures: Foundations of Economic Anthropology* (Boulder, Colo., 1996).

32. Daniel Miller, ed., *Material Cultures: Why Some Things Matter* (Chicago, London, 1998).

33. One of the most interesting discussions is monitored by Gerhard Haupt from the House of World Cultures in Berlin, "Cultural Exchange Via Internet," *http://www.hkw.de/forum/forum1/english.html*.

1 Background

John G. Blair

First Steps toward Globalization

Nineteenth-Century Exports of American

Entertainment Forms

We have something to learn about contemporary globalization issues by turning the clock back a century and more. To people around the world who express anxiety about the cultural hegemony they see implicit in all-too-successful exports of American popular culture, the powerful contemporary media themselves (film, television, the Internet) seem so "American" as to constitute a cultural Trojan horse threatening to breach the defenses of cultures naive or "weak" enough to accept such imports. Such a statement obviously exaggerates the fears, but there are real issues to be debated. I examine here the earliest American entertainment forms that succeeded outside the United States. By focusing on a time when modern media did not even exist, we can begin to separate out what cultural factors affect the processes of acceptance and adaptation. Cultural exports of this sort are not simply shipped out at random; they arrive in specific cultures at specific times. Bi-national factors that may vary profoundly from one time and place to another affect the ways and the degrees to which any given cultural product takes hold and why.

The exemplary nineteenth-century instances involve two distinct entertainment forms and time frames. The first came to be known by mid-century as "blackface minstrels." The form began in New York in the early 1830s and quickly enjoyed equal success in London, launching a genre that was to flourish for decades. By the 1850s blackface-minstrel companies were performing all over the English-speaking world, including Australia and even South Africa. In contrast, all attempts to export minstrelsy to the continent of Europe failed, for differing reasons in different countries. My first test case, then, constitutes an exportation from the United States to the larger English-language world.

My second instance is Buffalo Bill's Wild West, an action-packed, proto-rodeo history pageant that flourished for three decades starting in 1883. Here the range of successful exportation was the Western world in its entirety (including Australia, which was visited by Buffalo Bill's competitors, though not by his own troupe). What permitted the wider range of acceptance was the downplaying of language-based entertainment in favor of horse-driven action depicting a civilization-scale triumph of Western humanity over the "primitive" nonwhite peoples of the world. The particular setting of this global confrontation was, of course, the American Great Plains, represented by real cowboys and authentic Indians (i.e., not white actors in costume). As became inescapably clear when "Buffalo Bill" Cody had his troupe act out the Boxer Rebellion conflict at the Battle of Tianjin in his 1901 season, his Indians by this time could stand in for the universal losers of colonial battles anywhere on earth (see chapter appendix).

I. Blackface Minstrels: From Innovation to Exportation

The differences in cultural reception of exported entertainments help to define the original American characteristics as well as to highlight characteristics of the importing culture. Blackface entertainment started with solo song-and-dance routines in the 1830s and developed into ensemble performances in the 1840s. In the beginning, audiences in the British Isles and the United States responded to virtually the same performances by the same performers; spectators were everywhere enthusiastic, but on opposite sides of the Atlantic they responded quite differently to the burlesquing of blacks and black subculture.

In the United States blackface minstrels flourished in American cities and towns, particularly in the North; their heyday lasted from the 1840s through the 1880s, the period when a whole evening of entertainment was assured by a company of performers in blackface.[1] Prior to and after that time blackface acts appeared as part of variety or vaudeville programs, extending up to World War II in the United States and much beyond in the United Kingdom.[2] By definition, the original performers were white (in fact most were Irish-Americans), who blackened their faces with burnt cork.[3] In doing so, they generated a new and complex representation of race suitable to northern cities in the decades preceding the Civil War. In New York, for example, the very last slaves became free in the 1820s, but few whites could imagine them as "belonging" in any sense. Ostensibly the blackface conventions served merely to elicit raucous laughter, but in the process they articulated a new sense of "white" as distinct from the laughably inferior "black." As Eric Lott points out, the new entertainment conventions "minstrelized racial encounters into imitative entertainments that were homologous with northern racial feeling."[4] Blackface, as Lott says, "reifies and at the same time trespasses on the boundaries of 'race.'"[5] Minstrel performers claimed to imitate plantation life authentically, but their audiences had no exposure to actual slave conditions and thus no ground from which to resist the farcical character types offered them.

The first blackface character was named Jim Crow. If "Jim Crow" means to us now a complex of laws and practices segregating black Americans from whites, formally sanctioned by the 1896 Supreme Court decision *Plessy v. Ferguson*, we must go back two-thirds of a century. Though the precise origins of blackface performance disappear into anecdote, by the 1830s Thomas Dartmouth Rice hit it big with his impersonation of "Jim Crow" as a pseudo-plantation slave. His raggle-taggle costume (tattered pants, oversize shoes with gaping holes) may have made him seem clownishly pitiful, but his rambling ballad narrative recounts fighting and drinking and encounters with women that echo white folklore figures like the Mississippi flatboatman Mike Fink. The "Jim Crow" figure not only had a rollicking ballad to sing but a vigorous and startling dance unrelated to standard reels and square-dance figures. This dance, like all the others it spawned, involved exaggerated, unnatural contortions as part of its appeal. Hans Nathan, as part of his recuperation of the blackface archive, summarizes the dance itself:

Rice, according to his own words, wheeled, turned, and jumped. In windmill fashion, he rolled his body lazily from one side to the other, throwing his weight alternately on the heel of one foot and on the toes of the other. Gradually, he must have turned away from his audience, and, on the words "jis so," jumped high up and back into his initial position.[6]

Reviews make it clear that Rice carefully varied his movements and his words so that each verse seemed to offer something new—no mean accomplishment when he might be called for dozens of encores.[7] This was a spectacular act, well suited for the growing urban populations of Jacksonian America. The primary audience, all studies agree, was young, male, and working-class—hence the appeal of the hard-drinking boastfulness of Jim Crow. The language was loaded with bombast or malapropisms. Nothing that took place in blackface seemed serious. Jim Crow is a dressed-down figure of fun, a dancing fool, a self-satirizing nobadaddy, a model for multiple generations of laughable black stereotypes.

In England, by contrast, blackface took on a more top-down appeal. In the 1840s, the Virginia Serenaders became the first four-man troupe to offer a full evening's entertainment in blackface, dressed in full concert regalia with wing collars and tails, which helped them attract packed houses patronized by socially prominent individuals. The initial appeal in 1843 is clear from a London *Times* review:

The spectators and auditors of the wonders exhibited at this theatre have during the week been amused by what is called an Ethiopian concert, by four Virginian minstrels, in which some of the aboriginal airs of the interior of Africa, modernized if not humanized in the slave states of the Union, and adapted to ears polite, have been introduced by the musical conductor of the theatre. . . . The performance itself has great merit and is characteristic and peculiar. (26 June 1843)

This contextualization of minstrelsy could not be imagined in the United States, where Africa interested only a few missionary groups. Ethnocentrism does its work on cultural importations so thoroughly that each culture assimilates the genre to its own preoccupations. The British by this twist could have it both ways, incidentally confirming their superiority to the Americans by viewing the latter as merely a half-way station between Africa and polite civilization. The reference to "slave states of the union" was, of course, total fantasy, since the minstrels had only the most distant and stereotypical ties with plantations and the life of slaves. Exoticism ruled the day on both sides of the Atlantic.

In 1846, this group of performers, now grown to five and reborn as the "Ethiopian Serenaders," issued in London an extraordinary promotional brochure of thirty pages, a copy of which is preserved in the Harvard Theatre Collection. The title tells the essential story:

*A List of the **ROYAL FAMILY**, NOBILITY & GENTRY, who have honoured the **ETHIOPIAN SERENADERS**, Germon, Stanwood, Harrington, Pell & White, With Their Patronage at the St James's Theatre, London, Together with the Opinions of the London Press.*

The highest patrons are identified as Her Most Gracious Majesty, THE QUEEN, and His Royal Highness PRINCE ALBERT, followed by a careful list of Duchesses, Dukes, Viscountesses, Baronesses, and so on, all identified in precise hierarchical order. For these gala entertainments the group offered a core program of minstrel songs with occasional variations, as was their habit on stage. The marketing strategy was brilliantly adapted to the British scene; from then on the legitimacy of blackface minstrelsy was unchallenged. An American named George Washington Moore stayed on to become the resident expatriate organizer of minstrel groups and performances for the rest of the century.

In terms of audience, then, the primary differences between Britain and the United States lay in aristocratic sponsorship in the former versus the actuality of race as a complex domestic issue in the latter. Thus the importation of an American entertainment form into Britain depended very much on local factors that cannot in any sense be construed as American in origin.[8] The point is not just how effectively the minstrels learned how to market their wares in England, but that the associations were upscale and exotic. The St. James Theatre remained dedicated to minstrels all the way through to its demolition around 1910. Even clergymen were reported to be common among its patrons. In the United States by contrast the social associations started downscale: working-class patrons who encouraged not only the caricaturing of blacks but the addition as of the 1850s of burlesque blackface versions of "higher" entertainment forms: opera, ballet, and "legitimate theater" including Shakespeare and other imported playwrights. Only gradually did middle-class spectators join in. The American tendency was *not* toward subtlety (as of the 1850s, New York minstrel theaters like the Bowery held up to three thousand spectators).

During the second half of the century, British and American troupes began diverging in their emphases. Harry Reynolds, for example, reads this history from a British point of view: "In the early days of burnt cork minstrelsy, the comedian usually depended upon the quaintness of the melody and the broken English dialect of the American negro—more than on the wit and humor of the words—to gain his comic effect" (58). As British puns began to triumph over American malapropisms, wit and humor increased in British troupes, as in stump speeches satirizing popular American concerns from politics to feminism to science. Malapropisms, though they implicitly condemn social and educational self-promotion, do not necessarily involve a display of wit. The overdressed urban black figure known as Zip Coon (the first of many names for this figure, later known as Jim Dandy) exemplified this critique of social climbing. American minstrels, in short, continued in a social-satirical vein, emphasizing the preposterous expressions of laughably inferior creatures.

Blackface minstrelsy spread early to Australia and South Africa. In Australian writing as early as the 1840s minstrel stage black dialect issued from the mouth of an aboriginal character, and presumably minstrel stereotypes affected Australian perceptions of the aboriginals in other respects as well.[9] Minstrelsy continued to be a popular form of stage entertainment in Australia through the rest of the century, and thereafter its conventions enjoyed a long afterlife as amateur fundraising entertainment for school and social groups. The Australians always had the choice to import U.S. or British troupes and tended to prefer the latter. To them the British were better musically, whereas the Americans were more satirical, sometimes to the point of being unwelcome when they probed too crudely into locally sensitive issues.

In South Africa the phenomenon worked very differently. Though the first companies were U.S. or British groups stopping at Durban for recoaling en route between Britain and Australia, the most long-lived and popular group was composed of African Americans well after the Civil War. The Orpheus Myron McAdoo company toured South Africa for most of the 1890s, performing primarily for whites. On occasion black spectators were permitted in segregated seats, or else whole performances were designated for blacks only. The outcome of this black minstrel presence was that minstrel conventions merged with black South African musical entertainment to the point where they came to seem indistinguishable from "folklore." Except as traceable through careful reconstructions by cultural and musical historians like Charles Hamm or Dale Cockrell, minstrelsy has disappeared into facial makeup and fancy costumes at Cape Town festivals or Durban cakewalks.

In short, we see major differences in the after-effects of exporting blackface minstrelsy from the United States to Britain, Australia, and South Africa.[10] These differences make inescapably clear that exportation is never more than half the story: the conditions of importation are controlled by local circumstances, and if these are not favorable then no cultural transaction takes place. To exemplify this latter case, take India, another outpost of the Empire in which minstrel companies made refueling stops going to and from Australia. There are a few traces of minstrel performances for segregated British-only audiences in India, but nothing ever came of them. For whatever complex of reasons, blackface premises did not prove adaptable to categorizing the populations of India for their white governors.

There were attempts to export minstrelsy from England to the continent of Europe, all of which failed, but for different reasons in different countries. In Germany the initial audiences expressed outrage when they learned that the "blacks" they were watching were only blackfaced whites. The very racial premise that originally allowed the genre to flourish in the United States condemned it in Germany, where ethnic authenticity was already a primary value (a factor which would help acceptance of Buffalo Bill's Wild West some years later). In France the issues turned on language: the elaborate word games of minstrel patter proved to be untranslatable, a reminder of just how central wordplay was to the genre in its English-speaking settings.[11]

Returning to our starting point, we can see that blackface minstrelsy presents a clear and perhaps even exemplary case of cultural exportation. Where receptivity was high, as in Britain, local social and cultural circumstances led to a rapid assimilation of the entertainment form, marked at first by local imitations, which went on to introduce their own variants and emphases until third parties, notably the Australians, could recognize and choose between "American" and "British" minstrels. At that point blackface minstrelsy had lost its identifiable Americanness, just as surely as brand names like Kleenex or Band-aid or Kotex lost their identity once they came to be used as generic names.[12] Exportation turned out to be the result, though limited to the English-language world, a limitation that Buffalo Bill's Wild West circumvented deftly.

II. From the Great Plains to the Western World

The second stage of American entertainment exports is represented by Buffalo Bill's Wild West, an extraordinarily successful dramatization in open air of the struggles for control of the Great Plains, taking the form of legendary presences that embody a historic reality. William F. Cody managed to make this show seem the epitome of the whole of Western colonization—not just the domination of North America but a world-scale suppression of native, nonwhite peoples.

The scale of his success is evident in the estimates of his spectatorship. In all, over three decades of existence, the show was witnessed by some fifty million people in more than a thousand cities in twelve countries.[13] Since every one of these spectators had to be physically within sight and sound of the spectacle, Cody habitually ran two showings a day, or rather, once lighting became available, as at Earl's Court in London in the 1880s, one show during the day and the other at night. Everywhere it went, the show was physically impressive, full of violent action, thundering hoofbeats, shrill war cries, and blasting gunshots. All this drama was immediately accessible to its audiences. Also, unlike any competing form of entertainment at the time, it was supranational. There was no need to translate more than the program in going from one European country to another because the action spoke for itself.

Europeans were involved in this spectacle from even before its beginning. In 1872 General Philip Sheridan assigned Cody the job of arranging a buffalo hunt for Grand Duke Alexis of Russia. Cody arranged with a band of Sioux following Spotted Tail to put on a demonstration of their group hunting techniques and to stage a "war dance." One account claims that 265 lodges or about one thousand Sioux participated. In another foreshadowing of Buffalo Bill's Wild West, the Second Cavalry band took part in the festivities.[14] Other wealthy Europeans, led by the Earl of Dunraven, came forward seeking similar safari spectacles. The step into show business basically meant taking the show to the spectators rather than the other way around.

In the 1870s Cody began with crude stage melodramas performed in the off-season in large American cities. However raw their performances, Cody and his stage partner, Texas Jack, struck the spectators as *authentically* Western. Urban audiences paid handsomely for this sensation. Like Owen Wister's later bestseller, *The Virginian* (1902), Buffalo Bill may have helped to heal sensibilities wounded by the divisions of the Civil War by calling attention to the West as a region where national unity could be reinvented against the backdrop of the Indian as an enemy all Americans could unite in opposing. The show, like the war before it, came across as a largely masculine melodramatization fraught with national significance. The ground of its appeal was best articulated by the Richmond *Enquirer*, which lauded the presence of "bonafide Indians on the stage."[15] Bonafide Indians and cowboys indeed packed them in year after year, at home and all over Western Europe.

When Buffalo Bill was finally launched as an outdoor traveling show, Cody was ready with appropriately large-scale gestures. As the Hartford *Courant* evaluated the first season, it was the "best open-air show ever seen.... Buffalo Bill ... sits on a horse as if he was born in the saddle.... He has, in this exhibition, out-Barnumed Barnum."[16] This last was the highest compliment available in the business of attracting public attention, for P. T. Barnum, as he boasts in his autobiography, was the inventor and/or master of every aspect of advertising and show biz. Besides the sheer spectacle, hard work went into the Wild West as well: Cody reportedly missed only nine performances in the first twenty-six years.[17]

The success of bonafide Indians and authentic paraphernalia led Cody to invest in one of the original Deadwood stagecoaches, which, wherever the Wild West went, served to transport local dignitaries in inaugural parades, thereby affirming their local importance in trade for their implied endorsement and patronage. Cody also marketed the show by collecting an honorary title as Colonel in the Nebraska National Guard, rightly believing that the military associations would further his reception as an authentic Indian fighter. With the box office in mind, Bill was willing to pay Sitting Bull more than the going rate because this Indian, identified in popular fantasy as "the killer of Custer," could be given top billing under the slogan "Foes in '76—Friends in '85."[18] These elements of advertising and showmanship were just as applicable in Europe as they were in the United States. The combination of the authentic and the exotic proved unbeatable.

For the troupe's first European tour the shipboard party included 97 Indians, among them the Sioux visionary Black Elk, plus 180 horses and 18 buffalo. The enthusiasm of royalty and other public figures was skillfully managed, just as with the blackface minstrels of the 1840s. The Prince of

Wales, the future Edward VII, led a delegation for a private showing at Earl's Court before opening day. The greatest triumph was a command performance for Queen Victoria, who had not attended public entertainments for a quarter of a century since the death of Prince Albert. The queen won over the Americans at once by bowing in stately fashion to the American flag. Her evident pleasure in the Wild West led to another command performance on 20 June 1887, for royalty from all over Europe who had assembled for Victoria's Golden Jubilee. This success in turn ensured bookings in all major continental countries. The Deadwood Stage was driven by Buffalo Bill himself that day since it held "four kings": those of Denmark, Greece, Belgium, and Saxony.[19] Buffalo Bill's Wild West would ultimately play about half of its first twenty seasons in Europe, confirming that it offered not just exoticism and authentic primitives but also a narrative that invited Western self-congratulation wherever it went.

Verbalization played a minimal role in the show itself; the program could be issued in any language, but the performers had virtually nothing to say. Their job was to act out an "authentic" representation of a civilization-scale triumph of whites over lesser humans. The action was vigorous and rousing, essentially mindless, the marksmanship and horsemanship skills impressive in an era when horsepower was central to the way of life everywhere in the Western world. The latest technology, for example in lighting and railroad transportation, was skillfully exploited, even as a point of advertising. Marketing was conscious and skillful, capitalizing on existing social structures as well as emphasizing family and education, which suited the rising middle classes everywhere in the Western world: entertainment was surely no waste of time when the presence of authentic Indians proved the historical accuracy of the implicit narrative. The inherent superiority of all white cultures was vividly present in what was advertised to Europeans from the outset as the "Drama of Civilization."[20] Through the flamboyance of spectacle, this message could come alive even for the illiterate, thus reaching those who escaped the basic acculturation of newspapers and popular fiction.[21] The show's international appeal was enhanced in the 1890s by including elite cavalry units from European armies under the label Rough Riders of the World.

Just how far Cody might range beyond the American West in his dramatizations is illustrated in the program for 1901 reproduced at the end of this chapter. Here he takes the Boxer Rebellion in China for spectacular re-enactment, conveniently ignoring the fact that the largest of the nine army corps working to suppress the Boxers was Japanese. Instead, Buffalo Bill's Wild West conceived itself as celebrating the triumph of Christian civilization over paganism. There is no question which members of his troupe acted out the part of the Chinese losers.

III. Americanization?

Putting together these two primary steps toward the globalization of American popular culture, we can isolate some basic factors. Blackface minstrels, like Buffalo Bill's Wild West, initially sought audiences abroad in their quest for paying customers. Where they found acceptance, they also spawned imitators on the local scene, who proceeded to exploit the original entertainment premises in their own way. In the case of black-face minstrels, these imitators found diverse ways of adapting the imported genre to local tastes. In the case of Wild West shows, the imitators were essentially American,[22] but the spirit of the Wild West lived on in other modes. In Germany and Austria in particular the Indianer clubs flourished, meticulously mimicking the lifestyles of one favorite tribe or another.[23]

The impulse toward ethnological authenticity spawned many exhibits of "primitive" peoples and their modes of life. These were concentrated in national or international expositions or else in museums designed or adapted for the purpose. One early example is the display of Bushmen from the Kalahari in Africa at London's Egyptian Hall in 1847.[24] In my own university's city of Geneva, a Senegalese village was implanted near the center from May to October, 1896. This living museum was self-consciously contrasted with a "Swiss Village" erected as part of the Second National Exposition. About two hundred Muslim Africans from near Dakar participated, including several mothers who gave birth during their stay in Geneva.[25] In all such cases the fundamental message was the same as that dramatized by Buffalo Bill's Wild West: white European–based hegemony around the world was not just military and technological, it was justified by civilizational superiority, a "natural" phenomenon.

In short, the Americanness of the original imports was largely lost as time and adaptation went on, a process that, based on the nineteenth-century evidence, should be expected everywhere in cases of cultural exports. It still takes two to tango, even in an era of intensive media development like our own. Entertainment exports cannot be imposed either far out or in deep, even in cases where they are backed by centralized imperial power, as in the case of the Soviet Union in relation to its dependent republics for most of this century. Where reasonable liberty of response exists, we should expect to see local adaptations and imitations coexisting or even replacing the import from afar.

A single example from our contemporary world must suffice to suggest that the nineteenth-century models studied here are still relevant to cultural issues current today. MTV is one of the "successful" exports of American popular culture in recent years, yet press reports in early 1996 suggested that in a number of diverse television markets around the world, MTV is losing ground to local imitators who adapt its formulas but use local language and locally popular performers (*International Herald Tribune*, 26 March 1996, front page). These markets include large or sensitive areas like Brazil, Argentina, Japan, Hong Kong, Italy, and Germany. In such cases the putative "Americanization" carried by the original U.S. exports is either obscured beyond recognition or else acknowledged only indirectly by local innovations that take on a life of their own. MTV, of course, continues to be available via cable or satellite transmission, but its popularity is seriously challenged by these local competitors.

Exoticism can sell entertainment for a time, as in the initial perceptions of blackface minstrels or wild-west shows, but over the medium term these entertainment premises will likely either drop out of sight or prolong their appeal through local coloration. Globalization of American popular culture, as we know and debate it today, may well prove to be a temporary phenomenon, an issue internationally only so long as it takes to generate a local response that tests which premises can be successfully adapted to local circumstances and expectations. In cultural matters change is more or less continuous, so we do ourselves a disservice if we focus too exclusively on one artifact and on too narrow a time frame for analysis. This excursion back into the last century has had precisely the goal of testing such issues against depth in time.

Appendix I: Blackface Minstrelsy in Performance

What follows is a rare document: a summary description of a minstrel skit performed by the classic Christy's Minstrels as recounted in the humor weekly *The New York Picayune* (vol. 10, no. 6, 1 May 1858). The journalist's summary gives a good idea of how fast paced and how superficial minstrel skits were. He claims to have been haunted for a month by posters of "an enormous sleigh, containing a miscellanous [*sic*] party of 'culled [colored] persons,' drawn by four spanking greys"—the chief attraction of the third part of Wood and Christy's performance at the Music Hall. The first two parts can be passed over quickly as constituting, by this time, standard minstrelsy: "the performance started with a lot of singing, by a party of colored individuals, armed with fiddles, drums, bones, and other musical weapons. To this part of the entertainment we paid but little attention, our purpose there being solely to see the Sleigh ride. The singing was followed by dancing, to the merits of which we were equally oblivious, and then the sleigh ride commenced":

Scene the First—Half a room with four doors; if the other half which we didn't see has as many entrances as this half, it must be a cold room, two niggers come on, inform each other, and then each informs the audience that a sleighing party are to meet there immediately—darkies go off.

Scene Second—Two colored wenches, one with a deep bass voice, the other with a superb soprano, make the spectators acquainted with the important fact that they are in love with a couple of gentlemen, members of the aforementioned Christy and Wood's Minstrel Company. The two individuals thus favored enter at once and cheer the hearts of the ebony virgins by assuring them in strains poetic that their passion is responded to; other sleighers arrive—one carrying a basket of broken crockery which he hands to Fox. Fox, in going with which, takes especial care to knock it against the coat buttons of a dark gentleman six feet high; basket falls, broken crockery rattles. Fox declares that the china am all broked, stage folks all laugh expecting audience to do ditto; audience goodhumoredly comply. George Holland, his mother and little brother enter. Holland jumps a rope girl fashion, plagues his mother, upsets a chair, cries, laughs, and performs several other feats as naturally as life. George Christy announces the arrival of the sleigh, which announcement meets general approval. Little darkey becomes excited, dances a jump round, and winds up by sticking a pin in Holland's rear. Nigger informs the audience in a rich Irish brogue that it is time to depart; upon which a melancholy darkie sings a melancholy song to the effect that they'll all "Go a sleighing, a sleighing, a sleighing," and all take their departure vociferating a responsive chorus.

Scene Third—Broadway. A canvas sleigh, minus horses, in which all the party are seated, George Christy on the box, attaches behind the scenes, firing balls of cotton at them, party pick them up and return fire. Spectators are informed that "all are aboard," music strikes up and off the sleigh starts—not a bit of it; off the houses start, sleigh perfectly still, houses running a race; Burton's, the St. Germain, and building after building runs by. On every second house is a sign informing us that "The Ravens are at Niblos." "Cheap Carpets at Bore-em Sandersons." "The Owl on a stump, sings in the Leader." "The Picayune is out," and other important items, showing a new wrinkle in the phizog of advertising; houses still keep running. This struck us as an excellent mode of sleigh riding, so handy and comfortable; just jump into a sleigh and wait until your destination arrives at you—not you at your destination. Soon Bloomingdale's comes along, party adjourn to bar-room.

Scene Four—A phantom bar-room. Sleighing party enter, call for drinks, and the bartender being *non est* they retire without them.

Scene Fifth—Inside of the sleigh. (Here we noticed a wonderful transmogrification: the horses which weren't there in the Broadway Scene, had been transformed into a steam engine and the driver into a Conductor. George Christy comes on drunk and insists on levying subscriptions on the company; somebody behind fires a gun, sleigh falls to pieces, two wooden niggers are hoisted up to the top of the stage with ropes, while the flesh and blood ones fall upon the stage; a pack of fire crackers are let off, powder fizzles, and Fourth of July takes place generally. This is called The Railroad Explosion, and winds up the sleigh ride.

Appendix II: Buffalo Bill's Wild West in Performance

Herewith the official program of Buffalo Bill's Wild West and Congress of Rough Riders of the World for the season 1901, which was spent partly in North America and partly in Europe. Original in the Harvard Theatre Collection, The Houghton Library.

1—**Overture,** "Star Spangled Banner" . . . Cow-boy band, Wm. Sweeney, Leader.

2—**Grand Review** introducing the Rough Riders of the World—Indians, Cowboys, Mexicans, Cossacks, Arabs, Scouts, Guides, and detachments of fully equipped Regular Soldiers of the Armies of America, England, Germany, and Russia.
    Detachments from the contending forces in **South Africa** (wounded and invalided veterans); **Canadian Mounted Rifles;** Commando of **Transvaal Boers; Canadian Strathcona Horse** (Mounted Police), and a band of **Baden-Powell's Defenders of Mafeking.**

3—**Miss Annie Oakley,** Celebrated Shot, who will illustrate her dexterity in the use of fire-arms.

4—**Race of Races.** Race between a Cowboy, a Cossack, a Mexican, an Arab, a Gaucho and an Indian, on Spanish-Mexican, Bronco, Russian, Indian and Arabian horses.

5—**U.S. Artillery Drill,** by veterans from Capt. Thorpe's Battery D, Fifth Regiment, U. S. Artillery.

6—**Illustrating a Prairie Emigrant Train Crossing the Plains.** It is attacked by marauding Indians, who are in turn repulsed by "Buffalo Bill" and a number of Scouts and Cowboys.

7—**Pony Express.** A former Pony Post Rider will show how letters and telegrams of the Republic were distributed across our Continent previous to the building of railways and telegraph.

8—**A Group of Mexicans** from Old Mexico will illustrate the use of the lasso and perform various feats of horsemanship.

9—**Johnny Baker,** Celebrated American Marksman.

10—**A Group of Riffian Arab Horsemen** will illustrate their style of horsemanship, together with native sports and pastimes.

11—**Life-Saving Service Drill.** Illustrating the methods of saving lives when a vessel is wrecked. This Drill will be executed by a full crew of veteran members of the Life-Saving Service of the United States from the stations on the New Jersey coast. Every man of this crew has a record for skill and daring in his hazardous profession.

12—**Cossacks,** from the Caucasus of Russia, in feats of horsemanship, native dances, etc.

13—**Indian Boy Race.**

14—**Cow-boy Fun.** Picking objects from the ground, lassoing wild horses, riding the buckers, etc.

15—**Indians** from the Sioux, Arrapahoe, Brulé and Cheyenne tribes will illustrate the Indian mode of fighting, war-dances and games.

16—**Veterans from the Sixth U.S. Cavalry** in military exercises and an exhibition of athletic sports and horsemanship.

Note.—The men will wear the uniforms adopted by the U.S. Army on the frontier. The horses are Western range horses, used in this manner for the first time in history. The Army and National Guard use the "American" horse.

17—**Hold-Up of the Deadwood Stage Coach.** Being an exact reproduction of an event in the history of this identical coach.

18—**Three Minutes with the Rough Riders of the World.**

19—**Col. W. F. Cody** ("Buffalo Bill") in his unique feats of sharpshooting while riding at full speed.

20—**Buffalo Hunt,** as it was in the Far West of North America, by "Buffalo Bill" and Indians, exhibiting the last of the only known native herd of buffalo.

21—**The Battle of Tien-Tsin.** This episode introduces detachments from the allied armies of the world. The mise en scène is correct in every particular, and is carried out with strict fidelity to the subject.

Scene 1—Assembly of the powers. Cavalry Drill. Camp episodes, and the Advance on Tien-Tsin.

Scene 2—The walls of Tien-Tsin. The Royal Standard of Paganism floats proudly defiant of the Christian world. The Alarm, the Attack, the Defense and the Storming of the Walls. The Royal Standard comes down and the Banners of Civilization take its place.

> Up towards the crystal gates of Heaven ascending,
> The mortal tempest beat,
> As if they sought to try their cause together
> Before god's very feet.

N.B.—The colors carried by each detachment denotes the army to which the detachment belongs.

[A discreet footnote indicates that endorsement advertising was already in practice: "Col. Cody uses Winchester Rifles and Winchester Ammunition exclusively in all his exhibitions."]

Notes

1. Before 1845, the time by which the genre was fully established among theatergoing publics, the sheet music publications of their songs quite often showed the performers both in and out of blackface. This practice reflects at the outset a palpable need to reassure American audiences that they were NOT watching black performers. After the Civil War some black companies did succeed in attracting audiences, but only at the price of respecting the conventions and stereotypes long established by white actors.

2. For example, in the "Black-and-White Minstrel Show" so popular on BBC television till driven off the air by the Race Relations Act of 1977.

3. "Recipe for burnt cork: Take a quantity of corks, place them in a tin pail or dish, saturating them with alcohol, then light. Let them burn to a crisp, when burned out, mash them to a powder, mix with water to a thick paste, place the mixture in small tin boxes and it is ready for use. In applying it to your face it is better first to rub the face and hands with cocoa butter, which can be purchased from any druggist at a small cost, as when removing the black it can be rubbed off easily with a dry cloth. It is not necessary to use carmine for the lips to make them appear large. All that is required when applying the black is to keep it about one-half an inch away from the mouth, or more if a larger mouth is wanted. This applies only to end men. The balance of the company should black close to the lips so as to appear dignified and neat in appearance." (Jack Haverly, *A Complete Guide to Negro Minstrelsy* [Chicago: Frederick J. Drake, 1902], 6–7).

4. *Love and Theft: Blackface Minstrels and the American Working Class* (New York: Oxford University Press, 1993), 38. This is the best recent study of minstrelsy.

5. "White Like Me: Racial Cross-Dressing and the Construction of American Whiteness," in Amy Kaplan and Donald E. Pease, eds., *Cultures of United States Imperialism* (Durham: Duke University Press, 1993), 476.

6. Hans Nathan, *Dan Emmett and the Rise of Early Negro Minstrelsy* (Norman: University of Oklahoma Press, 1977), 52.

7. In 1836 Rice first appeared at lower-echelon houses like the Surrey and the Adelphi. Two years later the *Times*, citing a New York paper, marvels that to date Rice had sung and danced 37,000 verses in the United States, England, and Ireland (25 October 1838).

8. The difference in perceptions of race in the two countries as of the 1850s surfaces in responses to Dion Boucicault's 1859 play *The Octoroon*. In the original New York version, the beauteous octoroon is denied the possibility of marrying her handsome true love because of the taint of her one-eighth black blood; hence she commits suicide. In London, audiences were horrified at this violation of romantic conventions. Boucicault, ever with an eye on the main chance, rewrote the ending to satisfy them.

9. See Elizabeth Webby, "The Aboriginal in Early Australian Literature," *Southerly* 40 (1980): 45–63.

10. For a more detailed treatment, see John G. Blair, "Blackface Minstrels as a Cultural Export: England, Australia, South Africa," in George McKay, ed., *Yankee Go Home (& take me with u)* (Sheffield: Academic Press, 1997), 67–77.

11. In Holland, Dr. Pieter R. D. Stokvis of the Open University at The Hague has turned up visual evidence of a performance in Amsterdam in 1847 by the "Lantum Ethiopian Serenaders," but no reviews have yet surfaced that might explain why minstrelsy did not take hold in Holland.

12. I do not mean to imply an unduly sophisticated marketing mentality among the early minstrels; they were simply seeking paying audiences wherever they might be found.

13. Sarah J. Blackstone, *Buckskins, Bullets, and Business: A History of* Buffalo Bill's Wild West. (Westport, Connecticut: Greenwood Press, 1986), 92.

14. Nellie Snyder Yost, *Buffalo Bill: His Family, Friends, Fame, Failures, and Fortunes* (Chicago: Swallow Press, 1979), 52–54.

15. As quoted in Don Russell, *The Lives and Legends of Buffalo Bill* (Norman: University of Oklahoma Press, 1960), 200.

16. Russell, *Lives and Legends*, 297.

17. Blackstone, *Buckskins, Bullets, and Business*, 92.

18. Russell, *Lives and Legends*, 316. In fact, Sitting Bull came with quite an entourage. He was paid $200 a month for four months plus a bonus of $125 and sole right to sell his photographs and autographs. He was accompanied by five Sioux warriors at $25 a month each, three women for $15 a month each, and William Halsey as interpreter for $60 a month. Transportation to and from the show was also provided.

19. Russell, *Lives and Legends*, 327ff.

20. William Brasmer, "The Wild West Exhibition and the Drama of Civilization," in *Western Popular Theatre*, ed. David Mayer and Kenneth Richards (London: Methuen, 1977), 133–56.

21. The magnitude European illiteracy might attain as a cultural factor is indicated by the estimate, according to the census of 1861, that 78 percent of the Italian population could neither read nor write. See Naila Clerici, "Native Americans in Columbus's Home Land: A Show Within the Show," in Christian F. Feest, ed., *Indians and Europe: An Interdisciplinary Collection of Essays* (Aachen: Edition Herodot, Rader Verlag, 1987), 417.

22. Don Russell, *The Wild West or, A History of the Wild West Shows* (Fort Worth, Tex.: Amon Carter Museum, 1970).

23. There was a strong and persistent tendency to see the Sioux as the prototypical Indian nation so that their teepees and long feathered headdresses represented universal Indian practice. For example, when in the early 1980s a delegation representing several Indian tribes came to Geneva to lobby at the United Nations for their independent rights of self-determination as peoples, they got no attention from the local media until they put on Sioux-style paraphernalia. Sioux had become the visual equivalent of Indian-in-general, thanks substantially to Buffalo Bill's Wild West.

24. See Richard Altick, *The Shows of London* (Cambridge, Mass.: Harvard University Press, 1978).

25. See Bernard Crettaz and Juliette Michaelis-Germanier, *Une suisse miniature, ou les grandeurs de la petitesse* (Geneva: Musée d'ethnographie, 1984).

References

Cockrell, Dale. "Of Gospel Hymns, Minstrel Shops, and Jubilee Singers: Towards Some South African Musics." *American Music* 5 (1987), 417–32."

Hamm, Charles. *Afro-American Music, South Africa, and Apartheid.* I.S.A.M. Monograph 28. New York: Brooklyn College Conservatory of Music, 1988.

Reynolds, Harry. *Minstrel Memories: The Story of Burnt Cork Minstrelsy in Great Britain from 1836 to 1927.* London: Alston Rivers, 1928.

James T. Campbell

The Americanization of South Africa

I. Introduction

An American arriving in South Africa today cannot help but be struck by how familiar it seems. South Africans, black and white, drink Coca-Cola, eat Kentucky Fried Chicken, and spend exorbitant sums on Nike shoes and sportswear. They shop in sprawling suburban malls, modeled on American prototypes and offering a dizzying array of American commodities. The local cineplexes carry the latest Hollywood blockbusters, while television, which the apartheid state prohibited until 1976, serves up an endless stream of American commercial programs. The same process is evident in the realm of politics. While South Africa's history as a British colony is reflected in the country's parliamentary system and its renewed membership in the Commonwealth, many of the controversial political issues debated in South Africa today—federalism, judicial review, minority rights, affirmative action—revolve around concepts appropriated (some might say misappropriated) from American political discourse.

Examples could be cited almost indefinitely, but the point is clear. When the Union of South Africa was established in 1910, its political, economic, and cultural metropole was unquestionably a product of Great Britain. Today, Britain's role has been usurped by the United States. The object of this essay is to unravel the process of this shift in cultural influences.

Before proceeding, it may be useful to anticipate a few potential objections. To highlight the American presence is not to imply that the United States is the sole foreign influence on South Africa, nor to deny the profound imprint of other societies—among them Great Britain and the Netherlands, Germany, Australia, Israel, Mozambique, even Brazil, which provided a crucial model for architects and town planners during the 1930s and '40s. Nor is it to suggest that American influence is somehow universal or smoothly spread across the country. In a society as riven by racial, class, ethnic, and generational cleavages as South Africa, the process of "Americanization" has inevitably been uneven, contingent, and contested. Manifestly, U.S. influence has been most marked in urban areas, pre-eminently in Johannesburg, which is, in a more than figurative sense, a product of American knowledge and inspiration. American influence has typically spread along generational lines, with young South Africans, black and white, appropriating American music, fashion, and even slang as a means to distinguish themselves from their more conservative, more Anglicized elders. Last but not least, the process has been distinctly racialized. While both black and white South Africans have proved extraordinarily receptive to American culture, they have typically embraced different aspects, while entertaining profoundly different ideas about the nature of the American experience and its relevance to South Africa.

This qualification prompts another. An inquiry like this one invites a kind of argument by accretion, trying to prove one's case through an endless catalogue of "Americanisms" in South African life. Such data, however, represent the beginning rather than the end of the analytical problem. The immense popularity of Hollywood westerns, for example, is obviously a significant datum, but it tells us nothing in itself about the mechanisms by which such movies were introduced in South Africa or about what they meant to different audiences. The same might be said about shopping malls, the post–World War I penchant for Tuskegee-style industrial education, or *The Cosby Show*, which had the bizarre distinction, during the twilight of apartheid, of being the highest rated television show among both white and black South Africans. In short, Americanization involves processes of reception—of selection and reinterpretation—as well as of transmission. While the vast differences in national size and power have often made it difficult for South Africans to resist American penetration, it would be misleading to portray them as helpless victims of American imperialism. In many cases, they have sought out American goods, ideas, and images, grafting them onto their own experiences to produce new ways of understanding and acting upon their worlds. One of the chief challenges of an inquiry such as this is to do justice to these myriad moments of appropriation and refashioning without succumbing to the simplifications of "cultural imperialism" on one hand or unfettered agency on the other. In today's brave new world of globalization, Marx's famous dictum is more pertinent than ever: people make their own history, but not exactly as they choose.

One other potential line of criticism also involves issues of selectivity and balance, but in a different way. Put simply, why pick on South Africa? What country today is not plagued by Coca-Cola, Nike, CNN,

Baywatch, or other manifestations of Generica America? Fair enough. But even if one concedes the point, the historical particularities of the process in different societies are surely worthy of careful analysis. As it happens, South Africa is something of a special case. In few if any societies in the world did the process of Americanization begin so early; in few if any has it been so thoroughgoing, so replete with irony, or of such central historical significance. When, to take a singularly obnoxious example, the 1939 Mixed Marriages Commission convened, its first act was to dispatch a representative to the U.S. Library of Congress to find American precedents. (For the record, the researcher found over a hundred antimiscegenation laws on the books, in thirty-seven different states.) American experience was likewise invoked, implicitly or explicitly, in the elaboration of segregation; in the creation of radio and television broadcasting; in the establishment of suburbs; in changing fashions, in music, dress, and interior decoration; in inter- and intra-racial debates over political strategy and tactics; in conservation policy (including the inflammatory apartheid-era policies on stock limitation); in the creation of bantustans; in the political negotiations that culminated in the end of apartheid; and in innumerable ongoing debates about apartheid's legacy. In short, Americanization is a deeply rooted, complex, contested historical process, with profound significance for South Africa's past, present, and future.[1]

II. Antecedents

Individual Americans surface throughout South African history, often in the most paradoxical or portentous places. The leaders of the 1807 Slagtersnek uprising, whom later generations of Afrikaner Nationalists would embrace as martyrs, were prosecuted not by an Englishman but by a Dutch-speaking American, Jacob Cuyler, from Albany, New York (hence the Eastern Cape city of Albany.). The voortrekkers who set out into the South African interior three decades later were serviced spiritually by an American, the Reverend Daniel Lindley, who left his post at the American Zulu mission to accompany them. ("The cheapest, speediest, easiest way to convert the heathen is to convert the white ones first," he explained in a letter to his supervisors.) During the American Civil War, the Confederate raider *Alabama* did a booming business in Cape waters, seizing one Union vessel right in Table Bay, an episode memorialized in the still popular folksong "Daar Kom Die Alabama."[2]

Such anecdotes are more or less familiar to South African historians. What historians have been slower to recognize is the substantial commercial foundation upon which such encounters took place. Traders in New England and Cape Town conducted a lively trade in the eighteenth century, often in defiance of both British mercantilist and Dutch East India Company regulations. New England slave ships, en route from Madagascar, regularly stopped at the Cape to take on provisions, leaving a portion of their human cargoes as payment. In the years after American independence, upward of two dozen American ships per year put in at Cape Town; today's Victoria and Alfred Waterfront, a tourist mecca modeled on San Francisco's Fisherman's Wharf, stands near the site of what Capetonians two centuries ago called "the American wharf." Settlers in the Cape ate American grain, built homes out of American timber, and aged wine in American-made barrels, some of which was later quaffed in New England taverns. With the outbreak of the Napoleonic Wars, transatlantic commerce swelled still further, to the point that the United States stood briefly as South Africa's largest trading partner.[3]

The boom of the Napoleonic era proved short-lived. British annexation of the Cape in 1806 was followed by a series of new commercial restrictions, culminating in a special Order in Council barring U.S. ships from access to African ports. At the same time, Thomas Jefferson, fearful that the United States might be drawn into war with Europe by some incident on the high seas, imposed a unilateral embargo on foreign trade. Ironically, however, the developments of 1806–1807 helped lay the foundations of future commerce. British annexation paved the way for substantial white settlement, enlarging the potential market for U.S. producers, once they were finally readmitted to South Africa in 1830. In turn, Jefferson's embargo, together with the war and the new tariff regime that followed it, precipitated America's industrial revolution, and with it a robust demand for South African primary products. By the 1830s and '40s, hundreds of U.S. whalers plied South African waters, harvesting the spermacetti that lubricated the humming looms of Lowell and Chicopee. The wool boom that transformed the Cape economy in the mid-nineteenth century was propelled by American manufacturers, who purchased over a third of local output. The burgeoning U.S. shoe industry provided an insatiable market for South African skins and hides. A single firm, the G. S. Holmes Company, the first American firm to open operations in South Africa, shipped over 200,000 hides per year from the Cape to Boston in the 1850s. Many Union soldiers in the American Civil War wore boots manufactured from South African leather and slept beneath blankets woven from South African wool, which helps to account for the presence of a Confederate raider in Cape waters.[4]

Some of the United States' surging industrial output found its way back to South Africa. While paltry as a percentage of total American exports—

historically, South Africa has accounted for roughly one percent of total U.S. foreign sales—this commerce had a significant impact on South Africa, concentrated as it was within a few sectors of what was still a relatively small market. The U.S. farm implement industry, one of the bellwethers of American manufacturing, quickly cornered the local market. Cyrus McCormick's reapers were available in the Cape in the early 1850s, just a few years after their introduction in the United States. The market for ploughs was likewise dominated by American imports, sold through local agents and sporting such brand names as the Yankee, the Eagle, and the American Planet, Jr. Barbed wire, at once the most prosaic and the profound symbol of colonial rule, was likewise imported from the United States, beginning in the 1870s. By century's end, Americans supplied virtually all of South Africa's sewing machines, typewriters, bicycles, cash registers, cameras, and canned meats. American dominance was perhaps most conspicuous—and certainly most enduring—in fuel oils, initially in kerosene and later in gasoline or "petrol." If nineteenth-century South Africa had an equivalent of today's ubiquitous Coca-Cola can, it was the bright red five-gallon tin with the Standard Oil logo.[5]

III. Americans and the Mineral Revolution, 1880–1903

As significant as these early linkages may have been, the process of "Americanization" began in earnest only with the mineral revolution. The discovery of diamonds at Kimberley, followed a decade and a half later by the opening of the Witwatersrand gold fields, ignited in southern Africa one of the most compressed and ferocious industrial revolutions in the history of the world. Significantly, this transformation coincided with sweeping changes in American life, particularly in the scale and scope of economic activity. One of the industries affected most profoundly was mining. Across the American West and later the world, the pick-wielding digger was displaced by vast, highly capitalized mining operations, overseen by professional mining engineers. Schooled at new institutions like Yale's Sheffield School and the Colorado School of Mines, as well as at the more established Freiberg School of Mines in Germany, this new class of "scientific" miner possessed expertise in mineralogy, metallurgy, chemistry, engineering, and management, all with an eye to extracting the greatest amount of ore at the least possible cost.[6]

By the late nineteenth century, American mining engineers were spread across the globe, from Nevada to Australia, California to Peru. Southern Africa drew them like a magnet. Kimberley was home to at least a thousand Americans, the most famous of whom, Gardner Williams, doubled as U.S. consul and chief operating officer of Cecil

Rhodes' DeBeers Company. Easily twice as many Americans found their way to the gold fields of the Witwatersrand, which posed many of the same technical problems as the hard rock mines of Nevada. By the mid-1890s, over half the mines on the Rand were managed by Americans, and a chain of new cities had sprouted along the Reef, with names like Denver, Cleveland, and Florida. In the wake of the engineers came a motley collection of American journalists, entrepreneurs, and adventurers, all eager to sample life in the world's latest, greatest boom town. Americans established Johannesburg's first hotel, its first steam laundry, and its short-lived horse-drawn tram system. One U.S. expatriate made a handsome living importing used stagecoaches from California. Americans even dominated the Rand's underworld: the so-called "Bowery Boys," a network of Eastern European Jewish criminals expelled from their base on New York's Lower East Side in 1894, relocated to Johannesburg and quickly cornered the local prostitution market.[7]

It is no exaggeration to say that Americans built South Africa's gold industry. It was an American, John Hays Hammond, chief engineer of Cecil Rhodes' Consolidated Gold Fields, who first persuaded skeptical Randlords that the unprecedented investments required for deep level mining could be made to pay, notwithstanding the low grade of ore. Hammond's judgment was confirmed by Hamilton Smith, an engineer from the Nevada silver fields who was brought out by the Rothschilds in 1893 to assess the Witwatersrand; and by George Becker, head of the U.S. Geological Survey, who produced the first comprehensive surveys of the Witwatersrand complex three years later. The list goes on and on. As Mark Twain, an old digger (not the celebrated American author) who passed through Johannesburg in 1896, put it, "South Africa seems to be the heaven of the American scientific mining engineer. He gets the choicest places and keeps them."[8]

Most of the capital goods required by the growing industry came from the United States. The elevators and skips that carried men and machines underground and hoisted ore back to the surface were supplied by the new Otis Elevator Corporation. Underground electricity was supplied by generators from General Electric, one of the first American companies to create a South African subsidiary. The Ingersoll Corporation enjoyed a monopoly on rock drills, while Fraser-Chalmers supplied many of the massive stamp batteries needed to pulverize the gold-bearing reef. Everything from the cyanide used in the retorting process to the Oregon pine used for timber packs and in miners' homes came from the United States.[9]

It is important, of course, to maintain a sense of proportion here. The flood of people and products from the United States was focused on the Witwatersrand and obviously not characteristic of South Africa as a whole. Great Britain still outstripped the United States in the total value of exports to South Africa and, with occasional brief exceptions, would continue to do so for the next eighty years. Finance capital remained emphatically British, thanks to a tangle of British, U.S., and Cape laws that prevented American banks from opening branches in South Africa. The absence of U.S. banking facilities, in turn, inhibited large-scale investment by American capital. Aside from a consortium that briefly held the concession to build the rail line from the Transvaal to Lourenzo Marques, Americans played no role in the explosion of railroad building in industrializing South Africa. More surprisingly, mining capital remained almost exclusively European, despite the enormous contributions Americans made to the industry in terms of technical and management expertise. No American mining house arose on the Rand, a fact that sharply distinguishes the South African case from, say, Rhodesia, Zambia, or the Congo, where American mining capital would come to wield enormous economic and political power. The obvious exception, the massive Anglo-American Corporation, launched in 1917 with the help of J. P. Morgan and future president Herbert Hoover (himself a veteran of the South African mining industry), is more apparent than real: by 1930, most of the American interests in Anglo had been bought up by De Beers' Ernest Oppenheimer.[10]

Yet even admitting these qualifications, there is no gainsaying the growing American presence in South Africa. Indeed, curtailing American influence became one of the chief objectives of the imperial officials sent out to "reconstruct" the Transvaal after the South African War of 1899–1902. One of High Commissioner Milner's first acts was to impose a special "permit system" on interior travel for nonimperial citizens, impeding the return of American mining engineers and entrepreneurs to the Rand. (The system had the additional benefit of curtailing the movements of African American missionaries of the African Methodist Episcopal Church, which had entered South Africa in 1895 and quickly attracted thousands of adherents away from European missions.) Milner also moved to stem the flow of American imports, which had swelled to unprecedented levels in the immediate aftermath of the war. Under Milner's new "imperial preference" policy, U.S. trade with South Africa plummeted; American grain sales, a staple of the transatlantic trade for a century, were wiped out almost completely. To be sure, the policy was not airtight. Several U.S. companies qualified for imperial preference by incorporating themselves in Canada. American firms continued to dominate the oil and farm equipment industry, as well as the emerging automobile market. Unquestionably, however, Milner's intervention slowed the process of Americanization, while drawing a newly united South Africa firmly into the orbit of the British Empire.[11]

IV. Creating a Consumer Society, 1919–1938

If the aftermath of the South African War marked the end of the first phase of South Africa's "Americanization," the aftermath of World War I marked the commencement of the second. As historian David Kennedy has shown, the outbreak of war in Europe represented a windfall to American producers, who not only fed and supplied the belligerents but gained a foothold in colonial markets previously dominated by the British. While Kennedy focuses on Latin America, his insight applies equally to Africa, particularly South Africa, which by 1915 had become the United States' fifth largest overseas market. Trade accelerated still further after the war ended, as the British economy languished. Spurred by pent-up wartime demand, the total value of U.S. exports peaked in 1920 at over $60 million; for a brief moment, the United States stood yet again as South Africa's largest trading partner. So enticing was the South African market that some Americans began to consider direct investment. "There are splendid openings here for energetic men with sufficient capital to finance the undertaking and employ the large forces of cheap native labour found in most parts," the U.S. consul in Cape Town declared in 1921. Two years later, the Ford Motor Company launched Ford, South Africa. (The venture was technically sponsored by Ford, Canada, to ensure that the new enterprise qualified for imperial preference on imported components.) By the end of 1923, the first Model-T had rolled off the company's assembly plant in Port Elizabeth.[12]

The entrance of American capital was facilitated, paradoxically, by the 1924 election of the Nationalist-Labour "Pact," an avowedly anti-imperialist government explicitly committed to enhancing South Africa's economic independence. The 1925 Tariff Act raised customs and duties on imports to unprecedentedly high levels, in a bid to nurture local manufacturing and provide jobs for "civilised"—i.e., white—labor. In most particulars, the act succeeded: manufacturing industry grew spectacularly, eventually outstripping mining in its contribution to national GDP; hundreds of thousands of white workers, male and female, secured decently paid work in match factories, canning works, automobile plants, textile mills, and later in the embryonic steel and chemical industries. Whether the act enhanced South Africa's autonomy, however, is a different question. As Richard Hull has shown, the new tariff regime essentially forced overseas firms with an interest in South Africa either to abandon the local market or to establish their own manufacturing subsidiaries inside the country. Dozens of U.S. corporations chose the latter course. For the first time, American capital began to enter South Africa in substantial amounts.[13]

Once unleashed, the flow of American investment continued, undeterred by the onset of depression or by a series of major political realign-
ments in South Africa. The economic boom that followed South Africa's
withdrawal from the gold standard in 1933 prompted another spurt of
investment, as U.S. corporations raced to enter what *Businessweek* called
"one of the most spectacular markets in the world." In 1936, Firestone,
which had recently secured new sources of raw rubber in Liberia, established a factory in Port Elizabeth. Coca-Cola arrived in 1938. By the end
of that year, the book value of American direct investment in the country
exceeded $70 million.[14]

Even with the investment of the 1920s and '30s, total U.S. direct investment in South Africa continued to lag far behind investment from
Great Britain. Yet American capital had a disproportionate impact, concentrated as it was in manufacturing, the most dynamic sector of the
economy. Like their predecessors on the diamond and gold fields, the
American engineers and managers who came to South Africa in the
1920s and early 1930s brought with them a wealth of new, "scientific"
techniques. Assembly line production, time and motion studies, and
other techniques of so-called scientific management were all introduced
in South Africa by Americans. These innovations in production were accompanied by even more revolutionary innovations in the realm of consumption, or marketing. Someone, after all, had to buy the output of all
these new, prolific factories. Particularly in a society like South Africa,
where extreme maldistribution of wealth radically reduced the size of the
aggregate local market, the future of manufacturing capital hinged less
on productivity than on persuading people to consume.[15]

The devices employed by American capital in the 1920s to close the
widening gap between production and consumption are familiar enough
to historians: installment plans; the introduction of "yearly models" (an
innovation pioneered by General Motors and initially resisted by Henry
Ford); the endless elaboration of superficial differences in functionally
similar products. Advertising blossomed as a professional industry, complete with its own associations and journals, as well as its own vernacu-
lar, borrowed from the developing science of psychology. Ultimately, of
course, such initiatives did not forestall the Great Depression, but they
did help to consolidate a culture of consumption, in which individuals'
status, personal happiness, even identity came seemingly to hinge on pos-
sessing this or that commodity.[16]

Given South Africa's elaborate tradition of labor repression, historians
have naturally focused more on production than on consumption, yet
even a cursory glimpse at the sources suggests that South Africa, too, experienced a significant shift in the nature and meaning of consumption in

the interwar years, with American capital and technique playing vital roles in the process. At the risk of overstating the point, one can see in South Africa in the 1920s and '30s the emergence not only of a consumer culture but of an enduring association of Americanness with certain forms of consumption and display. The auto industry offers perhaps the best example. Given South Africa's size and the considerable distances between cities, the country's love affair with the automobile was probably foreordained, but it was American automakers who first fueled the romance. Like their American parents, Ford and General Motors used advertising to associate their products with wealth, sophistication, and personal freedom, encouraging buyers to express their individuality by choosing particular models, colors, and features. (In G.M.'s case, advertising was also used to associate the company with the Pact's "civilised labour" policy: all G.M. ads included the legend: "100 per cent. White Labour.") Advertisements routinely cited the latest U.S. sales figures for particular models, to ensure South Africans that they were obtaining the best that America had to offer. Through such techniques, American auto manufacturers soon controlled over 90 percent of the local market.[17]

As in the United States, the search for new customers gave rise to a professional advertising industry, serviced by its own trade journal, *South African Business Efficiency*, launched in 1934. Dozens of local agencies emerged, all faithfully following American practice, by striving to endow particular commodities with an air of distinction, leisure, youth, or sex appeal. Surely the most blatant evidence of American technique was the proliferation of advertisements featuring women in undergarments, a development that scandalized at least some potential customers.[18]

This new consumer ethic was not uniformly embraced; on the contrary, its spread was uneven, contested, and shaped by all of South Africa's myriad racial, class, and ethnic fault lines. Most early mass marketing campaigns were directed at English-speaking whites, a population that was, by South African standards, not only cosmopolitan, but disproportionately urban and affluent. The premier medium for reaching this market was *Outspan*, the most prominent of a new generation of mass circulation weekly magazines that appeared in South Africa in the years after World War I. Like the American *Saturday Evening Post*, on which it was apparently modeled, *Outspan* was a lavishly illustrated affair that offered wholesome, general-interest articles while zealously excluding any reference to "politics." Designed to appeal to the entire family, the magazine included features on health, fashion, and romance, game parks and golf, movies, music, and dance, as well as a regular column for youngsters ("At the Children's Outspan") and a virtually endless stream of articles on automobiles ("Motoring Etiquette," "When an Engine

Lacks Power," "Motoring Days of Yesteryear"). Each issue also included literally hundreds of advertisements, for everything from imported "Frigidaires" (". . . truly modern. It saves work, worry, money and time . . . with every corner of every compartment chilled to the scientifically correct degree") to Odo-Ro-No underarm deodorant for women ("Dancing, tennis, riding—why should your enjoyment of them be spoiled by that horrid, nagging doubt—the doubt of your personal daintiness . . . ?"). Taken as a whole, *Outspan* conjured a vision of the South African good life, American style—a vision of material progress, ample leisure, and domestic comfort, unruffled by financial insecurity or political dissension.[19]

Among African readers, *Umteteli wa Bantu* played a similar role, though in radically different circumstances. Founded by the Chamber of Mines in the early 1920s to wean "responsible" African opinion away from militant organizations like the Industrial and Commercial Workers' Union (I.C.U.), *Umteteli* targeted an emergent black, urban "middle class." The problem for the paper, and indeed for the target group itself, was how to distinguish members of this class from other Africans. Given the reality of urban segregation, entrenched in the 1923 Natives' (Urban Areas) Act, as well as the ongoing political assault against all forms of African accumulation and autonomy, members of this aspirant elite lived cheek by jowl with the working class and urban poor, often in equally parlous circumstances. In such a context, consumption acquired enormous personal and political significance. Dress, hairstyles, leisure activities, furniture, even the bric-a-brac that cluttered one's sitting room, became coveted markers of difference, purchased even at risk of falling perilously into debt. In keeping with this priority, *Umteteli* devoted considerable column space to advertisements, peddling pianos, patent medicines, and everything in between. The influence of the United States, mostly implicit in *Outspan*, was utterly explicit in *Umteteli*. Not only did the paper carry regular columns on the achievements of African Americans; it also routinely invoked black America in its advertisements, presenting this record or that beauty treatment as the "latest" thing from the United States.[20]

Afrikaners presented an even more complex case. Over the first quarter of the twentieth century, Afrikaners poured into cities, driven from the land by the accelerating capitalization of the countryside. While many, indeed most, of these first-generation urbanites were poor, they also represented a substantial potential market. Developing this market became one of South African manufacturing capital's most urgent priorities. This priority, however, ran afoul of another. As Isabel Hofmeyr has shown, the first decades of the twentieth century represented a pivotal period in the history of Afrikaner Nationalism. The Second Language Movement, the emergence of Malan's National Party, and the 1914 Rebellion all reflected and advanced a growing sense of "volkskap," of shared nationhood and identity. Like nationalists in other places and times, Afrikaner Nationalist ideologues viewed commerce with a jaundiced eye. The flood of alien commodities sapped Afrikaner vigor and independence; it smacked of "Englishness"; it diluted the national distinctiveness that was God's gift to all peoples. The comments of Die Huisgenoot, the largest-circulation Afrikaans weekly, were representative: "Our biggest daily papers, the cinemas, the school system, the language of our courts, the shops with their fashions and merchandise, the furniture in our house are all bastions and agents of a foreign culture which claims for itself the right to overrun and conquer the world." In the years that followed, Afrikaner Nationalists would coin a revealing neologism for this alien plague: "bioskoopbeskawing," or the culture of the movies.[21]

Fortunately for Die Huisgenoot (which, like Outspan, was sustained by advertising revenue), the imperatives of volkskap and consumption could be reconciled. The solution, as Hofmeyr suggests, lay not in resisting commerce so much as in incorporating it, by identifying certain forms of consumption and leisure as authentically Afrikaans. Die Huisgenoot itself led the campaign, helping to establish through its advertisements, articles, and illustrations the boundaries of legitimate consumption in everything from meat to movies, furniture to fashion. A "regte" Afrikaner would not eat marmalade, but he would eat "Gold Reef Konfyt" or, to take a slightly more contemporary example, "Ouma" rusks, still made according to grandmother Grayvenstein's old Karoo recipe. Thus did consumer culture infiltrate even those quarters that were most overtly hostile to it. Indeed, one might even suggest that Afrikaner intellectuals had, for a brief moment, outrun the wizards of Madison Avenue, who, in their rush to sell tomorrow's product today, had yet fully to grasp the vast commercial possibilities of yesterday.

V. Mass Media: Music and Movies

As the lament of Die Huisgenoot suggests, the development of an American-inflected consumer culture was intimately related to the rise of mass media. In the quarter century that followed the creation of Union in 1910, South Africa was transformed by powerful new forms of mass communication, from advertising and mass circulation weekly magazines to gramophone records, radio, and Hollywood movies. Each of these media had its roots in the United States; each carried a host of American associations, ideas, and images.

Consider the world of music and entertainment. Even before the mineral revolution, South Africans, black and white, had begun to exhibit their apparently insatiable appetite for American performance styles. The most popular form of mass entertainment in the nineteenth century, save perhaps the circus, was the minstrel show, an American import, in which performers in blackface aped the antics and music of an imagined slave South. With the opening of the Witwatersrand, a host of new musical idioms, from ragtime to Tin Pan Alley, found their way to South Africa, borne on a tide of inexpensive American sheet music. The 1890 arrival of Orpheus McAdoo's Virginia Jubilee Singers, an offshoot of the celebrated Fisk University Singers, awakened an enduring taste for African American spirituals, especially among African Christians. Vaudeville made its appearance in the early twentieth century, serving in South Africa, as in the United States, as a waystation between minstrelsy and movies. South Africa even hosted a touring Wild West show, run by a man named Texas Jack and featuring a young cowboy named Will Rogers. By ironic coincidence, this visit by a man who "never met a man I didn't like" overlapped with the visit of another who never met a man he did: W.C. Fields, who arrived with a touring American vaudeville troupe.[22]

The cultural traffic from the United States accelerated in the 1920s, thanks largely to the gramophone, Thomas Edison's inexpensive, mass-produced device for reproducing recorded sound. Periodicals like *Outspan* and *Umteteli wa Bantu* carried regular advertisements for dozens of different models, most American made and all available on convenient installment plans. Weekly bulletins alerted customers to the latest American recordings to reach South African shores, from Louis Armstrong to "Dixie" pioneer Jimmie Rodgers, whose yodeling style harked back to the slave "hollers" of his native Mississippi even as it laid the foundation of country and western. In the late 1920s, two of the premier recording companies in the United States, Gallo and Columbia, opened South African subsidiaries, vastly expanding access to American music while creating new recording opportunities for local artists. Tragically, many of these early recordings appear to have been lost, but those that survive almost universally betray American, and especially African American, influence. *Mbaqanga,* for example, the "African jazz" tradition that dominated urban African music in the 1930s and '40s, was a self-conscious blending of *marabi,* an urban proto-jazz of the early twentieth century, with American swing. Its most celebrated exponents—groups like the Jazz Maniacs and the Harlem Swingsters—expressed their identification with America not only in their music, but in their names, their dress, their swagger. For such groups, comparison with the

American original became, in musicologist Christopher Ballantine's words, "the ultimate stamp of approval."[23]

The swelling popularity of American music was intimately related to the rise of another, even more emphatically American medium. As early as 1895, exhibitors from Europe and the United States had introduced South Africans to the wonders of the "kinetoscope." In the years after the South African War, moving pictures—typically single-reel affairs, lasting perhaps a minute—became a regular attraction in vaudeville programs, and later in dedicated theaters. In an industry with no uniform specifications, different exhibitors relied on slightly different technologies, one of which—the "bioscope"—became South Africa's generic term for the cinema.[24]

The history of South African cinema is, to an extraordinary extent, the story of one man: Isadore W. Schlesinger. Schlesinger was born in the old Austro-Hungarian Empire in 1871, one of nine children of Jewish parents. He arrived in the United States in 1884, settling, inevitably, on New York's Lower East Side, where he worked as a peddler. A decade later, for reasons that remain unclear, he embarked for South Africa. He arrived in Johannesburg in early 1895 and found his way to a bicycle shop owned by two Americans, whom he asked for a job. "I'm good at selling things," he allegedly said. To test the proposition, the men entrusted him with a large consignment of American chewing gum, an unfamiliar novelty that they had found impossible to sell. Schlesinger returned a few days later having sold the lot, an achievement noted in passing by the aforementioned Mark Twain. From chewing gum Schlesinger graduated to insurance, and in the years before the South African War he accumulated a small fortune as a traveling agent for the Equitable Insurance Company of New York. By the time of his death half a century later, this astonishingly neglected figure had parlayed that initial stake into the Schlesinger Organisation, a vast empire of ninety companies that embraced, at various times, insurance, banking, real estate, advertising, agriculture, hotels, newspapers, radio, and, most importantly, cinema.[25]

Schlesinger's genius lay in applying in South Africa methods and techniques perfected in the United States. His African Realty Trust, for example, developed some of the first of South Africa's leafy white suburbs, including Mount Pleasant in Port Elizabeth and Orange Grove, Parkhurst, and the "prestige" suburb of Killarney in Johannesburg. Following a model pioneered by American developers a generation before, African Realty sold lots on a monthly installment plan, promising buyers all the comforts of country living combined with proximity to the city. In 1926, Schlesinger launched the African Broadcasting Corporation, South Africa's, and indeed the continent's, first radio network. (A.B.C. was amicably handed over in 1936 to the newly established South African Broadcasting Corporation.) He even revolutionized South Africa's citrus industry, through the introduction of time and motion studies, assembly line packing, and U.S. refrigeration technology. The list of Schlesinger's American-inspired innovations goes on and on, from South Africa's first amusement parks to an abortive attempt to introduce commercial aviation, from a chain of American-style "drugstores" to the creation of the Miss South Africa pageant.[26]

It was Schlesinger's career as a movie mogul that best exhibited his distinctively American genius. In 1913, he bought The Empire, a failing vaudeville house in Johannesburg. In the space of just a few years, he built that investment into African Consolidated Theatres, which, with its sister company, African Film Productions, dominated South Africa's cinema industry until 1956, when the Schlesinger Organisation sold its movie interests to Twentieth-Century Fox. Like his counterparts in Hollywood, Schlesinger was quick to recognize the value of vertical integration, of bringing production, distribution, and exhibition all under one roof. Indeed, he went further than most American studios, creating companies to oversee theater catering, film advertising, even the production of newsreels that accompanied features. The heart of Schlesinger's domain was Johannesburg's Commissioner Street, South Africa's "Great White Way," which featured Broadcast House, headquarters of the A.B.C. radio network, and three massive movie theaters, The Empire, His Majesty's, and The Colisseum, which among them seated more than six thousand people. Like the contemporary "picture palaces" of New York or Los Angeles, Schlesinger's theaters pandered to dreams, offering not only movies and fine dining but a variety of luxurious appointments, from arches and classical statuary to the famous vaulted ceiling of the Colisseum painted to resemble the night sky. For generations of South Africans, the "evening out" for dinner and a movie became a cherished weekly ritual—a ritual that, with the delayed advent of television, persisted far longer in South Africa than in the United States. By the time television finally arrived in the 1970s, South Africa boasted the eighth largest movie audience in the world. Needless to say, the movies that locals flocked to see were predominantly—and, by the 1930s, almost exclusively—American. Westerns, swashbucklers, gangster films, MGM musicals: all did robust business in South Africa, among both black and white audiences.[27]

In South Africa as in the United States, the emergence of cinema generated enormous controversy, with critics proffering ominous predictions about the new medium's effects on the individual, family, and nation. In substance and tone, such attacks were virtually identical to those showered on the film industry in America, but they were inflected in distinctively South African ways. How could the superiority and reputation of "white civilisation" be upheld when Hollywood filmmakers insisted on representing white people in the worst possible light—as gangsters and adulterers, prostitutes and thieves? Would impressionable "natives" be capable of distinguishing reality from what they saw on the silver screen? Faced with such questions, South African officials lurched instinctively toward censorship. As early as 1910, authorities prohibited screening of the Jack Johnson—Jim Jeffries fight, on the grounds that it had provoked race riots in the United States. For the next eighty years, South African censors would continue to monitor movies, in a vain quest to prevent the infiltration of "dangerous" and "inappropriate" ideas from the United States.[28]

Afrikaner Nationalists were particularly uneasy with "bioskoopbeskawing," focusing not only on its moral corrosiveness but on its tendency to dissolve divinely ordained differences between nations. Leaders of the secretive Broederbond published a two-volume investigation into ways to harness cinema's extraordinary power, to make a medium that was volksvreemde (alien to the people) volkseie (the people's own). Largely at the instigation of Afrikaner Nationalists, a succession of South African governments from the 1930s to the 1970s maintained a lucrative subsidy system for South African films, particularly for films in Afrikaans, essentially guaranteeing a profit for anyone with a movie camera. Yet, while the system did help to sustain a small local industry, it did not upset the dominance of Hollywood. As late as 1969, a full 98 percent of South African films were imported from overseas, the vast majority from the United States. Ironically, most of the dozen or so low-budget features produced annually by South African filmmakers were bound for that most American of venues, the drive-in theatre.[29]

There was an even deeper irony here. The same Afrikaner Nationalists who denounced "die bioskoop," who decried the United States' commercialized, mongrelized world, on acceding to power in 1948 enacted policies that drew South Africa ever deeper into America's embrace.

VI. Apartheid and Cold War, 1945–1963

On the surface, the years after World War II marked a period of sharp divergence between the United States and South Africa. The war ushered in unprecedented economic advance for African Americans, while laying the seeds of a political realignment that would bring the civil rights issue into the center of the Democratic Party agenda. In 1947, Harry Truman became the first American president to address a meeting of the National Association for the Advancement of Colored People. Later in the same year, the Truman administration published *To Secure These Rights*, a manifesto that pledged to use the power of the federal government to prevent violations of blacks' civil rights. To be sure, such pronouncements were propelled by Cold War calculations as much as by sincere sentiment, and they were honored more in the breach than in the observance. Nonetheless, in the two decades after World War II, the United States took a giant step on the road to nonracial citizenship. The situation in South Africa could not have been more different. While the war years produced many of the same structural transformations—accelerating urbanization, the large-scale movement of black workers into secondary industry, growing black political assertiveness—the result was not civil rights but the triumph of Daniel Malan's National Party on a platform of apartheid. The years that followed brought population registration, the Immorality and Mixed Marriages acts, group areas, separate amenities, Bantu Education, intensified urban influx control, rural labor bureaus, forced removals, and a violent assault on all political opposition. Yet, paradoxically, these years of divergence produced a dramatic intensification of economic, cultural, and political links between the United States and South Africa.[30]

As has happened so often in the past, U.S.–South African commerce was propelled by war. In the first two years of World War II, the American share of South African imports doubled; by the end of 1941, the United States had once again displaced Great Britain as South Africa's largest trading partner. Transatlantic traffic increased further at war's end, just as it had after World War I. With the British economy moribund, American commodities poured into South Africa. Total American sales, which had increased threefold between 1938 and 1945, nearly tripled again in the war's aftermath, peaking at nearly half a billion dollars in 1948. In that most portentous of years, South Africa consumed nearly 4 percent of total American exports. U.S. direct investment also grew substantially, if less spectacularly. Goodyear Tire, for example, which had marketed its products in South Africa for more than three decades, opened a factory in 1947 in Uitenhage, not far from the factory opened by its rival, Firestone, a decade earlier. (General Tire opened its factory two years later, giving the Port Elizabeth area a trio of American tire plants.) The flow of investment capital was encouraged by the influential *Fortune* magazine, which hailed South Africa as "one of the latter-day world's amphitheaters of ante-Delanian [i.e. pre-Roosevelt] rugged individuals." While acknowledging that South African prosperity hinged on labor repression, the magazine also noted the country's "fantastically low operating costs," which created "opportunity and to spare for venture capital."[31]

Fortune's assessment was shared by the U.S. government, which saw in South Africa's appetite for American commodities and capital a perfect complement to the American economy's need for overseas markets and investment outlets. Significantly, U.S. policymakers were unconcerned by the rising Afrikaner Nationalist challenge to the United Party government of Jan Smuts. Indeed, a 1945 State Department report suggested that the Nationalists' antipathy to Britain might play into American hands. "Americans would try to break down the walls of Empire preference from the outside while the Afrikaners would seek to do so from the inside," the report projected. "[T]he Nationalist ideal of a South Africa independent, economically and politically, is obviously in accord with the American hopes of freer world trade without discrimination."[32]

The State Department's prediction came true, though the process was more complicated than anyone had anticipated. Malan's Nationalists were indeed determined to assert South Africa's autonomy from Britain. On coming to power, they announced that South Africa would no longer market its gold through the Bank of England, overturning a system in place since the South African War. Instead, the country's entire gold output from 1948 was shipped directly to the United States, to pay for the flood of American imports. A short time later, however, the government took steps to halt the flow of imports, which, together with the flight of British capital, had left national reserves dangerously depleted. The year ended with a battery of new import restrictions, including high tariffs, local content rules, and outright prohibitions on certain nonessential consumer goods. Over the next two years, the value of American exports to South Africa fell by more than 75 percent, while the American share of the South African import market fell by half.[33]

Yet even as they stemmed the flow of American imports, Afrikaner Nationalists welcomed American investment with open arms. Like its Pact predecessor, the Malan government was anxious to promote local manufacturing, in order to enhance national autonomy, expand white employment, and reduce the influence of pro-British mining capital. It was particularly eager to acquire new technology and management techniques. Where else to turn but the United States? While a few Nationalist leaders warned of the dangers of replacing one imperialism with another, the Malan government set out to entice U.S. investment capital, offering generous policies on taxation and repatriation of profits, while waiving tariffs and license fees on companies with local subsidiaries. In effect, the Nationalists in 1948 did deliberately what their predecessors in the Pact had done half-wittingly in the 1920s, compelling companies with an interest in South Africa's expanding market to set up operations locally.

The result was a torrent of new American investment. Virtually overnight, direct investment in South Africa increased threefold. By the end of the 1950s, it had more than doubled again, until it represented over half of American investment on the African continent. More than forty American firms, including such giants as Timken Bearings, Dow Chemical, John Deere, IBM, Kellogg, Quaker Oats, and 3M, established local subsidiaries in the years after 1948. A host of others, most notably General Motors and Johnson and Johnson, dramatically expanded operations. In 1953, Mobil Oil built South Africa's first oil refinery, enabling the country to process locally more than a quarter of its annual fuel requirements. The investment surge was most dramatic in pharmaceuticals, an industry dominated before the war by German firms. Thirteen American pharmaceutical companies opened South African subsidiaries in the late 1940s and early '50s; no fewer than ten manufactured their products locally. So conspicuous was the capital flow that the U.S. Department of Commerce began to issue an annual publication on South Africa for potential American investors, touting the country's commitment to "capitalism and individualism," as well as its political stability and quiescent labor climate.[34]

As in the 1920s, the post–World War II investment surge had profound cultural consequences. Birdseye Corporation, for example, introduced South Africans to frozen food, an innovation made possible by the explosion in the (American-dominated) home refrigerator industry. The whole phenomenon of processed food, which swept across South Africa in the postwar decades, was quintessentially American, enshrining values of consumption, convenience, and speed. Perhaps the most portentous new arrival was IBM, which established a South African subsidiary in 1953 and began to market its then state-of-the-art 700 series computer. In the years to come, American computer companies, and IBM in particular, would revolutionize the working lives of South Africans as fundamentally as American mining and manufacturing engineers had transformed the lives of previous generations.[35]

From the perspective of investors, of course, such considerations were secondary to profits. And make no mistake: investments in apartheid South Africa paid off spectacularly, generating rates of return that were consistently the highest in the world. In 1950 alone, the rate of return on U.S. direct investment in South Africa was 27 percent. In the mid-1960s, it still hovered around 20 percent, more than half again higher than in Japan, which ranked second in the world, and nearly three times higher than in Canada, which ranked third. One former managing director of an American company in South Africa recalled a thirteen-year streak in which his group won the trophy that the parent company awarded to the international subsidiary generating the highest return on investment. Even in the early 1980s, as apartheid crumbled and economic growth stagnated, U.S. companies still reported an average rate of return of 18 percent.[36]

The United States' deepening economic involvement in apartheid South Africa was accompanied by a profound change in the political relationship between the two countries, to the point that one can begin meaningfully to speak of the United States as South Africa's political metropole. This process was inseparable from the Cold War. Where previous American administrations had tended to view relations with South Africa through the prism of Great Britain, the Truman administration and its successors saw them unequivocally in East-West terms. By those lights, South Africa represented a vital ally. Not only did it command the Cape sea routes, but it also boasted thirteen of the twenty-four minerals listed in the U.S. strategic stockpiling program, including massive deposits of uranium ore, conveniently embedded in the gold-bearing conglomerates of the Witwatersrand. And uranium, as historian Thomas Borstelmann has shown, was regarded by American policymakers as the key to national survival in the Atomic Age.

The Truman administration was determined not only to exploit the Witwatersrand uranium deposits, but to ensure that they remained securely in Western hands. In June 1948—one month after the National Party's accession—negotiations commenced between the South African government, the local mining industry, and the "Combined Development Trust" of the United States and Great Britain. The eventual agreement, signed in November 1950, guaranteed the Western alliance (in actual practice, the United States) a uranium monopsony. In exchange, the United States committed to design, build, and finance six uranium processing plants. The deal also included a series of less explicit *quids pro quo*. In February 1951, Secretary of State Dean Acheson announced that the United States would henceforth give "the most sympathetic consideration" to South African requests for military equipment, despite a confidential C.I.A. report that stated that "South African military planning, to a degree unknown in North Atlantic Treaty states, focuses on the basic requirement of internal security." At the same time, the United States used its considerable influence in the United Nations to shield South Africa from international censure, by forestalling and, on occasion, vetoing antiapartheid resolutions. (This policy, as Acheson himself conceded, had the dual purpose of defending an ally and denying a precedent to those who wished to introduce the subject of American race relations on the floor of the United Nations.) Thus did one of the most unfree nations in the world become a bastion of the "Free World."[37]

Most importantly, the 1950 uranium agreement gave South Africa unprecedented access to American capital, some of it from commercial banks but the bulk of it channeled through the Export-Import Bank, a government body, or the World Bank, an international agency dominated by the United States. It is worth looking closely at this process, if only to contrast the largesse of the American government and its international proxies during the early apartheid years with their extraordinary stinginess today, when a democratically elected government struggles to redress apartheid's legacy. In January 1951, two months after the uranium agreement was signed, the World Bank announced a $50 million loan to the South African government, $30 million of which was earmarked for ESCOM, the state-owned electricity supplier, and $20 million of which was intended to modernize the country's transportation network. Lest there be any doubt that the loan marked a deliberate shift in American policy, a consortium of eight American commercial banks unveiled a $30 million dollar loan to the South African government on the very same day. A few months later, the Ex-Im Bank granted a $35 million loan to the mining industry to facilitate the uranium project. In the years that followed, American capital continued to pour into South Africa. Of the nearly $200 million in Ex-Im grants, loans, and credits to Africa between 1946 and 1955, roughly $150 million—75 percent—was directed to South Africa. Over 60 percent of World Bank investment in Africa over the same period likewise went south of the Limpopo. (The lion's share of the balance went to Rhodesia.) World Bank and Export-Import Bank money overhauled the country's road network, modernized its harbor facilities, funded new rail lines and rolling stock, and vastly increased the productive capacities of ESCOM and ISCOR, the state-owned power and steel producers. South Africa's vaunted "modern infrastructure" was built with American dollars.[38]

The importance of American capital was vividly illustrated in the aftermath of the Sharpeville massacre in March 1960, when South African police fired on unarmed African protestors, killing sixty-nine and wounding over two hundred. The massacre provoked an international outcry and massive capital flight. Over a quarter billion rands in investment left South Africa; gold and foreign exchange reserves fell by nearly 60 percent. All of this is familiar enough to historians. What is less often observed is the American role in containing the panic. In late 1960, a consortium of American investors, led by Charles Engelhard, a mineral and chemical industry baron with close links to the Kennedy administration, arranged a $150 million loan for the South African government. A few weeks later, the World Bank and the IMF stepped in with loans totaling more than $40 million, pumping up South African reserves and calming nervous investors. American corporations also helped to calm the waters. In May 1961, the South African government funded a twenty-page insert into the New York *Times*, aimed at potential investors. The insert included lavish testimonials from the managing directors of Coca-Cola and General Motors, both of which announced substantial new investments. "My corporation does not idly play with this kind of money," the director of Coca-Cola declared, referring to a $3 million investment in new bottling facilities. "We believe in South Africa and the new plant is a demonstration of faith on our side." Buoyed by such support, the South African economy weathered the crisis and embarked on a decade of unprecedented economic growth. By the end of the 1960s, American direct investment topped $1 billion.[39]

The ironies in all this are palpable. At the very moment that the United States began tentatively to confront the problem of racial inequality, it was deeply implicated in the elaboration of apartheid in South Africa. Stranger still, the resources that poured into South Africa in the 1950s in the name of western values of individualism and free enterprise underwrote a dramatic increase in state ownership and control of the economy, a process particularly evident in the steel and energy industries. The situation was equally ironic from the South African perspective, as a rabidly nationalist government, intent on asserting its autonomy from imperial Britain, pursued policies that drew South Africa into the embrace of imperial America.

VII. The 1970s and Today

Given constraints of space, this article can only touch briefly on the final two periods in U.S.-South African relations. The first began in the mid-1970s, a period of declining economic growth and intensifying opposition to apartheid, at home and abroad. Three themes merit mention. The first and most obvious is the introduction of television, specifically the launch of the state-controlled South African Broadcasting Corporation in January 1976. Rob Nixon has described the Afrikaner Nationalists' long refusal to admit this quintessentially American medium, and the combination of circumstances that caused them ultimately to relent. Suffice it to say that much of what they feared—an avalanche of American commercial programs promoting values foreign to "the South African way of life"—has come to pass. Between the high costs of local production and the South African boycott by the British union Equity, an increasing percentage of American shows appeared on South African screens. The most successful—*Rich Man, Poor Man, Dallas,* and *Dynasty*—were not only

American in origin but served further to entrench South African (and especially white South African) assumptions about American wealth and power. Even the vaguely countercultural shows that began to appear in the 1980s—*Miami Vice* (dubbed into Afrikaans, as *Misdaad in Miami*) and *The Cosby Show*—portrayed an America of astonishing glamor and material comfort. As in many other countries, the rain of American shows stifled the growth of a local industry, a problem that continues to this day. The sheer size of the American market has made it possible for American television producers to recoup costs locally, enabling them to sell overseas rights for a fraction of what it costs to produce a program from scratch. According to current S.A.B.C. figures, producing a local hour-long drama costs at least sixteen times more than licensing an American program—the difference, say, between four or five hundred rands per minute and upwards of eight thousand rands per minute.[40]

The second process is spatial. The erection of the first shopping malls in the 1970s—malls modeled on American prototypes and, in several cases, designed by American firms—heralded a profound spatial reorganization of South African urban life, a suburbanization of economic life, embracing commerce, consumption, and, increasingly, white-collar work. The process has accelerated since the collapse of group areas and influx control, which had prevented black people from settling in central cities. The end result is a new, eerily American peri-urban landscape of shopping malls and cluster housing, interspersed with fast-food outlets and landscaped corporate office parks, all bound together by a network of multilane roads.[41]

The third process is financial or, more accurately, political-financial. Facing slowing growth rates, continuing capital outflows, a massive increase in state spending (defense spending alone increased more than 1000 percent in the 1970s), and a dangerously low level of domestic savings (itself an artifact of American-influenced consumption patterns amongst white South Africans), the Nationalist government did what any government would do in the circumstances: it borrowed money. Large-scale government capital projects were increasingly funded through short-term loans from American commercial banks, which offered far lower interest rates than those available locally. In 1974–1975, for example, Citicorp lent $150 million to ISCOR, the steel parastatal, and another $30 million to ESCOM, to aid in the development of nuclear power. The need for short-term money increased after the Soweto uprising of 1976, which prompted another bout of capital flight. By the early 1980s, more than forty U.S. banks had made substantial loans to the South African government, the total value of which peaked at $4.7 billion in 1984. One consequence of this dependence on American commercial loans was that the South African government found itself vulnerable to the swelling pressure for disinvestment in the United States. In 1985, New York banks refused to roll over South African loans, precipitating a run on the South African rand so destructive that the South African government was forced temporarily to suspend all foreign exchange transactions. When the definitive history of the end of apartheid is written, this chapter will loom large. For present purposes, the episode is significant as perhaps the final step in the century-long process by which the United States displaced Great Britain as South Africa's cultural, political, and economic metropole.[42]

Which brings us to the present. Perhaps not surprisingly, the years since 1994 have accelerated the process of Americanization, while introducing a raft of new ironies and paradoxes. The ongoing process of privatization of the television industry has, if anything, increased the predominance of American shows and movies, but the "demographics" of the shows has changed dramatically. Determined to shed its reputation as a bastion of "white" South Africa, the S.A.B.C. saturated the airwaves with African American situation comedies. Precisely what messages are being absorbed by South African viewers is, as always, difficult to ascertain, but it seems safe to say that images of black Americans sitting in middle-class homes and in college fraternities and sororities have a particular impact on South Africa's rapidly growing black middle class. At the same time, images of African American ghetto life, transmitted through rap, hip hop, and movies such as *Boyz in the Hood* and *Wild Style,* have permeated township life, giving rise to a self-consciously Afro-American-style gang culture. Just as "the Americans," the leading criminal gang in 1950s Johannesburg, drove tail-finned Cadillac sedans, sported zoot suits, and appropriated the argot of Hollywood gangster films, so today do gangs in the "Coloured" Cape Flats affect African American speech, sport stars and stripes "do-rags," and "tag" buildings with neon tributes to the late gangsta rapper Tupac Shakur. And just as the visit of the McAdoo Jubilee Singers spawned a host of African imitators in the 1890s, so has the recent entrance of hip hop given rise to local bands such as Blade, Vulcan, and the all-female Ghetto Luv.

As always, these inroads in the realm of "culture" have been accompanied by important economic changes in the realms of both production and consumption. While the promised flood of American investment in postapartheid South Africa has not materialized (despite the current government's slavish devotion to a U.S. and World Bank–mandated structural adjustment program), the post-1994 years have seen the entrance of new U.S. investors, as well as the return of some old investors. Perhaps the most portentous new arrival is the McDonald's Corporation, not only because of McDonald's status as the largest (and surely one of the most notorious) private employer in the United States, but also because of what the McDonald's regime implies in terms of speed, standardization, and the structure of domestic life. Postapartheid South Africa has also provided fertile ground for American management consultants. Like the "scientific" mining engineers of the late nineteenth century or the "time and motion study" experts of the interwar years, consultants from Arthur Anderson, Deloite and Touche, McKenzie and Associates, and other U.S. management firms offer South African businesses knowledge, expertise, and information—all in pursuit of the grail of "efficiency."

Last but not least, the postapartheid years have sparked increased political traffic between the United States and South Africa. The A.N.C.'s election campaign in 1994 was managed by President Clinton's house pollster, Stanley Greenberg, himself the author (back in his academic days) of an important comparative history of the United States and South Africa. Deval Patrick, Clinton's advisor on race relations, has played a central role in helping South Africa's Ministry of Labour to draft affirmative action codes, and in providing the computers that the Ministry will need to interpret incoming data. (Embattled defenders of affirmative action in the United States might be forgiven for wondering whether such computers were available because of the dwindling home market.) Vice President Al Gore has made several trips to South Africa, and serves, with his counterpart, Thabo Mbeki, as co-chairman of a new, permanent U.S.–South African Commission. President Clinton himself arrived in early 1998, finding in the august presence of Nelson Mandela a welcome respite from domestic scandal. During his visit, Clinton extolled open markets and stressed that the future of U.S. relations with the country and the region lay in "trade, not aid." Americans, he opined, owed South Africans nothing. What, one wonders, do South Africans owe the United States?

Notes

1. Union of South Africa, *Report of the Commission on Mixed Marriages in South Africa* (Pretoria, 1939), 41–49. For studies of parallels and encounters, see George Fredrickson, *White Supremacy: A Comparative Study in American and South African History* (New York, 1981); Fredrickson, *Black Liberation: A Comparative History of Black Ideologies in the United States and South Africa* (New York, 1995); John Cell, *The Highest Stage of White Supremacy: The Origins of Segregation in South Africa and the American South* (New York, 1982); and J. Campbell, *Songs of Zion: The African Methodist Episcopal Church in the United States and South Africa* (New York, 1995).

2. Eric Rosenthal, *The Stars and Stripes in Africa*, 2nd ed. (Cape Town, 1968), 23–28. Lindley's statement is quoted in Robert Kinloch Massie, *Loosing the Bonds: The United States and South Africa in the Apartheid Years* (New York, 1997), xviii.

3. Richard W. Hull, *American Enterprise in South Africa: Historical Dimensions of Engagement and Disengagement* (New York, 1990), 2–15; Rosenthal, *Stars and Stripes*, 13, 39–48; Massie, *Loosing the Bonds*, 13–14. On Cape Town's waterfront, see Nigel Worden, "Unwrapping History at the Cape Town Waterfront," *Public History* 16, no. 2 (1994): 33–50.

4. Hull, *American Enterprise*, 25–27; Massie, *Loosing the Bonds*, xix. On American whalers in southern African waters, see Rosenthal, *Stars and Stripes*, 52–58.

5. Hull, *American Enterprise*, 38–39, 69–77, 119–20; Rosenthal, *Stars and Stripes*, 222–24. Perhaps the most influential of these American commodities was the Singer sewing machine, which revolutionized working and domestic life in countries all over the world; see Robert B. Davies, *Peacefully Working to Conquer the World: Singer Sewing Machines in Foreign Markets, 1854–1920* (New York, 1976).

6. Clark C. Spence, *Mining Engineers and the American West: The Lace-Boot Brigade, 1849–1933* (New Haven, 1970). Probably the best examplar of this new class was John Hays Hammond, who studied at Yale and Freiberg, before making his fortune in the American West and in South Africa; see Hammond, *The Autobiography of John Hays Hammond*, 2 vols. (New York, 1935). On the transformation of American life in the late nineteenth century, see, *inter alia*, Robert H. Wiebe, *The Search for Order* (New York, 1976); and Alfred DuPont Chandler, *The Visible Hand: The Managerial Revolution in American Business* (Cambridge, 1977). On the wages of South Africa's mineral revolution, see Charles van Onselen, "The World the Mineowners Made: Social Themes in the Economic Transformation of the Witwatersrand, 1886–1914," in *Studies in the Social and Economic Transformation of the Witwatersrand, 1886–1910*, vol. 1, *New Babylon* (London, 1982).

7. For a contemporary portrayal of Kimberley from an American perspective, see "Life on the Diamond Fields," *Harpers New Monthly Magazine* (Feb. 1873): 325–26; and Gardner Williams, *The Diamond Mines of South Africa* (New York, 1902). See also G. R. Bozzoli, *Forging Ahead: South Africa's Pioneering Engineers* (Johannesburg, 1997), 59–62; Hull, *American Enterprise*, 67–69, 89–90; Enid De Waal, "American Black Residents and Visitors in the S.A.R. before 1899," *South African Historical Journal* 6, no. 1 (1974): 52–55; and Rosenthal, *Stars and Stripes*, 121–28, 131–35. (Rosenthal includes an appendix listing American place names in South Africa; see pp. 228–29.) On the "Bowery Boys," see Charles van Onselen, "Prostitutes and Proletarians, 1886–1914," in *New Babylon*, 118–35.

8. Hammond, *Autobiography*, 291–306; Rosenthal, *Stars and Stripes*, 131–35; Bozzoli, *Forging Ahead*, 49–54, 62–73. Twain's comment is quoted in Massie, *Loosing the Bonds*, xxi.

9. The fullest account of Americans in the period before and after the raid is Hammond, *Autobiography*, 309–429 ff. See also Thomas J. Noer, *Briton, Boer and Yankee: The United States and South Africa, 1870–1914* (Kent, 1978), 21–68; Rosenthal, *Stars and Stripes*, 141–48; Hull, *American Enterprise*, pp. 69–77; and Shula Marks and Stanley Trapido, "Lord Milner and the South

African State," in P. Bonner, ed., *Working Papers in Southern African Studies*, vol. 2 (Johannesburg, 1981), 65–67. On American equipment, see Enid De Waal, "American Technology in South African Gold Mining before 1899," *Optima* 33, no. 2 (1985): 88–96.

10. Rosenthal, *Stars and Stripes*, 137–40; Hull, *American Enterprise*, 24–25, 36–37, 65–66, 77–82, 218. On the rise of Anglo-American, see Duncan Innes, *Anglo: Anglo-American and the Rise of Modern South Africa* (New York, 1984), 75–96.

11. Noer, *Briton, Boer and Yankee*, 91–110 ff; Hull, *American Enterprise*, 120–23. On state policy and the A.M.E. Church, see Campbell, *Songs of Zion*, 150, 222–26.

12. David Kennedy, *Over Here: The First World War and American Society* (New York, 1980); Hull, *American Enterprise*, 138, 153, 365.

13. Hull, *American Enterprise*, 132–34. On the Pact, protection, and the growth of South African manufacturing capital, see D. Hobart Houghton, *The South African Economy*, 3rd ed. (Cape Town, 1973), 116–42, 236–39; and Robert H. Davies, *Capital, State and White Labour in South Africa, 1900–1960: An Historical Materialist Analysis of Class Formation and Class Relations* (Brighton, 1979), 177–244.

14. Hull, *American Enterprise*, 138–40, 182–89, 369. On G.M., see Eric Rosenthal, *The Rolling Years: Fifty Years of General Motors in South Africa* (n.p., 1976). On Coca-Cola, see Affinity Advertising and Publishing CC, *Brands and Branding in South Africa: Key Success Stories* (Johannesburg, 1993), 68–69. The comment in *Businessweek* is quoted in Thomas Borstelmann, *Apartheid's Reluctant Uncle: The United States and Southern Africa in the Early Cold War* (New York, 1993), 49.

15. See Belinda Bozzoli, *The Political Nature of a Ruling Class: Capital and Ideology in South Africa, 1890–1933* (London, 1981), 190–200, and passim.

16. On advertising and the rise of a consumer culture in the United States, see Roland Marchand, *Advertising the American Dream: Making Way for Modernity* (Berkeley, 1985); and Richard W. Fox and T. Jackson Lears, eds., *The Culture of Consumption: Critical Essays in American History, 1880–1980* (New York, 1983). Revealingly, one of the avatars of the industry, Edward Bernays, was Sigmund Freud's nephew; see *Biography of an Idea: Memoirs of Public Relations Counsel Edward L. Bernays* (New York, 1965).

17. The G.M. ads appeared regularly in *Outspan*; see below. Special thanks to Glenn Adler for information on the early history of the South African automobile industry.

18. Articles cited are from *South African Business Efficiency* 1, no. 10 (Sept., 1934). The complaint about indecent advertisements is from *S.A.B.E.* 1, no. 11 (Oct., 1934): 327–28.

19. The first issue of the journal announced "the avowed intention of *The Outspan* to introduce no politics," see *Outspan*, 4 March 1927, p. 3. The quoted advertisements are from *Outspan*, 4 March 1927, p. 46; and 19 December 1930, p. 60.

20. I pursue this theme further in Campbell, "T. D. Mweli Skota and the Making and Unmaking of an African Petty Bourgeoisie," paper delivered to the History Workshop conference, Johannesburg, February 1987. On urban areas legislation and its impact on elite accumulation, see Rodney Davenport, "African Townsmen? South African Natives (Urban Areas) Legislation Through the Years,"

African Affairs 68, no. 1 (1969): 95–109; and Davenport, "The Triumph of Colonel Stallard: The Transformation of the Natives (Urban Areas) Act Between 1923 and 1937," *South African Historical Journal* 2, no. 1 (1970): 77–96.

21. See Isabel Hofmeyr, "Building a Nation from Words: Afrikaans Language, Literature and Ethnic Identity, 1902–1924," in Shula Marks and Stanley Trapido, eds., *The Politics of Class, Race and Nationalism in Twentieth-Century South Africa* (London, 1987). The quoted passage is on p. 110.

22 Veit Erlmann, *African Stars; Studies in Black South African Performance* (Chicago, 1991), 21–53, 59–68, 112–55; David Coplan, *In Township Tonight: South Africa's Black City Music and Theatre* (Johannesburg, 1985), 37–41, 94–110; Thelma Gutsche, *The History and Social Significance of Motion Pictures in South Africa, 1895–1940* (Cape Town, 1972), 1–40, 149 n.3, 327; Rosenthal, *Stars and Stripes*, 157, 168–73. On the origins of minstrelsy, see Robert C. Toll, *Blacking Up: The Minstrel Show in Nineteenth-Century America* (New York, 1974). On the sheet music industry, the global impact of which is still under-appreciated by historians, see R. Charles Hamm, *Yesterdays: Popular Songs in America* (New York, 1983, orig. pub. 1975).

23. Christopher Ballantine, *Marabi Nights: Early South African Jazz and Vaudeville* (Johannesburg, 1993), 3–7, 12–28, and passim. (The quotation is on p. 15.) On *marabi* and *mbanqanga*, see Coplan, *In Township Tonight*, 94–110, 113–39. To sample the eclecticism of the period, listen to "Aubuti Nkikho," recorded in London in 1930 by jazz impressario Griffiths Motsieloa and included in the musical sampler accompanying *Marabi Nights*. While the tune preserves elements of *marabi*, it also utilizes "Dixie" yodeling and Hawaiian guitars, apparently played by two Afrikaner musicians working in the same studio at the time.

24. On cinema's origins, see Robert Sklar, *Movie-Made America: A Cultural History of American Movies*, 2nd ed. (New York, 1994), 3–64. For the introduction of the medium to South Africa, see Gutsche, *History and Social Significance of Motion Pictures*, 1–95.

25. For a person of his stature—he was, by some calculations, the largest employer of labor on the African continent—Schlesinger is a remarkably elusive figure. This account is culled from John R. Shorten, *The Johannesburg Saga* (Johannesburg, 1970), 365–66, 631–38; W. J. De Kock and D.W. Kruger, eds., *Dictionary of South African Biography*, vol. 2 (Cape Town, 1972), 632–33; and L .E. Neame, *City Built on Gold* (Johannesburg, n.d.), 181–82, 207–8, 227.

26. Shorten, *Johannesburg Saga*, 342–46; Neame, *City Built on Gold*, 229–30, 236. On the citrus industry, see A. P. Cartwright, *Outspan Golden Harvest: A History of the Citrus Industry* (Cape Town, 1977); and Rosenthal, *Stars and Stripes*, 195–99. On the beginnings of radio broadcasting, see Eric Rosenthal, *'You Have Been Listening . . .': The Early Years of Radio in South Africa* (Cape Town, 1974).

27. Gutsche, *History and Social Significance of Motion Pictures*, 199–231; Neame, *City Built on Gold*, 181–82; Trevor Philpott, "The End of an Innocent Age," *The Listener*, 8 July 1976, p. 4. I discuss the history of African Film Productions, Schlesinger's studio, in Campbell, "The Americanization of South Africa," paper presented to Institute for Advanced Social Research Seminar, Johannesburg, October 1998. On the advent of television, see below.

28. On censorship, see Gutsche, *History and Social Significance of Motion Pictures*, 283–306; and Keyan Tomaselli, *The Cinema of Apartheid: Race and*

Class in South African Film (London, 1989), 9–28. For parallel developments in the United States, see Sklar, *Movie-Made America*, 161–74. Despite censorship, black South Africa soon blossomed into a major cinema market—a market, moreover, with distinctly American tastes. See Peter Davis, *In Darkest Hollywood: Exploring the Jungles of Cinema's South Africa* (Johannesburg, 1996), 9–11, 20–59.

29. On the subsidy system, see Tomaselli, *Cinema of Apartheid*, 29–51. On Afrikaner Nationalist attempts to harness the medium, see H. Rompel, *Die Bioskoop in Diens van die Volk*, 2 vols. (Bloemfontein, 1942).

30. *To Secure These Rights: The Report of the President's Commission on Civil Rights* (New York, 1947). See also Alonzo Hamby, *Beyond the New Deal: Harry S. Truman and American Liberalism* (New York, 1973); and Borstelmann, *Apartheid's Reluctant Uncle*, 64–68.

31. Hull, *American Enterprise*, 126, 200–2, 210. Borstelmann, *Apartheid's Reluctant Uncle*, 49, 96. (*Fortune*'s endorsement is quoted in Borstelmann, p. 72.)

32. Quoted in Borstelmann, *Apartheid's Reluctant Uncle*, 49.

33. Hull, *American Enterprise*, 205–9; Borstelmann, *Apartheid's Reluctant Uncle*, 105–6.

34. See U.S. Department of Commerce, Bureau of Foreign Commerce, *Investment in Union of South Africa: Conditions and Outlook for United States' Investors* (Washington, 1954). On American investment, see Rosenthal, *Stars and Stripes*, 223–25; Massie, *Loosing the Bonds*, 76–78, 112; Borstelmann, *Apartheid's Reluctant Uncle*, 96–97; and William Minter, *King Solomon's Mines Revisited: Western Interests and the Burdened History of Southern Africa* (New York, 1986), 73–83.

35. Hull, *American Enterprise*, 212; Affiliated Advertising, *Brands and Branding*, 115.

36. Massie, *Loosing the Bonds*, 274; Hull, *American Enterprise*, 210, 250, 319. Special thanks to Colin Urquhart for sharing his experiences as managing director of a South African–based U.S. subsidiary.

37. Borstelmann, *Apartheid's Reluctant Uncle*, 164, 187–88. See also Rosenthal, *Stars and Stripes*, 212–15; Hull, *American Enterprise*, 213–17; and Minter, *King Solomon's Mines Revisited*, 105–10, 130, 138.

38. For a pioneering analysis of the role of American grants and loans in Africa, and in South Africa in particular, see W. Alphaeus Hunton, *Decision in Africa: Sources of Current Conflict*, 2nd. ed. (New York, 1960), 76–90. See also Borstelmann, *Apartheid's Reluctant Uncle*, 165; Hull, *American Enterprise*, 204; and Rosenthal, *Stars and Stripes*, 215.

39. On the United States and South Africa in the aftermath of Sharpeville, see Minter, *King Solomon's Mines Revisited*, 187–203; Hull, *American Enterprise*, 245–55; and Massie, *Loosing the Bonds*, 88–89, 169–70, 214–15. (The statements by Coca-Cola and G.M. managers are quoted in Massie, pp. 88–89.). For the post-Sharpeville economic boom, see Houghton, *The South African Economy*, 209–29.

40. On the television debate, see Union of South Africa, *Report of the Commission of Inquiry into Matters Relating to Television* (Pretoria, 1971); Rob Nixon, *Homelands, Harlem and Hollywood: South African Culture and the World Beyond* (London, 1994), 43–76; and Trevor Philpott's four-part series in *The Listener*, 8–29 July 1976.

41. Nigel Mandy, *A City Divided: Johannesburg and Soweto* (Johannesburg, 1984), 68–76, and passim. On the ongoing process of suburbanization in post-apartheid South Africa, see K. Beavon, "Nearer My Mall to Thee: The Decline of the Johannesburg Central Business District and the Emergence of the Neo-Apartheid City," paper presented to the Institute for Advanced Social Research seminar, Johannesburg, October 1998.

42. Hull, *American Enterprise*, 266–67, 297–309, 349; Massie, *Loosing the Bonds*, 93, 170, 204, 368, 500, 591–93. In 1986, as in the aftermath of Sharpe-ville, a South African deputation hastened to the United States, visiting the State Department, the IMF, and nineteen commercial banks to plead for new investment capital, as well as for patience in repaying existing loans. In contrast to the earlier period, they received no satisfaction.

Oliver Schmidt

No Innocents Abroad

The Salzburg Impetus and American Studies in Europe

Heretoforth Americans have come to Europe as students, whether as
passionate pilgrims with Henry James, or more irreverently with Mark
Twain as innocents abroad. But now we come not to study your
culture, but bringing our own.

With these words Francis O. Matthiessen, the literary historian and foremost Americanist of his time, inaugurated the first Salzburg Seminar in
American Civilization, on 15 July 1947.[1] Welcoming an eclectic group of
ninety young Europeans and twenty Americans, Matthiessen depicted his
vision of an intellectual exchange in which Americans would be both
guests and hosts, students and teachers at the six-week summer school at
Schloss (castle) Leopoldskron. "You will recall," the Harvard professor
told his audience, "the classical advice to beware of Greeks bearing gifts.[2]
We cannot even make a claim to being Greeks, as everyone knows who
wants to press the analogy: we Americans are the Romans of the modern
world." However, he added, "none of our group come as imperialists of
the pax Americana to impose our values upon you. All of us come nonetheless with a strong conviction of the values of American democracy"
and also "with what I take to be a saving characteristic of American civilization: a sharp sense of both its excesses and its limitations."[3]

Such statement of purpose, delivered with conviction, confidence and
constraint, was no mere rhetorical device. Matthiessen was deeply convinced that American hegemony after 1945 was different from old-world
imperialism, in line with the idea, as Ron Robin put it, "that moral influences and persuasion could eliminate the need for naked power in the
management of global affairs."[4] If the United States was bound to retain

its leading role on the global stage, its cultural mission abroad must be guided by the values of American democracy and the study of previous empires. Matthiessen's advocacy of humanistic principles as guards against the imperial temptations of superpower aligned him with the conventional wisdom shared by many American educators at the time. It resonated with a tradition that promoted acculturation of newcomers through education, and reflected their commitment to revive intellectual exchange as a political symbol. Matthiessen's Christian socialism may have been idiosyncratic in many ways; yet I submit that his liberal, internationalist agenda lay at the very heart of the enterprise in Salzburg: Both his pride and his aesthetic prejudice in promoting American studies abroad constituted a source of inspiration for fellows and faculty alike.[5] In the eyes of its founders, the first Salzburg summer school in 1947 was indeed nothing if not "the first experiment in international education in postwar Europe."[6]

Over the intervening years, over 370 sessions involving more than 16,000 participants from 123 countries have paid tribute to a one-time experiment that commentators have christened a "cultural and intellectual Marshall plan."[7] Reinvigorated by its fiftieth anniversary in a post–Cold War Europe, the Salzburg Seminar has been experiencing something of a rebirth of its original mission.[8] In an attempt to account for the institutional longevity of the Salzburg Seminar, I suggest that it is not adequately evaluated as either an "intelligent and refined form of cultural imperialism"[9] or a "quasi-official conclave,"[10] to use but two of the competing interpretations. Nor is the seminar duly captured when interpreted as yet another slide projecting the emerging Cold War consensus of national security abroad.[11]

Instead, I take the origins of the seminar to be an apt case study of American cultural diplomacy competing for cultural hegemony in Western Europe under the conditions of an emerging international liberal order.[12] To understand the particular evolution, dilemmas, and paradoxes of the Salzburg Seminar in its early years, I would like to single out four factors that marked the emergence of a pattern, or trademark, for what may arguably have become the most illustrious center of American studies in Europe.

I. Private impetus. A joint venture cf student enthusiasm and professorial curiosity, "American Civilization" was initially introduced as a common point of reference for students to discuss both "Americanism" and "Europeanness," and hence the postwar world.[13] The first improvised summer session generated both a sustained interest in and the elements of a powerful founding myth. The legend features the castle as a stirring setting that blended Old World tradition with New World élan, and aristocratic splendor with democratic practice; a generous gesture of good will; an optimistic creed centered on cross-national communication and civic responsibility; and finally, a privileged cast including American volunteers and hand-selected young Europeans.

II. Containing contradictions. The founding myth, soon incorporated into an efficient fundraising strategy, helped blur original contradictions. Just as American cultural diplomacy came to align itself with the prerogatives of the emerging Cold War, the Salzburg Seminar learned to accommodate the ambiguities of the democratic promise. As early as 1948, heterodoxy and freedom of expression had to be compromised "in the name of democracy." Seminar administrators feared that a public debate over U.S. Army controls might well have undermined its reputation as an independent and merely philanthropic enterprise.

III. European demand for a _lingua franca_. Much of the initial impetus for an American study center came from the Europeans themselves. The seminar encouraged them to explore the boundaries of transatlantic affinities and inter-European and national identities. European responses were strongly shaped by the memories of war, Nazism, and anti-Soviet dispositions. In most instances, initial suspicions and animosities among European guests yielded to intellectual curiosity, scientific interest, and, above all, a desire for mobility and international contacts after years of isolation.

IV. Informal networks. Confidence in the permissive patronage of intellectual elites and their domino effect in society characterize the founding phases of the Salzburg Seminar, from experiment (1947) to its incorporation (1950) and ensuing fermentation as an institution. While the transition required the active support of the State Department, American foundations and academic institutions sponsoring the seminar continued to dispel fears of official propaganda and indoctrination. The seminar displayed little coordinated effort in building institutional networks—with the exception of the European Association for American Studies, founded at Leopoldskron in the spring of 1954.[14]

I.

Forsaking the details of the intriguing chronicle leading up to the establishment of the first summer session, it seems fair to say that much of this exchange project was driven by the romantic adventurism and the _chutzpah_ of a few students, the improvisation of many others, and the intellectual passions of all involved.[15] The idea for the Salzburg Seminar took shape in early 1947, when Clemens Heller, a thirty-year old graduate student at

Harvard and the son of a prosperous Viennese publisher, met with Helene Thimig, actress and émigré widow of the Austrian impresario Max Reinhardt. Encouraged by letters he received from European students, Heller had persuaded the Harvard Student Council to share its surplus from a food drive in support of European students. Joined by Richard Campbell and Scott Elledge, Heller wanted to bring together future leaders of European thought and education to study well-defined subjects of common interest to both Europeans and Americans. Together, this trio sought to provide agreeable working and living conditions for students, who had been cut off from international exchanges by fascist regimes or the dictates of war.[16] Charmed by Heller's enthusiasm, Thimig offered what had been the Reinhardt residence until the couple fled Austria in 1938, Schloss Leopoldskron.[17]

Barely half a year later, ninety European scholars and advanced students joined twenty American scholars for six weeks of common study at the castle. One hundred "potential leaders" from sixteen countries ranging as far East as Greece, Czechoslovakia, and Finland, some of whom with only a basic command of English,[18] were squeezed into facilities described by one historian as "a rather curious mixture of Eighteenth century Rococo, early twentieth century Reinhardt, and postwar army surplus."[19] The Harvard student trio had used personal and professional connections across Europe in order to locate, interview, and select candidates for the seminar. Preference was given to "those who teach, who have entered public life, and who intend to do so."[20] Their average age was twenty-seven, and their political background varied, as did their wartime experiences. An assembly of keen intellects, and not the co-optation of friendly elites in distant provinces, was what the founders around Heller had in mind. In the end only Warsaw and Moscow failed to send their hoped-for representatives, on the pretext of an alleged anti-socialist bias displayed in the reading lists.[21]

Managing the logistics of such a project in 1947 was no small feat. The winter of 1946–1947 had been a particularly harsh one; Austria and Germany were still occupied, refugees abounded, and essentials of life were still in very short supply. The U.S. Army headquarters did not object in principle to the seminar idea, but refused to offer any material support. The Harvard "establishment" showed little interest in the student initiative. Alarmed by concerns over politics and prestige, University President James B. Conant thought the proposal to be "too idealistic, too impractical, too premature."[22] Undeterred, the Harvard Student Council pledged $2,000 and the equivalent of $4,000 from a university food drive and sought cooperation with the World Student Relief in Geneva.[23] In teamwork, the students gathered support through a respectable fundraising committee that included leading educators and cultural diplomatists such as Ben M. Cherrington, the first Director of the Cultural Affairs Division in the State Department, and George N. Shuster of Hunter College. By the summer, they had collected the necessary $23,500 to secure the six-week seminar[24] and rallied a distinguished faculty, including the literary critics Alfred Kazin and Francis O. Matthiessen, the economists Wassily Leontief and Walt Rostow, and the anthropologist Margaret Mead.[25]

The academic curriculum itself turned out to cover the wide, interdisciplinary, eclectic survey of American civilization. In the field of literature, Matthiessen lectured on Emerson, Hawthorne, Melville, James, Mark Twain, Dreiser, Eliot, and gave a seminar on "Topics in American Literature." Alfred Kazin discussed a complimentary series of authors from Thoreau, Whitman, Melville, and Henry Adams to Hemingway, Dos Passos, and Cummings. With his thick Russian accent, the émigré and later Nobel laureate Wassily Leontief spoke on the "Economic Structure of the United States" and discussed "Problems in Economic Theory" in the afternoon, while Margaret Mead taught social science methodology through a series of field studies on the Schloss campus. In addition to guest speakers, European participants such as Frank Thistlewaite and Arie N. D. Den Hollander volunteered to give special lectures. The antifascist historian Gretna Salvemini stopped over on his remigration from Harvard to Italy to deliver a keynote address for the other implicit theme of the summer: "European reconstruction."[26]

All obstacles notwithstanding, the Heller initiative seemed to grow on fertile soil. Support for the American studies movement was running strong at Harvard and elsewhere, and the field brimmed with intellectual excitement.[27] Many philanthropies and private sponsors, although still hesitant to invest in freewheeling exchange projects in Europe, were committed to the prevention of further isolation of the occupied zones in Germany and Austria.[28] American universities, in turn, while struggling to accommodate demobilized soldiers flooding the campuses, were anticipating an expansion and internationalization of higher education in the wake of the GI bill. A seemingly unlimited supply of importable goods back home and favorable exchange rates and PX privileges abroad (often enhanced through black marketing) reduced the material cost and risk for the student organizers running the seminar. Furthermore, the State Department had begun to support and promote information programs abroad and worldwide exchange programs, which could build on the Fulbright Act of 1946 and the Smith-Mundt Act of 1948.[29] Paradoxically, the flaring of the Cold War increased official interest in the young institution that had been founded to overcome, or subvert, the Manichaen choices the superpower conflict increasingly imposed in Europe.

II.

The Cold War did not make a detour around the Salzburg Seminar, and its warriors soon began to interfere with the presumed free flow of exchange traffic. Despite the State Department's support of the program, criticism of the United States by participants, voiced in heated discussions, aroused the suspicion of counterintelligence (CIC) officers overtly and covertly observing the seminar. The alarmist intelligence report on "Communist Activity at Harvard Summer Seminar," although of dubious quality, triggered the alarm bells of Samuel F. Williams, Head of the Education Division of the U.S. Allied Command, Austria (USACA), who soon called for more "virile college men"—and more supervision.[30] Heller, the founder of the seminar, faced denunciation as a communist—a charge that was never substantiated—and had to stay out of the U.S. zones of occupation.[31] Matthiessen was similarly accused, his socialist humanism branded as un-American even before the publication of his intriguing, if politically controversial, report, *From the Heart of Europe* (1948). Unlike Heller,[32] Matthiessen never returned to Salzburg; in the spring of 1950, disillusioned and deeply depressed for both personal and political reasons, the humanist jumped from the twelfth floor of the Manager Hotel in Boston.[33]

At first, the State Department did not agree with the more or less overt pressures toward conformity exercised by the U.S. Army. Yet, as self-righteous anticommunist sentiment grew at home, the State Department increasingly came under attack for its presumed soft stance on Soviet foreign policy designs, a trend that, in early 1948, unbeknownst to the Fellows recruited for the second summer school, began to threaten the Salzburg Seminar altogether. The coup in Prague and the tensions in Berlin heightened the uncertainty and distrust among the four powers controlling Austria, cementing USACA's change of tactics. Rather than pursuing a *Staatsvertrag* for Austria (still the "official" policy), the military initiated its secret rearmament program, helped dispense Marshall funds, and reinforced its cultural diplomacy.[34] By mid-1948, when the Heller controversy reached its crescendo, Williams did not want to close the seminar; he merely aimed to reassert his personal control and to make the seminar safe for his version of occupation.

If the Harvard Summer School (as the seminar was called in the bureaucratic correspondence) survived the political challenge, it was to a significant degree due to the support of key scholars back home, and to a political officer of the American legation, Martin Herz.[35] In a dispatch to the Secretary of State, Herz lauded the "fairly high standard of intellectual communication" and the "new respect" the seminar had infused in American teaching methods. What really distinguished the Salzburg Seminar from other educational exchanges, he reported, was its influence "by indirection" on students, many of whom arrived rather skeptical, and its "healthy mix of the typical with the atypical, the orthodox with the heterodox," which helped to maintain "the unofficial and unsponsored character of the Seminar." It would be "fatal," Herz concluded, if the military gave "evidence of hand-picking people for their conformance." For "here, if it is left to develop in its own way, is a peculiar and unique instrument for the effective projection of American democracy."[36]

Thus, while Herz considered the seminar by no means an extension of the State Department, it seemed to him a most subtle channel to communicate one of Washington's main postwar messages: its claim that a free exchange of ideas was a touchstone of the "American" value system reflecting both cultural *and* political relations with friends and foes. If we take the reports of both faculty and fellows at face value, the Europeans were positively struck by the open and frank atmosphere. Within the privileged confines of the Schloss, the Americans appeared to have put their educational philosophy on its feet. "In listening to the way in which Americans participated in discussions," the anthropologist Margaret Mead concluded in a long evaluation report after the first session, "many of them experienced, probably for the first time, the particular quality of a democratic tradition which valued the existence of differences of opinion."[37] Little did they anticipate, know of, or talk about, the expulsion of Heller and Matthiessen from the proclaimed free flow of ideas.[38]

Their suppression did not squash the Salzburg impetus, but it surely altered its course and ended—to pick up Mark Twain's aforementioned trope—its brief innocence. Tensions among Americans revealed several faultlines—between civilians and the military, between Yankees and Southerners, between "100 percent Americans" and "long-haired theorists and radicals," between war veterans and a postwar generation. Fear of heterodoxy alone, however, could not terminate the educational experiment. The seminar not only learned to live with its own contradictions but also eventually succeeded in building them into its institutional identity. In a report on the 1948 summer school, Herz mentioned the pending Heller case while at the same time extolling the seminar's function as "a live demonstration of the fact that freedom of speech and academic freedom do indeed exist in the United States."[39] Annual internal reports later reinterpreted these early conflicts as proof of "independence from government interests." As early as 1947, the schizophrenia of Cold War culture had begun to reshape the presumably private character of cultural exchange without ever overwhelming it altogether.[40]

III.

Yet even those critics who interpret the Seminar's submission to U.S. Army demands as "ideological compliance" (*Gleichschaltung*)[41] concede that invitations to Leopoldskron continued to strike a receptive chord among many young Europeans. If the rationale of the seminar corresponded with its self-image as mediator, arbiter, and teacher, we should keep in mind a fact often neglected: that, from the very beginning, European students had invited their American colleagues to organize an exchange forum. Letters, applications, and evaluation reports indicate over and over young Europeans' dual interest in, and suspicion of, the emerging formula of the "American way of life."

To disarm lingering reservations among the fellows, the seminar staff catered to European tastes and needs wherever possible, developing a peculiar mixture of American informality and European high culture. Blending previously derided visions of modernity with the distinctly traditional privileges such as the music festival in town, the Schloss environment opened European minds to American studies. Stanley Hoffmann, a Vienna-born French fellow in 1950 and later Harvard scholar, was by no means an exception when he recalls the seminar, somewhat ironically, as an experience that unlocked the door to a "new world of classical music."[42]

There was indeed little talk of imposition in the early years. On the contrary, one is prone to find Europeans using whatever opportunities the seminar has to offer for their own purposes. Some fellows saw the seminar as a stepping stone toward studies abroad, others considered it a stimulating vacation time, and others again hoped to meet with like-minded professionals or intellectuals. Individual agendas differed and could be social, scientific, spiritual, or ideological in nature. Education chief Williams and Matthiessen were of course not the only observers to have strong opinions on contemporary political affairs in Europe. If "America" was one way of talking about "Europe," the latter often turned out to be a starting point for discussion about the nation states reformatting themselves after Europe's Thirty-Year War. Nowhere was this link more apparent than for those fellows from the erstwhile Axis countries. The seminar was a welcome stage for many visitors to reposition themselves in a post-Nazi era. The Austrian foreign minister Karl Gruber delivered a fine anticommunist speech, the socialist internationalist and economist Adolf Sturmthal (disregarding Williams' less than subtle discouragement) discussed labor relations, and the zoologist Konrad Lorenz talked about what some American students remembered as "distasteful" biologism. No passive recipient of American studies either, the resistance fighter and Austrian patriot Fritz

Molden turned out to be a particularly agile seminar guest, being called upon as a witness in "the Heller case" by *both* sides.[43]

Even those students arriving with a good deal of suspicion, left with a sense that the seminar had no strings attached—visible or invisible—other than those the Europeans wished to tie for themselves. The first meeting of the European Association for American Studies (EAAS), organized at Leopoldskron on 16–19 April 1954, illustrates the point. Thirty-eight (primarily Western) European "Americanists," including four Americans and three Yugoslavians, accepted on short notice an invitation to the extracurricular session to discuss the resources for research, teaching, and development of American studies.[44] On the top of a wish list for future research in Europe that was solicited from American scholars were the issues of the American impact in Europe and the "allegedly unique features of American civilization." As Daniel Boorstin put it in his letter to seminar president Dexter Perkins:

[S]cholars who have lived most of their lives outside of the United States and hence are less likely to accept unquestioningly the supposed uniqueness of American civilization might be especially well qualified to ask embarrassing and refreshing questions. . . . [T]he non-American has a peculiar vantage point. His superior knowledge of a culture other than that of the United States qualifies him to ask those very questions [which] might never occur to the American student of the subject. In this area, therefore, the European scholar would be qualified to make a more profound, even if perhaps less "scholarly" contribution. And also a contribution which we Americans might be incompetent to make.[45]

If the suggestions of Boorstin and his American colleagues is anything to go by, critical reflection of both exceptionalism and universalism—and no celebration of American values—is what was being asked for. "American Civ" made in Europe was to be a corrective, a regenerator, and a detector of American blind spots, and no mere agenda in the grand scheme of authentic Cold War containment. The planned panel on the role of the Salzburg Seminar in the development of American studies was eventually taken out of the official program. However, the appointment of the seminar's assistant director, Robert O. Mead, as secretary of the newly founded EAAS signals the key role the Salzburg Seminar played in aiding what Sigmund Skard, the director of the Amerikansk Institute in Oslo and chairman of the meeting, described as "the growth of American studies in Europe."[46]

IV.

Five years later, in his classic work on American Studies in Europe, Skard concluded that "the influence of the Salzburg seminar can be hardly overestimated."

In a period when American studies were being organized all over Europe, under great difficulties and sometimes against resistance, the Seminar has served as a spearhead by offering unobtrusively to the postwar generation of European scholarship a brief and informal, but solid introduction to the field. . . . [L]ocated in a small neutralized nation with no ax to grind, the Seminar has avoided the political suspicions of skeptical Europe; and the quality and objectivity of its work have ensured its lasting success.[47]

While one could take issue with Skard's depoliticized view of Austria as a "neutralized nation,"[48] there can be little doubt that the Salzburg Seminar has served as a conduit for intellectual exchange between Europe and the United States. During its first decade, sojourns at Leopoldskron attracted considerable academic talent, particularly in American studies and the social sciences.[49] Most certainly they have contributed to transnational, professional networks among functional elites and served as useful venues for continuous transatlantic dialogue.

There is equally little doubt, if one contrasts goals and achievements, about some of the seminar's shortcomings. All in all, alumni associations have not taken deep root; recent attempts to revive this form of self-organization seem to indicate less a growing assimilation on the parts of Europeans than an apprehension about the benefits of tax-deductible contributions. One may also question to what extent the recruitment of fellows has increasingly tended to favor the converted over the unconvinced and heretic. The historical record indicates that during the first two decades the Salzburg Seminar never became the East–West exchange station it aspired to be.[50] At least in the short run, then, cultural diplomacy did not prove to be the avant-garde of détente. In rewriting the early history of the seminar, we need to disentangle political constraints from institutional choices, the commodification of its foundation myth from historical practice, and the context of social privilege from the script of promoting ideas about "democracy." These themes require further exposition elsewhere.[51]

By way of conclusion, suffice it to say that if cynics did well to denounce an invitation to Salzburg as bribery, others like Matthiessen preferred to call it a gift (with all its connotations). I, myself, may go along with Margaret Mead in positing that the Salzburg forum permitted young Europeans to experience "some of those aspects of American culture which the best intentioned army of occupation is unfitted to convey."[52] Now that the U.S. Congress has unwrapped its Cold War presents and redefined American presence in Europe, it might well be worth studying the challenges and legacies of that immediate postwar generation. A double promoter of American civilization and American studies, the Salzburg Seminar serves as an intriguing case study of cultural diplomacy. It allows us to illuminate a complex and often contradictory set of aspirations among private and public American actors, and a variety of expectations, needs, and responses of their guests, as they met, exchanged ideas, and often enough—we now know—managed to learn about and from each other. As part of a new American mission on the old continent, the Salzburg impetus at the heart of Europe was no longer passionate pilgrimage, nor innocence abroad.

Notes

1. I would like to thank Amy Farber, Campbell Craig, Rebekah Davis, Tim Ryback, and Mitchell Schechter for their comments, Luisa Passerini for her ongoing support, and John Lewis Gaddis for his early encouragement. An earlier version of this essay was presented to the workshop "Concepts and Methods for United States Studies in Europe" at the European Association for American Studies conference, Warsaw, 21–25 March 1996.

2. Matthiessen refers to the famous speech by the Trojan priest Laocoon, who is trying to dissuade his fellow Trojans from bringing the wooden horse, filled with Greek warriors, inside the city walls. "Don't trust the horse, Trojans," he says, *quidquid id est, timeo Danaos et dona ferentes.* "Whatever it is, I fear Greeks, even when they bear gifts." His warning is all but ignored. Once Laocoon and his two sons are killed by serpents, the Trojans open their gates and bring the horse in, thus setting up the fall of Troy. Cf. Vergil's *Aeneid* 2.49.

3. F. O. Matthiessen, typescript, July 1947, Box 1 "1947," Salzburg Seminar Archives/Salzburg (herein cited as SSAS).

4. Ron Robin, *The Barbed Wire College: Reeducating German POWs in the United States during World War II* (Princeton, 1995), 27

5. One must not underestimate the degree to which Matthiessen, like many of his fellow teachers challenging culturally ingrained biases against American anti-intellectualism, relished being taken seriously as what another Salzburg Faculty, years later, flippantly called "a new kind of ambassador—the thoughtful American" (Alvin Toffler, "Seminar at Salzburg," *Saturday Review*, 17 August 1963). We need to keep in mind that in 1947 only very few permanent institutions in Europe—among them, the universities of Uppsala, London, Oxford, Cambridge, and the Collège de France—were offering systematic studies of American culture. Sigmund Skard would launch the American Institute in Oslo in early 1948.

6. The advertisement for the 1947 summer seminar was not altogether correct (Program sheet, Box 1 "1947," SSAS). Anticipating the Seminar by two years, the Internationalen Hochschulwochen in Alpbach, a village in Tyrol, have a more credible claim to be the first "European experiment." The symposium, still thriving today, was instigated in the summer of 1945 by the newly founded Österreichische College under the tutelage of Otto Molden and Simon Moser, an erstwhile student of Heidegger. Otto Molden, "Die unsichtbare Generation," in Paula von Predarovic and Otto Molden, *Alpbach* (Wien, 1952), 6. Otto Molden, *Der andere Zauberberg: Das Phänomen Alpbach* (Wien, 1981).

7. Sigmund Skard, *American Studies in Europe*, 2 vols. (Philadelphia, 1958); more recently, André Kaenel, "Les Etudes américaines en Europe, modèle et con-

quête," in Jacques Portes, ed., *L'Amérique comme modèle, l'Amérique sans modèle* (Lille, 1993), 171.

8. For the recent expansion of seminar activities particularly into Eastern Europe, cf. Presidential address, President Olin Robison, Annual Reports, Salzburg Seminar in American Studies, 1992–1996; and Robert Marquand, "Austrian haven for scholars bounces back," *Christian Science Monitor*, 22 August 1994.

9. Marcus Cunliffe, "American Studies in Europe," in Robert H. Walker, ed., *American Studies Abroad* (London, 1975), 47, paraphrased in Wagnleitner, *Coca-Colonization in Austria: The Cultural Mission of the United States in Austria after the Second World War* (Chapel Hill, 1994), 168.

10. Richard Pells, *Not Like US: How Europeans Have Loved, Hated, and Transformed American Culture since World War II* (New York, 1997), 185.

11. André Kaenel, "Les Etudes américaines en Europe," 168.

12. Robert Latham, *The Liberal Moment: Modernity, Security, and the Making of Postwar International Order* (New York, 1997); Emily Rosenberg's *Spreading the American Dream: American Economic and Cultural Expansion, 1890–1945* (New York, 1982); Frank Ninkovich, *Diplomacy of Ideas. U.S. Foreign Policy and Cultural Relations, 1938- 1950* (Cambridge, 1981).

13. In his heuristic argument on "Americanization," Volker Berghahn has put much emphasis on the need for a *tertium comparationis* in postwar Europe; idem, *The Americanization of West German Industry, 1945–1973* (New York, 1986).

14. While sketching some elementary forces marking the seminar's formative years, this essay is primarily concerned with the tension between the founders' aspirations and the U.S. Army's need for control. For a more systematic account of the seminar's institutionalization during the 1950s, I refer to my 1999 doctoral dissertation on American exchange programs after 1945. Meanwhile, I welcome responses and personal recollections by seminar alumni.

15. Aside from feature stories and essays written by participants, literature on the Salzburg Seminar is mostly descriptive. F. O. Matthiessen's chapter "Salzburg: July and August," in idem, *From the Heart of Europe* (New York, 1948), 3–66, and Alfred Kazin's recollections in *A Lifetime Burning in Every Moment* (New York, 1996) remain the most vivid accounts of the origins in 1947 and 1948. Thomas H. and Louis J. Eliot's *The Salzburg Seminar* (Ipswich, 1987) and Timothy W. Ryback's concise synthesis "Salzburg Seminar—A Community of Fellows" in the seminar's picturesque autobiography, *Schloss Leopoldskron* (Salzburg, 1994), provide reliable institutional histories rich in anecdotes.

16. *Salzburg Seminar: 40th Anniversary, 1947–1987* (Salzburg, 1987), 32. In 1947, food and shelter were scarce resources not taken for granted by thousands of DPs and refugees in nearby camps.

17. Located on the outskirts of Salzburg, Leopoldskron was built in 1736–1744 for the Archbishop Leopold Firmian. After a history of changing proprietors it was Max Reinhardt, co-founder of the Salzburg Festival, who restored its original splendor, surrounded by seventeen acres of land and a scenic, if artificial, lake. C. W. Thomsen, *Leopoldskron: Early History, the Reinhardt Era, The Salzburg Seminar* (Siegen, 1983).

18. Benjamin F. Wright, "Seminar in Salzburg," *Harvard Alumni Bulletin* (spring 1948).

19. Ryback, *Salzburg Seminar—A Community of Fellows*, 160

20. Promotional pamphlet, n.d., folder "Student Council Salzburg Seminar, 1947," Harvard Archives, HUD 3808.679.

21. Relying on his powers of persuasion, Heller personally went to see the Polish Minister of Education—to no avail. Interviews with Clemens Heller, 4 September 1996, and Scott Elledge, 26 October 1996. In the eyes of Heller, the creation of the Seminar is testimony to an "optimistic generation, which acted on its own convictions rather than on orders coming from governmental instances" and a belief that "a new world could be constructed on the basis of a worldwide dialogue and scientific collaboration." Letter of Clemens Heller to the President of the Salzburg Seminar, Dr. Olin Robison, Lausanne, 23 February 1995.

22. As quoted in *Salzburg Seminar—A Community of Fellows*, 157.

23. The World Student Relief (WSR) united aid agencies such as Pax Romana, International Student Service, and the International Union of Students. American donations were raised through the World Student Service Fund, New York. When contacted by the Harvard students, the WSR was already managing rest centers in Cambloux, France, Ashton Hayes, U.K., and Rocca di Papa, Italy.

24. According to the Seminar's budget table, nd., Box 1 "1947," SSAS, the breakdown was as follows: $9,000 food, $7,000 transportation, $3,000 rent, $2,000 administration, $1,500 repairs, $1,000 books. While neither faculty nor staff received any salary, living expenses were free for all participants. Careful budgeting notwithstanding, the Student Council registered a deficit exceeding $5,500. While considered manageable by Heller, rising debts would eventually trigger a financial crisis in the fall of 1949, and the incorporation of the seminar in early 1950.

25. Correspondence, Box 1 "1947," SSAS.

26. The other faculty members were: Vida Ginsberg, New School of Social Research, "The American Drama"; Richard Schlatter, Rutgers, "American Historiography"; Elspeth Davies, Sarah Lawrence, "US Foreign Policy"; Benjamin Wright, Harvard, "Theory of American Government"; Neil McDonald, New Jersey College for Women, "Government in the United States"; Walt Rostow, Oxford, "Economic Influences on American Policy"; Lyman Bryson, Columbia, "Mass Communication." Among the special lecturers: Mario Praz, University of Rome, on "Poe, Hemingway, and Eliot"; James Sweeney, former director of the Museum of Modern Art, New York, on "Painting and Architecture in the U.S." See "Report on the 1947 Seminar," Student Council Salzburg Seminar, 1947, Harvard Archives, HUD 3808.679.

27. F. O. Matthiessen was succeeded in the following years by students of his and other epigones in the young discipline, such as Henry Nash Smith, Daniel Aaron, and R. J. B. Lewis who, in 1950, served for one year as academic director in Salzburg.

28. The Rockefeller Foundation, for instance, funded its vital contribution through its German emergency program, aided early on by the Old Dominion Foundation and the Commonwealth Fund; Rockefeller was also instrumental in winning the Ford Foundation as a major sponsor beginning in the mid-fifties.

29. Enacted ten years after FDR had initiated the first official cultural exchange program, the so-called Smith-Mundt Act distinguished between international information ("to disseminate abroad information about the United States") and educational exchange ("to cooperate with other nations in the interchange of persons, knowledge, and skills"). While the Fulbright Act was sponsored by foreign currencies owed to the U.S. government for war surplus materials, the Smith-Mundt-Act allowed for the expenditure of hard U.S. dollars. Cf. *Public Law 402, 80th Congress, the Information and Educational Exchange Act*

of 1948, January 1948. Contrary to Heller's hopes, the occupation of Austria and Germany delayed bilateral agreements—and thus the arrival of the first Fulbright grants—until the early 1950s. Direct government grants played only a minor role in the seminar budget until the Kennedy administration.

30. Re: "Communist Activity at Harvard Summer Seminar," 26 July 1947, "Mr Heller–Harvard Seminar File," Box 8, RG 260, Records of U.S. Occupation Headquarters, WW II, U.S. Allied Command Austria (USACA), Education Division, General Records, National Archives and Records Administration (NARA), Washington, D.C. The zoologist Samuel H. Williams became the central figure in this dispute behind the scene that was to last for almost twelve months. As a scientist he favored free inquiry, yet as an army officer in occupied Austria he sought control over experiments. This tension was apparent from his first visit to Leopoldskron. "Now that the session is over, we are most happy to report its success in achieving *most of its aims*. The Seminar was well directed and the deportment of the staff and students was commendable" (my italics). At the same time, Williams reported that "it was imperative that we guard against any activities which might negate the occupation mission or which might be deleterious to the interests of our Government's beneficent attempts to reestablish Austrian autonomy. Our continued scrutiny of Leopoldskron was, therefore, a necessary defense measure." Letter, Williams to President Conant, 3 September 1947, Box 1 "1947," SSAS.

31. Relying primarily on the original CIC report, plus circumstantial and contradictory evidence, High Commissioner Gen. Geoffrey Keyes upheld the verdict: "I am confident that Mr. Heller, in making the above statement, went beyond the reasonable scope which could be attributed to intellectual freedom. Such statements touch on very vital questions . . . and I believe that you will agree that such statements should not be made in an occupied area. . . ." Gen. Keyes, Vienna, to Merle Fainsod, Dept. of Government, Harvard University, 24 May 1948, "Mr. Heller–Harvard Seminar File," Box 8, RG 260, NARA.

32. Despite his exclusion, Heller remained the Seminar's *spiritus rector* well into the early 1950s. Although no longer a front man, he inspired the next generation of students to pursue the seminar idea even as the seminar's governance shifted from students to scholars under the new president, Dexter Perkins (1950–1961). Heller settled in Paris and remained a center of gravity for intellectual exchange as Fernand Braudel's chief administrator at the Sixième Section des Hautes Etudes and, later, at the Maison des Sciences de l'Homme in Paris. In a fitting epitaph for the unwarranted actions in 1948 (brought to my attention by Perry Anderson), Immanuel Wallerstein dedicated his recent work, *After Liberation*, to the founder of the Salzburg Seminar.

33. When Matthiessen committed suicide amidst the high tide of McCarthyite redbaiting and homophobia, political observers on the Left were too quick to see him as a victim of the Cold War. His farewell note seemed to support such a conclusion: "I am exhausted. I have been subject to so many severe depressions during the past few years. . . . How much the state of the world has to do with my state of mind I do not know. But as a Christian and a socialist believing in international peace, I find myself terribly oppressed by the present tensions." Seminar administrators have grappled with the question whether the conflict with the U.S. Army in Austria may have contributed to his desperate state of mind. According to Dexter Perkins, Matthiessen had signed up as a member of the Salzburg faculty in the summer of 1950, but was yet again denied a visa. Daniel Aaron, a student

and close friend of Matthiessen, maintains that the suicide was primarily related to Matthiessen's unresolved grief over the loss of his partner. Dexter Perkins, *Yield of Years: An Autobiography* (Boston, 1969), 69; William E. Cain, F. O. *Matthiessen and the Politics of Criticism* (Madison, 1988); Paul Marlor Sweezy, ed., *F .O. Matthiessen, 1902–1950* (New York, 1950); interview with Daniel Aaron, 25 May 1996.

34. Bischof, "Prag liegt westlich von Wien," in G. Bischof and J. Leidenfrost, *Die bevormundete Nation* (Innsbruck, 1988), 324.

35. The same age as Heller, Herz was born in New York in 1917 and spent much of his youth and adolescence in interwar Vienna. An American citizen, he returned to the United States in 1936 and completed his undergraduate degree at Columbia University before he was drafted into the Army. His bilingual skills predestined Herz for work in the Office of War Information. He entered Austria in the spring of 1945 with the "Psychological Warfare Division" and joined the State Department after a stint at the U.S. Allied Commission in Austria. Cf. also Oliver Rathkolb, ed., *Gesellschaft und Politik am Beginn der Zweiten Republik: Vertrauliche Berichte der US-Militäradministration aus Österreich 1945 in engl. Originalfassung* (Boehlau, 1985), 415.

36. Memo by Martin F. Herz to Mr. Erhardt, Vienna, 16 January 1948, "Harvard-Leopoldskron, 1948," Box 1, RG 260, Records of U.S. Occupation Headquarters, WW II, USACA, Education Division, General Records, NARA; also, Reinhold Wagnleitner, ed., *Understanding Austria, The Political Reports and Analyses of Martin F. Herz, 1945–1948* (Salzburg, 1984), 413.

37. Margaret Mead, evaluation report on summer session 1947, Box 1 "1947," SSAS.

38. Interviews with Carl Kaysen, Robert and Barbara Solow, and Herbert Gleason, spring 1996. Alfred Kazin, *A Life Burning in Every Moment* (New York, 1996).

39. Reinhold Wagnleitner, ed., *Understanding Austria*, 464.

40. For points of departure in discussing a cultural cold war, cf. Christopher Lasch, "The Cultural Cold War: A Short History of the Congress of Cultural Freedom," in Barton Bernstein, ed., *Towards a New Past: Dissenting Essays in American History* (New York, 1968); Stephen Whitfield, *The Culture of the Cold War* (Baltimore, 1991); Amy Kaplan and Donald E. Pease, eds., *Cultures of United States Imperialism* (Durham, 1994), and Pierre Grémion, *Intelligence de l'Anticommunisme: Le Congrès pour la Liberté de la Culture, 1950–75* (Paris, 1995).

41. Reinhold Wagnleitner, *Coca-Colonization*, 165.

42. Interview with Stanley Hoffmann, 24 April 1996. Cf. Kazin, *A Lifetime Burning*, 90.

43. Interview, Robert and Barbara Solow, spring 1996. Adolf Sturmthal, *Zwei Leben: Erinnerungen eines sozialistischen Internationalisten zwischen Oesterreich und den USA* (Wien, 1989). Active in the Austrian resistance movement during World War II, Molden later married the daughter of the OSS chief and later head of the CIA, Alan Dulles. In the immediate postwar years, Molden served as transatlantic liaison for the conservative foreign minister Karl Gruber, emerging as a conservative journalist and publisher in his own right. Fritz Molden, *Besetzer, Toren, Biedermaenner. Ein Bericht aus Österreich 1945–1962* (Wien, 1980).

44. For a complete list of participants, see "American Studies Conference, April 16–19, 1954," Box "1954," SSAS.

45. Letter, Daniel Boorstin to Dexter Perkins, 8 April 1954; cf. letter, Robert E. Spiller to Perkins, 6 April 1954; letter, Arthur M. Schlesinger to Perkins, 1 April 1954, Box "1954," SSAS.
46. Schedule of meetings, April 16–19, 1954, Box "1954," SSAS.
47. Skard, *American Studies in Europe*, 636.
48. Cf. David S. Broder, "Neutral high ground," *Washington Post*, 29 May 1996, for a more recent illustration of an enduring metaphor.
49. An impressionistic list of German participants includes sociologists like Dahrendorf, Lepsius, Maynz, and von Friedeburg; the political scientists Hennis and Besson; historians such as Rüschemeyer, Kosselek, Bracher, Hans and Wolfgang Mommsen; the legal experts von Münch and Zeidler; the economist Giersch; the journalists Kaiser and Thomas von Randow; among the Americanists, A. Weber, Moltmann, Brumm, and Poenicke. However, one is hard pressed to support Skard's claim that, by the late 1950s, "great numbers" of Americanists "received their initiation" in Salzburg. Probably less than 10 percent of those researchers active in the field had gone through the Seminar by 1957. Salzburg Seminar Directory, 1947–1980, SSAS. Skard, *American Studies*, 679–87.
50. Between 1947 and 1961, the seminar invited 3,646 Western Europeans and 150 Eastern Europeans, among whom fellows from the former Yugoslavia predominated The trend in favor of "Eastern" Europeans (defined as "behind the iron curtain," including the Soviet Union), up to then hardly exceeding the Finnish quota, began to shift in the mid-sixties. SSSA, alumni database, F:/document/jt/alumni/fellows#.doc.
51. In order to come to grips with Skard's verdict ("lasting success"), much more is required than could possibly be done here—an analysis of the seminar as ritual and rite of initiation; an interpretation of the power of privilege bonding the select few invited to attend the seminar; an examination of Leopoldskron as a symbol of European patterns of allegiance and as a metaphor for (asymmetrical) exchange.
52. Evaluation report, "Salzburg Seminar 1947," by Margaret Mead, Box 1 "1947," SSAS.

II The World of Hollywood

Theodore A. Wilson

Selling America via the Silver Screen?

Efforts to Manage the Projection of American Culture

Abroad, 1942–1947

In late November 1944, shortly after President Franklin D. Roosevelt's sweeping victory in his campaign for a fourth term, Office of War Information staffer David Wilson submitted a memorandum to the organization's "think tank," the Washington Review Board. This document, entitled "Draft Outline of a Directive on Projection of America," was one of many generated within OWI during the three stormy years of its existence to confront the thorny, multifaceted problems of what visage America should show to the world following the inevitable victory and how best to frame and highlight that portrayal.[1] The paper triggered an extended if ultimately futile debate within OWI about how best to depict America's past, present, and future image abroad. Wilson's memorandum is noteworthy chiefly because of the double meaning found in its title—"projection" in the sense of forecast or prediction and "projection" as related to the most popular and presumably influential medium for communication about American culture during and after World War II, the motion picture. Examining that discourse—its origins, certain of the assumptions and ambitions that informed it, and what if anything constituted a relationship between the aims of official policymakers and the assorted reflections of America that emerged wherever a projector cast "moving pictures" onto a silvered screen, whitewashed wall, or grimy bedsheet—forms the substance of this essay. Much of what follows will perhaps be familiar, but revisiting these years and some of the films depicting them from a post–Cold War, post-triumphialist perspective may bring into sharper focus questions that have been both obscured and distorted over the years.

Wilson's thinkpiece began with the usual stipulation that his "draft outline" was precisely that. Nor was it particularly original, for a substantial OWI literature on the general subject of what he termed "Americana policies" had already been produced.[2] He further acknowledged that "the bulk of what we have to say about our own affairs cannot have universal interest; our projection of America must vary with the differing interests, intellects, economics, politics and cultures of our many target areas." However, there did exist an important part of "our American story" that deserved "to be presented to all audiences in fairly uniform fashion."[3] What did that narrative comprise?

The overriding aim, Wilson asserted, was the purpose that has driven "cultural diplomacy" in its various manifestations from America's entry into World War II. "Our projection of America," he asserted, "is not an end in itself. It is a means of making other peoples favorably disposed toward us, of diffusing among them an atmosphere of liking and respect for us which will aid in the implementation of our national policies."[4] What stood in the way of that goal? Generally speaking, it was the negative image of America that peoples elsewhere in the world had derived from watching all those horrible gangster movies, celebrations of exploitation, greed, crudity, and violence that had typified the films exported abroad before World War II, a time when American films dominated European and other markets. Wilson's memo cited a "representative collection" of OWI reports and analyses over the past several months:

"We are barbarian destroyers of older cultures."—*Operational Guidance on Documentary Films*

"A barbaric country without culture or taste."—*Long-Range Policy Guidance for Italy*

"All Americans are rich. . . . Americans lack cultural background and understanding. . . . Terrorism and gangsterism are an accepted feature of American daily life. . . . Americans lead a frivolous life.—*Long-Range Policy Guidance for the Netherlands*

"Europe expects Americans to be boastful, rash and superficial."—*Long-Range Guidance for Europe*

"Americans are ignorant of European nations and their achievements."—*Long–Range Policy Guidance for Hungary*

"Americans are materialistic and their greatest ambition is the accumulation of wealth and comfort. . . . immorality is prevalent. . . . America has far-reaching imperialistic designs."—*Long-Range directive for Syria and Lebanon*

"Alarm about our post-war commercial plans is becoming widespread in Great Britain and already dwarfs the fear that we will return to ostrich isolationism."—*Basic Directive for Great Britain*

Taken together, such observations added up to a picture of Americans as:

1. Uncultured; uninformed about and unappreciative of the cultures of other peoples.
2. Materialistic and grasping.
3. Intolerant of others' views and unconcerned about their problems.
4. Boastful, superficial, and undisciplined.
5. Unpredictable and unreliable.
6. Impractically idealistic.
7. Blind to injustices in our own society.

The memo admitted that replacing "an established group of anti-American ideas with a ready-made set of pro-American ideas" was an impossible task. But it argued that "by infiltration and expansion of bridgeheads we can hope in many cases to swing a preponderantly unfriendly viewpoint a measurable distance in our favor, and to do so in a reasonably short time, provided the themes we employ are simple, direct, plausible and skillfully disseminated." Wilson proposed to do so via a campaign—using speeches, writings, radio programs, and especially films—to drive home the following points:

First, Americans were well-informed about what was happening elsewhere in the world;

Second, Americans were well-intentioned, that they were committed to both individual freedom and to the opportunities for women, blacks, and other minorities, raising standards of living, and championing the rights of workers and the elderly and disabled, and that both national policies and public attitudes reflected "enlightened self-interest" in dealings with the rest of the world;

Third, Americans were not standardized, robotic consumers of mass culture, that one should not "jump to conclusions about American characteristics" that in reality were "as varied as the land itself." The aim was to "orient" foreign audiences to the "expression by Americans of divergent views on almost every topic," stressing that "'E pluribus unum' is more than a motto on a great seal," and emphasizing the proliferation of America's geographical locales, regional cultures and characteristics, ethnic and religious groupings, internal migrations, daily life, and occupational interests.[5]

The memo elicited assorted qualified responses and several vitriolic refutations. The most dismissive came from OWI political analysts. One observed that there may be occasions, in fact, "when we may not want a particular people to 'like' us or 'admire' us. We may want a people, for instance, to stand in a certain amount of fear of us. . . . [W]e know that the very size and power of this country will produce a certain amount of envy, suspicion, and even hatred. It may be better for these antagonistic feelings to vent themselves in a sneering or patronizing attitude toward American 'culture' than in hostile political thought or action." This rebuttal concluded: "I believe, therefore, that we should strenuously avoid any effort to 'sell' American culture (with the implication, which I believe emerges in the Draft, that we have a feeling of inferiority in this field) unless we select for projection such aspects of our culture which will promote specific and purposeful political reaction in foreign audiences."[6]

Generally, however, OWI senior officials agreed that foreigners (or at least European intellectuals) still largely viewed Americans as uncultured, obsessively materialistic, boastful, impractically idealistic, and blind to the blatant injustices prevalent in their own society and that these attitudes should be challenged. One stated that "even for Europeans, we have outlived the myth that we are still in coonskins and shouting in forests," but he urged that we "grow less sensitive about ourselves as barbarians."[7] If the pervasive American sense of inferiority persisted, "we shall lack the impulse and the poise to tackle the greater and graver problems that face us—i.e., the revelation that all is not heaven in the USA."[8] Another observed that OWI had been "constantly on the defensive when it comes to the presentation of American cultural achievements." That was wrongheaded, for "American culture is a popular culture; this is attested in all forms of art by writers like Mark Twain; musical compositions like 'Porgy and Bess'; the modern ballet," and particularly in motion pictures produced for a broad and diverse popular audience. Whatever happens, American culture should be presented in "a positive and non-apologetic manner."[9]

These issues and concerns had been simmering since OWI's establishment in June 1942 and, indeed, long before. The conviction that people in other countries held erroneous and/or unfortunate ideas about the United States and American society and that those attitudes derived chiefly from the stream of motion pictures churned out by Hollywood and blithely exported to Europe, Latin America, and other regions was as pervasive as the presumed American inferiority complex. There appeared to be objective support for such a conclusion. In a 1937 study, 1,000 British teenagers were asked to identify their principal source of information about the United States. The cinema came out far ahead (with 583 assigning it first place) of newspapers, schoolbooks, or teachers.[10] This and similar data seemingly confirmed the views of foreign observers that cinematic portrayals "of "brigandage, . . . racketeering, and sensuality" degraded America's world image. "Do they not realize," wrote a British reviewer of *Scarface* in 1932, "that such vivid concentration by American film directors and companies upon the putrid spots of their big cities . . . is gradually quite destroying the respect of the world for American citizenship, American manners and morals, and bringing the world to the suspicion that the whole American nation consists of a lot of perverts or fools, a pack of worse than worthless weaklings and wrong-uns."[11] That view generally held until World War II.

Between 1942 and late 1944, as Clayton Koppes and Gregory Black have informed us in their authoritative account of OWI and Hollywood, significant control was exercised over the movies being produced by Hollywood for commercial distribution.[12] As well, a collaborative effort between the War Department and some Hollywood directors led to such documentary films aimed at shaping domestic opinion as the "Why We Fight" series.[13] OWI's Bureau of Motion Pictures (BMP) erected a second code for Hollywood via its "Government Information Manual for the Motion Picture Industry," stressing self-censorship and uplift.[14] Although export of Hollywood films dropped off sharply (because such markets as Germany, Italy, and France were blocked and because of shipping and financial constraints), OWI, along with the Hays Office and the Department of State, agonized about the impact of Hollywood fare—once Europe was liberated and pent-up demand for America's celluloid products was unleashed—and scrutinized scripts with great diligence. Indeed, OWI's power over the movie industry largely derived from the ability of its Foreign Branch (which took control of the BMP in 1943) to award export licenses.[15]

OWI oversight had the dual aims of, first, ensuring that movies not insult—either intentionally or otherwise—America's allies and other nations deemed important to the war effort, and, second, that they avoid depictions of such "unattractive" aspects of American life as gangsterism, racism, materialism, and anti-intellectualism. A Twentieth Century–Fox Film Corporation internal memo in March 1943 discussed the four pillars of the government's War Information Program for Hollywood. First, it was necessary to ask: "will this picture help win the war?" Obviously, most movies would (and should) be "pure entertainment" films. "But even in non-war pictures care should be taken," the OWI emphasized, "not to do anything which might harm the war effort, such as presenting a false picture of American life which might mislead foreign audiences." Second, ensure that every film treat its subject honestly and realistically. "We don't want to make pictures which will appear as false and ridiculous 20 years from now as some World War I pictures appear today." Third, take care that films dealing with the war remain valid when screened eight months or a year after being approved for production.

Fourth, be especially circumspect about producing movies that can be sent overseas. "Misrepresentation of American life, of our allies, or of the world we live in could do incalculable harm in those areas which have had nothing but Axis propaganda for years."[16]

Using the club of national security, OWI pressed (sometimes with less than total success) Hollywood filmmakers to forego such prewar stock-in-trade stereotypes as buffoonish, effete British aristocrats lapping up champagne in English country houses and exploiting the natives everywhere else. For example, *Adventure in Iraq*, a Warner Brothers remake of the George Arliss film *Green Goddess*, was deemed "horrible" and unsuitable for showing to foreign audiences because of its misleading portrayal of Iraqis as "devil-worshippers" and as uniformly pro-Axis, but especially because one of the villains was an English valet who was "such an unsavory character" that British audiences would be alienated—though Irish moviegoers would likely have cheered. Although initially cleared for export, in March 1944 the film was shelved indefinitely by Warner Brothers with the hope that "sometime after the world is straightened out we may be able to release it then." Sensitivity to national/ethnic stereotyping triggered similar responses to Charlie Chan movies (in fact, to most American-made films about China such as *Dragon Seed*, *China*, *Keys of the Kingdom*, and the fortunately-never-released *Beast of the East*) and to movies featuring Hispanic characters.[17] Although much got through that strikes our sensibilities as odd or outrageous, these films marked a notable advance on the world-as-envisioned-by Hollywood before Pearl Harbor. While reviewers trashed these films as insulting, melodramatic, and mostly silly, OWI considered *Dragon Seed*, which had been reworked in significant ways to meet objections of the Motion Picture Division, "a document not only of the fighting Chinese people but, by implication, of people all over the world who have united to fight aggression."[18]

OWI worried that Danny Kaye's zany comedy *Up in Arms* (1944), which had Danny singlehandedly capturing twenty Japanese soldiers, would be taken literally by foreign audiences. "The tendency on the part of past American films to extol the glorious achievement of the Yanks to the exclusion of the . . . other United Nations has been deeply resented overseas," remarked one OWI official. "The war is not a subject for musical comedy." Both OWI's New York Review Board and the War Department opposed overseas distribution of *Up in Arms*.[19]

The second censorial function performed by OWI and collaborated in by Hollywood involved the attempted avoidance of plots and characterizations that offered negative portrayals of American life. That proved a hard nut to crack, for tough kids and ex-cons in urban shoot-'em-ups, movies introducing rural rubes to big city life (whether via the political satire of *Mr. Smith Goes to Washington* or bucolic farces), and stereotyping of blacks, immigrants, labor organizers, and corrupt politicians had been staple fare in 1930s Hollywood films.[20] Despite a public outcry that such films as *Secret Six* and *Public Enemy* made racketeers and gunmen into heroes and the view that "the movies were so occupied with crime and sex stuff and are so saturating the minds of children the world over with social sewage that they have become a menace to the mental and moral life of the coming generation," Hollywood continued its waltz with murderer's row.[21]

Mowing down the thugs proved only marginally easier in wartime. OWI made effective use of rules promulgated in December 1942 by the Office of Censorship that, among other things, prohibited depiction of "labor, class or other disturbances since 1917 which might be distorted into enemy propaganda."[22] Films such as *Mr. Lucky* (a 1943 RKO film in which Cary Grant played a crooked gambler) and *Lucky Jordan* (Paramount, 1942), featuring Alan Ladd as a draft-dodging swindler were rewritten to meet BMP objections. Despite OWI's opposition, however, such wartime films as *Clancy Street Kids* and *Cowboy in Manhattan,* emphasizing lawlessness and the vulnerability of ordinary Americans to gangsters, were released.[23] OWI experienced even less success at persuading Hollywood to downplay escapist screwball comedies/society takeoffs (exemplified by Preston Sturges's *Palm Beach Story,* released by Paramount in November 1942). An OWI official termed *Palm Beach Story* "a libel on America at war," and asked what America's allies would think of the "unbridled extravagance" and "childish irresponsibility" it celebrated.[24]

On the positive side were those films that dramatized America's contribution to the Allied war effort (focusing on the role of the U.S. armed forces, production miracles, home front sacrifices, and related themes) and movies that celebrated American ideals and institutions. In the former category belonged the saga of American nurses on Bataan, *So Proudly We Hail* (1943), *Sahara* (1943, especially pleasing to OWI because it featured an international platoon), the many-times critiqued *An American Romance* (1943), and David O. Selznick's sentimental ode to the American home front, *Since You Went Away,* which was an Academy Award contender in 1944.[25] Koppes and Black have rightly described *Since You Went Away* as "a virtual compendium of OWI-approved vignettes of American life as changed by the war."[26] After a review of the film script, OWI's Ulrich Bell rhapsodized about the "tremendous importance" of *Since You Went Away* "from the standpoint of picturing to the outside world the serious way in which Americans take the war and regard the future."[27] Producer David Selznick had argued that the film's dramatization of a family's awakening to the need for sacrifices on the home front was extremely effective. "I should think," he said, "that the Government would wish to show this in foreign countries where the impression undoubtedly exists that most Americans are still living on the fat of the land."[28] Interestingly, a British Institute of Public Opinion poll of what one British expert termed "this rather sentimental American film" was conducted in early 1945. Moviegoers in Bedford and in London were asked what they liked and did not like. Many said they did not like the "emotional parts, the sob-stuff and weeping," and about one-fifth believed the film was not true to life, that the picture of family life was too perfect. But when asked if they understood America better after seeing *Since You Went Away,* 54 percent in Bedford and 62 percent in London said "yes."[29]

OWI (and, indirectly, the Roosevelt administration) invested great hopes in those films—documentaries and features—that directly confronted the question: why are we fighting? It has to be said that mostly these films—*Mission to Moscow* and *Wilson,* for example—were box office disasters and generally failed to win converts at home or abroad to the message of liberal internationalism.[30] James Agee judged that Darryl Zanuck in *Wilson* had reduced "an extraordinarily grandiose prospect of powerful and original cinema to a high-grade sort of magazine illustration. . . . Although foreign audiences were eager for [evocations] of American politics, cinema-goers in London and Paris preferred Tarzan over Woodrow Wilson."[31]

In large part, what happened reflected not intervention—successful or not—from Washington but Hollywood's "guesstimate" about what the American (and potential foreign) moviegoer would pay to see. During the years 1942 to 1944, some 1,402 feature films were released. According to Dorothy Jones, once head of OWI's Film Reviewing and Analysis Section in Hollywood, films dealing chiefly with the war totaled 374, or 26.1 percent. Films dealing with the enemy (mostly espionage movies such as the B-quickies *Enemy Agents Meet Ellery Queen* or *Secret Agent of Japan*) represented approximately 30 percent of that total, though releases plummeted after 1942. Movies about the armed forces totaled 95 and held steady between 25.9 and 33.2 percent of all "war films" released. At the other end of the spectrum, Jones identified 43 feature films that told "why we fought," 40 films about the home front, and a mere 21 movies that dealt with the war effort and production. Her judgment was that only a relative handful, perhaps 45–50 of all those released during the first three years of the war, "aided significantly, both at home and abroad, in increasing understanding of the conflict." Reflecting a deeply rooted antipathy to the values she encountered in Hollywood and to the movies as a cultural medium, Jones concluded that the reason was that Hollywood's love affair with "formula musicals, domestic comedies, westerns, and murder mysteries" left the industry unable to grapple with actual social and political problems.[32]

Historians have reached a somewhat different conclusion—that moviegoers, whether American, British, French, Irish, or Italian, tended to be bored by and to tune out philosophical or ideological sermons preached on the silver screen. It was not that Hollywood was unable to grapple with real life issues, but that there was a manifest lack of enthusiasm for films that ignored major complexities of life—such as sex, fear, jealousy, greed—and, therefore, that the films produced did not ring true for their makers or for their eventual audiences. In rebuttal to those who claimed that Hollywood was merely responding to the preference for escapist fare of ticket-buying, popcorn-munching audiences, the noted New York *Times* film critic Bosley Crowther wrote that "the public is not tired of war's realities, but of woefully cheap make-believe. What we want in our war films is honest expression of national resolve and a clear indication of realities unadorned with Hollywood hoopla."[33] Crowther subsequently observed that filmmakers confronted a great challenge, for they knew that Americans had acquired a greatly expanded understanding of world affairs and of other cultures. "They know," he asserted, "that the mind of the masses, awakened to sharp realities, will not henceforth be susceptible to unmitigated 'escape.' They know that our films of the future will have to come to a closer grip with life."[34]

That insight goes some distance toward reconciling what otherwise stands as an apparent paradox. When one recalls the American mood in the final year of World War II and the first years of peace, terms such as "triumphalism" and "the arrogance of power" come to mind. Countless politicians from the president down repeated that smug refrain: "We won [are winning] the war, and now we must win the peace." America's self-absorption in those years has been thoroughly chronicled. Historian Richard Pell has written: "The American memory of the war is peculiarly parochial, disconcertingly innocent. For millions of Americans, the war brought no terror and suffering, but renewed prosperity and a better way of life after ten years of staggering economic depression."[35] Also well documented has been the turn to the right in politics and economic life that began with "Dr. New Deal" becoming "Dr. Win the War." It proceeded via the Democratic Party's rejection, in the person of Henry A. Wallace, of domestic liberalism and openhanded internationalism and of the program built upon the Economic Bill of Rights that FDR proudly proclaimed in January 1944 and then permitted, malnourished and ignored, to expire.[36]

During his last months, Roosevelt seemed disinterested in putting flesh on policy aims, contenting himself with pronouncements about the Ten Commandments, the Atlantic Charter, and Woodrow Wilson's Fourteen Points as "something pretty good to shoot for."[37] Apparently, FDR and his advisers believed the American people, eager to see the war over, gave no thought to the future. "Just as soon as the news of our victories comes, everybody wants to put on his coat and stop working. The curious characteristic of our noble people in the U.S. is that they have no more notion that they are in a war or the sacrifices which are involved or needed—just so many children," Secretary of War Stimson complained to General Marshall.[38]

In such a triumphalist milieu, and given the people's presumed obsession with "normalcy," Hollywood logically should have returned to the prewar patterns that had served so well. Flush with wartime profits, primed to reclaim and extend the foreign markets it had dominated before Pearl Harbor, and freed of the objections from OWI ideologues and bureaucratic fussbudgets, filmmakers might have given expression to what some commentators at the time and many historians since have perceived to be the national mood. Instead, there was, arguably, a brief shining hour in which Hollywood did confront and elucidate important social and political issues of the day and did justify, to a degree, the convictions of those who believed that motion pictures could change minds, penetrate to the heart, and stir souls.[39]

In support of this assertion, look briefly at some of the Hollywood films that confronted important aspects of American life, while (of course) still seeking to attract crowds to the theaters at home and abroad. At war's end, *The Story of GI Joe* (1945), a fictionalized version of Ernie Pyle's account of American combat soldiers in North Africa and Italy, offered a gritty, unsentimental portrait of what this war had been like. It excised the high-flown speeches about why American fought in favor of an honest depiction of individual soldiers and their buddies trapped in circumstances beyond the reach of rational discourse.[40] A contrasting treatment of the American democratic outlook—far removed from the flagwaving patriotism of so many wartime films—was the sentimental yet moving adaptation of John Hersey's novel *A Bell for Adano* (1945). Reviews of these two films, released during the victory summer of 1945, noted their striving for realism and evocation of the stubborn strengths of a democratic system.[41]

Hollywood revived the gangster film, but the subject was now viewed through the dark, morally ambivalent lens of film noir. Of the numerous movies within this genre, including *Detour* (1945), *Gilda* (1946), and *The Killers* (1946), *Mildred Pierce* exemplied the dual themes of social realism and high entertainment characteristic of the immediate postwar years. *Mildred Pierce* offered a great part to Joan Crawford and stands as a milestone in Hollywood's depiction of women. Begun by Warner Brothers in early 1944, the film was made over the Hays Office's vehement objections that the story contained "so many sordid and repellent elements" as to make filming it impossible.[42] On the film's release in September 1945, OWI termed *Mildred Pierce*'s main characters "largely self-seeking and unsympathetic" and saw the film as stressing the "ruthless pursuit of money and social position" in America. But it conceded that overseas audiences were not likely to infer that these larger-than-life characters and sordid situations were "typical of Americans as a whole."[43]

Also deserving of mention are Hollywood's groundbreaking encounters with such social problems as alcoholism (via Billy Wilder's *The Lost Weekend*, winner of four Academy Awards in 1945); mental illness (as seen through the windows opened by *Spellbound* (1945) and *The Snake Pit* (1948), despite the latter's pollyannaish ending and trusting acceptance of Freudianism and electric shock treatment); and antisemitism, notably in the 1947 Oscar-winning film, Elia Kazan's *Gentleman's Agreement*.[44]

Admittedly, Hollywood failed to grapple in any serious way in these years with America's deepest-rooted problem, racism. Several socially progressive short films were made during the war, and the incorporation of positive black characters in such films as *Lifeboat* (1947) and *Home of the Brave* (1948) raised hopes that the film industry was ready to confront racial issues with honesty and sensitivity.[45] But the story of what happened to the script and filming of *It Happened in Springfield* (1946)—when a message about attacking the influence of racial bigotry in a "typical" American community was hopelessly diluted by box office compromises and the copout that racism and bigotry were alien viruses and not reflections of basic problems in American society—soon offered an object lesson in the limits of cinematic progressivism. Such films as *Pinky* (1949), in which a white actress, Jeanne Crain, portrayed an educated African American's struggle with racial prejudice, affirmed that Hollywood mirrored those values dominant in the larger society.[46] The chief concern of Production Code Administration head Joseph Breen was that, "From the standpoint of general good and welfare, we strongly urge that you avoid physical contact between Negroes and whites throughout the picture."[47]

On the positive side, two films now generally considered classics—*It's A Wonderful Life* (1946) and *The Best Years of Our Lives* (1945)—were instrumental, historian Garth Jowett has argued, in "freeing social and political themes from the narrow reformist confines of the problem film genre and defining new . . . approaches to political concerns."[48] Both films dealt with individual tensions and constraints imposed by changing social norms and political and economic pressures. George Bailey's story as told in *It's A Wonderful Life* is now so universally known as not to require elaboration. One need merely observe that its subsequent characterization as the quintessential "feel good/nobility and steadfastness triumph over adversity" holiday movie has tended to obscure the complex, dark vision of postwar America conveyed by the film. Historians have correctly noted the multiple ironies that infused Frank Capra's seemingly innocent story and have placed it squarely in the genre of film noir.[49]

The Best Years of Our Lives directly engaged pivotal themes with which American society was wrestling—that category of neurosis now termed post-traumatic stress disorder, attitudes toward those with physical disabilities, alcoholism, divorce and gender relations in general, greed and exploitation on the home front, bureaucratic blundering, and the dislocations associated with demobilization and reconversion at war's end. This was emphatically not sentimental fluff. *The Best Years of Our Lives* was made despite a barrage of protests from Joseph Breen and the Hays Office about its treatment of adultery, allusions to the sexual act, and alleged endorsement of divorce, and it reflected the labor unrest, rampant inflation, shortage, uncertain international climate, and bitter political conflict of the times.[50]

Did these films embody the U.S. government's broadly defined effort to modify the negative images about America that existed elsewhere in the world? Yes. But they did so not because of overt pressures from bureaucrats in Washington but because of the determination of writers, directors, and producers to tell marvelous stories that both attracted large audiences and evoked and elucidated important social and political issues.

The chief conclusion appears to be that the mature handling of complex issues in these films and greater sensitivity to the concerns and perceptions of a global audience suggests, as former OWI representative turned film chronicler Dorothy Jones once claimed, that the American film community was growing up.[51] A contrary conclusion is that the fact that this body of films was produced during the period of America's transition from war to peace may have resulted from a unique set of circumstances, opportunities, and individual ambitions. If the latter view is correct, then there was, besides a mere maturing, a budding of artistic sensibility allied with moral conscience that might well have flowered fully had not its development been stopped by the frigid blasts of the Cold War, domestic repression, and the movie industry's financial difficulties after 1947. Viewed in this way, the labor conflicts, the militancy of disillusioned black soldiers, the rejection by them and their white counterparts of a social and economic system that enshrined class and privilege in such institutions as the U.S. Army, and the political turmoil that led to such quixotic crusades as the formation of the Progressive Party and Henry A. Wallace's candidacy for president in 1948 were healthy and encouraging.

Responding in early 1945 to Dave Wilson's memorandum on the projection of America, one OWI media specialist welcomed the suggestion "that we are to tell all—the good and the bad. I assume we are to tell all in balanced proportions and perspective. But then what about the numerous bans now in force on the melting pot, negro [sic] question, etc. etc? If this directive is to mean anything, all the bans should be reexamined and some new decisions made at the very highest level. . . ."[52] Similarly, Norman Cousins, then head of OWI's USA Division, argued that explicit guidance was needed for dealing with "controversial questions being asked about America—questions concerning minorities, races, injustices." How should OWI (and by extension Hollywood), for example, "counteract the growing feeling abroad that the U.S. is embarking on a period of commercial imperialism as apart from military or political imperialism?" Cousins chastised his colleagues for their lack of confidence in the ability of people in the United States and elsewhere in the world to discriminate between actual and manufactured realities. Truth, Cousins asserted, was the most powerful message Americans could impart to the world. When a film or a novel or a political broadcast spoke truth—as conceived by its creator and as fully articulated as possible in given circumstances—then America had nothing over which to agonize.[53]

If Cousins was correct, then "selling America" via the medium of Hollywood films was not so much a hypothesis or a question as a non sequitur. The question to be posed is not whether a Hollywood film triggered certain responses from its viewers or whether individually and collectively the movies were manifestations of a conspiratorial drive for ideological hegemony; rather, one must ask, what meanings did this myriad of wonderful and atrocious films, considered as symbolic associations and representations of a vanished era, convey to audiences in Peoria, Illinois, Paris, France, and Portsmouth, England, about that America constructed by our past selves?

Notes

1. Dave Wilson to Washington Review Board, OWI, "Attached Draft Outline of a Directive on Projection of America," 30 November 1944, OWI: Projection of America folder, Box 7, Charles Hulten Papers, Harry S. Truman Library, Independence, Missouri.

2. For example, see "Government Information Manual for the Motion Picture Industry," summer 1942, and subsequent revisions of 22 April 1943, and January 1944, Box 15, OWI Records, National Archives and Records Administration (NARA), Washington, D.C. Helpful overviews are in Allan M. Winkler, *The Politics of Propaganda: The Office of War Information, 1942–1945* (New Haven, Conn.: Yale University Press, 1978); Clayton R. Koppes and Gregory D. Black, *Hollywood Goes to War: How Politics, Profits, and Propaganda Shaped World War II Movies* (New York: Free Press, 1987); and Thomas Doherty, *Projections of War: Hollywood, American Culture, and World War II* (New York: Columbia University Press, 1993).

3. Wilson to Washington Review Board, OWI, "Attached Draft Outline of a Directive on Projection of America," 30 November 1944, OWI: Projection of America folder, Box 7, Charles Hulten Papers, Harry S. Truman Library (HSTL). Hereafter cited as Wilson Memo.

4. Wilson Memo.

5. Wilson Memo.

6. O. W. Riegel, Deputy Assistant Chief for Policy, Operations Bureau, New York, to Alice Curran; subject: "Draft Outline of the Directive on Projection of America," Box 7, Charles Hulten Papers, HSTL.

7. Ben Sills, Chief, Special Programs Section, Operations Bureau–New York, to Alice Curran, n.d., OWI: Projection of America folder, Box 7, Charles Hulten Papers, HSTL.

8. Ibid.

9. Joseph Handler, Acting Regional Specialist for France, New York Review Board, to Alice Curran, n.d., OWI: Projection of America folder, Box 7, Charles Hulten Papers, HSTL.

10. Richard Heindel, "American Attitudes of British School Children," *School and Society* 46, no. 1200 (25 December 1936): 838–40, cited in Garth Jowett, *Film The Democratic Art: A Social History of American Film* (Boston, Mass.: Little, Brown, 1976), 285–86.

11. Sidney Carroll, Sunday London *Times*, quoted in "A Thug Symphony," *Literary Digest* 114 (30 July 1932): 14.

12. See especially the chapter "OWI Takes the Offensive"in Koppes and Black, *Hollywood Goes to War*, 82–112.

13. Frank Capra directed the "Why We Fight" series. For government-commissioned films, see David Culbert, ed., *Film and Propaganda in America: A Documentary History*. 5 vols. (Westport, Conn.: Greenwood Press, 1990–1993); Frank Capra, *The Name Above the Title* (New York: Macmillan, 1971); Richard Dyer MacCann, *The People's Films: A Political History of U.S. Government Motion Pictures* (New York: Hastings House, 1973); and Richard Shale, *Donald Duck Joins Up: The Walt Disney Studio During World War II* (Ann Arbor, Mich.: UMI Research Press, 1982).

14. Jowett, *Film the Democratic Art*, 312–13; Richard R. Lingeman, *Don't You Know There's A War On?* (New York: G. P. Putnam's, 1970), 184.

15. Koppes and Black, *Hollywood Goes to War*, 140–41.

16. William Goetz to All Producers, Directors, Writers, and Heads of Departments, 20th Century–Fox Film Corporation, 5 March 1943, Box 12A, OWI Files.

17. An internal assessment of the Charlie Chan movies in July 1943 argued that caricaturing the Chinese as "inscrutable" speakers of "pidgin English" retarded "the better understanding between all peoples necessary to establish a just

and lasting peace." Script Review, *Charlie Chan in Secret Service*, OWI Overseas Bureau, Motion Picture Division, 29 July 1943. OWI ruled that this and other Charlie Chan films, while "not objectionable," contributed "nothing to American-Chinese relations," and overseas distribution was banned. Script Review, OWI Los Angeles Overseas Bureau, Motion Picture Division, 23 March 1944, Box 3529, OWI Files, RG 208, NARA. A useful analysis of the stereotyping of Chinese and blacks in such films is Gregory D. Black, "Charlie Chan Meets the O.W.I.: Racism in World War II Films," *American Classic Screen* 3, no. 4 (November-December 1978).

18. Script Review, *Dragon Seed*, 10 September 1942, 15 September 1942, Box 3525, OWI Files, RG 208, NARA.

19. Script Review, *Up in Arms*, 11 May 1943, Box 3528, OWI Files, RG 208, NARA.

20. Gregory D. Black, *Hollywood Censored: Morality Codes, Catholics, and the Movies* (New York: Cambridge University Press, 1994), 107–11.

21. Fred Eastman, "Our Children and the Movies," *Christian Century* 47 (22 January 1930): 110.

22. Quoted in Koppes and Black, *Hollywood Goes to War*, 126.

23. See the discussion of these films in Koppes and Black, *Hollywood Goes to War*, 128–31.

24. Quoted in Koppes and Black, *Hollywood Goes to War*, 91–93.

25. In the judgment of OWI's Hollywood office, "SAHARA is a film which makes an outstanding contribution to the Government's War Information program," precisely because it espoused such themes as the unity of the fighting forces of the United Nations, contrasted the nature of American soldiers with the arrogance, cruelty, and treachery of the enemy, and ensured that "what we are fighting for, the nature of the peace, is shown in simple terms throughout the script." Memos re *Sahara*, 1 February 1943, 8 July 1943, "Sahara" folder, Box 3524, RG 208, NARA.

26. Koppes and Black, *Hollywood Goes to War*, 156.

27. Ulrich Bell to David Selznick, 14 October 1943, Box 3525, OWI Files, RG208, NARA.

28. Selznick asserted that *Since You Went Away* sent a powerful message about such issues as rationing and the black market, David Selznick to Ulrich Bell, 30 September 1943, Box 3525, OWI Files, RG 208, NARA.

29. Ruth Hooper, "Memorandum on BIPO Poll *re* 'Since You Went Away,'" 17 April 1945, Box 3525, OWI Files, RG 208, NARA.

30. In a frank letter to President Franklin D. Roosevelt, Darryl F. Zanuck claimed that *Wilson* had been "exceptionally successful in the larger key cities where there is a big labor population or where a 'liberal attitude' exists," but he acknowledged that it had "experienced difficulties" in smaller communities, the Midwest, and the South." Darryl F. Zanuck to FDR, 28 October 1944, Box 3518, OWI Files, RG 208, NARA. Generally, audiences agreed with reviewer Manny Farber's summation: "costly, tedious, and impotent." *New Republic* 3 (14 August 1944): 187.

31. James Agee, "Films: *Wilson*," *Nation*, 159 (19 August 1944), 221.

32. Dorothy Jones, "Hollywood War Films, 1942–1944," *Hollywood Quarterly* 1 (1945): 1–19. Jones backhandedly absolved the film industry by observing that "faced with the task of making films which would educate the public about the war, most Hollywood movie makers did not know where to begin. They

lacked experience in making films dealing with actual social problems. And, like the rest of America, they themselves lacked real understanding of the war." Ibid., 13.

33. New York *Times*, 23 May 1945, quoted in Lewis Jacobs, "World War II and the American Film," Arthur F. McClure, ed., *The Movies: An American Idiom* (Rutherford, N.J.: Fairleigh Dickinson Press, 1971), 167.

34. Bosley Crowther, "The Movies," in Jack Goodman, ed., *While You Were Gone* (New York: Simon and Schuster, 1946), 532.

35. See, for example, Richard Pells, *The Liberal Mind in a Conservative Age* (New York: Harper and Row, 1985), 6–7.

36. John M. Blum, *The Price of Vision: The Diary of Henry A. Wallace* (Boston: Houghton Mifflin, 1972), 26–29; Norman Markowitz, *Rise and Fall of the People's Century* (New York: Free Press, 1974), 65–74. Also see Richard Polenberg, *War and Society* (Philadelphia: Lippincott, 1972), and Alonzo Hamby, *Beyond the New Deal: Harry S. Truman and American Liberalism* (New York: Columbia University Press, 1973).

37. "Those Fourteen Points weren't all attained, but it was a step toward a better life for the people of the world," Roosevelt commented at a presidential news conference in December 1944. 985th Press Conference, in Franklin D. Roosevelt, *Complete Presidential Press Conferences of Franklin D. Roosevelt*, 25 vols. (New York: DaCapo Press, 1972), 24:319.

38. Henry L. Stimson to George C. Marshall, 6 December 1944, Chief of Staff folder, Secretary's "Safe" File, RG196, NARA.

39. Notably, the American film industry enjoyed its biggest year ever (in terms of profits and audience numbers) in 1946, and then began a steady decline for the next thirty years. Jowett, *Film: The Democratic Art*, 334–35.

40. Koppes and Black, *Hollywood Goes To War*, 304–8. Reviews were universally enthusiastic. James Agee, indeed, said of the film: "Coming as it does out of a world in which even the best work is nearly always compromised, and into a world which is generally assumed to dread honesty and courage and to despise artistic integrity, it is an act of heroism, and I cannot suggest my regard for it without using such words as veneration and love." *Nation* (15 September 1945): 264.

41. "Unsunny Italy," *Commonweal* 42 (27 July 1945): 318–19; "Heart of Gold: The Films in Review," *Theatre Arts* 29 (October 1945): 578–83.

42. Joseph I. Breen to Jack Warner, 2 February 1944, Box 3521, Production Code Administration Files, Library of the American Academy of Motion Picture Arts and Sciences, Beverly Hills, Calif.

43. Print Review, "Mildred Pierce," 26 September 1945, Box 3521, OWI Files, RG 208, NARA.

44. Also deserving mention is *Let There Be Light*, John Huston's documentary film about veterans suffering from combat fatigue and other psychological problems. Completed in 1945, this film was not released because of War Department objections to its antiwar tone, even though such critics as James Agee hailed it as a masterpiece. *Let There Be Light*, when finally shown commercially in 1981, struck many as an "ingenuous and naive" paean to Freudian psychiatry, but it still serves as a cultural artifact of a more optimistic, confident time. Leonard Quart and Albert Auster, *American Film and Society Since 1945* (New York: Praeger, 1984), 1, 7.

45. OWI made sincere efforts to remove or reduce manifestations of overt racism and racial stereotyping from Hollywood-produced films and to press for

increased attention to the role of African Americans in the war. See the extended discussion in Koppes and Black, *Hollywood Goes to War*, 84–90, 178–84. However, the blunt observation by Philleo Nash, a highly placed OWI official who later was an adviser to President Harry S. Truman—"It is not and should not be the responsibility of the Office of War Information to attempt to solve the problem of Negro-White relations"—represented the viewpoint of the Washington bureaucracy. Philleo Nash, "Recommendations," n.d. [1944], Box 19, Philleo Nash Papers, Harry S. Truman Library, Independence, Mo.

46. Quart and Auster, *American Film and Society Since 1945*, 30–34; "New Films [Confronting Racial Issues]," *Newsweek* 34 (10 October 1949): 88–90.

47. Joseph I. Breen to Jason Joy, 28 February 1949, Motion Picture Producers and Distributors of America (MPPDA) Files, Academy of Motion Picture Arts and Sciences (AMPAS).

48. Jowett, *Film: The Democratic Art*, 336–37.

49. Peter Roffman and Jim Purdy, *The Hollywood Social Problem Film: Madness, Despair, and Politics from the Depression to the Fifties* (Bloomington: Indiana University Press, 1981), 270–71; Quart and Auster, *American Film and Society Since 1945*, 22–23.

50. Joseph I. Breen to Samuel L. Goldwyn, 1 August 1945, MPDA Files, AMPAS Archives. Having viewed the final print, Breen protested that the film's ending was "a definite indication and justification of the breakup of a marriage" and demanded that Fred's assertion that his divorce had freed him to marry Peggy "be eliminated." In this instance, claiming that no violation of the Production Code's provision "regarding the sanctity of marriage" had occurred, Goldwyn–RKO Radio refused to budge. Patrick Duggan to Breen, 24 June 1946, ibid.

51. Dorothy Jones, "Tomorrow the Movies IV: Is Hollywood Growing Up?," *Nation* 160, no. 5 (3 February 1945): 125.

52. A. A. Micocci, Regional Specialist for Central and Southeastern Europe and Acting Regional Specialist for Italy, New York Review Board, to Alice Curran, n.d., OWI: Projection of America folder, Box 7, Charles Hulten Papers, HSTL.

53. Norman Cousins (U.S.A. Bureau) to Sam Williamson (Washington Review Board), n.d., OWI: Projection of America folder, Box 7, Charles Hulten Papers, HSTL.

Aurora Bosch and M. Fernanda del Rincón

Dreams in a Dictatorship
Hollywood and Franco's Spain, 1939–1956

1. The Cinema and Spanish Post–Civil War Society

General Francisco Franco's forty-year dictatorship—the longest of any in Western Europe in the twentieth century—effectively divided Spanish society into the victors and vanquished of the bitter fratricidal civil war of 1936–1939.[1] However, Franco shared one passion with his fellow Spaniards irrespective of their political allegiances: the cinema. Not only were special film showings held for the dictator at his Pardo Palace outside Madrid, but Franco occasionally wrote film reviews (also under a pseudonym) for the Madrid newspaper ABC. He also pseudonomously wrote a film script, *La Raza,* which reached Spanish screens in 1942.

Not suprisingly, the dictator's film script depicted his vision of the causes and antecedents of the civil war as seen through a family that had anti-Republican and Catholic persuasions similar to his own.[2] The only exception is one character, a son who argues in favor of the legally established Republic. This son—loosely based on the general's brother, the aviator Major Ramón Franco—loses the arguments, of course, and the film vindicates General Franco's 1936 military uprising against the Republic. The film's title, *Race,* indicates Franco's attachment to the "authentic" virtues and values of traditional and antiliberal Catholic sectors of Spanish society.

Raza was hailed by Catholic critics as depicting a "brotherhood of men united, in time and space, in the service of an eternal ideal inspired by the spirit of God. . . ." In this view, the family members portrayed in the film "incarnated the eternal principles of our race, religion, military spirit, chivalry and family values. . . ."[3]

From the moment of his civil war victory over the Republic in April 1939, Franco imposed a military dictatorship in which the Catholic Church and the government's profascist political party, FET y JONS, controlled all elements of social and political life. Morality, ideology, education, customs . . . everything fell under their stifling sway. Anyone who had not supported Franco in the civil war could expect, at best, to be jailed; at worst, to be shot.

The end of World War II, and the defeat of the Axis powers in 1945, resulted in the Spanish profascist political party losing its previous dominance in favor of the Church, and a form of social control known as National-Catholicism was born. The post–World War II years brought hardships over and above the harsh physical repression of all those who had supported the Republic before and during the civil war, and the continuing suppression of any political or cultural dissidence. The 1940s brought near famine conditions and the international isolation of Spain for its support of the Axis during the War.

In these harsh post–civil war and post–World War II years, movies provided one of the few means of evasion open to Spaniards.[4] Not only was the cinema cheap; it was also warm in winter and cool in summer. There were movie theaters in every neighborhood of the large towns, and at least one in most of the rural villages. In these pre-television times, entire families could, by attending a film, literally escape the cold or the heat of their own homes and the tribulations of daily life, as well as the asphyxiating Spanish cultural climate. Parents with young children and babes in arms went together, their meager suppers carried in bags. Children paid no admission, but were expected to fall asleep after eating their sandwiches, while their parents spent the next three hours absorbed by the screen. And the films they most enjoyed were those made in Hollywood.

In 1947, Spain had a total of just over 3,000 movie theaters and an average capacity of 525 seats, making it second in the Western world behind the United States in per capita cinemas. (Spain had one for every 8,666 persons as compared to 7,277 for the United States.)[5] The cinema's popularity in Spain was obvious to those foreigners who visited the country in the post-war period. In 1949, Gerald Brenan, the British writer and historian of Spain, affirmed that no other West European country had as great a passion for the cinema as the Spaniards. In Madrid, he observed, there were few churches, but more than 70 cinemas, and almost all of them were doing a flourishing business.[6]

This passion for the cinema was not new. It had existed under the Republic (1931–1936) and during the civil war, when, in addition to domestic productions, 500 films, the majority American, were imported every year. As soon as the Republic was declared, the U.S. consul-general in Barcelona, Claude I. Dawson, contacted the State Department with his fears that the new regime might take protectionist measures against the import of Hollywood movies in order to protect Spanish filmmaking. In his confidential report he referred to the popularity of American films:

American motion picture films unquestionably hold first place in the Spanish market. . . . Of the 500 feature films brought into Spain about 300 were sound films of which nearly 80% were American. . . . From 60% to 70% of 200 silent films were American.

American motion pictures are the most popular and successful pictures in Spain and are the only ones having long runs. The record run in Spain was "The Love Parade" which was shown in one Barcelona theater for six months straight. In fact all the big successes are American films and the writer knows of no films of other countries which can compare with them in popularity.[7]

Hugh Thomas, one of the best-known British historians of the war, points out how, during the civil war, films made a great impression on the Spanish working class.[8] Shirley Temple in *The Little Colonel* enjoyed great success; the Marx Brothers' *Duck Soup* also was particularly popular. (Given the Republican politicians' failure, despite ample warning, to take preventive measures against the military uprising, Groucho Marx, looking like any Spanish politician with a report in his hand, invariably brought the house down with his line: "A four-year-old child could understand this report. Run out and find me a four-year-old child.")

Although the Spanish cinematic enthusiasm was not new, it gained an even wider and deeper base during the first period (1939–1956) of Franco's military dictatorship. At this time, illiteracy was still relatively widespread, particularly in rural areas, which gave film an ascendancy over the printed word. But the cinema, at this time of great poverty, was also the one entertainment available to all, including women, who could attend alone or in groups. In a predominantly male chauvinist society, the cinema was the one socially acceptable venue of entertainment for a woman to attend on her own. The dictatorship inevitably tried to control and use the cinema for its own ideological and political ends, but certain values and lifestyles depicted by Hollywood films of the 1930s, 1940s, and early 1950s subtly escaped the regime's control.

Despite censorship, Hollywood's representation of American lifestyles, fashions, and values was taken up by groups of privileged youths, especially in Madrid. The grandiloquent official rhetoric, endlessly repeated, about the "eternal values" of Spain, and the constant emphasis on woman's role as virtuous wife and mother, could not ameliorate the drab, harsh reality these youths saw around them; and they reacted by creating the so-called topolino subculture. The name "topolino" was borrowed from a small Fiat car popular at the time.

The young women topolinas were self-assured and carefree in their relationships with their fellow male topolinos, and the barriers between them were less perceptible and ceremonious than those traditional Spanish society required of male-female relationships. Moreover, they danced freely to foreign music that most people, during the moralistic times, considered "indecent." The topolinas had their own style of dress: thick-soled, heelless shoes, sometimes with open toes, short skirts, a long jacket, and a long lock of hair fixed back from the forehead high over the head. Members of this subculture came from the urban monied elite, which, unlike the average Spaniard, was not suffering from the rampant hunger of the postwar years; young topolinas were known for having money to spend or for at least surrounding themselves with others who did.

2. Hollywood Cinema of the 1930s and 1940s

Classic Hollywood films dominated Spanish screens from the end of the civil war to the early 1950s. Directly or indirectly, American films of the 1930s and 1940s were influenced first by the Depression and then by World War II. Many directors, including Lang, Capra, Ford, and Hawks, reacted to the Depression with an undeniable liberal-radical New Deal thrust. Trying to capture the hard social realities of the times, they interpreted them not in terms of class or collectivities but rather as an individual's struggle to rise above economic threats in the name of traditional, individualistic American values. It was the comedies, however, such as Leo McCarey's *The Awful Truth,* George Cukor's *Holiday*, Howard Hawks' *Bringing Up Baby*, and Frank Capra's *You Can't Take It With You* that best reflected the hard times by satirizing the race for power and wealth, and by focusing more on cultural than on economic considerations.

Charlie Chaplin and the Marx Brothers must be recognized for achieving the funniest and the most penetrating social commentary and criticism of American society at the time. And so, too, must the singular case of Orson Welles, the only radical director tolerated (grudgingly) by Hollywood. In general, though, these decades were outstanding for the combination of good actors, great directors, and fine scriptwriters who, among them, achieved a remarkable synthesis of cinematic quality and public appeal never bettered by Hollywood before or since.

In the 1940s, radicalism began to give way to a stress on democratic values and the fight against fascism. This became a staple of the World War II movies, and the trend continued until the formal beginning of the Cold War in 1947. Both the Depression and the world war changed many social roles and brought in their wake a greater permissiveness in social customs, which was amply reflected in the cinema of the times.

3. Franco's Dictatorship and Hollywood Cinema

Apart from the democratic and liberal values exemplified by American films of the period, one of the major social changes they represented was the new roles that had opened for American women as a result of the Depression and World War. Thus, films suddenly depicted independent women with professional jobs who had the right to compete with their male co-workers; divorced women who fended for themselves in a male-dominated world; women involved in triangular love affairs; and even women prepared to kill to achieve their aims. *The Postman Always Rings Twice, Gilda, The Lady from Shanghai* . . . Barbara Stanwyck, Rita Hayworth, Lana Turner, Ava Gardner, Lauren Bacall, Katharine Hepburn, Joan Crawford . . . These films and film stars showed women in a new light, especially to Spanish audiences. For one thing, these women were not passive. They were a far cry from the homemaking female whose sole destiny, according to the Franquista regime, was marriage and maternity.

Hollywood's portrayal of these new American moral values and social roles had struggled to survive the strict regulation of the 1934 Hays Code, which laid down rigorous norms about what could and could not be shown, particularly with respect to explicit representation of sex and violence. But despite these restrictions, self-imposed by the studios to prevent federal censorship, the image of American society and particularly women's new roles went dead against everything the Franco dictatorship had exalted since 1939—the image of Spain as a "spiritual" nation that would lead the West to moral salvation. In Franco's Spain, a woman was, above everything else, a Catholic and a mother, the bedrock of family life and values, and submissive to her husband. Her inner world and the rearing of children were her destiny and recompense. To this chaste and virtuous female, sensuality and sexuality were, of course, forbidden; so too was divorce or even separation.

National-Catholic criticism extended to the American family, as represented in *The Hardy Family*, a famous MGM series of films between 1936 and 1946 about a "typical" small Midwestern family, which won a special Academy Award in 1942 "for furthering the American way of life." This family, thundered the *Ecclesia*, bore no relation to our "Christian, Spanish family . . . it is a lay, puritanically moral family . . . without solid, well-founded moral norms," which, when the series took the family on vacation, inevitably found difficulty constraining "the natural impulses of its children in the corrupt American beach-life."[9]

As the Franquista weekly, *Destino*, clearly saw, Spanish and American values clashed head on. "Everything 'made in the USA' is an assault on us—rich and poor alike, by the grace of God. . . ." the journal wrote in September 1939. "The U.S. has not propagated openly a national and religious ideal. Among some sectors of European youth there has been a dangerous enthusiasm for American lifestyles and cinema . . . always accompanied by contempt for the deepest and truest in ourselves. . . . Mimicry is the first step toward the dissolution of a fatherland."

This "dangerous enthusiasm" certainly continued to exist amongst Spanish youth in the immediate post–World War II period, in contrast to the regime's particularly sharp anti-Americanism. In 1945, the newly created United Nations had declared Spain to be isolated from the international community for Franco's support of the Axis powers during the war and for his hostility to liberal democracy and the "West" in general. U.S.–Spanish relations were at a nadir. But the official beginning of the Cold War in 1947, and Franco's experience—and survival—of diplomatic isolation began to change perspectives on both sides. As Western Europe's leading anticommunist, Franco sought to use his position to seek a rapprochement with the United States at the moment when the American government began to take account of Spain's military and strategic potential in the new Cold War situation. In an attempt to break the still-growing tension between the two countries, the U.S. Congress voted in 1950 to authorize President Truman to give Spain $62.5 million on credit through the Import-Export Bank. By 1952, the United States and Spain were actively negotiating a pact. In September 1953, the military and economic pact was signed, and it lasted for the rest of Franco's life and well into the reign of his successor, King Juan Carlos. The agreements were decisive for Spain because they ended its international isolation, a fact confirmed by President Eisenhower's official visit to Madrid in 1959—the first head of state to visit Spain since the end of the civil war.

But how, in the first seventeen years of his rule, from 1939 to 1956, could the dictatorship square the circle and continue to allow the showing of Hollywood films that so clearly stood for everything that, in its hatred and fear, the regime tried to repress? It seems paradoxical that the dictator would even have stimulated their release to Spanish audiences, who so obviously preferred them to non-Hollywood products.

The reason behind this paradox lay in the regime's cinematographic policy, which, while aiming to imitate Mussolini's and create a powerful national industry, in fact weakened local productions, since the postwar Spanish cinema's profits came from importing Hollywood films and not from domestic production.

In Italy, the fascist regime had decreed in 1934, as part of its policy of autarchy, to stimulate national cinema production. Outside Rome it built the gigantic Cinecittà studios, and it promoted the showing of Italian films and created prizes for those with the greatest box-office successes, with the idea of encouraging entertainment cinema rather than propaganda films. By law, all foreign films had to be in Italian, a nationalistic measure that served to make films more readily accessible to the cinemagoing public. As a protective measure against American film exports, the regime adopted in 1938 a quota system regulating the number of films that could be imported each year from abroad—a measure that immediately provoked reprisals from Hollywood.

The Spanish movie industry before the civil war had shown a certain incipient vitality[10]; but the war and the subsequent repression meant that many of the best actors and technicians went into exile or, if they remained in Spain, were arrested, jailed, refused permission to work, or had their films destroyed. Antonio del Amo, a film director who had shot documentaries in the Republican zone during the war, was arrested and condemned to death; though the sentence was commuted, he was not allowed to direct any more films until 1947. The actress María del Carmen Merino was arrested in 1941 while in the middle of shooting a film, and the director Benito Perojo had to watch the authorities destroy the negatives of his film *Nuestra Natacha*.

With a weakened industry and amidst the difficult post–civil war economic situation, Franco promoted patriotic films exalting military values or the glory of Spain's imperial past with a suitable admixture of folklore and myth.[11] To this strictly controlled native fare was added, during World War II, the salt and pepper of Nazi and Italian fascist films. Franco's film policy was rounded off with a system of prizes for Spanish films. Ironically, these consisted of the concession of licenses to import Hollywood films, which, after 1941, had to be dubbed in Spain (previously, Hollywood had produced the Spanish-spoken versions). Thus filmmaking became "not a matter of premiering a film and achieving success, but rather a business centered round achieving import permits which, transferred to foreign distributors in Spain, brought in income sufficient not only to pay for the film but could mean profits of 100% on the capital invested."[12]

To win the highest prize—three to five import licenses—a film had to demonstrate "an advance in some aspect of production"; simply being "of sufficient quality" was enough to win two to four licenses. Once in the producer's hands, the licenses could be transferred to third persons or, more accurately, sold in the black market to distributors. The granting of these "prizes" was highly arbitrary and politically motivated; if the Classification Commission, appointed by the Ministry of Industry, decided that a film was of especially high quality, the number of licenses awarded could increase. Not surprisingly, the prize films were always those that defended National-Catholic values.

As a result of this system, the preoccupation of Spanish filmmakers became the gaining of licenses. It was an arrangement that suited all concerned: the regime got "its" films, the producers got massive profits, and the public got the Hollywood films they liked. But there can be little doubt that the license policy damaged the quality of Spanish filmmaking since films were now shot as rapidly as possible with only one real aim in mind.

The license policy came in for criticism from the falangist (profascist) sectors of the regime on the grounds that it was responsible for the public "fleeing" from Spanish films. As F. Vizcaino Casas wrote, "This highly grave situation has come about because filmmaking has been turned exclusively into a business affair, and the cinema has been denied all value."[13]

The contemporary Spanish film historian Juan Antonio Cabero agreed with this criticism. The cinema-going public, he wrote in 1949, went out of its way to see anything "from abroad" and depreciated "home production," so that the license system was the only means of paying for domestic filmmaking. "In reality," he stressed, "Spanish films cost between one and four million pesetas to make, sums that can only with difficulty be earned at the box office by even the most successful among them. If so much money is spent on producing a film, it is only in the hope of winning import licenses for films that cost only a quarter of Spanish production budgets to import and that, saddest of all, find favor with the public."[14]

Despite the falangists' criticism, the regime made almost no changes in its film policy during the 1940s. As a result, not only did Hollywood films continue to dominate Spanish screens, but the distribution industry gained greater weight than the production sector. This, as we have seen, was a paradoxical outcome since the content and value system of Hollywood films in the 1940s and 1950s ran directly counter to the anti-American discourse of the various nuclei of powers.

But there was little that could be done while the regime continued to insist on hammering home its propaganda message. Wooden and thoroughly predictable "regime" films exalting the traditional values of "the nation," "the (Hispanic) race," and the authoritarian family, stood little chance against Hollywood's realism, spontaneity and thematic diversity, which corresponded more closely with the diversity of Spanish society and its need for evasion. Even Mussolini's far more subtle fascist attempt to appeal to broad sectors of ordinary people by producing entertainment films faced stiff competition in the realism and quality of Hollywood's products, which appealed to the Italian cinema-going public in the 1930s.[15]

It was not until 1951, when, as the failure of the regime's policy in defending national film production became more apparent, changes were made. The major one was to end the relationship between film production and licenses to import American films. Instead, in imitation of earlier Italian policy, import quotas were established for each foreign country; also, from 1955 on, a distribution quota obliged cinemas to show a growing percentage of Spanish-produced films. American distributors retaliated with a boycott of Spain, refusing to supply films to the country between the summer of 1955 and March 1958.

This new policy had definite and favorable results for Spanish film production, leading to the birth of what has been called the "New Spanish Cinema," which, in its quality and thematic content, bore no relation to the first post–civil war franquista cinema. Even so, during the 1950s Hollywood retained its pre-eminent position, with a market quota of 30.5 percent. Spanish-produced films came in a distant second with 17.8 percent.

4. Censoring Hollywood

The Franco regime did not allow any and all American films to be shown. A direct censorship could be and was applied to all whose social or political themes ran counter to the dictatorship's political practice and ideology: his outlawing of liberal democracy, strikes, and any form of "class struggle," of Communism, Freemasonry, and republican allegiance. All popular opposition to the dictatorial regime itself was, of course, automatically proclaimed "communistic" and banned. *The Grapes of Wrath*, *How Green Was My Valley*, *To Be Or Not To Be*, and *The Great Dictator* never showed on Spanish screens until after the dictator's death in 1975.

Apart from outright prohibition, cutting and dubbing were the two main techniques used to try to keep Hollywood within the bounds of Franquista National-Catholic moral propriety. The 1941 decree that foreign films has to be dubbed in Spain of course gave the regime additional lattitude to manipulate content. The censors' cutting and dubbing resulted in some ludicrous—and often unintelligible—changes, of which the following are but a few examples.

In *Waterloo Bridge*, Vivien Leigh's past as a prostitute became that of an actress whose husband had been devoured by a tiger so that her relationship with her lover should not be adulterous. In *Arch of Triumph*, while Ingrid Bergman clearly shakes her head in reply to the question "Is that your husband?", the Spanish public heard her answer simultaneously with a ringing "Yes." The married couple played by Grace Kelly and Donald Sinden in *Mogambo* was turned into a sibling couple to make morally acceptable Kelly's relationship with Clark Gable. Needless to say, in Orson Welles' *Lady from Shanghai*, the protagonist's past in the International Brigades (the Comintern-organized forces that had fought Franco's armies in the civil war) vanished from the screen.

Government censorship was exercised by the Superior Censorship Committee (Junta Superior de Censura), made up of a military officer, a falangist, and a representative of the Catholic Church. The latter, moreover, maintained an unofficial censorship of its own which, until 1946–1947, coincided with the government's criteria. However, after 1950, when these no longer seemed sufficiently intransigent to the Church on moral questions, the Church put out its own views on what Catholics could and should not see.

Until 1942, the committee depended on the Ministry of the Interior; in that year, the Vice-Secretariat of Popular Education was created and the committee came under its aegis. Its censorship affected political, religious, military, moral, and sexual matters, although the principles by which it made its judgments remained (probably deliberately) vague. It could just as easily censor a film for attacking "public decency," especially in sexual matters, as for offending Catholic dogma or the Church itself, or, of course, the regime and any of its institutions or personalities. On these grounds, not only new films were banned, but those made even before the outbreak of the civil war. *The Scarlet Pimpernel* (Harold Young, 1935), Richard Boleslawski's *The Painted Veil* of the same year, and *China Seas* (Tay Garnett, 1936) were notable among the outlawed films.

Films that passed the censorship were classified as "recommended," "authorized," and "allowed to under sixteen-year-olds." Undefined in its principles, censorship was applied with the same meticulous arbitrariness that characterized the dictatorial regime generally, keeping Spaniards in a state of tremulous suspense as to what might or might not be permitted— a form of social control that served the regime well in its early years. At the level of film, a snip of the censor's scissors could leave two hundred years of Western political culture on the cutting room floor. This, for example, was the fate of a scene in *Ruggles of Red Gap* (Leo McCarey, 1935) in which Charles Laughton, playing an English indentured servant, secures his freedom from his master on arrival in the United States by invoking the principle of the equality of all men. This scene was deemed a subversive principle, one that had "ruined" Spain and that Franco's rising was destined to correct. In a lesser, but still significant case, *Mutiny on the Bounty* (Frank Lloyd, 1935), was, upon its first showing in 1945, renamed *La Tragedia del Bounty* (this despite the fact that the same film had premiered in Spain in 1936 under the title, *Rebelión a Bordo*.) Mutiny and rebellion were subversive concepts to be eliminated, although in fairness it must be said that the film's portrayal of the crew's mutiny against the Bounty's captain was not changed.

The outcome of World War II caused some of the censorship criteria to be slightly relaxed, leading to accusations by the Catholic Church of "sexual permissiveness," which in turn led to serious differences and eventually to the official separation of government and Catholic censorship.

It was the showing of *Casablanca* in 1946—the film having been suitably purged of all Bogart's dialogues referring to his participation in the Spanish civil war—that opened the rift between government and Catholic censorships. To the Church, the cutting of references to the civil war was insufficient, for it had "grave moral objections" to the film because of its "crudeness, brusque realism and its scabrous motives. Violent passions of all sorts aroused in a climate of low-class bars and roulette. And around the gaming table men without scruples or morals."[16]

The following year, Billy Wilder's *Double Indemnity* provoked the Church's even greater wrath. It was called "a morbid monstrosity" in which "a repugnant, morbid evil lurks that even remorse, being completely ineficacious, can neither stop nor make any compensation for."[17] But the culminating point in the Church-government rift came with Charles Vidor's *Gilda*. To a public whose expectations were aroused by the publicity as well as by Rita Hayworth's Spanish origins, the film was premiered in Spain at Christmas 1947. Popular opinion held that the censors had cut the strip-tease Gilda was said to perform. Despite the aura of scandal surrounding the film, the only reaction came from the Church. "Gilda is a spectacle in which the woman who incarnates the central character has been used to make alluring publicity for lechery. The moral qualification (this) deserves is even more extreme and severe."[18]

The Church's opposition to *Gilda* went as far as setting up picket-line protest demonstrations outside cinemas showing the film and in the refusal of the Catholic press to publish publicity for it. The subsequent showing of *Leave Her to Heaven* (John M. Stahl, 1945) and, in 1949, of *Gone with the Wind*, displaying Scarlett O'Hara's "sexual voracity," only served to drive in the last nail. The Church was now aware that it had to act—and act for itself, since the official censorship had permitted such monstrous films. Thus, in 1950, the Church set up its own national censorship office (Oficina Nacional Clasificadora), depending on the Episcopal Commission, with its own classifications of films that were propagated through every parish in the land. (The categories were: "permitted for children," "permitted for youth," "for adults," "for adults—though with criticisms" (3R), and, finally, "seriously dangerous").

Despite the Church's attitude, numerous examples show that govern-mental censorship in relation to public decency and sex had not relaxed in the 1950s. Wilder's *Some Like It Hot* was banned "even if only to keep up the close season on queers."[19] All passages referring to the civil war in Henry King's *The Snows of Kilimanjaro* were excised because they took place on the Republican side, and passionate love words were turned into a religious prayer. Burt Lancaster's and Deborah Kerr's love meeting on the beach in Fred Zinnemann's *From Here to Eternity* immediately brought out the government censors' scissors; while the impotent hus-band in Joseph L. Mankiewicz' *The Barefoot Contessa* was turned into the female protagonist's brother in order to cover up adultery.[20]

In these years, Hollywood films reached Spanish screens, especially those in villages and small towns, after passing through a triple filter: go-venment censorship, ecclesiastical censorship, and that of the local au-thorities or regime figures: the mayor, the priest, the schoolmaster, the fa-lange delegate, and the police chief. On many occasions, these figures interrupted films in the middle of showings, or hid a sequence, while the audience booed them.

None of this prevented the world created by Hollywood from remain-ing the favorite form of collective Spanish evasion. Nor could it prevent Hollywood's values and lifestyles from penetrating the popular mind, al-lowing older generations to recall the permissive, pre–civil war Spain and creating new and future possibilities for those who had not lived through that experience.

5. Models of Hollywood Femininity and the Topolino Girls

Very few Spaniards could, of course, imitate Hollywood styles in the Franco years. Shortages and rationing dominated their material lives, while the Catholic Church's moral repression controlled their leisure time, entertainment, and love lives. One of the major obsessions of the time was to reduce to the minimum the possibility of physical contact between the sexes. On beaches, men and women were obliged to remain separate and to wear bathrobes. Modern dancing was considered a sin by the Church, especially those foreign dances like the tango, fox-trot, one-step, swing—not to mention the jitterbug; such dances had been "born in the fetid pools of rotting peoples, in the moral carrion of Europe, in the bestial outburst of the most depraved tribes on earth. . . ."[21] It was quite normal, therefore, for such dances to be prevented by governmental au-thorities acting on their own account. The only possibility of physical contact that remained was in the darkness and anonymity of the movie theater—although even this was to run the risk of detection by the police who attended each session.

The moral barriers exclusively surrounding women were even harsher. With a stroke of the pen Franco had abolished the conditions of women's equality that the Republic had legally recognized in the 1930s. Women were deprived of the vote, of the right to abortion, and of juridical status; divorce and civil marriage were banned. In place of women's previous equality, the regime tried to impose on them the most reactionary ideas of womanhood, indoctrinating them in the contribution that woman-mother had to make to the aggrandizement of the state and the future empire. Their position was in the home and the family, their role to be passive and subordinate to their husbands, their major virtues modesty, submission, reserve, and a spirit of sacrifice.

The instrument used for indoctrinating women was the falangist Sección Femenina, in which all young women had to serve for a period of time (as all young men were traditionally conscripted for military service). In the words of the Sección Femenina, Spanish women were to be "heroic, military, but feminine. A rifle in a woman's hands dishonors the rifle, the poor, unhappy woman who shoulders it, and the men who see her. . . . [Women's role] is limited to the field of purely feminine activities: religion, works of charity, hospitals, pediatrics, music, art, the office. . . ."[22]

The Church, meanwhile, instructed women that they must "bury to the maximum their bodies, which were 'the house of sin.'"[23] Dresses must not be tight-fitting, sleeves must reach at least to the elbow, décolletage, see-through, and lace dresses were forbidden. Women who refused to obey these rules were punished by being refused communion in church, denied the right to be godmothers at baptisms and, in extreme cases, by being barred from entering a church.

The Church also laid down the norms for engagements. The young engaged woman must never be alone with her fiancé, or ride a bicycle (for fear of rupturing her hymen), or walk through the streets arm-in-arm or hand-in-hand with her fiancé.

These imposed and rigid forms of behavior obviously formed a strong contrast with the feminine models and lifestyles shown in American films, but only a tiny minority of Spanish women in the 1940s and early 1950s could break with the rigidity in order to imitate what they saw on the screen. These were the aforementioned "Topolino Generation." They were young, upper-middle-class Madrileños, children of the victors in the civil war, who enjoyed sufficient economic means and the necessary social tolerance to lead a frivolous, free-and-easy life in the midst of scarcity and the harsh moral strictures of the postwar Church and regime. Such lack of inhibition, quite common after a war, was summed up for the young

Topolino women in the slogan, "drink, smoke and kiss,"[24]—a far cry from what the Sección Feminina was laying down as their duty to the fatherland.

Criticism of the "topolino" culture was quick in coming. Their wealth and their style of dancing was viciously attacked. "Do we have to leap and jump about like clowns from 'over there'? . . . It is not good taste to imitate the savages of the middle of Africa and the colored men who show off the freedom they enjoy at the feet of New York skyscrapers," wrote a critic in *La Hora* in March 1947.

In general, the young Topolino women were criticized for their frivolity and lack of dedication, which, it was claimed, would ruin their lives. This was well expressed in the words of a character in the novel, *Una Chica "Topolino,"* whose heroine suffers precisely this fate. "They start to go out at fifteen or sixteen, and by the time they're twenty they've lived four or five intense years of life. They're bored, tired, have seen it all. . . . They've been kissed a hundred and one times. No one stops them, nothing matters to them. . . . At twenty they look more than thirty. . . . If they fall in love, the young man in question is frightened off. . . . They're destined to grow old and fat with the suppers they eat, the bars and dances they go to, where they backbite their friends, especially the ones who've been lucky enough to get married."[25]

Although, given the times, this was a mild enough criticism of Topolino behavior, the charge of "frivolity" was one of the principal criticisms—and perceived dangers—of Hollywood films. As the author of *Una Chica "Topolino"* wrote, "As their titles indicate [these] do nothing but invite people to frivolous enjoyment of the pleasures of life. 'It's A Wonderful Life,' 'Live To Enjoy,' 'The Pleasures Of Living,' 'Live The Life You Want.'" Such titles indicated "an extravagant, boastful attitude which, in order to affirm the rights of man, breaks with an established (order) . . . that is thought to be tyrannical."[26]

Although only a wealthy elite could at that time imitate the styles and fashions of Hollywood, American films of the period certainly allowed the popular Spanish cinema-going audiences to escape the immediate reality and desire a different life in which they could talk, express themselves, and establish relationships "in another way." When the economic development and moral permissiveness of the 1960s finally permitted it, the values and lifestyles of Hollywood could at last be imitated by a majority.

5. Conclusions

The post–civil war moral values dictated by the Catholic Church and the profascist single party (FET y JONS), as well as Franco's pro-German and Italian policy of World War II, coincided in condemning American cinema and society as "consumerist," liberal, and of low moral standards.

Already popular before the civil war, the screening of Hollywood films was nonetheless boosted by the Franco regime, which, obviously aware of their continuing popularity, saw in the concession of import licenses the major way of securing and financing Spanish production of films supporting the dictatorship politically and ideologically. Woodenly repeating the regime's grandiloquent rhetoric, these films until the early 1950s bore no relation to the daily lives and experiences of Spaniards at the time. Of poor quality, they had no popular appeal. Hollywood cinema won out with the public precisely because of its realism, because its protagonists spoke like real people, and because it dealt with real problems of life. It did not seem to matter that this life was very different from that being lived by the majority of Spaniards and took place in countries or places by and large unknown to them. Of course, Hollywood won out in the real world, too, because the American film industry's financial power was infinite compared to the limited Spanish resources.

Despite the double filter of censorship and dubbing through which the Franquista regime in its first phase, up to the mid-1950s, tried to defend itself from the more "pernicious" Hollywood values, American films remained the general public's major form of evasion. Imitated in the 1940s and 1950s by a privileged minority of youth, the moral values and social roles these films portrayed on the screen began slowly to make headway against those of the Church and regime. This became apparent in the 1960s when economic growth led to the introduction of a consumer society, and when these values began to become those of a majority, widening the gap between the real Spain and official Spain. Although neither the former nor other new liberal cultural values—including the Spanish Church's astonishing about-face in the 1960s, largely under the effect of Vatican II—could bring the regime to its knees, they brought about a relaxation of its previous cultural and moral stance. And therein, too, lies an irony. By renouncing its aspirations to total control of moral and cultural values, Francoism almost certainly also ensured its own continuing existence for another twenty years.

Notes

1. The authors wish to thank Ronald Fraser for preparing the English-language version of this article and for his many helpful suggestions and critical comments.

2. Only in its upper-class social origins does the family of *La Raza* differ from Franco's more ordinary roots as a naval officer's son.

3. *Ecclesia*, 10 Jan 1942.

4. The radio represented another, and "soaps," though written and presented more like nineteenth-century popular newspaper serials than today's soaps, became highly popular. But radio production could be ideologically controlled with far more ease than American movies, even allowing for the censor and dubbing.

5. *ABC*, 1 Jan 1947, article by Henry Buckley, Reuters correspondent in Madrid.

6. Gerald Brenan, *The Face of Spain* (London, 1950).

7. Department of State. Spain, Internal Affaires, 1930–1939. Part II, reel 2.

8. Hugh Thomas, *The Spanish Civil War* (Harmondsworth, 1986), 400, n. 1.

9. *Ecclesia*, 5 March 1941.

10. A token of this is that in 1936 more Spanish-produced films opened in the United States than in any other successive year up to and including 1955. See Alfred Charles Richard, Jr., *Censorship and Hollywood's Hispanic Image. An Interpretive Filmography, 1936–1955* (Westport, Conn., 1993).

11. The dictatorship created a state-run cinematic news enterprise, NODO, but left the feature film industry in private hands.

12. F. Vizcaino Casas, *Historia y Anécdota del Cine Español* (Madrid, 1976), 87.

13. *Primer Plano*, leading editorial, 2 June 1943.

14. Juan Antonio Cabero, *Historia de la Cinematografía Española (1896–1948)* (Madrid, 1949), 662.

15. E. R. Tannenbaum, *The Fascist Experience: Italian Society and Culture, 1922–1945* (New York, 1972), 320.

16. *Ecclesia*, 4 Jan. 1947.

17. *Ecclesia*, 15 March 1947.

18. *Ecclesia*, 31 Jan. 1948.

19. José María García Escudero, *La Primera Apertura. Diario de un Director General* (Barcelona, 1978), 54. Quoted by Roman Gubern, *La Censura: Función política y Ordenamiento Jurídico Bajo el Franquismo* (Barcelona, 1981).

20. Gubern, *La Censura,* 137.

21. *Ecclesia*, 1 Sept. 1941, and J. Roca I Girona, *De La Pureza a la Maternidad. La Construcción del Género Femenino en la Posguerra Española* (Madrid, 1996), 85.

22. Radio Nacional de España, *La Hora Femenina*, Guía de Emisión, 10 Feb. 1942, A.G.A.

23. Catholic Church Circular, 1945.

24. Jesús Marchamalo, *Bocadillos de Delfín: Anuncios y Vida Cotidiana en la España de Posguerra* (Barcelona, 1996), 200.

25. José Vicente Puente, *Una Chica "Topolino"* (Madrid, 1945), n.p.

26. Gonzalo Anaya, *El Español*, 3 June 1944.

Giuliana Muscio

Invasion and Counterattack

Italian and American Film Relations in the

Postwar Period

The history of film relations between Italy and the United States after World War II is usually studied from a Cold War point of view. Although such an approach is relevant insofar as Cold War alignments facilitated the penetration of American cinema into Italy,[1] it is possible to reinterpret this history in a less mechanical way. The key element not fully accounted for is the concept of national identity. In the postwar period, Italy was re-elaborating its weakened sense of national identity,[2] and cinema, in particular neorealist cinema, with its sensitive reporting of national images and sounds and its national-popular project, played a key role in this process.[3]

American cinema and American popular culture flooded Italy after the war. Americanization—the export of the American dream and of democratic values, as well as a more generalized model for modernization—is also a process of establishing socio-cultural hegemony that reaches different age and social groups with different and sometimes contradictory impacts.[4] Europe is not Americanized from above, but it receives, and either rejects or accepts, the proposed models of Americanization, often adapting them to its own needs and its own internal politics. For example, while the Democratic Christian Party, which governed the country after the war, was politically and internationally pro-American and anticommunist, Catholic culture of the 1950s was nationalistic, conservative, and anticonsumerist, and thus not always appreciative of Hollywood cinema. On the other hand, some neorealists and supporters of the Gramscian concept of the *national-popular* were fascinated with American cinema and literature and had been so even in fascist times.[5]

In the United States, increased engagement in foreign affairs favored a more intense and widespread contact with European culture. American culture became internationalized in the postwar years, opening itself to Italian and French cuisine, fashion, and cinema. Distribution of European cultural products was no longer limited to elites, but one could find them readily available in department stores and in film clubs. In this respect, we could study the neorealist influence on American social films (as Italian film magazines have often argued), or the work of Italian actors, technicians, and filmmakers in America or in American productions in Italy, as well as the statements by Italian-American filmmakers such as Martin Scorsese, Francis Coppola, and Abel Ferrara in reference to the influence of Italian cinema on their work. We should also take into account the impact of European films on the development of a more mature American cinema, as the censorship case of *The Miracle* seems to indicate.[6]

Cultural relations do not seem bound by political motivations in this period; rather, they reveal a rich and contradictory trajectory that never moves only in one direction—that of dominance—from the United States to Italy, but takes unexpected turns and engages in many complex interactions.

American Cinema and the Italian Screens

With the landing of the American troops in Sicily in 1943, the American film companies began planning the systematic reappropriation of every inch of the Italian screen lost to them with the closure of the Italian market in 1938.[7] Hollywood sought to recover the old markets and to preempt the resurgence of protectionist legislation and continuation of the fascist effort to construct a modern national film industry in Italy. The plan of U.S. film companies was favored by the new political legitimation Hollywood had acquired during the war from its production of celluloid propaganda in cooperation with the Office of War Information (OWI). In his essay in this volume, "Selling America Via the Silver Screen?" Theodore A. Wilson re-examines OWI's strategies in "projecting" America on the screen and clearly defines the propaganda plans developed by the agency in this period.

World War II had seen a boom in film attendance globally, Italy included, and this made film production an attractive business. In the fall of 1944, therefore, Italian film producers put pressure on the government to secure a regular resumption of production activities in Rome.[8] The allied answer was clear: the Italian studios of Cinecittà were to be used as a refugee camp, thus preventing any resumption of film production in the main Italian film structure. Neorealism was born outside the studios, therefore, on the streets and not centered in Rome, because of structural necessities and not simply as an aesthetic choice.

For the Motion Pictures Producers Distributors Association (MPPDA), however, the main point was that Italy was "the very best" market for American cinema in Europe.[9] In fact, in July 1945, a group of Hollywood executives flew into Western Europe on a military plane to better plan the definitive stage of the invasion. As during the hot war, mass media now mobilized for the Cold War. Hollywood cinema in particular was seen as a useful antidote to totalitarianisms, which included nazism and fascism, as well as communism. Thus, after the war, American cinema received even stronger governmental support for its activities abroad, organizing its foreign policy more efficiently by moving the MPPDA offices to Washington. Because all relations enjoyed by American cinema abroad are strongly affected by the political relations of a particular country with the United States, postwar Italy, being completely dependent on the Marshall Plan and American support, initially showed little political resistance to the Hollywood invasion.

The Italian market was more than ready for American cinema. Audiences were anxious to see the spectacular Hollywood films they had missed during the war. Exhibitors wanted the best possible business. The political establishment supported Hollywood cinema as a kind of "quick vaccination" against fascism, and one that included antibodies against communism. The Hollywood film invasion was successful also because it was partially supported by the Catholic Church. While the clash between Catholicism and Hollywood films in Spain, as argued by Aurora Bosch and Fernanda del Rincón in their essay in this volume, "Dreams in a Dictatorship," produced a separation between official and Catholic censorship, in Italy the general attitude of the Church, especially in the 1940s, was favorable to American cinema, although not without contradictions.

In this very early phase, almost everybody—audiences, intellectuals, and politicians—liked American cinema, because it seemed to represent an innocent escape that kept people calm and content and offered them new hope. Hollywood films already had enjoyed a strong following in Italy since the 1930s. Even left-wing intellectuals had developed a love for American cinema and literature, and fascism never seriously hindered Hollywood's monopoly of cinema. Immediately after the war, communist intellectuals regarded American films with curiosity, but neorealist cinema claimed their loyalty: after 1948, being a communist implied a rejection of American culture, which meant that one's love for American culture had to become a private cult. And yet there is a distinct Hollywood influence in some neorealist films, such as Germi's *In nome della legge*, with its Western-like Sicilian landscapes and its military hero *à la*

John Ford; or *Senza pietà* by Alberto Lattuada, which is essentially a film noir in terms of thematic structure and cinematography.

After the war and throughout the 1950s, Italian theaters showed hundreds of American films of many kinds: small independent films, new major releases, older movies that had not previously been released in Italy, propaganda films, and small films noir. This represented a diverse and somewhat confusing mix, which ultimately left Italian audiences with a kind of cinematic "hangover."

Indeed, Hollywood invaded the Italian screens: six hundred films were shown in the two-year period from 1945 to 1946 alone. Obviously this invasion provoked defensive attitudes, mirroring patterns of reaction determined mostly by Cold War strategies. Leftists and neorealist-oriented film critics defended Italian cinema and criticized Hollywood films because they were industrial assembly-line products. They identified American cinema with mass culture, not with popular culture. Hollywood was perceived as the cultural "otherness" and always criticized as unrealistic, glossy, and false. Under the pressure of this uneven competition, Italian film producers and filmmakers expressed their negative reactions, too. But the film theaters almost exclusively screened Hollywood productions.

The decade between 1945 and 1955 saw an incredible growth in the consumption of films in Italy. The number of cinemas doubled from five thousand to ten thousand, not counting those five thousand parochial theaters which only operated on Sundays. Cinema was everywhere, on mural advertisements and posters; everywhere photos of film stars could be seen. The very visibility of American cinema therefore challenged the traditional local culture at the crucial moment when Italy was changing from a rural country to an urbanized society. In the immediate postwar period, when "the modern" remained distant and almost as unattainably exotic as a Hollywood film, the onrush of consumerism and modernization encountered an ideological void in a country that had suffered severe socioeconomic damage during the war and lacked a secular culture. American culture therefore became an important instrument of modernization. Hollywood cinema undoubtedly was one of the most efficient channels of Americanization, but its reception was mixed: it was both loved and hated.[10]

The best source for analyzing these contradictions is the Italian popular film magazines, which were devoted almost entirely to American cinema and played a key role in the modernizing of Italian attitudes. These magazines played an important cultural role during the Cold War period. Since many Italians still had serious problems with reading, the film magazines, with their illustrations, photos, and simple titles, acquired a sudden and enormous popularity. They were not targeted merely to film fans. In addition to film criticism and gossip, they contained investigative journalism, fashion articles, and homemaking and cooking tips, hoping to appeal to women who had just acquired the right to vote in 1946, as well as to young people and a general readership. For many Italians, film stars became the new role models for social mobility.[11]

Simultaneously, Italian-American film relations drastically changed. The looming "red peril," the emergence of neorealist left-wing cinema, and the facts of the Italian economy created new fronts. Most important, Italy did not have the necessary dollars to pay for a massive import of American cinema. At the same time, the United States needed Italy to remain firmly within the Western camp, and thus its economic and political stability were seen as essential ingredients of postwar politics. The Italian government proposed an agreement to cap the number of imported American films in order to avoid the export of film rental money from the country. The economic conflict was resolved only in late 1949 when Giulio Andreotti proposed the Cinema Law, apparently a piece of protectionist legislation, which established obligatory screen time for Italian films. While these mandatory screenings were never really enforced, the law did establish that the money derived from the showing of American films in Italy had to remain in the country, although this money could be used to build film plants or film theaters, or to develop local film activities. This political solution encouraged the American majors to invest in Cinecittà, to resume production in Italy, or to co-produce films with Italians. This was a very practical solution indeed, because Italian labor was much cheaper than Hollywood's and because Italy offered good locations. So, ultimately, Andreotti's law was not as negative toward American cinema as it had originally appeared.

Hollywood at Cinecittà

The production of *Quo vadis?* kicked off a stream of American film productions in Cinecittà, all of which were widely covered by Italian film magazines.[12] By the early 1950s, there was a sort of "Hollywood on the Tiber." Not only did American films invade Italian screens, but American film personalities also migrated to Italy.[13] American stars crowded Via Veneto, enlivening Roman night life. Actually, drastic changes within American cinema itself motivated this partial migration to Italy. The crumbling of the studio system and the expansion of independent production, encouraged by the resolution of the Paramount antitrust suit, weakened the central role of the old majors.[14] Politically engaged and artistically restless directors, writers, and actors began shooting independent projects on location. These films often featured relevant social content, a strong inclination to pessimism, and a film noir sensibility. Indeed, quite a few similarities existed between this search for authenticity and political engagement and neorealism, as has often been emphasized by Italian film critics.

During the anticommunist witch hunt, blacklisting made it impossible for some American filmmakers to work.[15] After 1951, the blacklist expanded beyond the "Hollywood Ten" to include liberals and those radicals who had participated in the political and cultural fervor of Hollywood in the 1930s. This situation encouraged migrations: from Los Angeles to New York, that is, to Broadway; to television and theater; or to Europe.

The beginning of co-productions in Italy coincides chronologically with the witch hunt in Hollywood. It is therefore hard to distinguish between the migration that took place for political reasons and that which was for creative reasons; or to determine how many filmmakers emigrated because the Hollywood system was becoming too tight and how many moved to Rome because they had been sent by a studio to work in Cinecittà. The filmography of the blacklisted filmmakers who worked in Italy is extensive, but studies of the period have never investigated the specific motivations for the presence of American film people in Italy in these years.

In the early 1950s, blacklisted filmmakers Jules Dassin, John Berry, and Ben Barzman moved to France; Michael Wilson, Cy Endflied, Bernard Vorhaus, and Joseph Losey went to London. Each of these men made at least one film—usually their first production as émigrés—in Italy. Orson Welles, Robert Rossen, Joseph Manckiewicz, and John Huston also worked in Italy. The arrival of these American film personalities provoked comment. Leftist film magazines such as *Cinema nuovo* usually supported the victims of American anticommunism. In addition to political solidarity, these magazines expressed a sense of belonging to an ideal front of realist cinema, reversing the model of Americanization in order to argue for a direct influence of neorealism on the realist American social cinema.[16] Film magazines thus identify leftist American filmmakers in a broad definition of neorealism, which would suggest that they were the natural allies of the leftist Italian filmmakers who were suffering a cultural and political persecution in Italy similar to that endured by blacklisted Americans. But quite the opposite happened. When blacklisted American filmmakers came to Italy they did not work on neorealist films, possibly because Italian neorealist filmmakers, as the self-appointed builders of national-popular culture, were strongly anti-American and, most of all, anti-Hollywood.

The fact that blacklisted American filmmakers could find work in Europe is not surprising. They were competent professionals who could be usefully employed by the reborn national film industries without interference from the weakening majors, who had determined the blacklisting policy, or by the United States Government, which continued to keep a close watch on them.[17] But the presence of American filmmakers in Italy did not create a cultural and political alliance, or an international project toward a "different" cinema that was anti-Hollywood, anti-American, neorealist, and communist. While American émigré filmmakers played a key role in the birth of British "Free Cinema," the traces of their work in Italy are very weak, despite the fact that Italy would seem an ideal place for their work at that historical moment. In the free zone of Cinecittà, we instead see a Babel, not a socialist International: in the daily work on the sets, political colors were less relevant than nationalities and cultural (and possibly technical) traditions.

American Cinema and Its Changing Influence in the Fifties

In the 1950s, Italy continued to be the largest importer of American films in Europe. David Ellwood, who has made important contributions to the study of this phase of Italian-American film relations, stresses "the central role of American myth and [the] American model in forming and directing Italy's tumultuous modernization experience in the 1950s."[18] But this was also at a time when Italy was attempting to rediscover its own national identity, making the interaction between socioeconomic transformations and cultural-ideological processes a highly complex one. In the 1950s, the swift modernization of the country—bringing a rise in living standards and, above all, urbanization—forced Italians to cope with "the modern" (i.e., the American) at the same time they were trying to determine the parameters of *Italian* culture.

As we have seen, the history of Italian reactions to American cinema is inscribed in popular film magazines. An interesting article in *Hollywood* (17 October 1949), entitled "Il quinto potere" (The fifth estate) attributed to American cinema "an influence that overcomes the diversity of language and customs, of age and belief," affecting "slang, export of typewriters, women's hairdos." This writer distinguishes two sources of this influence, "the films and the stars," separating the impact of the films themselves from the more general effects achieved by the *myths* evoked and the way the stories are narrated, and also from the more specific impact of the behavioral models offered by the star system, as acted out in the popular press. The article, full of early insights into the influence of

American cinema, continues: "The *longa manus* of Hollywood reaches every sector of the behavior and costumes of our time, without touching ... ideologies." American producers, the article goes on, did not want to deal with controversial issues and preferred making "pleasurable fairy tales," knowing that "maximum profit attends maximum innocuousness." This was the typical representation of American cinema as pure evasion, seen as nonideological because it did not transmit an explicit political message, whereas its ideological efficacy resided precisely in its "transparency" and universality.

This article represents a very early perception of an Italian cultural phenomenon and gives a detailed description of the influence of American cinema on Italian culture. It was an influence detectable "in every house and in every store, or just [by] looking into a mirror"; it was revealed in the form of "indirect lighting, modern furniture and sparkling bathrooms," as well as in "the hat raised in the front, invented by Hollywood to avoid shadows on the faces of the beautiful dolls of the screen." One of the more common interpretations of the phenomenon is summarized by this writer: "Sociologists have commented on the role of cinema in creating a new mentality about marriage and divorce, about the way of courting a woman, about the reactions to problems in family life. The movies ... bridge the eternal gap between the rural and the urban, undermining provincialism."

Popular film magazines such as *Hollywood* were not always scholarly or friendly in their treatment of the American film invasion, especially of the American film crews then arriving in Rome. In a 20 December 1947 article, *Hollywood* took a thinly disguised swipe at American filmmakers in saying, "Let them come and shoot in Italy, but with grace and discretion." The writer, Francesco Callari, criticized the American crews shooting in Cinecittà as domineering barbarians and faulted them for not using Italian film workers. A few years later, however, in a November 1951 article, the magazine triumphantly boasted "America is Here," referring to the incredible number of Hollywood stars then working in Italy. In 1953, the film magazine *Festival* published "Euphoria in the Hollywood on the Tiber," a feature article delighting in the fact that thirty American film productions were going to be shot in Europe, mostly in Italy. At the same time, both in leftist and popular film magazines, American film production in Italy began to be seen as a manifestation of economic and cultural imperialism that should firmly be challenged, in light of the superior cultural quality of Italian film production and the high standards of Cinecittà crews. Theodore Wilson has shown earlier in this volume that American officials were well aware of Italian criticism of America as "a barbaric country without culture and taste." But on the other side was the excitement about the presence of American stars in Italy, and so an ambivalence developed between love of "home-made" Italian products and fascination with the products imported from Hollywood.

In the 1950s, American film stars played a complex role in the process of modernization, as their depiction in scenes of daily life and family situations in fan magazines indicates. Many American stars were pictured cooking in their beautiful "American kitchens," wearing an apron, and smiling; or sitting in the living room, often in front of a fireplace, with their spouse and children. Irene Dunne was publicly complimented by *Hollywood* (3 June 1950) for being a "fervent Catholic," and for keeping "religion, family [she had been married for twenty-two years to the same man], her neighbor and her art" all at the top of her priorities. When American film stars had children, the newborn child was often pictured in the arms of its smiling mother. But if the mother had just divorced, there were bitter remarks about the instability of Hollywood marriages. Divorce remained shocking in 1950s Italy, a reaction that appears to have been cultural and not simply religious and political. Divorce and the lack of respect for family values were criticized even in leftist film magazines. A continuous tension ran through the pages of these magazines: on the one hand was the promotion of consumption and modernity in association with America's icons and stars; on the other was criticism of divorce, excess, unruly behavior, and Hollywood extravagance. This contradiction was anchored in the ideological persistence of the ideal of the patriarchal family, of the rural and Catholic mentality that still dominated Italy during the 1950s.

The images of American actresses in a domestic environment served several functions: to give a positive response to this ideological tension, to promote consumption in the modern home, and, last but not least, to side with the prevailing political force after 1948, the Democratic Christians. American celebrities were often presented during an official visit to the Vatican. They seemed to pay their homage not so much to Christianity as to the public spirit of the Cold War, which had taken on a crusade-like aspect in Italy.

In the immediate postwar period, American stars embodied the American dream in the form of lavish clothes, beautiful houses, modern appliances, and big cars. In the early 1950s, however, while making films in Italy, they began buying Italian products. Magazines from this period show Humphrey Bogart buying shirts in a famous store in Rome, or other film stars ordering shoes and clothes at famous Italian stores. During this period, Italian fashion gained international appeal, challenging the dominance of Parisian fashion. The astounding popularity of Italian fashion and crafts was an entirely new phenomenon that seemed to come from nowhere; it became a key "modernizing" factor in Italy's economy and incidentally bolstered Italian self-esteem.

Hollywood stars were highly visible in Italian high society in the 1950s. When Tyrone Power and Linda Christian decided to get married in Rome, the newsreels and the popular Italian press dubbed the nuptials the "marriage of the Century." But American stars also married Italians, starting with the scandalous marriage of Hollywood star Ingrid Bergman to Roberto Rossellini, and continuing with Vittorio Gassman marrying Shelley Winters, the love affair of Ava Gardner and Italian comedian Walter Chiari, and later the liaison of Pier Angeli with James Dean. These relationships were significant in that they brought American stars and Italians together in the popular imagination. As the 1950s progressed, therefore, the gulf between them had narrowed, and at the same time better economic conditions allowed Italian audiences to begin thinking in terms of a reasonable consumerism—always with an eye to the international high society that was acting out the dreams of the community.

In a diachronic study of this period, it is evident that American cinema had a strong impact on Italian culture of the 1940s. But by the 1950s, the influence seems to have become more interactive and balanced. The Italian economy was fast moving away from reconstruction into a boom period. Italian versions of appliances and American kitchens (that is, industrial products made in Italy by a rapidly developing industry) entered Italian homes as the American dream was recast in Italian products.

A similar phenomenon occurred in cinema. The national characteristics of Italian films were strong, but instead of opposing itself to American films, Italian cinema slowly developed an exploitative attitude. Italians simply stole the tricks of the super-spectacular shows, making cheap but well-crafted and internationally appreciated historical costume films (*sandaloni*). The appeal of these Italian films depended on the reformulation of popular genres, and on such long-lasting traditions in Italian cinema as the historical spectacle, which was revived by the presence of a popular, muscular hero, such as Hercules or Maciste.

Italian cinema also developed its own stars, especially the new, heavily "breasted" divas Loren and Lollobrigida, the so-called "maggiorate," who expressed the new, healthy, and more active condition of Italian women. "Maggiorate" were beautiful women, valued for their bodies in a way that resembled Hollywood's pinups. But there were crucial differences in their cultural profile: they were Mediterranean beauties, with strong maternal qualities; and yet they belonged to a more modern and emancipated gender culture.

These Italian stars and the new popular film genres, the *sandaloni* and the new comedy, won immediate and wide popularity with Italian audiences. "Pink neorealist comedies" such as *Pane amore e fantasia* used the energetic interaction between Vittorio De Sica, working here as an actor, and Gina Lollobrigida to present the conditions of rural Italy and changing sexual customs. This type of Italian comedy, which continued in the late 1950s and 1960s up until *Il sorpasso* by Dino Risi, always took notice of social change, reporting about both provincial and urban Italy, thereby registering changes in economy and thinking. Currently these films indeed represent a sort of social history of Italy. This innovative entertainment genre, soon dubbed "Italian comedy," was a combination of neorealist traditions with popular characters as protagonists and a continuous interest in social problems, but with the added attraction of stars like Loren and Lollo. Most of the best Italian filmmakers worked in this genre. The Italian comedy of the late 1950s and 1960s thus appears to have been the Italian way of adapting to modernization and to cultural changes—with laughter. These comedies maintained the neorealist search for reality but added more spectacular Hollywood touches, such as stars, and the use of deeply rooted generic conventions such as those of dialect theater.

Italian cinema stole the secret of another aspect of American film promotion as well: star portraits and publicity stunts. In the film magazines of the immediate postwar period, the photos of American stars had a superior quality that immediately exposed the inferior quality of Italian film publicity. Soon, however, photographers such as Luxardo created a new school of Italian portrait photography that had dignity and style, even by Hollywood standards. Anita Ekberg bathing in the Trevi fountain in *La dolce vita* epitomized the ability of Italian *paparazzi* to emphasize the new society life of Rome that was transforming the city into a magnificent virtual film set.

Popular film magazines indicate that Hollywood cinema was received with mixed reactions in 1950s Italy. It was perceived as an imperialistic venture because it had virtually invaded Italian screens. A wide-ranging coalition from the fields of business, politics, and culture fought against it because Hollywood strangled both Italy's newly resurgent national film industry and neorealism. Catholicism and Marxism, the two dominant cultures of the time, clashed with some of the values embedded in Americanization (i.e., consumerism, individualism). Industrial and economic considerations apart, Hollywood cinema was also criticized for offering escapist fare, both by the left, which was always looking for relevant social commentary, and, at times, by Catholic pressure groups, which did not like musicals with "almost naked" dancers, "materialist' or consumerist messages, or representations of social violence. Catholic publications strongly criticized Hollywood movies for representing life falsely and superficially and therefore lacking any educational value. Most of all, Catholics condemned the antifamily content of some American films. But in the end, at any small, parochial cinema, any American film was preferable to any communist neorealist film!

The Italian cultural resistance to American cinema thus comprised conservative, Catholic, and elite resistance to new attitudes, along with left-wing political opposition to the culture of the "Other." These pools of resistance were unified by their national-popular roots, their search for a new national identity, and a new moral strength drawn from their earlier participation in the resistance. This is why Americanization in Italy is "fragmented, marked both by pervasiveness and incompleteness," to the point that scholars have defined the Italian model as "half-americanized."[19]

But as soon as Italian film production gathered momentum and American production began to decline, the Italian market began to resist Americanization. Whereas in the early postwar period American films represented almost the entire popular filmgoing experience, in the long run, even though neorealist cinema lost its popularity, the new Italian films dominated the market. The new form was, to an extent, an Americanized version of neorealist cinema, involving stars, lavish studio productions, and the formulaic conventions of film genres. But it was a quality product with *added* commercial value, as exemplified in the new Italian comedy genre. By the 1960s, Italian cinema reached a high point in the author cinema of Fellini, Visconti, and Antonioni, which came to be called "author-superspectacles."[20] In the end, we might say that Hollywood defeated the neorealist model in merely economic terms, but it did not defeat Italian cinema.

Ultimately, Hollywood lost its control over the Italian popular audience. Saturated with the mass-produced, unrealistic Hollywood films, by the end of the 1950s Italian filmmakers had learned how to make high quality but popular films. The evolution of Italian film production in this period is impressive. Twenty-five films were produced in Italy in 1945; 62 in 1946; 148 in 1952; 201 in 1954. After a slight drop, the numbers subsequently remained stable. Cinecittà went back to work: 5 films were made there in 1950, 30 in 1951. In 1946, at the height of the Hollywood invasion and the first neorealist productions, only 13 percent of the box office went to Italian cinema, but in 1954 the share jumped to 36 percent. In 1962 it was 47 percent. In 1973 American cinema reached its nadir at the box office in Italy with only a slim 23 percent.

In a 9 December 1950 issue of *Hollywood,* journalist Italo Dragosei stated: "The box office receipts for national films have notably surpassed those of the feared American production." The 13 January 1951 issue of the same magazine included a U.S. Gallup poll showing that Italian cinema was the most popular foreign cinema in the United States, and Valentina Cortese the most popular foreign film star. In fact, many Italian film personalities went to Hollywood, among them Alida Valli, who acted in *The Paradine Case* by Hitchcock, Gina Lollobrigida, Vittorio Gassman, Pier Angeli, and Rossano Brazzi. This exchange has not received much attention thus far, but both American film artists in Italy and Italians in the United States are likely to have been affected by their professional experiences in a foreign country. This element represents another chapter of the more interactive contact between European culture and America: the internationalization of film sets.

In the second half of the 1950s, Italian cinema recovered the majority of its national audience through the fascination with new Italian film stars and the attraction of new popular genres. Soon, many of these Italian films—such as *La dolce vita*—found international popularity and were distributed globally. The improvised but very skilled local industry not only gained a position of dominance in its own market but also began a counterattack on American cinema's own ground—the western. In the 1960s, *spaghetti westerns* took revenge on Hollywood—appropriating the most American of American film genres.

The decline in appreciation of Hollywood cinema was encouraged by the increasing popularity of Italian cinema, in large part because neorealist cinema, "author cinema," and Italian comedies represented Italian reality and narrated the daily experiences as well as the complexities of Italian social life. In the late 1950s, the Italian public's overdose of American films, in combination with the peculiar political and social conditions of the country, produced a disaffection for the glossy product of Hollywood's assembly line. Italians seemed more reassured by their own elaboration of modernization through the familiar images of Italian cinema—a cinema that maintained the characteristics of a handcrafted product, warm and homey like the traditional kitchens of Italian comedy, with a *maggiorata* to offer a protective embrace.

Notes

1. On the Cold War, see Malvyn P. Leffler, *A Preponderance of Power: National Security, the Truman Administration and the Cold War* (Stanford: Stanford University Press, 1992); Lary May, ed., *Recasting America: Culture and Politics in the Age of the Cold War* (Chicago: University of Chicago Press, 1989). On the relations between the United States and Europe, see Ennio Di Nolfo, ed., *Power in Europe? Great Britain, France, Germany and Italy and the Origins of the EEC,*

1952–1957 (Berlin: De Gruyter, 1992). On the relations between the United States and Italy, see Christopher Duggan and Christopher Wagstaff, eds., *Italy and the Cold War. Politics, Culture and Society 1948–1958* (Oxford: Berg, 1995).

2. On the history of postwar Italy the most innovative work is Silvio Lanaro's *L'Italia nuova. Identità e sviluppo 1861–1988* (Torino: Einaudi, 1988). See also Paul Ginsborg, *A History of Contemporary Italy. Society and Politics 1943–1988* (London: Penguin, 1990). The elaboration of Italian national identity has been studied in the three-volume work *Luoghi della memoria*, edited by Mario Isnenghi (Laterza: Rome, 1996–1997).

When Italy was united in 1860, the struggle for national unity had been an elitist movement that involved the South only marginally. The new state was *piemontizzato*, that is, the administration, the king, and even the constitution of Piedmont were extended to the whole country. The new state and the nation—the people—did not develop a vital relationship, as political participation through suffrage was very limited. The relation of nation to state remained a problem throughout fascism. In 1943–1945, the Resistance movement represented a moment of possible national refoundation, although it was also a civil war. At the end of the war the Communist Party (together with the Socialists) and the Democratic Christians could boast of the political support of two almost equal halves of the Italian people. But when Italy, with the biggest Communist Party in the West and the closest proximity to Eastern Europe, became a crucial front in the Cold War, it was the Democratic Christians who gained the full (and decisive) support of their American ally.

3. Neorealism was an avant-garde movement elaborated by diverse film personalities such as Vittorio De Sica (*Sciuscià, The Bicycle Thief*), Roberto Rossellini (*Open City, Paisan*), Luchino Visconti (*Ossessione, La terra trema*), Giuseppe De Santis (*Bitter Rice*). It was an intellectual project developed by left-wing intellectuals who expressed their horror about nazi-fascism and their hope in the reaction of the Italian people, but also their desire to communicate with the audience through a realistic and popular representation. In the neorealist experience, "the screen is a mirror of the theater," bridging the division between filmmaker and audience. It was indeed a rare occasion in which cinema was able to develop a key political project, maintaining its relation with the audience and functioning not just as an expression of the desire for social change, but as an effective tool in the process.

Neorealist films were more spontaneous productions than industrial products. *Open City*, for instance, came about by the initiative of a director and a group of screenwriters making use of expired film stock and getting money from a couple of Americans, Geiger and Burstyn, who imported the film to the United States and gave Rossellini enough money to finish it. This was an important American contribution to the making and circulation of a masterpiece of world cinema. *Paisan* was not only produced in the same way, but it was developed from an idea by Klaus Mann, the son of Thomas, who had been in Italy and experienced the various episodes in the film as a member of the Psychological Warfare Branch.

On neorealism, see Gian Piero Brunetta, *Storia del cinema italiano*. vol. 3 (Rome: Editori Riuniti, 1993).

4. On Americanization, see Federico Romero, *"L'americanizzazione" e la storia italiana*, paper presented at the conference "L'Italia e Stati Uniti a 50 anni dal Piano Marshall," Rome 25–27 March 1998; and Pierpaolo D'Attorre, ed., *Nemici per la pelle. Sogno americano e mito sovietico nell'Italia contemporanea*

(Milan: F. Angeli, 1991); David Ellwood and Rob Kroes, eds., *Hollywood in Europe: Experiences of a Cultural Hegemony* (Amsterdam, VU University Press, 1994); in same, "The Long March of American Cinema in Italy," pp. 139–54; Robert Kroes, *If You've Seen One, You've Seen The Mall. Europeans and American Mass Culture* (Urbana: University of Illinois Press, 1996); Richard Pells, *Not Like US. How Europeans Have Loved, Hated, and Transformed American Culture since World War II* (New York: Basic Books, 1997).

5. On Gramsci's definition of *national-popular,* see David Forgacs, "National Popular: Genealogy of a Concept," and Dick Hebdige, "From Culture to Hegemony," both in Simon During, ed., *The Cultural Studies Reader* (New York and London: Routledge, 1993).

6. On *The Miracle* and the evolution of film censorship in the United States, see Ellen Draper, "'Controversy has probably destroyed forever the context': *The Miracle* and Movie Censorship in America in the Fifties," in *Velvet Light Trap* 25 (spring 1990): 70–79.

7. See Ennio Di Nolfo. *Documenti sul ritorno del cinema americano in Italia nell'immediato dopoguerra,* in Saveria Chemotti, ed., *Gli intellettuali in trincea. Politica e cultura nell'Italia del dopoguerra* (Padua: CLEUP, 1977), and David Ellwood, *Italy 1943–1945* (New York: Holmes, 1985). On the American penetration of international film markets in the postwar period, see Thomas Guback, *The International Film Industry: Western Europe and America since 1945* (Bloomington: Indiana University Press, 1969).

8. One of the main industries in Rome was indeed the film industry. The head of the Italian government, Ivanoe Bonomi, supported the Italian film producers' requests with American authorities soon after Rome was liberated, in June 1944, but received no positive answer.

9. "Very best" was the expression Carl Milliken of MPPDA used in addressing the State Department. David Ellwood, *Italy 1943–45.*

10. In the film *Un americano a Roma,* for example, comedian Alberto Sordi is obsessed by his passion for American culture and products and strongly influenced by his passionate frequenting of American cinema. But when it comes to food, he ends up refusing the American products he had wanted to try and goes back eating his dish of *macaroni.* David Ellwood, "Un Americano a Roma: A 1950s Satire of Americanization," *Modern Italy* 1, no. 2 (1996): 93–102.

11. These magazines proposed models of escapist social mobility, like beauty contests that promised quick popularity to young and beautiful Italian women. Lucia Bosé and Gina Lollobrigida, among many other stars, were "discovered" and became actresses after winning a beauty contest.

12. *Quo Vadis?* was such a Catholic superspectacle, full of martyrs, perfect for Cold War religious overtones and American grandiose vision of civilization, competition, and love. There were many promotional stunts for the opening of the film in Italy, which included a huge MGM *toga* party, the donation of two little lions (the lion is the logo of MGM and was connected to the circus scenes in the film) to the Roman zoo; most of all, an official visit of MGM executives to the Pope, which directly tied the film to the celebrations for the Jubilee or Holy Year, a Catholic celebration held every fifty years.

13. See Giuliana Muscio, "Lista nera sul Tevere," in *Acoma* 7 (spring 1996): 50–62.

14. On Hollywood in the fifties, see Robert Sklar, *Movie-Made America: A Cultural History of American Movies* (New York: Vintage, 1994, rev. ed.), and

Lary May, *The Big Tomorrow: Hollywood and the Politics of the American Way* (Chicago: University of Chicago Press, 2000).

15. On blacklisting and its background see Brian Neve, *Film and Politics in America: A Social Tradition* (London and New York: Routledge, 1992), and Lary Ceplair and Steven Englund, *Inquisition in Hollywood: Politics in the Film Community 1930–1960* (Garden City: Anchor Press, 1980).

16. Even the popular film magazine *Hollywood* discussed the work of Edward Dmytryk, describing him as a member of the "American neorealist school." *Cinema nuovo* (15 March 1953) compared the theatrical production of *Streetcar Named Desire* by Luchino Visconti and the same text as directed by Elia Kazan, in terms of realism.

The visit of radical documentary filmmaker Paul Strand to Italy implies complex cultural interactions. On the one hand, in the thirties and forties, Strand influenced the visual culture of Italian intellectuals. On the other hand, in Italy during the 1950s, he was influenced by the fascinating personality of Cesare Zavattini, the neorealist screenwriter and collaborator of De Sica. With Strand, Zavattini published a great photo-book, *Un paese*, about daily life in Luzzara, the village where the writer lived on the Po river.

17. Indicative of the FBI's attitudes were the tight controls on Charlie Chaplin.

18. See David Ellwood, "Un Americano a Roma: A 1950s Satire of Americanization," *Modern Italy* 1, no. 2 (1996): 3–102. Ellwood stresses the interaction between the socioeconomic changes in Italy and the relationship with (we could actually call it *dependence* on) the United States: "Urbanization (7 to 8 million people moved to the cities in the 1950s), the expansion of welfare, public development projects and the money spent by the government and its American allies convincing ordinary Italians to back the right in the Cold War: all these were factors pushing consumption upwards."

19. D'Attorre, ed., *Nemici per la pelle.*

Nosa Owens-Ibie

Programmed for Domination

U.S. Television Broadcasting and Its Effects on

Nigerian Culture

Introduction

The development of Nigerian television programming since its inception at the end of the 1950s has been characterized by a profound and relentless American influence. The increasing prevalence of American programs symbolizes the extent to which television has been a primary route for the mediation of America's colonial imperative in Nigeria. This paper attempts to explore the significance and impact of the Americanization of Nigerian television, and critically examines some trends through which the products of American culture permeate the globe. It locates the consolidation of American television programs within a nexus of historical, structural, political, economic, and cultural factors prevailing in Nigeria.

When Midwest Television was established in Nigeria in 1973, it embraced and incorporated a number of American programs into its roster. *It Takes a Thief*, starring Robert Wagner, was one such show. On a weekly basis, Mr. Monday proved that stealing was a worthwhile and lucrative venture and that all a successful thief needed was acumen, skill, bravery, and focus. For Mr. Monday, there was no *Mission Impossible,* and, although figures on the extent of his popularity are not available, avid viewers of the series, myself included, were fascinated by his exploits. We do not know how many of Mr. Monday's fans followed in his footsteps; but there is evidence that his message won him some following.[1] The popularity of *It Takes a Thief* mirrored the emerging impact of American television in the 1970s. The show was but one of many American programs signalling the Americanization of Nigerian television in that decade. This trend has since been consolidated in the programming at the local and national levels, demonstrating American culture's continuing impact upon Nigerian culture. Despite official attempts to control the increasing proliferation of American programs, the industry has, ironically, shifted itself further into the American sphere. Although a local framework puts quotas on foreign productions in programming schedules, the influence of American programs upon locally produced television has been profound.[2] The inroads made by programs from Europe and South America do not represent a shift away from American cultural productions, but rather reinforce Nigerian broadcasting's continued Americanization. For European and South American productions are in themselves distillations of the American influence in those parts of the world.

The Historical

The very origins of television in Nigeria established a basis for American influence. Britain, the colonial power until 1960, contributed to this process. The Western Nigeria Government Broadcasting Corporation, which midwifed the Western Nigeria Television (WNTV), went into partnership with Oversea Rediffusion Limited of the U.K.; in its first five years of operation, the WNTV spent a substantial sum on foreign films, many of which were American.[3] Following the launching of the WNTV on 31 October 1959, Nigeria's Federal Minister of Information, Hon. T. O. S. Benson, went to Europe and America in search of assistance in starting an external service for the Nigerian Broadcasting Corporation (NBC) and its television service. Discussions were held with, among others, the National Broadcasting Company of America (NBCA) and the Columbia Broadcasting System of America (CBS). The Radio Corporation of America was involved with the supply of equipment to the NBC. One of the terms offered by the NBCA was "programme formats and filmed programmes . . . at the lowest prices."[4] An agreement was eventually signed with the National Broadcasting Company International Limited (NBI) on 25 September 1961. The company was contracted to manage the new television service in its first five years. In addition to exercising powers in personnel matters, acquiring and maintaining equipment, and defining lines of organization, the NBI was responsible for producing, procuring, and scheduling programs. When the Nigerian Television Service (NTS) Channel 10, Lagos, was launched as an arm of the NBC on 1 April 1962, the director of programs was Roger Bower.

The station's initial daily transmission of programs was for only seventy-five minutes, of which thirty minutes were occupied by foreign programming.[5] This agreement with an American company favored the screening of American television series.

The Structural

The structure and organization of television have made the medium not just a pliable tool in the hands of its owners, but have made broadcasting dependent on sources outside the country. Under Decree 24 of 1977, the Nigerian Television Authority (NTA) is expected to produce and acquire television programs for mass reception.[6] However, maintaining a regular schedule without an indigenous technological base for hardware and software necessitated a dependency on foreign supplies and experts. The United States offered cheaper and ready alternatives which the NTA—the country's only television network—and the private stations have continued to exploit. In the precommercialization days when 60 percent of NTA's funds came via subventions from the federal government,[7] the most consistent complaint about programming was about the financial squeeze, which made the production of high quality programs difficult.[8] Such a weakened condition, combined with the grip American companies held on the global television programs market, and the popularity of such programs as the crime series *Through Every Conceivable Variation*,[9] reinforced American influence. Locally produced programs also suffered from what Olusola described as "The rather limited vision of the founding fathers . . . their failure to anticipate and plan for the content of television . . . too much emphasis on the gadgetry, the equipment, the installations of imported equipment, and very little thought given to the creative product of television."[10]

Operators of the medium whose task it is to interpret the fine print of the laws and other rules of operation, and who decide the content of television, either have American training or were weaned on the America-influenced curricula of Nigeria's mass communication and journalism schools. Other foot-soldiers in the industry who have undergone the same kind of education are also instruments of this influence. The industry bias, and the American-style programming it creates, are evident in the competition fostered, especially in the Southern and Middle Belt of the country, by the deregulation of broadcasting.[11] This competition is at its fiercest in Lagos, which has the single largest market in Nigeria.

The Political

Political considerations largely informed the establishment of WNTV, the continuing monopoly of the NTA of the very high frequency (VHF) band, and the proliferation of state government television stations, especially during the second Republic (1979–1983). Stations in the latter category were established in states run by political parties other than the National Party of Nigeria (NPN), which, by virtue of being in power at the center, controlled the NTA and its programs: Since television, and especially those stations controlled by government, have, with some variation between regimes, been an instrument of political competition, "neutral" foreign programs filled a gap. American programs fit this "neutral" category either as fillers or scheduled or unscheduled programs. They shared the spotlight in this regard with programs from other countries, but the balance tilted toward American programs.

The Economic

Previous emphasis on public service television, which relied basically on subvention from government, gradually gave way in the face of dwindling resources and erratic government funding. Decree No. 25 of 1988, which established a Technical Committee on Privatization and Commercialization (TCPC—now the Bureau for Public Enterprises), set the tone for subsequent programs. The signing of a performance agreement between the TCPC and government-controlled media, including the NTA, and the Federal Government, was the official mandate for wholesale commercialization.[12] This agreement represented a distinct phase of the Americanization of television broadcasting, and the trend was reinforced by the entry of private stations whose popular programming reflected their commitment to commercial broadcasting. News coverage was commercialized, and marketing departments were revitalized in order to shore up finances. NTA 2 Channel 5, Lagos, which was fully commercialized on 3 April 1988 and was "the network's goldmine,"[13] regularly screened American entertainment, children's, and sports programs. Studies by the Research Unit of NTA, Ibadan (formerly WNTV) and by myself[14] have shown that the station was the most popular of the six stations in its area of coverage.

Private television stations in Lagos, such as African Independent Television (AIT); Degue Broadcasting Network (DBN) Television; Murhi International Television (MITV); Galaxy Television in Ibadan, Minaj

Systems Television (MSTV) Obosi; Desmins Broadcast (Nigeria) Limited, Kaduna; and State Government television stations, have raised the tone of the competition through American and American-style programs that stations air within the 40 percent legal specification for foreign programs allowed on the schedule. Clapperboard Television, Lagos, which started as the first private station, was virtually an all-American Station until the National Broadcasting Commission (NBC) started enforcing controls.

Sponsorship of foreign programs on the NTA Network were the exception when *Roots, Capital,* and *Generations* were aired.[15] That policy has changed, essentially because of economic considerations. American programs and telenovelas from Mexico and Brazil are sponsored by multinational companies, both on government and private stations. That the telenovelas betraying a strong American influence are getting aired in spite of their age reflects economic factors.[16] Economic interests justify the involvement of the sponsors, many of whom have American connections. The popularity of the programs further fuels the enterprise.

The Cultural

Nigerian cultures have a very strong entertainment tradition. Such a tradition has favored the reception of American programs whose cross-cultural appeal makes them universal products. African American programs naturally have a ready following despite the problem of comprehension of the actors' diction by some viewers. There is, however, no defined pattern to the qualities of the preferred programs, beyond the fact of their being American. The general preference for dramatic entertainment during prime time[17] fuels the search for programs that program selectors expect to satisfy this criterion of popularity. In large part, the dominance of American-style entertainment, information, and educational programs or American products during prime time represents stations' attempts to reach out to the elite class who are cultural hybrids, as well as to the masses who are being steadily incorporated into a pro-American reality.[18]

Although Indian movies are very popular in the North, a sprinkling of American comedy, cartoons, and movies also dots broadcasting schedules there. Plateau Radio Television (PRTV), Jos—a state government station in the Middle Belt—tends to air more American programs than most stations in the North. This can be explained from the perspective of religion and culture. The core Northern states are predominantly Muslim. The commitment of the people to Islamic and local traditions also explains the immense popularity of local Hausa-language programs. Plateau State, on the other hand, has a sizeable Christian population. Popular local cultural productions such as the Yoruba language *Arelu* (drama) in the West of the country, and *Dambe* (wrestling) on NTA Kaduna, find an affinity with American programs of similar molds. *Arelu* was an action-packed series with a villain—Fadeyi Oloro—whose popularity contributed to the death of some viewers who attempted to recreate his invincibility,[19] while *Dambe* has the trappings of *Wrestlemania*. The appeal of both programs also cuts across socioeconomic lines.[20]

In contrast, the news broadcasting arena demonstrates a very class-specific, elite cultural influence on the Americanization of programming. Nigerian cultures have a strong information tradition. *CBN News Tonight* (CBN News), from Pat Robertson's Christian Broadcasting Network (CBN), is syndicated weekly on some stations, and DBN TV and Channels TV feature the *Jim Lehrer Newshour*, which competes with the NTA Network news on weekdays. However, it was the controversy surrounding the African Beamlink Network's introduction of the Cable News Network (CNN) broadcasts—based on an agreement with the NTA—that really put the elite culture factor into perspective. The agreement, which allowed for a nine-hour daily transmission of CNN programs during the dark hours, commenced on 11 February 1993; however, it was stopped through a directive by the NBC's director-general Dr. Tom Adaba on 11 March 1993, on the basis that it fails to promote "Nigerian indigenous cultures, moral and community life through broadcasting as required by law." Convinced that the CNN broadcasts would not compromise local culture, Lagos State legislators canvassed for the retention of the broadcasts.[21] A lawyer declared in a newspaper article that even its enabling decree did not empower the NBC to "unilaterally proceed to stop the NTA's CNN broadcasts."[22] Before the stoppage, advertising during the transmission was on the rise. Now, footage from CNN broadcasts is regularly used on government and private stations and there are now more private subscribers to CNN programs among the same elite vanguard who facilitate American cultural projection. According to Mallam Mohammed Ibrahim, its former director-general, even the NTA now plans to cover the world "like the CNN."[23]

Genres and Trends

Impact studies on, and analysis of, television affirm its capacity to moderate change.[24] Some such studies observe a positive relationship between the popularity of a station and its volume of entertainment programs.[25]

Nigerian television effectively provides a case study in Americanization through the instrumentality of the entertainment genre. American programs, marketers, and those who embrace American influence remain factors in this regard, and effectively bolster Americanization. However, the specific qualities of such programs, which include movies, soaps, sitcoms, sports, musicals, and cartoons, are extremely significant and do much to encourage the process. The programs are dynamic and tend successfully to project and capture the global cultural imagination. They therefore have a heavy impact on the popular culture, drawing on America's unique advantage as a cultural melting-pot able to fashion products with an appeal to peoples all over the world. The progression from various crime series to movies flows from this logic. While crime shows and other drama series are still featured, various American movies now offer a mixture of comedy, action, horror, adventure, romance, and thrillers to further seduce an already captive audience.

While *Sesame Street* is a perennial feature on many stations, considerable variety has been introduced to children's broadcasting, where American cartoons hold sway. *Barney*—the dinosaur who is all fun and gentle adventure—became a network program on the NTA. At the same time, American soaps thrive on a compelling story line, suspense, professional acting, technical finesse, and commercial appeal. These genres' ability to target an audience and mesmerize them by the sheer manipulation of plot, characterization, and other techniques (animation for children and teenagers, and more sophisticated plots for adults), continue to guarantee their popularity among Nigerian audiences. The enthusiastic reception of Alex Haley's *Roots* represented a phase in this progression. Kunta Kinte's incredible suffering and humiliation en route to and in America resonated powerfully with a Nigerian audience, who, still grappling with the consequences of that phase of their history, were able to experience feelings of shared consciousness.[26] Through *Roots*, Nigerians were able to appreciate again, reflect on, and discuss their colonial past and its consequences on their current dilemmas in development. Although the subsequent early 1990s crusade by the late Chief Moshood Abiola for reparations to Africa and Africans in the diaspora cannot be directly traced to the *Roots* series, it likely was influenced by it.[27]

Other landmarks in the progression of American shows include CBN's *Another Life*, a long-running sitcom that established a pattern of collaboration between a private American network and government-controlled television stations in Nigeria; *Rambo*, with its dose of glamorized violence; and the *Oprah Winfrey Show*, which catalyzed the growing fad of talk shows and inspired the locally produced *Mee and*

You, anchored by the late Mee Mofe-Damijo. The American shows have a clear advantage, owing to their technical quality, set, style of presentation, and sequence. American championship wrestling and basketball offer flexibility and dynamism, another explanation for the popularity of American programs. Both have influenced the local development of both sports, which has boosted the continuing airing of versions of the American programs and has guaranteed sponsorship. The evolution of American wrestling from the low-tech, relatively drab, production era of Dick "The Bulldog" Brower, Mighty Igor, and Mill Mascaras to the more flamboyant, advertising-oriented epoch of the Ultimate Warrior, Lex Lugar, and Hulk "Hollywood" Hogan, has become popular among the cultivated Nigerian devotees of American professional wrestling. Hulk Hogan and a retinue of other stars and heavyweight champions, whose stunts and gimmickry are spiced with music and the effervescent crowd support or boos, now considerably jazz up the shows. Basketball's exploitation of the success of Nigerian superstar Hakeem "The Dream" Olajuwon of the Houston Rockets has popularized the game and increased the number of teams locally and players internationally. Michael Jordan and his exploits with the Chicago Bulls were, up until Jordan's retirement, major media sports events in Nigeria.

Educational and informative programs of American origin are also popular, although not as popular as those in the entertainment genre. This may be due to the role of program selectors who, considering the profile of such American information and educative programs, tend to favor those that are racy, well-packaged, and glamorous. Many such programs may actually be classified as "infotainment" and "edutainment" programs because of their entertainment quotient. It may also be due to the emphasis of marketers, their understanding of what they think Nigerian viewers prefer, or what they believe these viewers deserve. According to Ifeoma Ndiolo, head of programming, Channels Television, the three principal reasons for the preference for foreign, and especially American, programs are that: (1) most local programs are of inferior quality in terms of standard programming requirements; (2) it is cheaper to procure foreign programs than to produce local ones; and (3) locally produced programs are not duly protected by the existing copyright laws. The influence of such marketers on program selection cannot be ignored, just as the biases of program selectors must be taken into account.

The resulting American dominance of the entertainment genre is mirrored in the tables in the appendixes to this chapter, which reveal that the proportion of American entertainment programs was never less than one-third on NTA 2 Channel 5, Channels Television or NTA Channel 10 during 1997 (see tables in chapter appendix). As the figures also show, Germany is making inroads as a source of educational television and programming in two of the randomly selected stations. This shows that a market exists for these genres, and is indicative of either the successful marketing of the German programs, the assessment of their quality by selectors, or other unclear incentives that won them a slot on Nigerian stations' schedules.

Controls

The NBC is constrained by factors in the environment, in spite of its attempt to apply the rules contained in the Broadcasting Code of 1993. For instance, it cautioned DBN TV against the airing of violent, basically American movies. The code seeks to regulate the content of television, specifying sanctions. NBC has closed some satellite/cable channels for not meeting the minimum of 20 percent local programming, but its efforts in cultural preservation have done little to reduce the growing number of American programs on Nigerian television.[28] This trend is observable both in the proliferation of American programs and in the American influence evident in the concept, context, presentation styles, costumes, set, and informality of some parts of otherwise serious Nigerian programs.

American-style Nigerian shows are popular, and incorporate segments on health, fashion, and music, as well as interviews with public figures and stars. Soaps reflect this influence, and their sheer popularity makes the task of the NBC more problematic. They are most often commercially sponsored, commercially appealing, and given to exploiting themes of love, crime, sex, intrigue, power politics, class conflict, and sleaze. Villainy is played up to excite viewers, and popular local acts are used to bolster local followings. New acts are groomed to star heights, with the print media assisting in the promotional strategy. Some of the more successful ones such as *Checkmate* (credited with being "the first indigenous soap opera to . . . have [a formal] ending on television"[29]) have the features of a typical Amerian soap opera and, in a sense, have recreated the kind of conflict, betrayal, rivalry, and secrecy evident in *The Bold and the Beautiful*.[30] These developments dim the prospects for stemming the tide of Americanization. Compounding the problem is the lack of sufficient local alternatives to challenge Nigerian dependence on foreign products. This, according to the director-general of the NBC, makes the task of regulating television more difficult for the commission, even when it is aware that stations are flouting the rules.[31]

Conclusion

To ignore the phenomenon of the United States' influence upon Nigeria and the Nigerian media is to take flight from reality.[32] The logic propelling the Americanization appears to be only partially related to economic progress. Poverty, which itself fuels escapism, bolsters television's role in helping to cushion social and economic pressures, and sustains escapist desires for the affluence depicted on American television. This has its cultural costs and may actually have sparked in many Nigerians the desire to emigrate to America, contributing to a steep increase in the number of Nigerian applicants for the American Visa Lottery.

The heavy direct and indirect presence in virtually every key area of Nigerian life assures continued Americanization, not just of television, but of other facets of Nigerian culture. There are even now attempts by some local, American, and America-related forces to image-engineer in favor of America, and television is a profoundly powerful instrument in this regard. Any notion of genuine bi-directionality in the content of television is, therefore, academic. Poverty hinders the export of Nigerian cultural products to the United States, the foot soldiers of American-style programming resist this, and existing economic and political structures ensure that Americanization will be allowed to continue unchecked. However, the future will be revelatory. Standing in the path of the tide of Americanization are Nigeria's deeply entrenched values and traditions. Whether they blossom into a genuine challenge to a global movement or allow American-style programming to survive will depend on a cultural awakening, flashpoints of which are evident not only in some locations in Nigeria but in other parts of the besieged world.

Appendix: Classification of Foreign Programming by Country of Origin

The following tables are based on research by Nosa Owens-Ibie. Program classifications are Edu (educational), Edu/TV (educational television), Ent (entertainment), and Inf (informational).

TABLE 1. NTA 2 CHANNEL 5, LAGOS[a] (January–March 1997 Programs)

Country of Origin	Program Type												
	Edu		Ent		Inf		Ent/Edu		Edu/Inf		Edu/TV		Total	
	No.	%	No.	%	No.	%	No.	%	No.	%	No.	%	No.	%
Germany	5	11.11	6	13.33					1	2.22			12	26.66
USA	3	6.66	20	44.44					3	6.66	1	2.22	27	60
Britain	1	2.22	2	4.44									3	6.66
USA/Britain			1	2.22									1	2.22
Mexico			2	4.44									2	4.44
Total	9	19.9	31	68.87					4	8.88	1	2.22	45	99.98

TABLE 2. NTA 2 CHANNEL 5, LAGOS[a] (April–June 1997 Programs)

Country of Origin	Program Type												
	Edu		Ent		Inf		Ent/Edu		Edu/Inf		Edu/TV		Total	
	No.	%	No.	%	No.	%	No.	%	No.	%	No.	%	No.	%
Germany	8	20.5	7	17.95			1	2.56	1	2.56	2	5.13	19	48.7
UK	1	2.56											1	2.56
USA	2	5.13	13	33.3	1	2.56			1	2.56			17	43.6
Brazil			1	2.56									1	2.56
Mexico			1	2.56									1	2.56
Total	11	28.2	22	56.4	1	2.56	1	2.56	2	5.13	2	5.13	39	99.98

TABLE 3. CHANNELS TELEVISION, LAGOS[b] (April–June 1997 Programs)

| Country of Origin | Program Type | | | | | | | | | | Total | |
| | Edu | | Ent | | Inf | | Ent/Edu | | | | | |
	No.	%	No.	%	No.	%	No.	%			No.	%
USA	2	16.6	4	33.3	1	8.33					7	58.33
UK							1	8.33			1	8.33
USA/UK	3	25	1	8.33							4	33.33
Total	5	41.66	5	41.66	1	8.33	1	8.33			12	99.99

[a] NTA 2 Channel 5 is a Federal Government–controlled entertainment television station.

[b] Channels Television is a privately owned news/commercial station.

EDU = Educational   ENT = Entertainment   INF = Informational   EDU/TV = Educational Television

Source (all tables): Nosa Owens-Ibie

TABLE 4. NTA CHANNEL 10, LAGOS[a] (January–March 1997 Programs)

Country of Origin	Edu		Ent		Inf		Ent/Edu		Edu/Inf		Edu/TV		Total	
	No.	%	No.	%	No.	%	No.	%	No.	%	No.	%	No.	%
USA			7	33.33			1	4.76					8	38.09
Germany	3	14.28	3	14.28									6	28.57
UK	2	9.52	2	9.52									4	19.05
Mexico			2	9.52									2	9.52
Africa	1	4.76											1	4.76
Total	6	28.57	14	66.66			1	4.76					21	99.99

TABLE 5. NTA CHANNEL 10, LAGOS[a] (April–June 1997 Programs)

Country of Origin	Edu		Ent		Inf		Ent/Edu		Edu/Inf		Edu/TV		Total	
	No.	%	No.	%	No.	%	No.	%	No.	%	No.	%	No.	%
Germany							1	6.25					1	6.25
USA	3	18.75	8	50.0			1	6.25					12	75.0
Britain	2	12.5											2	12.5
Mexico			1	6.25									1	6.25
Total	5	31.25	9	56.25			2	12.5					16	100

[a] NTA Channel 10 is a Federal Government–controlled public service commercial station.

EDU = Educational   ENT = Entertainment   INF = Informational   EDU/TV = Educational Television

Source (all tables): Nosa Owens-Ibie

Notes

1. For instance, in the years the show was on the air, it was customary for boys in our neighborhood to simulate his many antics. It may have been coincidental, but the incidence of gun robberies became slightly more pronounced following the airing of crime series like *It Takes a Thief*. The greatest advertisement for this development in the state renamed Bendel (later Edo State) was the Anini Saga of 1986, in which trigger-happy showboy Lawrence Anini and his gang of robbers unleashed a reign of terror on citizens and the police. The gang was eventually arrested, tried, and executed by firing squad.

2. In keeping with the official requirement for more local programs, the pioneer Western Nigeria Television (WNTV), now Nigerian Television Authority (NTA), Ibadan, witnessed a progressive decrease in the dominance of foreign entertainment (musical, drama, quiz) programs from 97.6 percent in 1962 to 58.1 percent in 1975 to 52.9 percent in 1979. Foreign programs remain common features on Nigerian television stations, however. In 1979, NTV Ibadan aired 14.5 percent foreign programs, NT Jos 36 percent, NTV Kaduna 18 percent, NTV Lagos 17 percent, and NTV Bauchi 19 percent. Of these, American and British programs were prominent, as the October 1962, April–July 1971, January 1976, and July–September 1979 program schedules of NTV Ibadan show. In a 1972 rating of the top twenty popular programs on WNTV, for instance, the American *Combat* ranked at a significant sixth position. (O. Ikime, *20th Anniversary History of WNTV* [Ibadan: 1979], 40–41, 109, 35–38, 56). *It Takes A Thief* was thus one of many American programs signalling the Americanization of Nigerian television in the 1970s.

3. O. Ikime, *20th Anniversary History of WNTV*, 4, 32.

4. O. Ladele, V. O. Adefela, and D. Lasekan, *History of the Nigerian Broadcasting Corporation* (Ibadan, 1979), 90–91.

5. Ibid., 97–103.

6. *NTA Handbook, 1981* (Lagos, 1982), 39.

7. M. Sule, "Here's the News on NTA," *Media Review* (April 1991): 25.

8. R. Mofe-Damijo, "Why NTA Can't Satisfy Viewers," *National Concord,* 10 July 1989, 11.

9. F. Wheen, *Television* (London, 1985), 127–30.

10. S. Olusola, "Words of Wisdom," *Media Review* (March 1995): 26.

11. N. Owens-Ibie, "Media/Cultural Imperialism and Nigerian Women: Whose Culture, Which Imperialism?" *Journal of Social Development in Africa* 7, no. 2 (1992): 49.

12. N. Owens-Ibie, "The Commercialization of the Mass Media in Nigeria: The Challenge of Social Responsibility," *The Journal of Development Communication* 4, no. 1 (June 1993): 65.

13. B. Ojediran, "Radio, TV . . . Cashing in on Commercial Broadcasting," *The Guardian* (10 July 1989), 11.

14. N. Owens-Ibie, "Audience Considerations in Viewing Different Television Stations in Lagos," unpublished M.Sc. research project, University of Lagos, July 1983, 32.

15. S. I. J. Wigwe, "Nigerian Television Authority: Philosophy, Objectives and Achievements," in T. Nnaemeka, E. Uvieghara, and D. Uyo, eds., *Philosophy and Dimensions of National Communication Policy,* vol. 1 (Lagos, 1989), 196–97.

16. T. Kolawole, "Ask Anyone, NTA's Gone to Mexico," *Sunday Concord,* 28 April 1996, M8; and Owens-Ibie, 1992, A8.

17. N. Owens-Ibie (Ombudsman), "Drama Versus Development," *The Guardian on Sunday,* 2 September 1989, 11.

18. In effect, elites who are already products of American influence are as much a target as members of the mass audience, who are similarly overwhelmed by the same products and who become instruments for sustaining American influence.

19. N. Owens-Ibie (Ombudsman), "Exciting Incitement," *The Guardian on Sunday* 20 September 1991, A6.

20. Although *Wasan Dambe* (Hausa traditional wrestling) as a game was meant for the entire society, it has since attracted the active participation of elites who sponsor the championships and select local bodyguards from the winners.

21. N. Owens-Ibie (Ombudsman), "Culturally Neutral News International," *The Guardian on Sunday,* 28 March 1993, A8.

22. F. Agbaje, "Why NBC Cannot Stop NTA Relaying CNN News," *The Guardian,* 5 June 1989, 30–31.

23. K. Ogundimu, "N.A. Plans Worldwide Reception," *Contact* (December 1996): 2.

24. Mohammed, J. B., "Democratization and the Challenge of Private Broadcasting in Nigeria," *Africa Media Review* 8, no. 1 (1994): 92; A. S. Tan, G. K. Tan, and A. S. Tan, "American TV in the Philippines: A Test of Cultural Impact," *Journalism Quarterly* (spring 1987): 66; R. Kroes, ed., *Within the U.S. Orbit: Small National Cultures Vis-a-Vis the United States* (Amsterdam, 1991), 131–71; Stuart Schoffman, "The Americanization of Israel," *The Jerusalem Report* (18 May 1995): 12–14; Tunde Ojo, "Television Violence," *The Guardian,* 2 August 1983, 9; C. P. Kottack, "Television's Impact on Values and Local Life in Brazil," *Journal of Communication* 41, no. 1 (winter 1991): 72; J. Tunstall, *The Media Are American* (London, 1977), 273–74; and L. C. Snyder, C. Roser, and S. Chaffee, "Foreign Media and the Desire to Emigrate from Belize," *Journal of Communication* 41, no. 1 (winter 1991): 117–32.

25. J. O. Onah, and A. V. Anyanwu, "Viewer Preference for TV Stations and Programmes: A Pilot Study," *Africa Media Review* 2, no. 3 (1988): 1–17.

26. The initial series of *Roots* received prominent coverage and positive reviews in local newspapers. It proved so popular that it is still occasionally rebroadcast.

27. The Group of Eminent Persons, *Facts on Reparations to Africa and Africans in the Diaspora* (Lagos, n.d.), 3–12.

28. E. N. E. Ume-Nwagbo, "Broadcasting in Nigeria: Its Post-Independence Status," *Journalism Quarterly* (autumn 1984): 589.

29. Nne Ukoha, "Are You Watching?" *TV Guide,* 1, no. 6 (July–September 1995): 9–10.

30. *The Bold and the Beautiful* is an American soap that revolves around the pursuit of wealth, love, and fame by members of its three principal families.

31. Tom Adaba, in "My Hands are Tied—Adaba Laments," *Sunday Times,* 24 November 1996, 4.

32. N. Owens-Ibie, "America, Our America," *The Guardian on Sunday* 26 August 1990, A6.

III   Rock, Rap, and All That Jazz

Elizabeth Vihlen

Jammin' on the Champs-Elysées

Jazz, France, and the 1950s

During the 1950s, the French attempted to forget the previous decade and to overcome the national self-doubt that had been caused by military defeat, foreign occupation, and collaboration with the Germans. Simultaneously, they experienced the process of Americanization on a scale greater than they had ever known. After the war, with the Marshall Plan and American economic hegemony, France faced an ever more powerful United States. At the same time, France sensed it might be losing its own global power and importance. During the 1950s, French national identity seemed unstable, and there arose a mounting uneasiness and tension over protecting and maintaining a distinct French national culture. Ironically, it was during these years that American jazz became extremely popular in France, albeit not as the culturally unidirectional, Americanizing force one might assume. A jazz public of professional critics, musicians, and fans had firmly established itself by the culturally insecure 1950s and continued to grow. This predominantly male public was located on the left of the political spectrum, and although it rarely advocated socialism or communism in an outward fashion, it consistently and openly criticized American capitalism, consumerism, and racism. As the most vocal political force in the French jazz scene, jazz critics assigned important meanings to the music they promoted. Jazz fans, who were primarily in their late teens and early twenties, certainly occupied different places along the political spectrum—if they were political at all—but the opinions of critics unquestionably influenced them. French culture continually assigned meanings to jazz that affected people as they danced or sat listening to jazz records. Therefore, despite the fact that jazz originated as an American music, many of its French fans actually used it as a vehicle through which they could express their criticism of the United States and selectively appropriate "America." The Cold War left its imprint upon

1950s French domestic politics, unleashing debates over communism and capitalism, the Soviet way versus the American way. As the French people struggled to stake out their own place in these debates, they regarded culture as existing on a continuous plane with politics.

French identity after World War II emphasized the nation's role in promoting and protecting French culture on an international scale. The Ministry of Culture was founded in 1959 under the leadership of André Malraux with this particular aim in mind. Both French people and their government asserted that France's place in global affairs largely hinged on the prominent place the nation gave to culture. French leaders, facing the United States' economic and military strength, worked to develop France's own economic and military resources, but maintained that it was the French people's high regard for culture that made their country great. This acute cultural self-consciousness accounts for jazz's peculiar role. Through media such as jazz, French cultural critics could both embrace and renounce different aspects of American culture and society. In appreciating jazz, French men and women on the cultural left criticized American racism, consumerism, and global authority, yet they also supported a unique American art form and its wide-reaching potential. Jazz made it possible for those French to assert their own identity in the face of an American threat.

On the whole, French people could deliberately decide whether to adopt or to reject different aspects of American popular culture, since a complete endorsement of "America" and all of its signifiers would have represented conforming to the American status quo. French jazz fans, who tended to be middle class, well educated, on the left of the political spectrum, and overwhelmingly male, accepted this form of popular culture coming from the United States while they and their countrymen concomitantly criticized American movies, automobiles, sports, and foods. Since well before the war, French commentators like Georges Duhamel had disparaged American fast food, football, Fords, and Hollywood.[1] Of course American movies were widely watched in France by the 1950s (two world wars and an aggressive American export policy had given the Americans global dominance in the film industry), and some genres, like film noir, were given critical acclaim.[2] But the French promoted jazz with a unique kind of enthusiasm. While Levi's jeans eventually became a youthful and countercultural symbol of America, especially in the sixties, in France, at least, they never carried the symbolic weight or the political meaning of jazz.

A wide French public took an interest in jazz, as evidenced by jazz-related articles that appeared regularly in French daily newspapers. American and European artists performed throughout France but most often appeared in Parisian performance spaces such as the Club Saint-Germain, the Salle Pleyel, or the Théâtre des Champs-Elysées. Specialized magazines for jazz fans also existed in the fifties, the most popular of which were *Jazz Hot* and *Jazz Magazine*. These periodicals displayed an almost uncontested Americanization through their focus on American musicians such as Charlie Parker, Miles Davis, Dizzy Gillespie, Louis Armstrong, Bud Powell, Art Tatum, Duke Ellington, and Sidney Bechet.[3] Critics also wrote about French musicians like Michel de Villers, Guy Lafitte, and Michel Legrand but much less frequently than they did about American artists.[4] In monthly columns, jazz magazines covered news and gossip coming from the United States. In advertisements, the influence of both American businesses and culture was apparent. The American record companies Capitol and Atlantic frequently used references to the United States in their French sales pitches, which often contained such expressions as "At the same time as in the U.S.A!" and "The most dynamic American trademarks."[5] References to the United States were also popular in French marketing strategies. A. Courtois promoted one of its trumpets as "adopted by the best American and French musicians."[6] In *Jazz Hot*, the American jazz magazine *Down Beat* was referred to as "our confrère." Critics and journalists discussed and reviewed American movies like *Pete Kelly's Blues* and *The Benny Goodman Story* that reflected the jazz tradition. For French jazz fans, understanding and promoting American jazz was an indispensable element of jazz appreciation in general.

One of the reasons that the French audience found jazz so acceptable was that it came from an African American tradition. Fans saw "black" jazz as the most authentic jazz and consistently portrayed it as superior to the music played by *les jazzmen blancs* (white jazzmen). African Americans had created jazz around the turn of the century, and both the experience of slavery and the endemic racial inequality that characterized American society were central to this creation. Jazz drew upon African musical traditions as well as newer African American, and even European, music. For Europeans, the jazz sound represented a new way of thinking about music: its unique use of syncopation as well as rhythmic and melodic tension made it radically different from other contemporary music.[7]

In the 1950s, French jazz fans were receptive to a number of the most important jazz schools of the period—especially bebop, but also the older New Orleans jazz and West Coast jazz.[8] Bebop, which had been founded in the forties by musicians like Charlie Parker, Thelonious Monk, and Dizzy Gillespie, was widely listened to in France (especially by the young), and musicians like Parker were lauded for their talent and originality. Its rhythmic jaggedness placed jazz firmly in the avant-garde,[9] although by no means was it uniformly accepted in France. Some critics, like Hugues Panassié, were hesitant to accept bebop and insisted on maintaining an understanding of jazz that looked backward almost exclusively to the New Orleans style.[10] The New Orleans revival was very real in France during the 1950s: the old and new music of Louis Armstrong was especially promoted in this context. West Coast jazz, which had its roots in the "cool" sounds of Miles Davis and others in the forties, was the domain of white Californian musicians like Stan Getz, Stan Kenton, Gerry Mulligan, and Zoot Sims, and it also received both critical and popular notice in France. Even though most French jazz critics tried to promote an understanding of jazz that included all of its divergent elements, ranging from the sounds of New Orleans and bebop to West Coast jazz, the music of black artists without a doubt received the most attention.

Most French jazz fans wanted to make a connection with what they saw as black, and, as a result, there occurred an almost complete bifurcation of jazz into black and white. André Hodeir, probably the most influential French jazz critic in the international jazz scene, asserted that undoubtedly, for him, the essence of jazz was contained in a certain "Negro spirit." In *Jazz: Its Evolution and Its Essence* (1956), Hodeir admitted that for a long time he had been convinced that the only way to appreciate jazz was to acquire a way of feeling like "the Negro's" and to completely abandon European culture. But, by the time he wrote this 1956 book, he had come to support the importance of finding an intermediary position between African American and European cultures and to interpret jazz as a complement to his culture.[11] For Hodeir, African American jazz could be used by Europeans without the risk of losing their European-ness. For most of the French critics, musicians, and fans, the blackness of jazz was precisely what made it unthreatening to French culture and therefore acceptable.[12] Yet French supporters in many ways essentialized blackness because their construction of jazz required its creators to be different from white Europeans and Americans. Black musicians were admired for having so-called inherent characteristics that whites did not have. French critics stressed the emotion, rhythm, and sexuality of black jazz musicians, musical assets that the French (and whites in general) supposedly lacked. Jazz's otherness in many ways made it appealing and culturally benign.

Non-French jazz critics readily highlighted this French tendency to praise black musicians at the expense of white ones. The British writer Leonard Feather, who thought that this behavior was discriminatory, criticized the French for their prejudice against white jazz musicians. He claimed that the former perceived black musicians as more authentic, and that a "true prejudice" existed against white musicians in France. Feather himself did not believe that there was a "white style" or a "black style"; for him, race was irrelevant.[13] Many French critics did not agree. For example, Charles Delaunay argued that "the majority of *true creators* are black, from the pioneers of New Orleans up until the modern champions of the school of 'bop'" (emphasis in original).[14] He agreed that European fans often discriminated against both American and European white jazz musicians, often preferring "black musicians of an inferior class."[15] For the French fan, blackness guaranteed a type of authenticity and vitality that seemed to be missing in white jazz musicians. Delaunay wrote, "[The] black musician, in a general way, is more spectacular, and . . . he shows to be more at ease, more relaxed (sometimes even inclined to a certain easy showing-off), than the white musician. For excellent that he is, the latter often seems uneasy and bored, and the spectator does not like this."[16] French critics often claimed that music was a fundamental part of the black personality, that blacks had "an inner taste for music."[17] People could love this music for its "intrinsic beauty," or as "a means to dance," but "the true fans are those sensitive to this music with the same intensity as the Blacks who gave it birth."[18] Jazz was therefore inherently connected to blackness. To be black meant to be emotional, virile, rhythmic, and active. A white jazz musician was thought to be more cerebral, refined, and polished, purportedly defying the essence of jazz.

Closely linked with this affirmation of blackness on the part of French jazz fans in the 1950s was the condemnation of American racism. Critics commonly discussed the subject of racism in the United States and brought up the issues of segregation, Jim Crow laws, and police brutality in their works. The jazz periodicals of the period consistently and directly addressed these issues as well. *Jazz Hot* recommended its subscribers read *Introduction à l'Amérique raciste* by Stetson Kennedy, *Segregation: essai sur le problème noir en Amérique* by Robert Penn Warren, and the autobiography of bluesman Big Bill Broonzy: all were meant to educate readers on the subject of American racism. The television work of Jean-Christophe Averty in the late fifties and the radio programs hosted by Hugues Panassié, Sim Copans, André Francis, and others also exposed audiences to the issue of racism.

The coverage that French jazz writers and journalists gave to American racism in this period was an extension of a persistent pattern: historically, French social observers had been critical of American racism. In 1835, Alexis de Tocqueville's *Democracy in America* had pointed to the problems of race in the United States; more than a century later, French social scientists who studied the United States almost without fail pointed to the problems of race and racism as central American weaknesses.[19] In the 1950s, the mainstream French media regularly reported on the dilemma of race in the United States—the jazz critics just tended to be more vocal and direct in their criticisms of the racialized American social situation; as jazz was historically connected to "blackness," this was a logical extension of their jazz appreciation.

In 1957, *Jazz Hot* took particular interest in the South after the Brown decision, especially in the fact that Louis Armstrong had "severely condemned the hesitant attitude of President Eisenhower" regarding public school integration, declaring that the President "lacked guts."[20] When the New York police took away Miles Davis' work permit at a nightclub after an altercation, *Jazz Hot* branded the entire episode an "inadmissible racial manifestation."[21] *Jazz Magazine* covered the story as well, and after recounting the "multiple wounds" caused by this "brutal attack," stated, "Here is what can happen to you if your face does not please a New York policeman—especially if you are black and the policeman is white."[22] In these articles, journalists attacked the United States, claiming that American society treated as social outcasts the black musicians who had created jazz and kept the music alive, and on whom the French as jazz fans depended. For jazz fans, social and political awareness went hand in hand with their appreciation of jazz; their condemnation of American racial inequality was the logical consequence.

Highly relevant in this context of antiracism was the issue of French racism. French jazz critic Lucien Malson, who eventually headed the Jazz Office of Radiodiffusion Française in the 1960s, was among the first to open up this subject for debate. Addressing the problem as early as 1951, years before many of his colleagues, Malson wanted to make French supporters of jazz aware that racism existed on both sides of the Atlantic. In the early fifties, the French had not widely discussed the issue of racism outside of the subject of antisemitism, largely because not many ethnic minorities had yet moved to metropolitan France. Of course men and (fewer) women from the French colonies lived in France and had been doing so for decades; but these individuals were largely members of the educated elite and remained for the most part in Paris. As the fifties progressed, this began to change. Throughout this decade, the French government, the army, and European colonials struggled to hold onto an Empire that was slipping away. As this happened, increasing numbers of immigrants from both North and West Africa began migrating to France, permanently changing the cultural and ethnic makeup of French society. In France, North Africans would feel the brunt of racial discrimination in the coming decades. By contrast, West Africans, Caribbean blacks, and African Americans would experience little if any racism at all in France.

Yet all of these groups were essentialized in some way in France based on the color of their skin.

This situation clearly fed into the way the French approached both the subject of jazz and the musicians who created the music. Lucien Malson thought that all stereotypes based on race needed to be abolished.[23] He stated that the French, too, conferred on blacks a "status of inferiority" by thinking of them primarily as athletes and musicians, or as being "close to nature," or even as being "large children."[24] Yet, he also believed that the level of prejudice that existed in France was less extreme than the type of racial discrimination blacks endured in the United States. In America, there was a "segregation of social space" and "a permanent hostility in regard to the black." Malson was aware of Southern lynchings and the high incidence of electric-chair executions of African Americans and recognized that "one does not judge in the USA men of color with the same rules that apply to whites."[25] In light of this reality, defending and supporting jazz for him became the same as defending and supporting blacks. He called for jazz to be recognized not as "a popular music, or foreign or sensual, but as that which it is, a black music. There comes a point when one is defending jazz that one is above all defending blacks and dissipating the false image that one traditionally makes of them."[26] Because jazz expressed "the black genius . . . with the most brilliancy" it would be able to uplift the image of blackness.[27] For men and women like Malson, endorsing jazz meant opposing discrimination and racism, especially the American variety that existed in the form of legal oppression. They expected jazz fans both to judge the actions of other people and to choose to act themselves in antiracist ways as these were the only means by which one could change the political climate.[28] Critics and fans argued that the French needed to be aware of racism—their own and others'—and work to defeat them both.

Jazz, in its most authentic form, was seen as anticommercial and therefore outside of, and defiant toward, American consumer culture. In the 1950s, Americans and Europeans alike viewed consumerism as one of the most defining elements of American society, and one that was easily exported to other parts of the globe. The idea that the production of manufactured goods in high numbers meant higher profits for businesses as well as lower costs for the consumers was central to this relatively new way of life. In the minds of many Frenchmen, however, American consumerism meant social conformity: everyone striving to own the same things and to define themselves through material goods. By the 1950s, the gospel of consumption had not only taken a very strong hold in America but it was also beginning to make an important impact on European countries. These countries had opened their borders to American investment, products, and ways of doing business, allowing standardized products, new spending patterns, higher wages, and increased social mobility to make inroads on their own economic and social systems.[29] In many ways, consumerism came to define postwar society; its materialistic outlook pushed people to orient their lives around buying—new cars, household appliances, clothes, and even jazz records.

Yet the French men and women who supported jazz challenged American consumer society in many ways. Jazz itself did not fit easily into the rubric created by a society obsessed with consumption. French fans and critics characterized improvisation, a central element of jazz's uniqueness, as "free" and "paraphrased" and therefore in conflict with the standardization and packaging of the market place.[30] Many French critics also lamented the fact that jazz musicians did not often benefit from American capitalism; these critics did so especially after the death of Charlie Parker in 1955. Parker died a poor man, provoking French jazz critics and fans to question the economic and social status of jazz musicians in the United States. Parker's case was not unique; it was just more widely publicized than others.[31] The high unemployment rate experienced by black musicians was a major problem. The strong postwar American economy did not necessarily reward these artists, and so even those who were famous often felt the pinch of financial need. It appeared that white musicians had it easier. As early as the 1920s, all-white groups such as the Rhythm Kings had commercialized their repertoire and become financially successful. The first widely known "jazz" musicians had been white imitators like Paul Whiteman and Red Nichols, who performed before the outbreak of World War II. Therefore, in the minds of French commentators, many white musicians became trapped in their commercialism and were unable to escape it.[32] In truth, although American radio and television programs gave them greater exposure, they were also subject to monetary concerns: *l'économie du jazz*.[33] Some were forced to change their music so that it could reach a wider audience and therefore be more profitable. The necessity of earning a living affected the music of all artists, black or white.

Still, the polarized imagery of wealthy white musicians and impoverished black musicians stuck. Through addressing the problem of black poverty and the overcommercialization of white musicians, these French supporters of jazz sought some sort of middle ground between the two extremes. Typical of the French in the 1950s, these critics pursued a "third way" for musicians between going hungry and selling out.[34]

A 1956 Jazz at the Philharmonic (J.A.T.P.) concert brought out many of these tensions. For twelve years, the American promoter Norman Granz had sponsored jazz concerts in the United States, Japan, Australia, and Europe. In the words of Swiss jazz critic Kurt Mohr, J.A.T.P. concerts were "in principle based on improvisation, on the 'jam-session,' . . . [and on the] a priori anti-commercial aspect of jazz."[35] But in reality and much to the chagrin of French fans, many aspects of the concert defied this anti-commercialism. For critics like Mohr, to announce "publicly a jam-session was already nonsense"—it worked against the very definition of such a gathering. Musicians were to play together for their own pleasure and not in order to sell tickets to the public. According to André Hodeir, there was no psychological tension for players who performed at a "pre-fabricated jam-session," and it was difficult for him to believe that an artist could "create during fixed hours."[36] Granz, the promoter, had even inserted planned dances into the performance, further defying what was understood to be an essential aspect of jazz—its undetermined nature. Another French critic and jazz musician, Michel de Villers, lamented the fact that even the physical surroundings of this concert were unrealistic: "a chair, a cigarette, a glass of beer are prohibited from the scene."[37] The results of this concert were "a frozen jazz" and a type of improvisation that had been "learned by heart." Because it was a predesigned spectacle, Granz even gave different musicians a specific role to play during the concert: "Flip Phillips, for example, is there for 'heat' whether he likes it or not."[38] As a result of its "inauthenticity," this J.A.T.P. concert did not succeed in France as it had in the United States. The European (and especially French) jazz fan was not as accustomed as an American fan to the expense or prefabricated conformity of such concerts. A fan in Europe wanted and expected originality, creativity, and improvisation from jazz. When a jazz concert resembled American consumer society in all of its monotony and rigidity, it was criticized along with the culture it reflected.

The French not only used jazz to address the problems of American consumerism but they also used this music as a means of addressing American global politics. In the second half of the 1950s, *Jazz Hot* was interested in the American government's use of jazz abroad as Cold War propaganda. As Penny M. Von Eschen's essay in this volume notes, between 1955 and 1958, many jazz musicians, including Dizzy Gillespie, Lionel Hampton, Benny Goodman, and Tony Scott, made European, African, and Asian tours with American State Department sponsorship. The Voice of America program *Music USA* with host Willis Conover played one hour of jazz daily to listeners across the globe, and French jazz fans themselves could tune into this show every night at nine o'clock. In 1956, *Jazz Hot* referred to jazz bands as the United States' "secret army," and in the same year, the New York *Times* wrote that Europeans could not understand why more money was not being spent to give financial support to jazz artists abroad.[39] Yet French fans found it difficult to criticize too strongly the propagandistic use of jazz bands on the part of the United States government: government funding of jazz abroad made the music cheaper and more accessible in France. So, although French jazz listeners could be critical of the American government using jazz for its own foreign policy needs, they were also pleased with the exposure it brought to the music. Despite the United States' self-serving co-optation of jazz, this music was being "officially" recognized for the first time.

Because of the importance and talent of American musicians, French jazz fans could not consistently call their country the capital of jazz. However, they freely referred to France as the European capital of jazz. In the 1950s, three International Salons of Jazz were held in Paris. The first was held in 1950; for a week different American and European musicians performed at the Salle Pleyel (the French equivalent of New York's Carnegie Hall).[40] Each time the Salon convened, it grew in number and importance. By the third Salon in 1954, journalists claimed that more than 50,000 visitors attended.[41] Yet more important than attendance was the way the French as hosts characterized themselves. In 1952, during the second Salon, Paris was called the "capital of jazz." One writer predicted that during this week Paris would be "the pole of attraction towards which people will converge from the four corners of Europe, musicians and fans of all nationalities."[42] Dozens of members of the international press attended in 1952 and Radiodiffusion Française transmitted the music from the event to seventeen foreign countries for those listeners who could not make it in person.[43] After the 1954 Salon, another critic claimed that Paris would become "the international city of jazz,"[44] that Paris and the Salle Pleyel had become for a week a "true global capital of jazz."[45] The French promoters of the Salon of Jazz wanted to make this event an integral part of French popular culture, and they placed it in the same tradition as the Salon of Automobiles or the cyclists' Tour de France.[46] Most importantly, they saw it as a French creation that could show the influence and importance of France in the world of jazz. In 1957, *Jazz Hot* was still claiming that "France is actually the most important center of jazz in Europe."[47]

Thus, despite its difference from French music of the classical or folkloric tradition, jazz was an important part of France's postwar cultural identity. This music grew out of an African American culture that greatly differed from the French one; yet the creativity, novelty, and emotion that characterized this music had important ramifications for French critics and fans, who claimed to understand jazz better than most Americans. Jazz taught the French about new musical innovations, and the blossoming interest in it came less than a decade after Jean-Paul Sartre's call for the circulation of "a little bit of fresh blood in this old body [of

Europe]."[48] In a period of self-doubt following the devastating experiences of World War II, the French sought new ways to enrich their culture without endangering French national uniqueness. As with Coca-Cola, Hollywood, and the beginnings of American multinational domination, French people had to find ways of mediating the "American invasion." Culture was an important site of arbitration and they were able to use it to negotiate "America" as well as to promote themselves in an international context. The French proponents of jazz co-opted this music to enrich what was seen as a dying and anachronistic European culture and to criticize American dominance. The construction of jazz required it to be emotional, sexual, and rhythmic, in direct contrast with a pensive and dull European classical and folkloric music. Through jazz, French fans could criticize American social, economic, and political practices: racism, rampant consumerism and commercialism, and the imposition of American culture on other nations. Because the French thought of jazz, first and foremost, as black, it did not represent these negative American characteristics; yet this perception, coupled with the insistence on the superiority of African American musicians, also revealed a tendency among French critics and fans to essentialize blackness—for them blacks possessed musical talents that whites did not or could not possess. Nonetheless, the French jazz scene did address the problems of economic, social, and racial inequality, through the music connected to a leftist political consciousness. Listening to jazz, the French could simultaneously criticize the United States, evaluate France's own cultural global strengths and weaknesses, and identify with an oppressed American minority.

All this while jammin' on the Champs-Elysées.

Notes

1. See Georges Duhamel, *America the Menace: Scenes form the Life of the Future*, trans. Charles Miner Thompson (Boston: Houghton Mifflin, 1931).

2. Through the Blum-Byrnes agreement of 1946, the American government insisted that French markets remain open to American movies as a condition of economic aid. The French movie industry's response brought an end to the agreement, but Blum-Byrnes still had lasting ramifications. See Patricia Hubert-Lacombe, "La Guerre froide et le cinéma français, 1946–53" (thèse de 3e cycle, Institut d'études politiques, Paris, 1981); Michel Margairaz, "Autour des accords Blum-Byrnes," *Histoire, économie, société* 3 (1982): 439–70; and Richard Kuisel, *Seducing the French: The Dilemma of Americanization* (Berkeley, Calif.: University of California Press, 1993).

3. In 1935, Hugues Panassié and Charles Delaunay founded *Jazz Hot,* which they co-edited until 1941. In 1947, Panassié severed his ties with *Jazz Hot* and later created his own journals, first *La Gazette du Jazz* and then *Le Bulletin du*

Hot Club de France, both of which had a small readership. Daniel Filipacchi and Frank Ténot created *Jazz Magazine* in 1954, and it and *Jazz Hot* continue to be published today. In 1959, critics associated with *Jazz Hot* and *Jazz Magazine* founded a new periodical based on the format of a literary journal, *Les Cahiers du jazz,* which is still in existence as well. In 1955, *Jazz Hot* printed 15,000 copies of each issue; *Jazz Magazine* 19,000 copies; and *Le Bulletin du Hot Club de France* 4,000. Jacques Lahitte, "Jazz-News: situation de la presse spécialisée," *Arts* 502 (9–15 February 1955): 4.

4. Frequently, French jazz musicians also worked as critics as it was difficult for them to support themselves solely as musicians.

5. *Jazz Hot* 98 (April 1955): 30–31; and *Jazz Hot* 148 (November 1959): 3.

6. *Jazz Hot* 97 (March 1955): 7.

7. Leroi Jones, *Blues People* (New York: William Morrow and Company, 1963); Lucien Malson, "L'universalité du jazz," *Jazz Hot* 116 (December 1956): 10; André Hodeir, *Jazz: Its Evolution and Its Essence,* trans. David Noakes (New York: Grove Press, 1956); Reinhold Wagnleitner, *Coca-Colonization and the Cold War: the Cultural Mission of the United States in Austria after the Second World War,* trans. Diana M. Wolf (Chapel Hill: University of North Carolina Press, 1994).

8. I am only mentioning these three types of jazz, but there were obviously other delineations such as hard bop, soul or funky jazz, Afro-Cuban jazz, Latin jazz, and modal jazz. I have chosen to focus only on bebop, the New Orleans style, and West Coast jazz here because they were most frequently discussed by French critics at the time.

9. Barry Kernfeld, *What to Listen for in Jazz* (New Haven, Conn.: Yale University Press, 1995): 191–95.

10. See *The Real Jazz,* trans. Anne Sorelle Williams (New York: Smith and Durrell, 1943), and his later book *La Bataille du jazz* (Paris: Éditions Albin Michel, 1965). Panassié played an important role in the promotion of jazz in France from the 1930s until 1947 when he ostracized himself from the larger French jazz community by refusing to recognize bebop as jazz. He was the founder of the Hot Club de France in the 1930s and continued to publish a journal by that name in the 1950s.

11. Hodeir, 10. Hodeir also wrote other important books on jazz such as *Toward Jazz* (New York: Grove Press, 1962) as well as contributed to periodicals like *Jazz Hot, Arts, The Jazz Review, Down Beat,* and *Jazz, A Quarterly of American Music.*

12. The positive reception of African American culture extended beyond music to embrace literature and art. A number of books have recently been published that study the lives and experiences of African Americans in France. See James Campbell, *Exiled in Paris: Richard Wright, James Baldwin, Samuel Beckett, and Others on the Left Bank* (New York: Scribner, 1995); Michel Fabre, *From Harlem to Paris: Black American Writers in France, 1940–1980* (Urbana: University of Illinois Press, 1991); and Tyler Stovall, *Paris Noir: African Americans in the City of Light* (Boston: Houghton Mifflin, 1996). The focus of these books is on African Americans themselves and, as a result, they do not examine in detail the French reception of these men and women's cultural productions. What these works do illustrate is the important presence African Americans had in France, especially after the Second World War.

13. Leonard Feather, "Préjugés," *Jazz Hot* 45 (June 1950): 11.

14. Charles Delaunay, "Préjugés ou malentendus," *Jazz Hot* 45 (June 1950): 12.

15. Ibid.

16. Ibid.

17. Frank Ténot, "Les chants religieux du peuple noir des Etats-Unis," *Jazz Hot* 88 (May 1954): 14.

18. Delaunay, 9. In general, the French jazz community accepted this view of "blackness" throughout the 1950s. Yet, during the following decade, critics like Hodeir and Delaunay moved away from such a strongly racialized framework and actually began having more positive assessments of white jazz musicians (both American and French). Yet Panassié and his followers remained skeptical about the talents of white jazz musicians, maintaining that African Americans were the only *true* jazz musicians. For more on Panassié's ideas about "true jazz," see especially his *Histoire du vrai jazz* (Paris: Editions Robert Laffont, 1959).

19. See for instance, Daniel Guérin, *Où va le peuple américaine?* (Paris: René Julliard, 1951), and André Siegfried, *America at Mid-Century*, trans. Margaret Ledésert (New York: Harcourt, Brace, 1955).

20. "Jazz Actualités: Eisenhower vu par Armstrong," *Jazz Hot* 125 (October 1957): 28.

21. "Jazz à la carte," *Jazz Hot* 147 (October 1959): 30.

22. L. F., "Sauvage agression contre Miles Davis," *Jazz Magazine* 52 (October 1959): 13.

23. Malson used cultural uniqueness to explain African American musical talent. See especially his article "Jazz noir; jazz blanc," *Jazz Hot* 102 (September 1955): 8. The critic Jacques Hess also claimed that culture (a musician's environment) was an important determinant of talent. He and Frank Ténot disagreed on this issue as Ténot claimed that the African Americans possessed more musical talent than whites. Oddly enough, Malson criticized Hess and sided with Ténot in this debate because Hess did not endorse the idea that African Americans were the best players. See "Le jazz est-il toujours un art nègre?" *Arts* 475 (4–10 August 1954): 5.

24. Lucien Malson, "Les Noirs," *Jazz Hot* 52 (February 1951): 7.

25. Lucien Malson, "Les Noirs," *Jazz Hot* 55 (May 1951): 11.

26. Malson, "Les Noirs" (February 1951): 7.

27. Lucien Malson, "Les Noirs," *Jazz Hot* 56 (June 1951): 11.

28. Especially see Frank Ténot, "L'Oncle Tom et le jazz," *Jazz Magazine* 14 (February 1956): 6.

29. Richard Kuisel, *Seducing the French: The Dilemma of Americanization* (Berkeley: University of California Press, 1993): 3.

30. L'exique du jazz," *Jazz Hot* 110 (May 1956): 34.

31. Lee Saner, "Le concert de Carnegie Hall à la mémoire de Charlie Parker," *Jazz Hot* 99 (May 1955): 29; also "Charlie Parker est mort," *Le Monde,* 16 March 1955: 6.

32. "Grandes orchestres: 1920–1930," *Jazz Hot* 119 (March 1957): 17.

33. Alfred Appel, Jr., "L'école de New York," *Jazz Hot* 128 (January 1958): 14.

34. During the Cold War, some French leaders, especially Charles de Gaulle, tried to find a "third way" between American and Soviet power and influence. See Jean Lacouture, *DeGaulle: The Ruler 1945–1970*, trans. Alan Sheridan (New York: W .W. Norton, 1993).

35. Kurt Mohr, "Le J.A.T.P.," *Jazz Hot* 107 (February 1956): 7.

36. André Hodeir, "Le J.A.T.P.," *Jazz Hot* 107 (February 1956): 7, 9.

37. Michel de Villers, "Le J.A.T.P.," *Jazz Hot* 107 (February 1956): 7.

38. Villers, "Le J.A.T.P.," 9.

39. Felix Helair, Jr., "The United States has a Secret Sonic Weapon—Jazz," New York *Times,* 6 August 1955; "Jazz à la carte: jazz et propagande," *Jazz Hot* 128 (January 1958): 40. See also, "Dizzy en Asie," *Jazz Hot* 111 (June 1956): 14. Also of interest on this subject is "Le jazz banni en U.R.S.S.: 'c'est une musique d'asservissement,' dit-on à Moscou," *Le Monde,* 3 May 1952, 6.

40. "Le premier Salon du Jazz," *Le Monde,* 2 December 1950, 12. On this Salon also see "Le jazz reçoit M. le Ministre et tout-Paris en son premier Salon," *Combat,* 2 December 1950, 2, "Avec son premier Salon le jazz fête son jubilé," *Paris-Presse,* 2 December 1950, 4; and "Le premier Salon du Jazz a pris un bon départ," *Paris-Presse,* 3–4 December 1950, 7.

41. "Plus de 50.000 visiteurs sont attendus au IIIe Salon International du Jazz," *Jazz Hot* 89 (June 1954): 7. Also on the third Salon see "Le IIIe Salon du Jazz ouvre ses portes à la salle Pleyel," *Le Monde,* 1 June 1954, 6, "Gerry Mulligan vedette de la 'semaine du jazz,'" *Le Monde,* 4 June 1954, 7; "Les prix de l'Académie du Jazz," *Le Monde,* 6–7 June 1954, 6; "Du 1er au 7 juin a eu lieu Salle Pleyel la semaine du jazz," *Arts* 467 (9–15 June 1954): 3; and Jacques André, "Quand le bon public acclame les nouveaux prêtres du jazz," *Combat,* 3 June 1954, 10.

42. "Paris, capitale du jazz," *Jazz Hot* 65 (April 1952): 7.

43. "Faisons le point," *Jazz Hot* 66 (May 1952): 7.

44. "Plus de 50.000," 7.

45. "L'énorme succès du IIIe Salon International du Jazz," *Jazz Hot* 90 (July–August 1954): 7.

46. "Paris, capitale du jazz," 7.

47. Marcel Romano, "Bilan et perspectives du Jazz en France," *Jazz Hot* 117 (January 1957): 30.

48. Jean-Paul Sartre, "Présence noire," *Présence Africaine* 1 (1947): 29. Important jazz critics like Charles Delaunay, Hugues Panassié, and André Hodeir contributed to *Présence Africaine,* a journal founded in 1947 by a group of black and white French-speaking intellectuals who sought to investigate and to help construct a "modern" African conscience. French intellectuals (the ethnologists Michel Leirus and Paul Rivet, as well as André Gide, Albert Camus, Jean-Paul Sartre, Emmanuel Mounier, P. Maydieu, and Théodore Monod) served on the founding Committee of Patrons for *Présence Africaine,* reinforcing their involvement in promoting African and African American culture, and Sartre's desire to circulate "a little bit of fresh blood in this old body [of Europe]." These intellectuals were interested in contributing to the postwar extension of the literary movement *negritude* as well as supporting other forms of "black" culture. For a detailed discussion of black literature by Sartre, see his introduction to Léopold Senghor's 1948 *Anthologie de la nouvelle poésie nègre et malgache* (Paris: Presses universitaires de France, 1948), entitled "Orphée noir," where he writes that "black poetry in the French language is, in our time, the only great revolutionary poetry." In 1947, Sartre also wrote "[Jazz musicians] are speaking to the best part of you, the toughest, the freest, to the part which wants neither melody nor refrain, but the deafening climax of the moment" ("Jazz in America," reprinted in Robert Gottlieb, ed., *Reading Jazz* [New York: Pantheon Books, 1996]: 711). After World War II, French intellectuals like Sartre looked beyond their own cultural heritage to such things as African literature and African American jazz to find the means to reinvigorate what some believed to be an increasingly obsolete French contemporary culture.

Penny M. Von Eschen

"Satchmo Blows Up the World"

Jazz, Race, and Empire during the Cold War

In 1956, Louis Armstrong performed before a crowd of more than 100,000 in Accra, Ghana. Commenting on the trumpeter's virtuosity in the face of the threat of nuclear disaster, Africa-wide *Drum* magazine quipped, "Satchmo Blows Up the World."[1] Indeed, the Cold War pun could not have been more appropriate. Sponsoring everything from international "Goodwill Ambassador" tours by jazz musicians such as Armstrong, Dizzy Gillespie, and Duke Ellington, to dance companies such as those of Martha Graham and Alvin Ailey, the U.S. government fought the Cold War with an astonishing number of forays into the performing arts. Situated at the intersection of three highly fraught issues in post–World War II America—foreign policy, government funding of the arts, and race and civil rights—the State Department-sponsored tours unleashed a complex negotiation over the meaning of the American nation. As the State Department exported its own vision of American culture, this vision was contested at home and overseas, not only by audiences, but also by the musicians and even, on occasion, by State Department personnel. This essay explores the implications of this contestation over the meaning of America by drawing on examples from tours by the jazz musicians Benny Goodman, Dave Brubeck, Louis Armstrong, Duke Ellington, and Randy Weston, and the dancer and choreographer Martha Graham.

In the past few years there has been an outpouring of interest—popular as well as scholarly—in the role of culture in the Cold War. When Willis Conover—the host of the Voice of America's jazz program—died in 1996, his New York *Times* obituary not only proclaimed Conover the most widely known and loved American worldwide; it further suggested Conover's unparalleled importance in bringing about the collapse of communism, a claim that Conover himself came to proudly embrace.[2] It has become commonplace in post–Cold War political discourse to claim

163

that the Cold War was ultimately won by Levi blue jeans and jazz. To be sure, the world witnessed an arms buildup as well as unfortunate "brush-wars" here and there, but the appeal of American consumer culture could only be held at bay for so long, and, in the end, free market capitalism triumphed over state socialism. In his nuanced discussion of the U.S./Soviet cultural exchange in his book *Parting the Curtain*, the historian Walter Hixson rejects what he terms "the crude and parochial triumphalist perspective on the end of the Cold War. Hixson argues that "the impact of Western culture on their [Soviet eastern bloc] consciousness was substantial, and perhaps even decisive."[3] For Hixson, it was the modern version of old-fashioned idealist diplomacy—with its belief in the inevitability of "the nation serving as a model of material success and democratic values"—not militarism, that "ultimately proved more effective in combating the Soviet Empire."[4]

I want to raise two objections to this view. One, this view of cultural exchange assumes the analytic and political separability, indeed the independence, of the categories "culture" and "militarism." Following the work of numerous scholars, including that of Tim Borstelmann, Irene Gendzier, and Bruce Cumings, I want to suggest that this separation of the cultural and the military ignores the extent to which the awesome material success of the United States in the post–1945 era was dependent on its domination of global resources, which, in the face of persistent attempts on the part of formerly colonized peoples to reclaim their resources, was in turn necessarily dependent on militarism.[5] Indeed, cultural exchange was the commodity that closely pursued the quintessential Cold War commodities, oil and uranium, along with many others critical to America's seductive abundance. Tracing the steps of the artists offers a window into the sheer enormity and originality—as well as the violence—of the U.S. global project of domination by way of modernization and development that increasingly replaced direct colonialism with Western domination in the post–1945 period.[6]

Secondly, by suggesting that the United States prevailed through the example of material success and democratic values, historians mute fundamental conflicts within the United States, suggesting a shared, core adherence to material abundance that ultimately transcended differences. However, as Reinhold Wagnleitner has brilliantly argued, it was often oppositional elements in American culture, and particularly those in African American culture, that proved appealing to disparate groups in various parts of the globe.[7] Indeed, the story of the cultural presentation programs is a story of pronounced differences in the aims of artists and government officials and an often sharp contestation over American culture.

Returning to the cultural presentation programs, this important cultural initiative must be situated in interlocking Cold War and Civil Rights contexts. The tours established during the Eisenhower administration were first financed by the President's Emergency Fund and run in conjunction with the National Theater Academy. By the early 1960s, cultural presentation programs were directly under the auspices of the U.S. Department of State.[8] Artists were chosen by committees of critics and patrons of the arts in music, dance, and theater.

The scope of these programs involved many realms of the performing arts. Yet the jazz tours received the most publicity and sparked the most controversy at home and abroad. Indeed, jazz was widely celebrated in establishment and middle-brow circles alike as a pivotal cultural weapon of the Cold War—in newspapers and magazines from the New York *Times* and *Newsweek*, to the *Reader's Digest* and *Variety*. In 1955, writing in the New York *Times*, Felix Belair proclaimed that "America's secret weapon is a blue note in a minor key," and named Louis (Satchmo) Armstrong as "its most effective ambassador."[9] For such writers, the jazz ambassador symbolized the legitimacy of American claims as leader of the "free world." While, as I argue below, jazz's status rested on its enormous appeal among audiences from Africa to the Soviet Union and Eastern Bloc nations, I would also suggest that an establishment and mainstream equation of jazz with the central Cold War trope of freedom depended, in part, on a highly racialized and deeply problematic assumption that what was fundamental to jazz was "spontaneity," not discipline, rhythm, or the nuanced conversations entailed in improvisation.[10] Moreover, the central place of *Playboy Magazine*, along with *Down Beat*, in promoting jazz for middle-brow white audiences in the 1950s and 1960s further suggests the association of the purported "freedom" of jazz with sexual license, underlining the layered meanings of freedom in masculinist Cold War culture. In the racialized crisis of masculinity of the 1950s, jazz became a way to fight the Cold War on a terrain of pleasure and leisure.

The first government-sponsored jazz tour was in 1956 when Dizzy Gillespie's integrated band, which also featured the trombonist Melba Liston at a time when female jazz instrumentalist were rare, toured the Middle East.[11] Despite their enthusiastic reception, early jazz tours were targeted by congressional critics and beset by political controversy and threatened cutbacks in funding. Representative John Rooney, a New York Democrat, led the attack, supported by southern segregationists such as Senator Allen Ellender of Louisiana. For Rooney and Ellender, to have bebop trumpeter Dizzy Gillespie representing the nation portended the end of the world as they knew it.[12] Although jazz certainly gained an enhanced stature and legitimacy, these criticisms affected the content of the programs, leading to the inclusion by the early 1960s of amateur musicians, including high school and college marching bands.[13]

While under attack by conservatives at home, jazz was a pet project of the State Department. Unlike classical music, theater, or ballet, U.S. officials could claim jazz as a uniquely American art form.[14] Officials and supporters of the arts alike hoped to offset what they perceived as European and Soviet superiority in classical music and ballet. In the cultural presentation programs, patrons and critics of dance and music who served on the selection committees saw themselves as competing with Soviet funding of the arts and responded directly to Soviet promotion of folk art and classical ballet productions. Seeking a distinctly American alternative to Soviet and European dominance in the arts, the program committees became venues for debating what was considered "modern" and "uniquely American" in dance, art, and music. It is noteworthy that cultural presentation programs in western Europe did not include jazz because jazz was considered already established, popular, and commercially viable.[15] However, in a very self-conscious competition with the Soviets, the U.S. government valued modern dance highly in western Europe because it presented a stark and appealing contrast to the excellence of the Bolshoi Ballet.

The work of the dancer and choreographer Martha Graham was especially esteemed in the early years; yet Graham ran into the same conservative opposition that had plagued the Gillespie tours. After Representative Edna F. Kelly of Brooklyn, NY saw Graham's State Department–sponsored production of *Phaedras* in Germany, Kelly and Peter Frelinghuysen of New Jersey accused Graham of portraying un-American values in her adaptations of Greek drama and mythology containing depictions of overt sexuality and incest. Graham's *Phaedras*, they charged, was not a proper cultural export. Frelinghuysen explained in a letter to his constituents that "the dance was shocking, portraying a mother who lusts after her stepson." According to Frelinghuysen, "they use couches, and there are a lot of men running around in loincloth. It is very confusing but the meaning is clear enough."[16] Worse yet, taxpayers' dollars were sending this production overseas as an example of American culture. Despite such opposition, Graham's company prospered as a result of the tours; the State Department cultural presentation programs proved to be a tremendous boon to the arts, especially for modern dance and jazz.[17]

As for jazz, State Department officials had picked up on the fact that there was avid interest in jazz in the Soviet Union and eastern Europe, providing officials with what they viewed as a unique opportunity to fight the cultural Cold War.[18] The fortunes of jazz in the Soviet Union had waxed and waned along with the relative openness or repressiveness of the Soviet government. Enjoying wide acceptance in the 1920s, jazz was driven underground during the purges of the 1930s, then revived again in the more tolerant years of World War II, only to be officially proscribed with the renewed clamp-downs of the Cold War, with many jazz musicians arrested and sent to labor camps during the repression of the late Stalin years.[19]

Through informal polls taken at exhibitions, State Department and USIS officials learned that Soviet citizens tended to resent what they regarded as heavyhanded didactic propaganda of Radio Free Europe. In contrast, they welcomed the cultural programming of Voice of America, and Willis Conover's jazz programs ranked as the most popular, to the consternation of Soviet officials who jammed the broadcasts. As the historian Walter Hixson has demonstrated in his study of U.S. cultural propaganda in the immediate postwar period, despite the expressions of sympathy for black Americans, Soviets resisted jazz, considering it "in the vanguard of a Yankee cultural assault."[20]

With the Krushchev thaw, the United States and the Soviet Union began an official program of cultural exchange in 1956. The Soviets now accepted "symphonic" jazz, while still rejecting modern or "decadent" jazz. Thus, in the aftermath of the Berlin crisis, Benny Goodman became the first jazz musician officially to tour the Soviet Union for the State Department in 1962, making thirty appearances in six Soviet cities from May 28 to July 8. With the Soviets waging a campaign against "decadent western abstract art," from their standpoint, Goodman was acceptable, in part because he was an accomplished classical musician in addition to being a jazz artist. Yet complaints issued from underground Soviet jazz fans, nourished by the Voice of America, who considered Goodman hopelessly out of date, declaring a preference for Miles Davis and modern jazz.[21] The tumult created by Goodman's tour led to a renewed party edict against jazz within the Soviet Union; this also could have been influenced by the Cuban missile crisis, which occurred just after his tour. At any rate, the Soviets did not accept another tour until 1966 and 1971, when the Earl Hines and Duke Ellington orchestras toured.

Just as important to the State Department as the Eastern Bloc interest in jazz was the prominence of African American artists in jazz. In high profile tours by Gillespie, Armstrong, Ellington, and many others, U.S. officials pursued a self-conscious campaign against worldwide criticism of U.S. racism, striving to build cordial relations with new African and Asian states. The glaring contradiction in this strategy was that the U.S. promoted black artists as "goodwill ambassadors"—symbols of the triumph of American democracy—when America was still a Jim Crow nation.[22]

This contradiction, as well as the foreign policy of the tours, was explored in a 1962 collaboration between Dave and Iola Brubeck and Louis

Armstrong called *The Real Ambassadors*. A jazz musical revue performed to critical acclaim at the Monterey Jazz Festival, *The Real Ambassadors* satirized State Department objectives, personnel, and protocol and voiced an unequivocal indictment of Jim Crow America.[23] Brubeck was concerned that Armstrong's contribution to the civil rights cause was largely overlooked even though official attempts to showcase Armstrong as a symbol of racial progress had imploded when Armstrong denounced President Eisenhower during the desegregation crisis at Central High School in Little Rock in 1957. Armstrong had been the State Department's first choice for a Soviet tour; however, after Little Rock he angrily declared that a black man has no country and refused to tour the Soviet Union for the government, adding, "I would rather play in Moscow than Arkansas because [Governor] Faubus might hear a couple of notes and he don't deserve that."[24] Still, Armstrong was widely criticized as an Uncle Tom, and, for many, compared unfavorably with a younger, more militant group of jazz musicians. Thus the musical opens with a reminder of Armstrong's militancy, as the hero—Armstrong—declares: "look here, what we need is a good will tour of Mississippi" and "Forget Moscow, when do we play in New Orleans?"[25]

Set in the mythical African country Talgalla, "the newest of new African nations," *The Real Ambassadors* satirizes the political motives for the African tours. "It had been unknown and unrecognized as a nation until the two great superpowers simultaneously discovered its existence. Suddenly, Talgalla was a nation to be reckoned with." The Russians had built roads. "U.S. equipment had cleared the airfield."[26]

The sensitive foreign policy context of the tours, as well as the troubling background of racial unrest in the United States is captured in "Cultural Exchange," from *The Real Ambassadors*.

> Yeah! I remember when Diz was in Greece back in '56.
> He did such a good job we started sending jazz all over the world
>
> The State Department has discovered jazz.
> It reaches folks like nothing ever has.
> Like when they feel that jazzy rhythm,
> they know we're really with 'em.
> That's what we call cultural exchange.
>
> No commodity is quite so strange
> as this thing called cultural exchange.
> Say that our prestige needs a tonic,
> export the Philharmonic,
> That's what we call cultural exchange!
> . . . when our neighbors call us vermin
> we send out Woody Herman.[27]

Lyricist Iola Brubeck's brilliant observation that "no commodity is quite so strange as this thing called cultural exchange" can only be fully appreciated in the context of the Brubeck and Armstrong tours. Indeed, as we shall see in those tours, cultural exchange was the commodity that closely pursued the quintessential Cold War commodities oil and uranium. An appreciation of the musicians' critique of the State Department's notion of cultural exchange must begin with the Brubeck and Armstrong tours. Both artists had participated in the tours; both artists had deliberately been sent into the front lines of major foreign policy crises. The Brubecks had toured eastern Europe and the Middle East in 1958.[28] Armstrong had only recently returned from a 27-city tour of the African continent during the Congo crisis. Brubeck's quartet toured Poland, Afghanistan, Turkey, India, and Pakistan in 1958. The trip had already lasted 120 days when Secretary of State John Foster Dulles unilaterally canceled Brubeck's engagements in the United States and extended the tour to Iran, and then Iraq and straight into the Middle East crisis of July 1958. Dulles ordered the quartet, Brubeck remembers, "to keep playing way longer than we had planned. They just kept us moving."

In Iran, the quartet played before elites in productions co-sponsored by the Iranian Oil Refinery Co. and United States Information Service.[29] Although the State Department had not briefed them on national and regional politics, to Brubeck and his band, things seemed dangerously amiss when they arrived in Baghdad, Iraq. Ill with dysentery and ordered not to travel, Brubeck nonetheless found a flight out of Baghdad through Istanbul. On July 14, the day after their departure, General Abdel Karim Kassim led a nationalist revolt that overthrew the Iraqi government and established a regime friendly to the United Arab Republic (UAR), disrupting the delicately constructed Baghdad Pact and challenging U.S. oil interests. As Kassim's troops rolled into Baghdad, clearing out the hotel Brubeck had just left, Lebanese President Camille Chamoun responded to the coup with an urgent request for military assistance from the United States.[30]

Ironically, alto saxophonist Paul Desmond had left the group as they went to Iraq and had headed to Beirut for what he thought would be a peaceful vacation on the beach. Desmond woke up, however, to 14,000 American marines wading onto shore amidst the sun bathers, to quiet the threat of civil war in Lebanon and warn the new Iraqi regime that any threat to Western oil resources in the area would not be tolerated.[31]

Armstrong's 1960–1961 tour of Africa—the first of numerous tours of the continent by jazz artists over the next decade—included stops in the Congo—home to the world's largest uranium reserves (along with huge supplies of cobalt, essential to jet engines) and two-thirds of the world's industrial diamonds. Armstrong liked to comment that he stopped a war when a truce was called for a day so both sides could hear him perform. However, Armstrong's rosy view of the Congo crisis was belied by the CIA-assisted assassination of Patrice Lumumba only two months after Armstrong's visit.[32]

As the satire of *The Real Ambassadors* implied, the complex projects and motivations of musicians often came into conflict with State Department objectives. Musicians viewed the performing arts as a sphere of struggle over working conditions and one's livelihood. For the musicians, overseas tours were first and foremost opportunities to work. And in an ongoing battle over the politics of representation of black people, black musicians and their allies perceived the State Department jazz tours as a global platform from which to promote the dignity of black people and their culture in the United States and abroad in the era of Jim Crow.

Musicians expressed conflicting feelings of patriotism at being able to serve their country alongside resentment at both their own treatment and the fact that they were being used for what they viewed as questionable political agendas. Gillespie later recalled that "I sort've liked the idea of representing America, but I wasn't going to apologize for the racist policies of America." He managed to avoid his official State Department briefing, noting that "I've got three hundred years of briefing. I know what they've done to us and I'm not going to make any excuses."[33] Musicians often felt that their own desires to play music and meet local musicians, as well as their own agenda of bringing jazz to new audiences, conflicted with the State Department's focus on indigenous elites as target audiences in fraught political circumstances. Deeply aware of the politics of the tours, Gillespie didn't hesitate to defy State Department and local convention, promoting his own vision of America, which was considerably more egalitarian than the State Department's. He later recalled that the tour skipped India because that country was nonaligned. His band played instead in Karachi, Pakistan, where the United States was supplying arms, and where Gillespie refused to play until the gates were opened to the "ragamuffin" children, because "they priced the tickets so high the people we were trying to gain friendship with couldn't make it."[34]

Ironically, the State Department cultural programs and tours helped foster the development of black international sensibilities. African American artists and musicians such as Gillespie used their status as good-will ambassadors to establish relationships with musicians in Africa and its diaspora. Music, and in that era particularly jazz, became a critical arena in which a militant internationalism thrived. In an article titled, "We Claim Jazz: Listen to Africa," a black South African writing in a Ghanaian newspaper affirmed the ties of Africans and African Americans through jazz. "The voice of Africa comes to us from thousands of miles away," even over "the splutter and meretricious ornament of Voice of America."[35]

As in the Gillespie tour, the State Department's views of cultural exchange were overtly challenged by members of the Duke Ellington Orchestra in their 1963 tour, which included Syria, Lebanon, Afghanistan, Turkey, India, Pakistan, Ceylon, Iran, and Iraq.[36] The tour forced one member of the State Department staff to rethink his and the State Department's assumptions. Thomas W. Simons, the African American escort officer for the 1963 Ellington tour, positioned himself as an advocate and interpreter for the musicians. Adopting the musicians' language, he discussed scheduling problems for example, by explaining that this orchestra never "hit"—that is, began their performances on time. When the musicians protested that they were only playing for elites already familiar with jazz when they had expected to play for "the people," Simons struggled to reconcile his role in the State Department with the musicians' view of "the people." The orchestra members, Simons explained, had a "different conception of what they were to do" than the State Department. Simons reported: The orchestra members had misunderstood the word "people" and were disagreeably surprised.[37]

As if his newfound identification with jazz musicians made him self-conscious about speaking as a member of the Department of State, and not attempting to mask his sympathy for the musicians' perspective, Simons referred to himself in the third person in his report:

He could point out that societies in that part of the world are less fluid and more highly stratified than American society, . . . that the "people," the lower classes do not in fact "count" as much as they do with us, and that we are trying to reach out to those who did count. . . . Few of these arguments made any real impression. Band members continued to feel that they would rather play for the "people," for the men in the streets who clustered around tea-shop radios. More rationally, they believed that the lower classes, even if unimportant politically, were more worthy of exposure to good Western music than the prestige audiences for whom they played.[38]

Embassy officials who encountered Ellington contended with the additional contradiction of the foreign policy of trying to win friends abroad by displaying integrated bands, while striving to manage the antiracist implications of this agenda for desegregation before audiences at home. When a picture of Ellington and his white European companion was published in the Turkish press, officials were mortified at the prospect of embarrassing the beleaguered State Department before conservatives at home. This particular dilemma was tragically resolved while the band was in Ankara, Turkey, when the tour was cut short by the Kennedy assassination. Ellington, a close friend recalled, "was beside being beside himself. The whole tour was already strange, and now the president went and died on him."[39] By strange coincidence, Ellington's friend may have been referring to the fact that the band had been playing next door when the presidential palace was attacked by Iraqi airforce jets in an attempted coup d'état on November 12. Unlike Brubeck however, Ellington had been warned by the State Department of an impending coup and had agreed to continue the tour.

The regional organization of the tours enables a focus on the relationship between these cultural and ideological campaigns and political, military, and economic strategies of empire. In addition to attempting to maintain the support of strategic allies in the oil-rich Middle East, win over potential dissidents in the Eastern Bloc, and court new African nations, cultural presentation programs targeted elites in Southeast Asia. Benny Goodman played for and with the jazz-loving, alto-saxophonist King of Thailand in 1957, and Stan Getz made another trip in 1967 to attempt to smooth over relations after Lyndon B. Johnson had offended the King at a White House Dinner. But the most significant tours were to Vietnam.

As testimony to the official capacity for self-delusion about the omnipotence of American culture, a 1968 report from the Saigon cultural attache described the year as one of "unexpected problems" brought on by the Tet offensive. Yet, he concluded, this made the programs all the more important. Cultural and educational programs would "give some balance to the overwhelming military presence . . ."[40] While initial requests for a major act were delayed, the program officers were able to deliver when the Martha Graham Company performed in Saigon in 1974, to sighs of relief from State Department officials and the media alike. In an eerie echo of the State Department desire to balance bombing with culture, a New York *Times* correspondent wrote: "For the first time in Vietnam, I felt proud of the U.S. . . . For two fleeting days, the U.S. showed a new face in Vietnam."[41]

Just as Southeast Asia represented a distinct area of focus for the tours, the U.S. escalation of the war in Vietnam made it the single most important foreign policy problem to be addressed by the tours throughout the globe. With demonstrations against U.S. intervention mounting in Europe, Asia, and Africa, including several incidents of bombings of USIA libraries, the convergence of the civil rights and antiwar movements in the United States could sometimes actually be an asset to the State Department. Indeed, the fact that the tours could invite an identification with black oppositional culture provided a way of identifying with America independently of American policies.

The subtle effectiveness of the "Goodwill tours" in addressing foreign policy crises is illustrated in the experiences of the black American pianist Randy Weston, who toured North and West Africa in 1966. Among the touring artists, Weston was especially self-conscious about seeing the tours in terms of a redistributive agenda, a way of funding black American art. He also regarded the tours as enabling ties between African and black American musicians. Weston relocated to Morocco following his second government-sponsored tour of Africa, and from Morocco he petitioned the State Department to set up more permanent programs to promote such collaborations. Weston's positive approach to the programs did not temper his strident criticisms of the ways the tours were handled. He was especially displeased with the escort officer for his tour, arguing that personnel with "colonial mentalities" had no business in African posts and were hurting the position of the United States.[42] Yet Weston's forthright criticism of the government illustrates how the tours worked, not despite, but because of these tensions. Declaring that "jazz speaks in a special idiom to many Algerians," an official in the American Embassy in Algiers praised Weston's response to Algerian militants criticisms of the United States. (Bear in mind that this is the U.S. official's rendition of the incident.)

Weston was approached by two twenty-year olds who rather belligerently asked him how he, a negro, [sic] could be playing when his country was committing atrocities in Vietnam. Weston, who towers six feet seven, answered, "War man, is a drag. There isn't just one Vietnam—there are lots of them, we have them in Mississippi, in Alabama and in the North. We're not just mouthing about them— we're trying to do something about them. You can't just mouth—you've got to *do* something—are *you*?[43]

The delighted official explained that Weston, a "sometime scholar of Schoenberg, does not use 'jive talk' in ordinary conversation—but it was clear that the two interrogators got the message."[44]

For the Embassy, which was by now deeply invested in proving the effectiveness of the tours so as to silence their critics, Weston's presence as an African American and jazz musician deflected criticism of U.S. policy. While my reading of the reception of the tours suggests that jazz tours did *not* persuade those in Algeria, the Congo, or elsewhere to support U.S. foreign policy, to the extent that Congolese or Ghanaians, for example, identified with Armstrong and also identified Armstrong with America, the tours did foster an appreciation of, if not an identification with, America. Indeed, the employment of African American artists in cultural presentation programs was far more sophisticated than earlier attempts to use intellectuals and liberal anticommunist spokespersons such as

Edith Sampson to insist, in Myrdalian terms, that racism was a fast disappearing aberration. No one had believed Edith Sampson or this kind of propaganda.[45] The State Department's deployment of black culture stepped away from such a didactic approach, gave a subtle twist to the earlier strategy, and proved effective not only in defending American race relations but also in deflecting, at least momentarily, critical scrutiny of U.S. foreign policy.

For the State Department, then, the tours were a legitimizing and humanizing force, one that tried to make critics of U.S. policy identify with America or the idea of America independently of American policies. Yet tracing the steps of the artists illustrates the intimate relationship of these cultural programs to military, political, and economic power, as well as the greater subtlety, innovation, and variety of forms of power exercised through these cultural efforts, challenging the epistemological, historiographical, and commonsense assumptions that continue to render U.S. empire invisible.[46] Moreover, this exported vision of America was often as contested and embattled as the nation it attempted to represent. The U.S. government recognized the power of African American culture and tried to enlist it for Cold War foreign policy by projecting abroad an image of racial progress. Ironically, the State Department jazz tours also provided a global platform from which to promote not only a civil rights agenda but a more egalitarian view of cultural exchange and, with it, a different vision of democracy. It was the simultaneity of the civil rights movement and African liberation—combined, paradoxically, with the emergence of the United States as the dominant global superpower—that projected the optimism and vitality of black American culture abroad. The battles over representation as well as the relationships forged through the tours point to ways in which the dynamic realities of cultural production have included a sometimes enabling, often fraught, relationship to the state. In the jazz tours, as in *The Real Ambassadors*, local and global democratic aspirations were elaborated not outside of but within the apparatus of the nation-state, reflecting the contradictions of Cold War America.

Notes

1. "Satchmo Blows Up the World," *Drum* (August 1956): 40.
2. "Willis Conover, 75, Voice of America Disc Jockey," Robert McG. Thomas Jr., New York *Times*, 19 May 1996, 35.
3. Walter L. Hixson, *Parting the Curtain: Propaganda, Culture, and the Cold War, 1945–1961* (New York: St. Martin's Griffin, 1997), 231.
4. *Parting the Curtain*, 232.

5. Irene L. Gendzier, "Play It Again Sam: The Practice and Apology of Development," Christopher Simpson, ed., *Universities and Empire: Money and Politics in the Social Sciences During the Cold War* (New York: The New Press, 1998), 57–95; Thomas Borstelmann, *Apartheid's Reluctant Uncle: The United States and Southern Africa in the Early Cold War* (New York: Oxford University Press, 1993); Bruce Cumings, *Parallax Visions: Making Sense of American–East Asian Relations at the End of the Century* (Durham: Duke University Press, 1999).

6. My characterization of this period draws on the work of Lisa Lowe and David Lloyd. See their introduction in Lisa Lowe and David Lloyd, eds., *The Politics of Culture in the Shadow of Capital* (Durham: Duke University Press, 1997).

7. Reinhold Wagnleitner, "The Empire of Fun, or Talkin' Soviet Union Blues: The Sound of Freedom and U.S. Cultural Hegemony in Europe," *Diplomatic History* 23, no. 3 (summer 1999): 499–524. See also the essay by Elizabeth Vihlen in this volume.

8. Records of the tours held in The Bureau of Educational and Cultural Affairs Historical Collection, J. William Fulbright Papers, University of Arkansas, Fayetteville, hereafter cited as Bureau Historical Collection.

9. Felix Belair, New York *Times*, 6 Nov. 1955, 1. See also "Good Will With Horns," *Newsweek*, 4 June 1956, 50; "Ambassador with a Horn," *Reader's Digest* (July 1957): 93–96; "State Department Pipes Up With Satchmo for the Soviets," *Variety* (31 July 1957).

10. Ingrid Monson, "The Problem with White Hipness: Race, Gender, and Cultural Conceptions in Jazz Historical Discourse," *Journal of the American Musicological Society* 48, no. 3 (Fall 1995): 396–422; Paul Berliner, *Thinking in Jazz: The Infinite Art of Improvisation* (Chicago: University of Chicago Press, 1995).

11. The tour, which began in Abadan, Iran, on 27 March and concluded on 21 May, included performances in Iran, Pakistan, Lebanon, Syria, Turkey, Yugoslavia, and Greece. Bureau Historical Collection, Series 5, Box 9, file, performers G–P. For an outline of the politics of the tour, see Penny M. Von Eschen, *Race Against Empire: Black Americans and Anticolonialism, 1937–1957* (Ithaca: Cornell University Press, 1997).

12. President's Special Emergency International Program, House Hearings, 1957; The Supplemental Appropriations Bill, 1957; Hearing before Subcommittee on Appropriations House of Representatives Eighty-Fourth Congress, Second Session, Part 2, 675–762. For a related discussion of congressional and conservative opposition to State Department support of abstract expressionism, see Jane de Hart Matthews, "Art and Politics in Cold War America," *American Historical Review* 81 (1976): 762–87. See also Serge Guilbaut, *How New York Stole the Idea of Modern Art: Abstract Expressionism, Freedom and the Cold War* (Chicago: University of Chicago Press, 1983).

13. See "Marking Time: Cultural Program Abroad is Modified to Win Congressional Support," New York *Times*, Sunday, 15 September 1963; Robert Bediner, "The Diplomacy of Culture," *Show* (April 1962): 51–54, 100. See also "Show Biz Pans Cultural Exchange; Pros Say Amateurs Hurt U.S. Image," *Variety* (18 Sept. 1963): 1.

14. See Advisory Committee on the Arts, Department of State, Minutes of Meeting, 10 May 1963, at Washington, D.C., attachment, Department of State, Bureau of Educational and Cultural Affairs, "Jazz in the Cultural Programs."

15. For an excellent exploration of U.S. Cold War cultural programs in a European context, see Reinhold Wagnleitner, *Coca-Colonization and the Cold War:*

The Cultural Mission of the United States in Austria after the Second World War (Chapel Hill: University of North Carolina Press, 1994); on jazz, see pp. 201–15. On the export of American culture abroad, see also Robert H. Haddow, *Pavilions of Plenty: Exhibiting American Culture Abroad in the 1950s* (Washington, D.C.: Smithsonian Institution Press, 1997).

16. "Legislator Asks Censorship Following Martha Graham Dance Sent Abroad," New York *Times*, 10 September 1963; "The Trojan, No the Cold, War," New York *Times*, editorial, 11 September 1963; "Mrs. Kelly Abroad: She Saw 'Phaedras' and Walked Out," New York *Times*, Sunday, 15 September 1963.

17. Through the sponsorship of artists in financially vulnerable art forms, critics exercised considerable influence over the development of the arts. Marshall Sterns and John Wilson were the jazz critics on the music committee. Dance critics are increasingly recognizing the importance of the jazz tours in shaping the world of dance. See, for example, Jennifer Dunning, *Alvin Ailey, A Life in Dance* (New York: Da Capo Press, 1998).

18. Here, the State Department was building on the Voice of America radio broadcasts of Leonard Feather (*Jazz Club USA*) and Willis Conover (*Music USA*), and a history of jazz in the Soviet Union. On the early VOA music programs and Leonard Feather's *Jazz Club USA,* see Leonard Feather, "Music is Combating Communism: Voice of America Shows Bring Universal Harmony," *Down Beat* (8 October 1952): 1–19.

19. S. Frederick Starr, *Red and Hot: The Fate of Jazz in the Soviet Union, 1917–1980* (New York: Oxford University Press, 1983); Walter Hixson, *Parting the Curtain: Propaganda, Culture, and the Cold War* (New York: St. Martin's, 1997). See also the essay by Michael May in this volume.

20. Walter Hixson, *Parting the Curtain.*

21. From: Amembassy MOSCOW; To: Department of State; Subject: Benny Goodman and his Band in the Soviet Union, 10 July 1962, pp. 1–19 and enclosures 1–9, Bureau Historical Collection.

22. I have discussed the political context and contours of these propaganda efforts in *Race Against Empire.* Mary L. Dudziak has explored related issues in "Josephine Baker, Racial Protest, and the Cold War," *The Journal of American History* (September 1994): 543–70.

23. Interview, Penny Von Eschen and Kevin Gaines with Dave and Iola Brubeck, 13 March 1997, Wilton, Connecticut. The Bureau of Educational and Cultural Affairs Historical Collection, J. William Fulbright Papers, University of Arkansas, Fayetteville, contain incomplete records of these early tours but have an itinerary for Brubeck's trip (Series 5, Box 9). The itinerary for Armstrong's 1960–1961 tour is also in the collection, Series 5, Box 9. It is also held in the Papers of Louis Armstrong, Queens College, Queens, New York; Scrapbook 58. See also scrapbooks 22 and 36, and photos box 30.

24. Gary Giddens, *Satchmo* (New York: Doubleday, 1988), 163; "Louis Armstrong, Barring Soviet Union, Denounces Eisenhower and Gov. Faubus," New York *Times*, 19 September 1957. I have discussed this incident in *Race Against Empire*, 179–80.

25. *The Real Ambassadors*, libretto, 3–4. "Dave Brubeck Collection," University of the Pacific, Stockton, California; from the personal collection of Dave and Iola Brubeck.

26. Ibid., 6.

27. "Cultural Exchange" from "The Real Ambassadors," lyrics by Iola and

Dave Brubeck, music by Dave Brubeck. "The Real Ambassadors," book by Iola Brubeck, music by Dave Brubeck, lyrics by Iola and Dave Brubeck, premiered on September 23, 1962, at the Monterey Jazz Festival in Monterey, California, with the following cast: Louis Armstrong, Dave Brubeck, Carmen McRae, Iola Brubeck, Trummy Young, Dave Lambert, Jon Hendricks, Yolande Bavan, Joe Morello, Eugene Wright, Joe Darensburg, Billy Kyle, Willy Kronk, Danny Barcelona, and Howard Brubeck as musical coordinator. A folio of fifteen songs and related narration from "The Real Ambassadors" was printed in 1963 and formerly published by Hansen Publications. That folio is no longer available. Twenty songs from "The Real Ambassadors" were recorded in September and December 1961 by Louis Armstrong, Dave Brubeck, Carmen McRae, Dave Lambert, Jon Hendricks, Annie Ross, and additional musicians, most of whom later performed at the 1962 premiere. Fifteen of those recorded songs were released by Columbia Records in 1962 on an LP entitled "The Real Ambassadors" (COL CL 5850). That LP is no longer available. In 1994 all twenty recorded songs were released by Sony Music Entertainment on the Columbia/Legacy label on a CD entitled "The Real Ambassadors" (CK 57663). Excerpts from "The Real Ambassadors" and "Cultural Exchange" copyright © 1962, 1963 (Renewed) Derry Music company. All Rights Reserved, Used by Permission.

28. For contemporary coverage of the tour, see "Dave Brubeck: The Beat Heard Round the World," *The New York Times Magazine*, 15 June 1958, 14–16; "Warsaw Extols Brubeck Jazz," New York *Times*, 13 March 1958; "Pianist Most Outstanding: Brubeck Concert Captivating," *The Times of India*, 4 April 1958.

29. Interview, Von Eschen and Gaines with Brubecks. Poster in possession of the Brubecks: The Iranian Oil Refinery Co. in cooperation with the U.S. Information Service presents the Dave Brubeck Quartet: Dave Brubeck, Paul Desmond, Gene Wright, Eugene Wright at the Taj Theater, Abadan, Iran, Sunday, 4 May (1958).

30. For a succinct narrative discussion of the Iraqi coup and Middle East Crisis of July 1958, see Walter LaFeber, *America, Russia and the Cold War: 1945–1990*, 6th ed. (New York: McGraw-Hill, 1980), 201–2.

31. Interview, Von Eschen and Gaines with Brubecks. LaFeber, *America, Russia and the Cold War, 1945–1990*, 201–2.

32. Papers of Louis Armstrong, area and country breakdown, July 1954 through March 1962, p. 1, Series 4, Box 1, Bureau Historical Collection; Madaline G. Kalb, *The Congo Cables: The Cold War in America—from Eisenhower to Kennedy* (New York: Macmillan, 1994); William Blum, *Killing Hope: U.S. Military and CIA Intervention Since World War II* (Monroe, Maine: Common Courage Press, 1995), 156–62.

33. Dizzy Gillespie with Al Fraser, *Dizzy: To Be or Not to Bop* (London, 1982), 414.

34. Ibid., 415–18.

35. "We Claim Jazz: Listen to Africa," *Voice of Africa*, Accra, July 1962.

36. Series 2, Box 9, Bureau Historical Collection.

37. Thomas W. Simons, Sr., Effectiveness Report, Ellington Tour 1963, Series 2, Box 9, 15–17; Bureau Historical Collection.

38. Ibid.

39. David Hajdu, *Lush Life: A Biography of Billy Strayhorn* (New York: Farrar Straus Giroux, 1996), 230–31. On the tour's early ending, see "Tour Curtailed,"

Washington *Daily News*, 29 November 1963; and "Jazz Seemed a Discord, Ellington Tour Ended," New York *Herald Tribune*, 29 November 1963, Series 5, Box 11, Bureau Historical Collection.

40. Amembassy SAIGON, Educational and Cultural Exchange: Annual Report, 16 July 1968; Country Files, Bureau Historical Collection.

41. From USIS Saigon to USIA Washington; Subject: Martha Graham Dance Company in Saigon, 21 October 1974, 9 Bureau Historical Collection.

42. Randy Weston to Thomas Huff, Office of Cultural Presentations, Department of State, 28 April 1967, and Report from Randy Weston on State Department Tour of West and North Africa (16 Jan. 1967–11 April 1967) Series 2, Box 31, Historical Collection.

43. Department of State Airgram, from the Amembassy ALGIERS; Subject, The Randy Weston Sextet in Algiers, p. 2; Series 2, Box 31, Bureau Historical Collection.

44. Ibid.

45. In propaganda efforts in the early 1950s, drawing on the economist Gunnar Myrdal's *American Dilemma*, the State Department developed a strategy acknowledging that discrimination existed, but hastened to add that it was a fast disappearing aberration. On Edith Sampson, see Helen Laville and Scott Lucas, "The American Way: Edith Sampson, the NAACP, and African-American Identity in the Cold War," *Diplomatic History* 20, no. 4 (fall 1996) 565–90.

46. I am indebted to the formulations of the critics Anne McClintock and Arif Dirlik. See Anne McClintock, *Imperial Leather: Race, Gender, and Sexuality in the Colonial Conquest* (New York and London: Routledge, 1995); Arif Dirlik, "The Postcolonial Aura: Third World Criticism in the Age of Global Capitalism," in Anne McClintock, Aamir Mufti, and Ella Shohat, eds., *Dangerous Liaisons: Gender, Nation, and Postcolonial Perspectives* (Minneapolis: University of Minnesota Press, 1997), 501–28.

Michael May

Swingin' under Stalin

Russian Jazz during the Cold War and Beyond

Oleg Lundstrem, at eighty-two, is considered the grandfather of Russian jazz, and he scolded me kindly but firmly, "I don't like it when you say 'Russian jazz.' There might be jazz that is somehow Russian, but never Russian jazz. Jazz belongs to the whole world. You know—at one time the Waltz was Viennese music, but now it is international. It is the same way with jazz. Once it is international—you can do nothing to stop it."

Jazz. The sound crept up from the Delta, cooked the melting pot, and soon bubbled over the border. In the Soviet Union, official attempts to stop jazz with the iron curtain were like trying to catch sound with a sieve. Unable to ignore its infectious influence, Soviet officials alternately attempted to coopt and contain jazz. At times the Soviet state embraced jazz as the revolutionary song of its black comrades overseas. Later, during the Cold War, jazz attracted an aura of undeniably Western decadence and was outlawed by decree.

The American government also had an ambiguous relationship with its hottest cultural export. There was a bitter irony in bending jazz to the goals of Cold War foreign policy when its progenitors suffered under Jim Crow. As both bureaucracies of the Cold War attempted to use jazz to reinforce nationalism, jazz musicians were, more often than not, simply caught in the fray.

Oleg Lundstrem was the only Russian swing band conductor who played during the fierce postwar Stalin years, and one of the few who continues to play today. In fact, the Guinness Book of World Records credits his band, which recently celebrated its sixty-second year, as the longest-running swing band in existence. His signature individualism, optimism, and ingenuity have allowed him to thrive under both the dull oppression of communism and the disappointing sting of capitalism.

After spending an afternoon talking with Lundstrem in his Moscow apartment, I had no doubt how he was able to survive. Although he claimed he hadn't spoken English in fifty years, his vibrant personality shone far beyond the limitations of his vocabulary. If anything, he used the language barrier to his advantage, answering not what inquiries he understood, but those he chose to answer. In the end, his story tells as much about him as an individual as it does about the times he lived in. To Lundstrem, Stalin's inhibiting cultural policies were simply another of life's challenges. He managed to spin his swing as nationalist Russian music rather than brazenly resist the state's anathema. He still colors his personal history with the pride of a survivor, which, in the end, tells us very little about the thousands of jazz artists who were forced to abandon their passion. In the end, our conversation left more questions unanswered than answered. But first, Oleg's story as he chose to tell it in late December of 1998:

Lundstrem's youth was spent in the Manchurian town of Harbin, where his father was working on the Chinese-Russian railroad. Here he discovered jazz. "I began to become acquainted with Jazz in 1932, but of course I looked at jazz as dance music. We danced the fox trot because the whole world danced the fox trot at that time," remembers Lundstrem. "When I went to buy some records at a store in Manchuria, I took from the stacks a record that nobody knew at that time—it was Duke Ellington and his Orchestra, 'Dear Old Stockholm.' We never knew about Ellington, nothing. The popular bands at the time were Guy Lombardo and Ted Lewis. I took it home and was astonished. This was something different, not only for dancing."

Lundstrem painstakingly transcribed the arrangement and called a small group of friends over to attempt the music. "There weren't enough of us to make it sound right. So one of the musicians said, 'Lets make a big band.' We said, 'yes, ok, but who will be the leader?' Somebody, I don't even remember who, said 'Oleg.' I was very surprised. There were much better musicians in the band than me. But they voted, and everybody voted for me. So, I became a leader, just like that."

Lundstrem's nine-piece orchestra became quite popular in Harbin, but in 1936 the Japanese took over the railway and the Russian community disbanded. The whole band decided to move to Shanghai, which was host to an international jazz scene. Over the next decade the Oleg Lundstrem Orchestra sharpened their chops playing alongside accomplished bands from America and Europe, and eventually rose to the top: house band at the posh Paramount Ballroom.

While the Oleg Lundstrem Orchestra incubated in jazz-friendly Shanghai, their contemporaries in prewar Russia fell victim to a fierce political debate. The overwhelming popularity of jazz bands during the 1930s had

put classical musicians, nationalists, and hardline communists on the defensive.[1] *Izvestiia*, the paper of the Soviet government, lashed out at jazz,
saying it was championed by "eager but semiliterate administrators,"
and demanded that Russians return to creating true Soviet music. *Pravda*,
representing the Communist Party, argued that while there was "decadent" American jazz, the "true Negro jazz" was, at heart, true proletariat
music and was "the joy and the love" of millions of Russians. Pravda
won this debate, but in the end, jazz music suffered the worst results of
both perspectives—elimination and assimilation. On the one hand, jazz
musicians were purged by Stalin for their Western influence, and, on the
other hand, the Soviet state earnestly attempted to create a "Soviet
jazz"—epitomized in the creation of the State Jazz Orchestra of the
USSR. The Jazz Orchestra played schmaltzy, nationalist, quasi-classical
pop, and was so bad that a concert for the Red Air Force nearly ended in
a riot.[2]

But the State Jazz Orchestra proved that jazz could be patriotic music
and, when World War II broke out, jazz musicians rushed to the front
lines to entertain the troops. For one brief moment during Stalin's reign,
jazz was accepted unconditionally. After all, it was Hitler who suppressed
jazz, and the Americans were now allies. Every military front had their
own jazz band, and many civilian bands enlisted to entertain the troops.
While much of the repertoire consisted of folk songs and patriotic songs,
such as "Slavic Fantasy," and "Song of Wrath," the collaboration with
America allowed Russian musicians, for the first time, to acquire sheet
music for many of the most popular American jazz hits.[3]

The war years produced an unlikely superstar—a trumpet-playing
Polish Jew named Eddie Rosner. Rosner, nicknamed "the white Louis
Armstrong" (a nickname signed and certified by Satchmo himself at a
cross-cultural cutting contest), fled the Nazi occupation of Poland in
1939. His escape alone was a breathtaking display of chutzpah. Rosner
marched into the Polish headquarters of the Gestapo, explained he was a
German with Italian blood and demanded provisions.[4] He swiftly collected them and headed for the Russian border. Rosner twirled between
multiple deadly obstacles like some hip, ethnic Indiana Jones; he barely
avoided the Nazi death camps, the thirties Soviet crackdown on jazz, and
the deportation of thousands of Poles to Stalin's labor camps in 1939. Instead, Rosner's revue, which included a chorus of scantily clad dancing
girls, became the darling of the Soviet elite. At his peak, Rosner was making more than 100,000 rubles a year, when a typical salary was 1500.[5]

Back at home, American jazz musicians struggled with the dilemma of
representing American freedom abroad while facing racism at home.[6]
When Louis Armstrong watched televised images of white people spitting

at a black girl trying to get into school in Little Rock, Arkansas, in 1957, he went public. He criticized Eisenhower for his weak response and told reporters that it seemed as if black Americans had no country. Then he said that he would rather play in the Soviet Union than in Arkansas.[7] Meanwhile, in the Soviet Union after the war, jazz played to a different political scene.

In 1947, Lundstrem and his orchestra decided to return to Russia. When I asked him why, he answered simply and proudly, "Because we are Russians." Of course, in ravaged postwar Asia, nothing was simple. Mao's forces had invaded Shanghai, officially ending its jazz era. In Russia, relations with the West were quickly dissolving, and, as before, the Russian people were to pay the price. Lundstrem and his orchestra returned, at best, to an uncertain future. "When the war ended, we were in Shanghai, and we were invited to play a victory concert in Russia. I said, 'Of course.' But then I thought, 'What to play?' The Cold War had started at that time," remembers Lundstrem. "Not Ellington, although I adore him. So I thought 'I must write something myself.' I had never pretended to be a composer, but I knew that I had to write something. I didn't even have access to Russian folk music. So I wrote 'Interlude,' based on Rachmaninoff. I was worried that I would finish and there would be silence. But then, they clapped like, like I don't know what."

Although Russians returning from abroad were generally treated with suspicion, Oleg says that the band could settle anywhere they wanted, as long as it was not near Moscow, "because after the war, everything was destroyed." So the band relocated to Tatar where they were to be the jazz band for the local conservatory.

Then, in 1947, things fell apart. Cold War cultural policies descended swiftly and brutally on both fronts. The State Jazz Orchestra was changed to the State Variety Orchestra.[8] Rosner was wrenched from his four-room deluxe apartment in exceedingly posh Moscva Hotel and sent to the harshest labor camp in Siberia (where, ever resourceful, he organized a gulag-touring jazz ensemble).[9] Stalin even attempted to banish the saxophone, collecting the instrument and assigning new instrumental duties to the now unemployed. This had the dubious effect of leaving an orchestra's worth of newly born, incompetent oboe and bassoon players. Propaganda further linked the saxophone's slinky curves and tones with depravity, violence, and imperialism. One slogan warned, "It's one step from the saxophone to the knife." Another dangerously punned, "Straighten up, saxophone!"

Frederick Starr explains in his book on Soviet Jazz, *Red and Hot*, that during this period the Soviet state reached a new height in paranoid zealotry: "They claimed that through the Marshall Plan, the United States was working to absorb other countries into its supranational empire. To achieve this, the Americans realized that supranational cultural forms, arts that reflected 'the wretched idolatry of dying capitalism' were also necessary." With jazz officially regarded as a stealth weapon, there was little room for its defense.

It seemed that Lundstrem's orchestra had walked into the lion's den. "We had seen rough times before. In Shanghai, when the war started, a nineteen-piece band was not supportable. So we thought, 'What can we do, war is war,'" Lundstrem remembers. "But then, when the cultural ministry said we couldn't play jazz, members of the band thought that we should commit suicide."

But Oleg laughs, "I didn't feel that. I didn't start moaning, 'ooohm-myooh.' No. I thought if they don't want jazz, then I will play classical music."

The remarkable thing is, the Oleg Lundstrem Orchestra did continue to play jazz. They played concerts and performed on the radio while many of their contemporaries were in labor camps. Lundstrem even remembers the era fondly, saying "I never felt like anybody oppressed me."

How did the Lundstrem orchestra deftly avoid Stalin's last purge? For one thing, they were in Kazan, far away from Moscow's central authority. The rest, Lundstrem explains, was simply a matter of marketing. "At the time they said about jazz, 'This is not our music, this is American, we must have jazz music that is Russian.' And I would say, 'Fine, we must try and have another, but this is not so easy to do all at once.' So I tried. Most other jazz bands at the time quit because they would only play the music they wanted."

Lundstrem worked within the imposed limitations, and found inspiration. "I started to arrange Tatar music. I wrote this music because I had to, but I have always liked folk music very much. So we made our own style, on the one hand it was traditional jazz, and, on the other, Tatar themes," Lundstrem recounts, his eyes sparkling. "No one said that it wasn't jazz. It was jazz. But they were astonished, they said, 'This is not American, this is Russian.' People still tell us that we are the only band outside of America playing in our own style, and I am proud of that."

Soon Lundstrem's Tatar-inflected swing was broadcast on the late radio show throughout Russia. One jazz fan remembers with bewilderment, "These were sounds of heaven, but coming not from New York or Paris, but from Kazan."[10] Even the regional cultural minister was a fan of the Lundstrem orchestra. "To tell you the truth I didn't pay much attention to what the politicians said. Making politics is their profession. They don't know music at all. Why even pay attention to what they say or not? I played for the audience," Lundstrem says with conviction. "And when

I looked down and saw the minister of culture in the front row, clapping like crazy, that's when I thought, if even the minister claps, we must be doing something right."

Stalin died on 5 March 1953 and the spring thaw began. Saxophone sections cautiously bloomed in the symphony orchestra, and Russian beatniks, the *Stiliagi* [from the word meaning "style"], began to emerge from the shadows. Tongues were loosened, and Lundstrem found himself an unlikely promoter. "After Stalin's death they brought together Russia's greatest composers to decide on the next direction for popular music," says Lundstrem. "They asked Shostakovich for his thoughts on creating the next Russian 'light' music. He answered, 'I don't like this term light music, popular music can be heavy also. To me, music is either good or bad, and I would rather listen to jazz played well than a bad symphony.' He then said that our band was the best popular music in the Soviet republic."

Lundstrem and company were immediately escorted to Moscow and provided with spacious apartments. The public was hungry for jazz music, and Lundstrem remembers playing forty-nine consecutive sold-out concerts. "From then until now we played what we wanted. People say, 'This can't be true, I know Khrushchev didn't like jazz,'" Lundstrem laughs. "Well, I didn't play for Khrushchev. I played for the Russian people."

In America, big band music, economically unwieldy and out of date, was in decline. In Russia, however, it was state supported and immune to the whims of the marketplace and the fleeting fancy of fashion. Big bands played well into the sixties, until the British invasion destroyed the nominal interest required. "After the Beatles came, we were the only big band left," Lundstrem laughs. "We were the first and the last."

From the fifties through the seventies Eddie Rosner and others were, once again, providing a competitive jazz scene in Russia. Lundstrem's band, however, was a cut above the rest, and the walls of his Moscow apartment attest to this fact. Rows of awards adorn the wood paneling, and elaborate ceramic trophies fill the shelves. Throughout our interview, Lundstrem sat like a king amidst this shrine, and he finished by laying down the gospel: "I think of jazz as international music. It cannot be defined by labels, American, Russian, Swedish. No. It is just jazz. It is something great in this world, something that brings people very good emotions when they hear it. No musician is trying to create a certain kind of political music when he composes, not any of the great ones anyway." Lundstrem motions to a poster of Ellington above his grand piano. "A musicologist once approached Ellington and asked, 'You are one of the great originators of jazz. Please settle the debate once and for all. What is jazz?' Ellington answered, 'I don't know, but I try and do the best I can.'"

Lundstrem laughed hysterically at Duke's wit, but I could not help feeling he was laughing at me too. He had become frustrated, as one does with a child, at my persistent questions about Stalin and the fate of jazz, about the Gulag and repression. I asked him no fewer than seven times, "What became of all of the other jazz players during the Stalin years?" Each time he answered with an assured tone and steady gaze and each time I was almost convinced he was answering the question I had asked. But no. Not even close. In fact, he was usually talking about an entirely different era. In the end, he had won. "So, you agree with me, right?" Agreed with him that jazz was not political, and that it was really not so bad under Stalin. I nodded wearily. One thing was certain: the oppression did not exist for Lundstrem. In fact, Lundstrem implied that the only musicians who failed, like always, were those too inflexible to adapt to the times. For Lundstrem? Hey, no problem.

A great story, but is it true? Frederick Starr's book, *Red and Hot,* is the most comprehensive English-language text on Russian jazz. It is meticulously researched, well crafted, and my best source for background information. The story of the Lundstrem orchestra in *Red and Hot* differs on several key points from Lundstrem's first-hand account. Starr tells of an orchestra that is desperate and trapped at the close of the war. "When Mao Zedong's Communists captured Shanghai in 1948, the city's nightlife closed down. The Russian jazzmen faced an impossible situation," Starr writes. "The United States, Canada, and most Western European countries would refuse them because of their Chinese or Stateless passports." So, according to Starr, the band, buoyed by accounts of the thriving wartime jazz scene, headed straight for Moscow's renowned Metropol restaurant, proudly brandishing their saxophones.

The restaurant's manager must have been astonished. Here was a group of eager young Russians in their late twenties proposing to play an evening of jazz as if they were in New York or London. Had they not heard by now that the very word "jazz" had been banned? But the risk was theirs, not his, so he allowed the performance to go ahead. A scandal broke out, and within days the entire band was banished to the Volga Tatar town of Zelenodols, near Kazan.[11]

Oleg Lundstrem, banished to Kazan? It seems hard to picture, but Professor Starr stands by his account of the events: "Three members of his orchestra reported on their one night stand at the Moscva Hotel. They played one night, had a great time, and the next day they were told, 'You are never going to play here again. Get out of town,'" Starr explained in an interview in April 1999. "But this is a guy who had driven from Shanghai to Moscow in two old American cars with an entire jazz band in 1948. A guy as gutsy as that is not going to be put off by merely being exiled to a provincial town. He's a survivor, and there he is still at it. It's an absolutely amazing achievement."[12]

The reason for the discrepancy is ambiguous and open to interpretation. Lundstrem has made the post-Soviet transition to capitalism more smoothly than most. An electronics manufacturer has put the band on its payroll and provided them with an in-house theater. Ingeniously, the Lundstrem Orchestra has flowed smoothly from state patronage to philanthropic patronage. Still, by all accounts, Lundstrem's band is a pale shadow of its glory years. Could it be that Lundstrem, privileged and successful under the Soviet regime, is unwilling to admit its shortcomings? He told the Moscow *Times* that he refuses to be "a martyr of Soviet jazz."

"I think you have to understand that Lundstrem's band became part of the establishment," says Starr. "They are grand people of the old school and the late Soviet era was very good to them. During the seventies and eighties all the solid old *babas* were still grooving to their music when the rest of the world had moved on and was listening to rock. But they were exiled to Kazan. No one would volunteer to go to Kazan from Shanghai, I mean, get real as they say. But they did well; they turned it to a plus and it is perfectly understandable that he might soft-pedal any complicated aspects of the experience."[13]

Still, it is important to note that Starr wrote *Red and Hot* during the Cold War, when he was advisor to several American presidents. "President Reagan was wide open, intellectually, a surprisingly open guy, and he had quite a number of meetings to discuss what was happening in the Soviet Union and I was honored to be part of those," Starr elaborates. "These were very small gatherings that would go on for a few hours, often over a meal. And I must confess that a significant part of what I brought to it were the insights that had come out of my rather idiosyncratic studies on Soviet jazz."[14]

Starr is deeply committed to the notion that jazz musicians were active agents of change, and portrays all official Soviet attempts at creating "mass culture" as inept and foolish. "The story that inheres in the fate of jazz in the Soviet Union is how the revolution from below, in this case jazz, in the end completely subverted, undermined, and triumphed over any attempt to reshape values from above," he says.[15] In contrast, Richard Stites, a professor of Russian history who writes on Russian popular culture, told NPR's *Morning Edition*, "I think it is unfair to say that culture which is produced and sort of modulated and fed to the people is somehow false and not popular, because at the most extreme moment of government control of culture, the time of Stalin, the songs that were produced at the time . . . were well received by the public because they contained elements put in by their creators that have wide, sort of universal popular appeal."[16]

This would explain Lundstrem's pride at being able to create a brand of jazz that was not technically mass culture, but was both able to fulfill nationalist goals and enjoy popular support. Jeffrey Brooks, author of *Thank You, Comrade Stalin*, feels that, in the case of Lundstrem and Starr, both perspectives are valid. "Is one more true than the other? I would say not necessarily so," Brooks said in March 1999. "During points of the Cold War when dissidents were persecuted it was quite natural for Soviet jazzmen to construct their experience in terms of that narrative, but once it was all over any other story could appear in which they were just making music. One of the marvels of history is that it is retold and retold and retold."[17]

I, too, found it difficult to maintain objectivity during my research and travels. I still saw Russia reflected in the Iron Curtain of the American imagination. One night on the train from St. Petersburg to Moscow, my subconscious preconceptions reared instantly and unforgettably . . .

26 December 1998, 3 a.m. The sleeping train car was unlit, but the figure looming above me was outlined by shadows in the shifting moonlight. That Soviet-style military hat, absurd and angular, and the commanding Russian words, impenetrable and severe—all signs pointed to a nightmare distilled from a Cold War adolescence. I had been deeply asleep. I knew that from the situation's fragmented urgency. But I was now unmistakably, painfully, and totally awake. I quickly pointed to the top bunk where Alan, my good friend and translator, slept.

He asked to see our tickets and quickly disappeared into the darkness. We waited apprehensively while the rest of the car slept peacefully. Why had we been singled out? What was our fate? Our dream-deluded minds wandered. The bombing of Iraq in December by U.S. forces had inflamed dormant tensions seething beneath diplomatic relations. At that moment, we were sure politics was about to get personal. For a brief, stark moment, glasnost's rosy hue was peeled away and we were back, shivering, in the dark, totalitarian Russia that inhabited the American consciousness for so long. We were powerless; we had lost our freedom.

After ten minutes of sitting in fear-induced silence, it became clear that, while we may have been denied our fundamental right to a good night's sleep, we were not on the way to our own private gulag. As the ice in my spine melted I began to accept that the official had probably forgotten to collect our tickets. But in that instant I realized the near impossibility of being an objective journalist in Russia. I was seeing Russia through red, white, and blue-colored glasses. I was here to cover the state of jazz, but in reality I hoped to uncover the historic battle of the State vs. Jazz.

The swinging, jiving, carefree jazz musicians blowing strong against the dark tidal wave of totalitarianism. As the Lundstrem interview had made clear, it was more complicated than that.

The Soviet system, after Stalin, had its disadvantages, but for jazz musicians, it did pay the bills. In the end, one does not have to be a Siberian bebop trombonist to worry about how to play jazz and feed one's family. Moscow's middle-aged musicians mostly remember the Soviet seventies and eighties with bemusement.

Eugene Ryabov, one of Moscow's most sought-after jazz drummers, enjoyed the steady salary but lost patience with the state-arranged tours. "The cultural commission would book you for five or six days a week. We would play to a sold-out crowd in a major city one or two nights and then spend four days out in the villages, jamming with the pigs and chickens," he remembers. "The villagers had no interest in jazz and seemed to view us with suspicion. We were once playing in front of a particularly dour audience and, in a desperate attempt to liven things up, the saxophonist motioned for a solo. The band stopped, and he tap-danced across the dirt floor—patatitata-ta-tata-ta-ta. Nothing. The audience didn't even blink. Oh man, that was depressing."[18]

The Soviet officials often displayed contrasting but equally dispiriting inclinations. "In the 1980s I was playing with a very tight mainstream jazz band, and we appeared before the commission for our review," Alex Rostotsky, bassist, remembers and chuckles. "We played through our set and looked hopefully at the head of the committee. 'You are so boring to watch,' was his only comment. 'Why don't you come back next week and put on a real show.' So we had to return the next week and . . . [rocking his body back and forth in faux ecstasy] we were given the stamp of approval."[19]

While many of the more repressive cultural policies were relaxed under Brezhnev, official musical appointments were often based more on party loyalty than musicianship. "I was playing in the government-run radio orchestra for a year. It was a typical Brezhnev-period orchestra— the salaries were always on time, and we had very good musicians in the band. For a while it was a jazz band, but that, I guess, was too good for them, and they dissipated it," says Victor Dvoskin, jazz bassist. "They kept many of the same musicians, but hired a new leader—he had been the director of a choir for retired communists. He was fierce, and absolutely unprofessional."

Dvoskin remembers that the repertoire became focused on patriotic themes, namely Lenin. "Now some of these songs were not so bad, because there was a high degree of professionalism among Russian composers. Of course, some were worse than junk," says Dvoskin. "Anyway, at one point we rehearsed the longest cantata about Lenin. We must have rehearsed for two full days, the band in one room and the choir in the other. Finally, it was time for us to play together. We were over a hundred musicians and singers, and it took about twenty minutes for everyone to tune and settle down. Then we begin to play and it was total cacophony. I mean, it was something unbelievable. The underqualified conductor got very scared and forced the band to start over and over. Finally, he asked some questions. Turns out we had rehearsed different songs—the choir had rehearsed "Lenin is with us," the band, "With us, is Lenin." They were in different keys, tempos, everything. The librarian had taken the wrong one off the shelf."[20]

In the waning years of the Soviet Union, the greatest obstacle for jazz musicians was obtaining Western jazz recordings. Diplomats traveling abroad were responsible for the majority of *plastiki*, that is, vinyl, but most of the jazz floated over the border on radio waves propelled by Willis Conover, host of *Music USA,* and courtesy of Voice of America (VOA). Conover went on the air in 1955, when America finally realized that to attract significant listeners in the Eastern Bloc they must feature jazz. They found the perfect conduit in Conover, who managed to play his role with subtlety and grace. Never an ideologue, he conveyed a simple love for the music unencumbered by propaganda. The formula worked, attracting an estimated 30 million listeners—even more remarkable when one considers that the whole audience was straining to hear the Soviet-jammed signal of *Music USA.* "A whole big band would sink into the buzz—a constant, almost impenetrable buzz," says Dvoskin. "The voice somehow came through. Willis Conover had this incredible voice, a deep bass, and you could always hear him."[21]

Whatever artists like Miles Davis and Dizzy Gillespie might have felt about the American government, once their music was packaged and sent to VOA, they were as American as Enola Gay. "Willis Conover is dead at 75, aimed jazz at the Soviet Bloc," the New York *Times* reported on 19 May 1996. "[Conover] proved more effective then a fleet of B-29s . . . Conover would bombard Budapest with Billy Taylor and drop John Coltrane on Moscow."

How Reagan must have felt, forced to share the credit for ending communism with Charlie Parker. "The thirst for freedom in the Soviet Union . . . has long been reflected in its people's love for Western music," *Billboard* magazine proclaimed in September, 1991. The magazine called for humanitarian aid for Russia—in the form of CDs—because, "like us, they do not live on bread alone: they need music to help keep their spirits up through the grim months ahead."

And the Soviet jazz musicians played along, trumpeting the call to freedom. From 1989 to 1991, jazz clubs and festivals featured Russian jazz musicians. In 1989, when the Igor Bril Quartet, with Victor Dvoskin on bass, performed with jazz legends Joe Henderson and Bobby Hutcherson in San Francisco, Reuters reported: "That jazz has been able to survive in the Soviet Union was incredible, considering the impediments to its development." Russian jazz musicians, it seemed, had torn the Iron Curtain from the inside.

For jazz musicians, the fall of communism has been bittersweet. "When jazz and rock music still had an underground component, everyone felt like there was a lot happening in basements across Russia," says Ryabov. "When everything was allowed, we realized that not much was really happening, and what did exist was largely a poor imitation of music in Europe and the United States. It went from an expression of innermost feelings, an expression of freedom, to nothing special. It was disillusioning for many musicians, when they realized, "Great, you play jazz, but who's going to listen to it?"[22]

A decade after the fall of the Soviet Union, there are many Russian musicians on a par with their Western counterparts. But now times are hard for everyone. The emerging Russian middle class had been dancing on rotting floorboards and, on 16 August 1998, the financial foundation simply crumbled beneath them. Under these conditions, it was difficult for the band to play on. The ruble, valued at six to the dollar in July, had slipped past twenty by the time I arrived in Moscow in late December. Bank accounts were frozen, so millions of Russians watched their rubles fade to paper, unable even desperately to spend them. For Russian jazz musicians, as for everyone else, optimism, along with other Western luxuries, could not be afforded. Two record labels committed to recording and marketing jazz talent had folded. With only two or three clubs open for serious music, many of Moscow's finest musicians make a living in fancy restaurants catering to the new Russians. "Well, since the crisis . . ." is a resignation offered in place of detailed explanation for why the gig was canceled, why they couldn't afford to go out, why there wasn't meat on the table. The evidence was everywhere, communist limitations had been traded for capitalist limitations.

But during this crisis—as with all the crises that define Russian history—art, culture, and music thrive. A jazz vocal festival at Moscow's Jazz Art Club plays to standing-with-no-view-of-the-stage-room only. A jazz quintet composed of eight- to ten-year-olds, already developing a strong tone and cocky swagger, tears through "Cantaloupe Island." I find the saxophone prodigy backstage, softly humming Thelonious Monk to himself. "Why do you play jazz?" I ask. "Because I can't live without it," he answers without missing a beat.

The grand irony is that jazz, once labeled "decadent," is now an oasis of Russian virtues—intensity, dedication, and soul—in a country drowning in American commercialism. Neon signs advertising Marlboro and Coca-Cola beam down on the Kremlin wall. Russian pop music, often in English, drives the staggering gyrations of Moscow's hedonism-happy youth. One thumping techno mega-hit repeats, "I'm horny, I'm horny, horny, horny," endlessly and everywhere. Conspicuous consumption seems to be the only kind of consumption in today's Moscow. You are either paying $50 to get into a nightclub or eating watered-down borscht in the old Soviet cafeterias.

Recently, Vladimir Danelin, a jazz piano player, went back to his childhood instrument, the accordion. I heard him play, at a small basement bar, "Crisis Genre." The rich pathos of the accordion melted into the bebop beat and sketched the sadness of the century into the drifting cigarette smoke. I realized, whatever the future holds, jazz had found another home.

Notes

1. S. Frederick Starr, *Red and Hot: The Fate of Jazz in the Soviet Union 1917–1991* (New York, 1994), 163.

2. Ibid., 176.

3. Ibid., 187.

4. Ibid., 198.

5. Ibid., 199.

6. See Penny von Eschen, "Satchmo Blows Up the World," in this volume.

7. See Laurence Bergreen and Jenny Minton, *Louis Armstrong : An Extravagant Life* (Broadway Books, 1998).

8. Starr, 215.

9. Ibid., 199, 214.

10. Ibid., 229.

11. Ibid., 223.

12. Interview with Frederick Starr, April 1999.

13. Ibid.

14. Ibid.

15. Ibid.

16. See also Richard Stites, ed., *Culture and Entertainment in Wartime Russia* (Bloomington: Indiana University Press, 1995).

17. Interview with Jeffrey Brooks, March 1999. See also Brooks, *Thank You, Comrade Stalin: Soviet Public Culture from Revolution to Cold War* (Princeton, 1999).

18. Interview with Eugene Ryabov, December 1998.

19. Interview with Alex Rostotsky, December 1998.

20. Interview with Victor Dvoskin, December 1998.

21. Ibid.

22. Ryabov interview.

Thomas Fuchs

Rock 'n' Roll in the German Democratic Republic, 1949–1961

The growing tension of the Cold War in 1948 (currency reform, Berlin blockade, coup in Czechoslovakia) strongly influenced not only foreign policies but also culture. The three western zones that formed the Federal Republic of Germany (BRD) in 1949 had already absorbed phenomena of American popular culture such as movies, fashions, Coca-Cola and chewing gum, Glenn Miller and boogie woogie since the end of the Second World War. Officials in charge of the development of popular culture in the German Democratic Republic (GDR) were extremely concerned about the "destructive and decadent" potential of American trash culture, such as chaotic and shrill music, comics, and other forms of trivial literature, gangster movies, pornography, and violent westerns. The specific problem of East Germany, in contrast to other members of the Eastern bloc, was the fact that the GDR was not a nation-state but the smaller part of a defeated, and therefore, divided, country. Unlike Poland or Hungary, East Germany always had to compete with a prosperous big brother on its western boundary that spoke the same language. Throughout the history of divided Germany there existed an ongoing fight between East and West for recognition as the legitimate heir of the "true" Germany. This struggle for the hearts of the Germans was especially intense from 1948 to 1955, when both Germanies joined their respective military alliances and it became clear that the division of Germany would remain a reality for some time to come.

Until 13 August 1961, however, the division of Germany did not mean an end to all contacts between West and East. Berlin remained the symbol for German unity—but also the prime locus for increasing ideological competition between the "free world" and the "democratic camp." Also, by the early fifties it became clear the neither West nor East would succeed in pulling the other part of Germany into its sphere of influence. Consequently, the competition between the ideologies shifted in the direction of

192

culture. Interestingly enough, East German officials strongly believed they had an advantage in the cultural realm.

East Germany played the national card continuously from 1949 until 1961. They pointed, with some justification, to the Americanization of West German culture. Since the foundation of East Germany, cultural officials emphasized the rebirth of German national culture, and not only workers' culture, but even more the "bourgeois heritage" of German high culture, especially the classics: Goethe, Schiller, Bach, Beethoven. This should promote a "healthy" form of German nationalism in preparation for the fight against "spiritual Marshalization through cosmopolitanism."[1] In addition to high culture, East German communists put a surprisingly strong emphasis on the resurrection of German popular culture, *Volksgut*, especially in the form of folk music and dances. The heritage of German pop songs from the 1920s, though, was neglected, as was the progressive modernist art and music of that same period.

Perhaps inevitably, both Germanies showed certain continuities with specific Nazi cultural policies. In the West, anticommunism was still hailed as appropriate to defend Western civilization against "bolshevik unculture." In the East, cultural nationalism was celebrated as an alternative to a decadent, degenerated, inferior, foreign, capitalist culture. East Germany regarded national German culture as a bulwark against Americanization. Manifestations of foreign culture—almost exclusively American popular culture—in West Germany were seriously regarded as components of psychological warfare. Consequently, American popular music played a completely different role in East Germany than it did in West Germany, where there was also opposition, but from nationalist-minded members of the educated middle classes and not cultural representatives of an increasingly repressive totalitarian government.

American popular culture was regarded as a frightening example of U.S. cultural imperialism, serving to water down and pervert the national German heritage. The destructive potential of this Trojan horse for a possible subversion of East German youth was regarded as a real danger. The complete inability of East German officials to look beyond narrowly defined confines of their horizons and to recognize, for example, the black components of U.S. popular culture is hard to comprehend, especially because communists had a long history of breaking the color line. East German publishers produced books that fiercely attacked racism, lynching, and the crimes perpetrated by the Ku Klux Klan.[2] The folk music of American blacks, such as slave songs, spirituals, gospel songs, but also "true" jazz, and the blues, were being hailed as genuine folk expressions of a suppressed minority. The multicultural dimensions of the origins of rhythm & blues were favorably reviewed. Andre Asriel, a prominent expert and critic of American poular music and a fan of jazz, in his influential study *Jazz*,[3] evaluated the mix of folk-blues, gospel, and big-band swing in rhythm & blues in positive terms.

Throughout the existence of East Germany, the well-known actor and singer Paul Robeson was adored as a representative of "the other America." The record company Amiga published his albums, and schools received his name. But Robeson was, of course, no rock 'n' roller. His artistic interpretations of spirituals, traditionals, songs of socialist agitation, and peace songs exemplified the musical tradition with which East German leadership had been familiar: traditional songs of international workers, the communist movement, and traditional folklore.

Why was it so hard for East German leaders to take one more step and discover the potential for progressive politics in the music and lyrics of *black* rock musicians such as Chuck Berry ("Brown-skinned handsome man"), Bo Diddley ("I'm a Man"), or Little Richard? Why did East German communists ape the negative reception of rock 'n' roll by archconservative West German guardians of high culture as well as American racists and clergymen, when they could have utilized this other music as an expression of urban black folklore and cultural protest for propaganda purposes, thus gaining recognition and respect among East German youth? Until 1972, boogie-woogie, rock 'n' roll, and beat were consistently reviled by East German officials. Needless to say, this had strongly negative consequences for the relationship between the party and the "future"—the young people of East Germany.

It is impossible to overemphasize the importance of East German youth, who were constantly portrayed as the future, as the source of leaders who would continue to build a socialist society. The Free German Youth (FDJ) was immensely significant, not only because the successors of Walter Ulbricht, Erich Honecker and Egon Krenz, were groomed for their leadership positions within the party and state through their leadership of the youth organization. Since its foundation, East Germany tried to present itself as a young country, where politics was run in the best interests of the youth. In striking contrast to West German chancellors like Adenauer, Erhard, Kiesinger, Schmidt, and Kohl (with the possible exception of Brandt), the East German leadership over the years tried desperately to present themselves as likable, as understanding young people's desires, and as having similar interests and backgrounds.[4]

East German leaders believed that their interpretation of progressive socialist popular culture, which had originated in the vibrant working-class culture of the Weimar Republic before World War II, still corresponded with the "people's cultural consciousness" of postwar youth. After all, revolutionary songs of the German working class as performed by Ernst Busch, music composed by Hanns Eisler or Kurt Weill, and lyrics by Erich Weinert or Bertolt Brecht together constituted a progressive song culture that everybody who believed in the creation of a new Germany simply had to like.

Until 1933 Ernst Busch, for example, had definitely been immensely popular with hits such as "Roter Wedding," and "das Solidaritätslied." Exiled and imprisoned during the Nazi era, he returned to Berlin in 1945 and founded the record company Lied der Zeit.[5] Supposedly, anybody desiring to buy records had to purchase a Busch record first, either for political reasons or simply to dispose of the high quantity of Busch records. But many buyers immediately destroyed these records and handed them back to the sales clerk for the raw materials customers needed to present in order to be able to purchase new records. According to Gisela Seeger, people objected to Busch's lyrics.[6] This indicates that even shortly after the war the cultural expressions of Weimar Republic working-class culture were no longer regarded as relevant by a large segment of the population. But Busch's opponents, people who failed to listen to classical music by German composers or to practice German folk culture in song or dance, were suspected of antisocialist activities. This was especially true of young people who dared to listen to the sounds of American "hot music," sung in the language of the class enemy.[7]

One of the problems of East German evaluations of cultural phenomena is the strange fact that culture was being regarded as something static, something that does not undergo changes. This attitude works fine in regard to both classical music and German traditional folk music, as well as for traditional working class songs. But American popular music, which after World War II achieved global supremacy among the youth, is and always has been dynamic. It experienced countless metamorphoses as a multicultural hybrid, no matter whether it was called swing, boogie woogie, rock 'n' roll, or rock. These dynamics were completely misunderstood by those in charge of East Germany's cultural policies. They rather helplessly interpreted "hot music" as indicative of a decline in German morals, standards, and culture. They even evaluated this music as being of inferior quality because they believed that it did not fulfill minimal standards of harmony and melody. They also attacked it as manifestations of drug addiction and petit bourgeois reformism. These were but a few of the reasons for the vilification of American popular music for at least two decades. Ironically, the East German communists used exactly the same arguments as their class enemy, the nationalist conservative bourgeoisie in West Germany.

But for East German youths, rock 'n' roll meant the same thing it did for rock fans all over the world: an exciting music that corresponded to their desires, that could be used as a sign of rebellion against the boring and retrictive world of the grown-ups' rules and regulations. The total opposition within East German leadership toward Anglo-American popular music did not end until 1973, when, during the Tenth World Games of Youth and Students in Berlin, it was deemed important to entertain the foreign visitors with the kind of music they were used to: rock.

In order to put East German reactions into perspective, we need to examine the West German reception as well. At first, rock was regarded as a variety of jazz, as every item of American popular music was misunderstood as jazz. Rock records were quite rare. Very few record stores carried them. Also, many records pressed in West Germany were geared toward the U.S. Army market. Crucial for the popularization in West Germany were two facts: the replacement of the unwieldy and fragile shellac record with the vinyl single, and the transnational cooperation between American, British, and West German record companies. Whereas East Germany had to pay dearly in hard currency for record imports from the West, the Telefunken company and American Decca, to cite just one example, cooperated through Teldec and traded German classical and pop music (*Schlager*) for American productions. Usually, Teldec was supplied with all the top ten U.S. hits, and stars like Pat Boone and Elvis ("Muss I denn zum Staedele hinaus") did German-language songs. There was little promotion done for rock, but the jukeboxes carried the music even to remote small towns. The allied military radio stations AFN and BFN and Radio Luxemburg played rock. But only one West German radio station ever played rock 'n' roll, the WDR. For many young Germans, the former "enemy stations" were taboo because of their parents' veto.

West Germans in general had mixed ideas about the United States. The parent generation admired economic achievements, superior technology, and standard of living. Some believed Germans should learn about democracy from the Americans. But in regard to culture many West Germans regarded the United States as inferior because of its supposed lack of high culture. West German society was split: conservative parents totally opposed rock. But those adults who regarded themselves as "modern" admired the United States in general and were more hesitant to condemn rock 'n' roll. In 1956 *Star-Revue* journalist Eva Windmoeller positively reviewed "Rock around the Clock" and contrasted its superior musical content with the German *Schlager*. But by far the most important print medium to popularize American culture and lifestyles was the youth magazine *Bravo*, which began publication at exactly the same time rock 'n' roll came to Germany, in the summer of 1956.[8]

In order to explain the popularization of American culture in West Germany, Kaspar Maase pointed to the central importance of attitudes modeled on the American way of life that arose from the economic "miracle." An enthusiastic and uncritical admiration of everything modern and "American" paved the way for an acceptance of rock among "progressive" young Germans. It helped that the United States was the dominant world force in artistic innovation, design, advertising, and other "modernisms."[9]

A major problem for German rock fans was the absence of the black originals on the German record market. Such rock, R&B, and doo-wop originals reached Germany only in the watered down versions of white cover artists. Even Fats Domino's "Ain't That a Shame" seemed too hot and was substituted by Pat Boone's plastic cover. This explains why, in both Germanies, during the 1950s black artists were hardly mentioned at all and why rock was seen as a white phenomenon. The first rock superstar in West Germany was Bill Haley. His excessive popularity rested on the movies and the soundtracks of *Blackboard Jungle, Don't Knock the Rock,* and the German production *Hier bin ich—hier bleib ich* (1958), and the song "Viva la Rock 'n' Roll." Bill Haley was not exactly "The Wild One." His stage act was tame. Still, riots broke out at concerts in Berlin, Hamburg, and Mannheim in 1958. All the pent-up emotions of the dreary fifties erupted during these concerts, as they had even during a Louis Armstrong concert in Hamburg in 1955. The biggest riots took place in Berlin's Sportpalast during the unfortunate pairing of Bill Haley with the Kurt Edelhagen Jazz Band, the last time that rock was regarded as being a part of the jazz universe. The young rock fans booed the highbrow Edelhagen band and chased them off the stage and, while in the mood, also rioted as soon as Haley took over. There were rumors that provocateurs from East Berlin had infiltrated the concert in order to protest against decadent, capitalistic American music. While some respectable German newspapers like *Hamburger Abendblatt* and *Die Zeit* attacked the "primitivism" of the new music, *Bravo* thrived on rock. Elvis became *Bravo*'s most prominent star, ensuring the success of the magazine in its first year of existence. In 1957 *Bravo* asked its readers to elect the "king of popular music" and named American and German stars to choose from. Elvis won by a mile.[10]

During the late fifties rock 'n' roll represented a rare opportunity for West German teenagers to retreat into their own world. Most grownups at the time did not understand English and rejected what they could not relate to as degenerate and primitive. Many teenagers, in turn, accepted anything coming from America as positive: fashions, hairstyles, *Bravo* star cuts. The fathers felt provoked by the laid-back, snotty attitude of their sons that represented such a contrast to the older generation's heel-clicking Nazi and war experience. But rock culture in West Germany was apolitical. It transcended class barriers, resembling youth rebellion more than political activism.

Similar things can be said about the early rock reception in the land of its origins, the United States. Opinion makers there condemned the rock phenomenon as harshly as their allies in West Germany *and* their enemies in East Germany. Rock, according to many American adults, inevitably led to a corruption of morals, juvenile delinquency, and violence. For many it represented a plot by the NAACP or even by the communists! In America, too, rock was a symbol of decadence, drug usage, and premarital sex. Yet its fans were outcasts mostly for their identification with *black* music. And this constituted the biggest difference with Germany: there, rock was *American* music, only very few Germans were aware of its black origins.

In the United States, campaigns against "dirty music" had been organized as early as 1954, always with a racist undertone. After all, the Civil Rights movement and rock mushroomed to prominence at exactly the same time in the same region: the deep South. "Clean-up drives" of disc jockeys playing "suggestive" music were initiated with the help of the major record companies, as R&B, and later rock, were often produced by small independent labels. Clearly the driving force behind mid-fifties U.S. anti-rock hysteria was the fear that undesirable aspects of black sexuality might infect white youth through interracial dances. Martha Bayles emphasizes the interracial dynamics of early 1950s R&B: it became impossible, even during the pre–Civil Rights era of the south, to keep R&B performances segregated, as many white youth flocked to such concerts. R&B bands were regularly hired for (white) high school dances and fraternity parties.[11]

Even conservative black organizations fought to clean up the airwaves by condemning sexually suggestive records. Radio stations had lists of banned records and launched crusades for better discs. It was no coincidence that the vast majority of blacklisted records were produced by black artists. Religious opposition was actually much more important in the United States than in Germany. A Catholic youth organization in Minneapolis even advised its readers to "smash the records you possess which present a pagan culture and a pagan concept of life."[12] In 1956 Alabama segregationists initiated a campaign to ban rock singles from jukeboxes because rock was "dirty, sexualistic, and immoral," and the "heavy-beat music of Negroes" was seen as a plot to pull the white man "down to the level of the Negro."[13] Various Christian denominations united in a rare ecumenical approach to "Knock the Devil out of Dancing." Among white artists, Elvis was singled out for his uninhibited stage sexuality as well as for promoting juvenile delinquency. In order to clean up Elvis's image, "Colonel" Tom Parker decided to have Elvis drafted as a regular into the U.S. Army.[14] The drive to clean up rock 'n' roll in the United States succeeded by 1958. The Payola scandals, novelty dance crazes, and syrupy pop songs all contributed to the decline of rock as an expression of youth rebellion.[15]

Only a few contemporary "American heroes" were known behind the Iron Curtain in the late forties and early fifties. Most of them were in some way associated with the CPUSA, for example the historian Herbert Aptheker, the writers Howard Fast and Albert Maltz, and the composer Earl Robinson. The most revered representative of the "other America" in East Germany, though, was Paul Robeson, the first black to play Othello in the United States. Also a great singer, he was blacklisted like so many other less prominent sympathizers of the communist cause in the United States. Robeson served as an example for the injustice and hypocrisy of an American society that had discarded the ideals of men like Abraham Lincoln and Franklin D. Roosevelt. Robeson was persecuted on account of his politics *and* his race—a persecution that, in East German eyes, proved the racist nature of capitalist American society. At the same time it was possible to accuse Americans of cultural ignorance and a witchhunt atmosphere. Robeson's music was art, not popular music, even his interpretation of rather simple songs based on the folk and religious heritage of black people. In that way, he became an ideal muse for East German image makers: a serious artist who was firmly grounded in his people's folk heritage and belonged to a suppressed minority. The fact that he also was a dedicated communist helped, of course.

In 1949 Robeson was scheduled to give a concert in Peekskill, located in the borscht-belt of the Catskill mountains north of New York City. During the concert, racist riots broke out that were also directed at the communist ties of the artist. The Dietz Verlag in East Berlin soon published an account of the events by Howard Fast.[16] In Fast's mind the riot of Peekskill constituted an "open manifestation of American Fascism." The local media had prepared the racist attacks through hostile editorials, and a drunken mob had attacked the concertgoers, shouting "We are Hitler's men and we will complete his work." Fast's interpretation that this proved that an American form of fascism had appeared and was rapidly gaining adherents within American society was passed on to East German readers in order to evoke sympathy for Robeson and the "other America." Nazi analogies were frequently used in East German media to discredit both the Adenauer and the Truman administrations. Events such as Peekskill came in handy because they seemed to support the notion of a United States drifting inevitably in the direction of fascism.[17] Robeson's image had changed from that of a World War II hero—on the home front—to that of a traitor, because he protested against the hostile attitude of the Truman administration toward the Soviet Union and demanded equal rights for black Americans.

In a 1957 interview in *Sonntag*, Robeson discussed aspects of the Civil Rights movement, which generally received a lot of coverage in East German media.[18] In celebration of Robeson's sixtieth birthday *Sonntag* published another piece full of praise for a man who stood by his principles: "Those people who deny Robeson his passport and civil rights are the same who threaten the world with nuclear war. They have the same interests as their West German clients who are responsible for the millions of dead Jews, Communists and Antifascists."[19]

The extreme anti-Americanism of East Germany is perhaps best illustrated in a famous propaganda song by Ernst Busch. The title sums up the official attitude: "Ami Go Home!" Busch recorded this song in 1949. The context was the Berlin blockade, airlift, and the Marshall Plan. The music reflects and criticizes certain contemporary characteristics of American popular music. The song begins with a shrill and menacing jazz inspired jingle and a 1-4-5-1 boogie-woogie riff. Busch employed these elements to criticize "degenerated" American music. Ironically, he was later criticized by *East German* authorities for having incorporated "undesirable" American elements in his work. Here are the lyrics in English:

> Ami Go Home
> Say what is life worth during war
> when the entire world is crumbling to dead sand
> but this is never going to happen because we do not want to perish
> therefore we are shouting all over our German nation
> Go home Ami, Ami go home
> split atoms for peace
> I'll say to father Rhine do not touch my daughter
> Loreley as long as you will sing Germany will remain free
> Clay and Cloy are having a good time behind the lines
> the German boys will do the dirty work and die in the sand
> as of yet the guns remain cold, but peace is not going to get old
> unless somebody holds his protective hand over peace
> Go home Ami . . .
> Ami learn the melody of the virgin Loreley
> who sits there combing her golden hair
> anybody breaking her comb is going to break his neck
> that is sad but true
> Go home Ami . . .
> leave the German stream alone
> because we will never adhere to your way of life
> you will never manage to influence us in any such way
> greetings from Lorchen the comb stays here
> Ami listen to good advice stay within your longitude
> because your Marshall brings us too much war danger

Why did an East German worry about the German symbol Loreley on the Rhine? In the early 1950s quite a few newspapers carried articles that referred to a secret emergency plan of U.S. military forces to blow up the Loreley and flood large parts of the Rhine and Main valleys in the event of a breakthrogh of Soviet tank forces that needed to be stopped along the Rhine river at all costs. These stories and the song underline the nationalistic approach of East German propaganda toward the United States.[20]

According to East German media, "Ami Go Home" became an international hit when it was performed by the German delegation to the Second International Festival of Youth and Students in Prague in the summer of 1950. *Junge Welt*, the official paper of the Free German Youth, reported that this hitherto unknown song was heard all over Prague and directed against the American occupation forces and their imperialist war policies.[21] *Junge Welt* underlined that "Ami Go Home" was by far the most successful and popular contribution of the German delegation in Prague because it was directed against "the politics of the American warmongers; this fact elevates this song to international significance."[22]

In the following years, the slogan "Ami Go Home" reappeared again and again. West German youth were being encouraged to paint grafitti on the walls of American barracks and army trucks,[23] photos of West German protesters inevitably featured an "Ami Go Home" banner. Those stories implied that the "Ami Go Home" movement had "taken on the dimensions of a giant people's movement in West Germany with millions of demonstrators. The massive resistance of the people of West Germany is a powerful force against the fascist schemes of the American imperialists."[24]

Busch performed two more anti-American songs. "No Susanna" focuses on the danger of German rearmament by Yankee imperialists. The music was based on the traditional "Oh Susannah"—not quite as upbeat was the "Koreasong" about GIs who know they will have to die and therefore blame President Truman and wrong American ideas for their predicament.

It may not be surprising that American foreign policy and Harry S. Truman received ill treatment in East German songs. But what about American popular culture? It was regarded as an especially mischievous trick by the American imperialists to brainwash the German population into accepting the American occupation, negate German culture, and promote decadence. Popular music constituted only one component of this cultural attack. Under the heading "Taxi girls and bankrupt theater," the *Junge Welt* in 1950 accused the Americans of having corrupted German womanhood by taking advantage of young girls who could be hired for a dance, a thinly veiled first step to prostitution. The introduction of woman's wrestling, trivial literature, brutal crime fiction, comics, and chewing gum was criticized as well. Even so, music was usually perceived as the major problem. When U.S. forces came to Celle—already a garrison town for the British—for maneouvres, "the inhabitants of Celle found themselves in an atmosphere of sex appeal and booze, jazz orchestras filled the streets with boogie woogie, and a hundred new bars were opened."[25]

The solution for combatting American popular culture by smashing records and boycotting the music mirrored contemporary campaigns in the American heartland. But such advice was not always adhered to. Articles throughout the 1950s either praised the producers of East German radio for finally having put the lid on a flood of inferior cosmopolitan dance music, or bemoaned the persistence of old habits and tastes. In 1959 a decree was issued that demonstrated the availability and popularity of American popular music in East Germany: the infamous 60/40 rule. At any public dance, in every radio program, at least 60 percent of the music had to have originated in socialist countries; Western music was allotted 40 percent at the most.[26] This desperate attempt to stem the ever-advancing tide of rock 'n' roll was destined to fail, as it was easy for East Germans to purchase "hot music" in West Berlin, or to listen to their favorites via RIAS (Radio in the American Sector Berlin) and AFN.

Michael Rauhut provides some revealing statistics about the origins of the popular music played on various East German stations between 1956 and 1960. Whereas in 1956–1957 songs from "nonsocialist countries" (chiefly West German *Schlager*) comprised around 60 percent of the total, this percentage had dropped dramatically to around 20 percent by 1959–1960. As Rauhut shows, the term "Americanization" also applied to West German productions and hits from the West in general, not just songs sung in English. This makes sense, as all Western culture in the East was regarded as corrupted by American imperialism.[27]

Ironically, the first American product that included a rock 'n' roll song was positively reviewed: the classic movie *Blackboard Jungle*, featuring Bill Haley's "Rock around the Clock" in the opening and closing credits. This film about juvenile delinquency, according to *Sonntag*, was regarded in West Germany as an "evil badmouthing of American schools, probably initiated by communist sympathizers, whereas this film actually reflected a realistic portrayal of undisciplined, demoralized, criminal big city youth who terrorize their teachers and try to rape their female fellow students. The film shows that these problematic young people are actually the victims of American wars."[28] No mention, as yet, was made of rock 'n' roll. In 1957 the DEFA film studios in Babelsberg tried their hand at a juvenile delinquency movie, including transistor radio music and featuring a mild form of youth gang, the well made *Berlin-Ecke Schönhauser.*

Jazz was hotly debated during the early years of East Germany's existence. Its surporters, surprisingly, included even the head of state Walter Ulbricht(!)[29] Its fans, like Asriel, Theo Lehmann, and Reginald Rudolf, pointed to the "vibrant folklore" it came from. But rock 'n' roll, quite to the contrary, had no East German decisionmaker on its side.[30] In a programmatic article, Alexander Abusch asked in 1957, "Why are we opposed to decadence?" and answered: Because decadence reflected the cultural decline of a disappearing bourgeoisie during the imperialistic stage. "The audience of West Berlin has already been conditioned to bourgeois nihilist philosophy through the decadent nonsensical trash of rock 'n' roll and other modish excesses. The imperialists are trying to smuggle this manifestation of imperialist rottenness into East Germany as part of the ongoing struggle between the two systems in order to divert the attention of our population from rebuilding our nation."[31]

Even West German media commented on the Communists' struggle with rock 'n' roll: many dance orchestras were mobbed by East German youth to play rock. Those bands which adhered to the 60/40 mix "soon played in front of empty halls."[32] During a jam session in Thuringia, an East German paper noted "the dancers went completely wild to the rhythms of an American hit song. One youth eventually stormed the podium and performed an Elvis Presley song despite the protests of the local FDJ secretary."[33] Still, to declare rock 'n' roll illegal and to enforce the declaration were two different things altogether. But East German officials, especially in the youth movement, were persistent. Lectures were organized in which speakers raved against the moral and political dangers of Western dance music. The *Neues Deutschland* warned that "Jazz is the fifth column of John Foster Dulles that will be utilized to subvert and destroy socialist culture."[34] Even Franz-Josef Strauss, the West German secretary of defense, was often quoted as an abhorrent example with his positive attitude about jazz orchestras in the West German army.[35]

As late as the end of the fifties the East German answer to rock 'n' roll was a "national German dance culture." For this purpose, an entirely new dance was being choreographed utilizing new compositions: the *Lipsi,* which turned out to be the biggest laugh since the Ford Edsel. But how else could the menace of cosmopolitan dance music be stopped? Peter Czerny, for decades an important ideological opinion maker in the field of popular music, summarized the dangers of Western dance music. Its purpose was "enticement to uninhibited rowdyism, a disregard of human dignity, ideological preparation for NATO." Dance music, of course, was "in the service of psychological warfare."[36]

East German television was also recruited for the battle against cultural barbarism. In 1960, the foreign affairs magazine *Objektiv* reported about riots at the Newport Jazz Festival caused by "the superhot rhythms of a big band." This was just another anachronistic evaluation proving that the number of East German experts on American music was rather small indeed. Elvis Presley's release from the U.S. Army in Germany even moved the editors of *Objektiv* to the following poem:

> 2 March 1960 in Frankfurt/Main
> enters history as a black day
> because Elvis Presley, U.S. scream idol
> top star in the devil's dance called rock 'n' roll
> has left the solders' ranks
> to return home to the states
> with sadness the fans of West Germany
> will remember him
> ecstatic and in wild pain
> the young hearts cramp up
> their legs in knots
> they experience extreme farewell pain
> we feel sad about those
> who adore this young man
> because of a lack of more appropriate ideals.
> But every country is offering to its youth the very best things
> it has to offer.

In summary: rock 'n' roll stars were regarded by Germans as puppets of American business, created to corrupt and degenerate first the American youth, then the West and East Germans. Rock 'n' roll was interpreted as an important aspect of psychological warfare and therefore needed to be eradicated by all means. "A Bill Haley, a Johnny Ray, or an Elvis Presley will neither be tolerated by our radio, nor our record companies, and will never reflect our taste."[37] Apparently, the African American roots of rock were not recognized at all. All the artists evaluated during the fifties were white. Rock 'n' roll was either criticized musically for being too syrupy (the crooning songs), or severely accused of promoting "excesses"—an accusation that, throughout the history of East Germany, was the most serious criticism that could be directed against any form of culture.

Notes

1. The ambitious monthly *Musik und Gesellschaft* has featured several programmatic editorials since 1951 focusing on the dangers of ideological corruption through American popular music. See Ernst H.Meyer "Realismus—die Lebensfrage der deutschen Musik," in *MuG* 2 (1951): 38–43; Georg Knepler "Musik,

ein Instrument der Kriegsvorbereitung," *MuG* w (1951): 56–58; Musikabteilung der staatlichen Kommission für Kunstangelegenheiten, "Um eine neue Tanzmusik," *MuG* 4 (1953): 69–70.

2. Civil Rights Congress, New York, 1951, *Rassenmord: Wir klagen an!* (Berlin, 1953); Stephan Hermlin, ed., *Auch ich bin Amerika: Dichtungen amerikanischer Neger* (Berlin, 1948); Stelson Kennedy, *Ich ritt mit dem Ku Klux Klan* (Berlin, 1954); Paul Robeson, *Mein Lied—meine Waffe* (Berlin, 1958); see also Theo Lehmann, *Nobody Knows . . . Negro Spirituals* (Berlin, 1961) and *Blues and Trouble* (Berlin, 1966).

3. Andre Asriel, *Jazz* (Berlin, 1966).

4. For a detailed discussion of the importance of the FDJ during the early GDR see Ulrich Mählert, "'Die gesamte junge Generation für den Sozialismus begeistern': Zur Geschichte der Freien Deutschen Jugend," in Jürgen Weber, ed., *Der SED-Staat* (Munich, 1995).

5. See Gisela Seeger, *Ernst Busch* (Berlin, 1987), for details on Busch's life and career.

6. Ibid., 257.

7. This attitude is by no means restricted to the hot phase of the Cold War during the early fifties: Stasi boss Erich Mielke started a surrealistic campaign against the few GDR punks as late as the early eighties because he felt personally insulted in his cultural understanding and regarded punks as a serious, subversive threat to socialism.

8. For a detailed but anecdotal discussion of the popularization of rock 'n' roll in the BRD see Ruediger Gloemeke, *Roll Over Beethoven: Wie der Rock 'n' Roll nach Deutschland kam* (St. Andrae-Woerdern, 1996).

9. See Kaspar Maase, *Bravo Amerika* (Hamburg, 1992).

10. See Bloemeke.

11. See Martha Bayles, *Hole in Our Soul: The Loss of Beauty and Meaning in American Popular Music* (Chicago, 1994), 112–15.

12. Linda Martin and Kenny Segrave, *Anti-Rock: The Opposition to Rock 'n' Roll* (New York, 1993), 26.

13. Ibid., 41.

14. See Martin and Segrave, 66–68.

15. Editor's note: In the late 1950s rock 'n' roll became domesticated for mass audiences. John Lennon always insisted that Elvis's joining the army was the end of rock 'n' roll, and every rocker with any respect for himself stopped listening to Elvis afterwards. He became a Hollywood and a Las Vegas act—and that also was the end of it. What would have been so new about the Beatles in 1962 if rock 'n' roll hadn't been dead because of Payola scandals, Pat Boone etc. etc.? It never was called rock 'n' roll after that but Beat or Rock music. Thus, there is a hiatus in "white" rock 'n' roll in exactly that period, reflected in a massive decline in sales. Of course, pop music still was alive in those four years but the most exciting thing happening in the mainstream music charts was the hula hoop and the twist, and those were novelties. Of course, the "Day the Music Died" refers to a plane crash, but for all hard rockers rock 'n' roll had been dead since the day Colonel Parker sent Elvis into the army to improve its image and Elvis accepted it. The effort to suppress rock 'n' roll was therefore successful and it needed the British invasion to bring the music back to its homeland.

16. See *Weltbuehne* 54 (1949).

17. *Aufbau* 57 (1952): 471–72.

18. *Sonntag,* 22 September 1957, 5.

19. *Sonntag,* 6 April 1959, 9.

20. "Hände weg von der Lorelei!" *Junge Welt,* 25 August 1950, 3.

21. "Überall in der Welt: 'Ami Go Home'" *Junge Welt,* 25 August 1950, 3.

22. Ibid.

23. See *Junge Welt,* 8 August 1950 and 15 June 1951.

24. *Junge Welt,* 2 February 1951.

25. *Junge Welt,* 14 March 1950.

26. For an excellent discussion of the relations between GDR political guidelines and rock music, see Peter Wicke, "Zwischen Förderung und Reglementierung—Rockmusik im System der DDR-Kulturbürokratie," in Peter Wicke, Lothar Müller, ed., *Rockmusik und Politik* (Berlin, 1996).

27. See Michael Rauhut, *Beat in der Grauzone: DDR-Rock 1964 bis 1972 — Politik und Alltag* (Berlin, 1993), 38–48.

28. *Sonntag,* 4 December 1955.

29. In 1958, at the height of the Bill Haley riots hysteria, Ulbricht was quoted in *Junge Welt* disclaiming that rock had anything to with jazz, "the negroes" having protested against such claims. Hanns Eisler, definitely more of an authority on American music as a famous composer and having spent years as an emigre in the United States, also denied that such "craziness and idiotic movements" had anything to do with the "real jazz" that Eisler had encountered in the United States during the thirties and forties. For a detailed analysis of American popular music in the GDR from the perspective of an American Marxist, see Edward Larkey, "Zur kulturpolitischen Rezeption der Rockmusik der USA in der DDR," Ph.D. diss., Humboldt University, 1986, 28–31.

30. Larkey also underlines that jazz increasingly became respectable in the GDR during the 1950s as an artistic expression of African American culture. He states that rhythm & blues was unknown in the GDR and that white rock artists were criticized especially for the country & western elements in their music, but black artists like Bo Diddley, Chuck Berry, and others were not personally attacked as Elvis Presley or Bill Haley had been, even though the black roots of rock were also critized. Larkey provides no sources for a 1950s discussion of *black* rock artists. Actually, there was very little knowledge in West and even less in East Germany that rock had black origins, and black artists were virtually unknown because white cover versions were produced for the German market instead of the originals. No wonder then that black artists were not singled out for criticism like Presley and Haley: they had never been heard of in the GDR. See Larkey, 31.

31. *Sonntag,* 27 October 1957.

32. *Der Tagesspiegel,* 19 April 1958.

33. Ibid.

34. *Neues Deutschland,* 15 February 1958.

35. *Junge Welt,* 22 January 1959.

36. H. P. Pehnert, "Wie steht es mit der Tanzmusik?" in *Junge Welt,* 22 January 1959. Larkey writes that rock was regarded as escapism from political activism, that this music degraded its fans into passive victims of manipulation by media corporations in order to divert attention from the pressing political problems of the GDR. Blue jeans and petticoats were regarded as "teenage uniforms" to prepare for a future wearing of the U.S. Army uniform. See Larkey, 34–35.

37. *Forum,* 3 November 1960.

Christoph Ribbat

How Hip Hop Hit Heidelberg
German Rappers, Rhymes, and Rhythms

From Elvis Presley to Kurt Cobain, from Janis Joplin to Madonna, American popular music has for decades provided the soundtrack to the lives of young Germans. Rebellion, alienation, hopelessness, the yearning for love, hippie anarchism, dance floor hedonism, the pleasures of sex and drugs—music carried this and much more across the Atlantic. Just as their peers in most other European countries do, young Germans, too, turn to American records for the magic that translates emotions into sound, and to singers whose voices speak to them in a language both foreign and intimately known. Do these (predominantly white) listeners care whether the singer is black or white? Apparently, they don't: Aretha Franklin, Whitney Houston, Michael Jackson, and Prince are only four of many African American superstars admired by millions of Germans. Why, then, introduce the category of race here if it appears unnecessary to draw a dividing line between white and black American music?

The case of rap music and the way it influences German youth culture in the 1990s prompts race-related questions that need to be explored. While, for example, both the music and the personae of Madonna Ciccone ("white") and Whitney Houston ("black") can be seen as hybrids of diverse American cultural traditions merged to please the taste of a mass audience,[1] rap is consciously, and by self-definition, black. (Too) simply put: its voice speaks from the ghetto, about the ghetto, to the ghetto. In contrast to this, "white" rock 'n' roll and its rhetoric of boredom, uncertainty, and rebellion can be tied much more easily into the fabric of German teenage lives. Middle-class adolescence looks pretty much the same on both sides of the ocean. Why, then, are young Germans so fascinated with rap, a collage of sound segments, monologues, and parodies that is so intricately interwoven with black American culture that it frequently remains almost incomprehensible for the American outsider, let alone the nonnative English speaker? It seemed extremely worthwhile to find out why young Germans even turn into rappers themselves: to explore the cross-cultural idiom they create as they follow in the footsteps of their African American idols.[2]

For me, the exploration of these questions started at a concert of a German rap group called Sons of Gastarbeita, who were performing at a club in Wattenscheid, a dreary industrial town in Germany's rust belt, the Ruhrgebiet. *Gastarbeita* is a conscious misspelling of *Gastarbeiter,* the label given to Southern European immigrants in the 1950s and 1960s—a term implying that the "guest workers" would, after a stint in German factories, return to their native Turkey, Italy, Greece. As we know, many preferred to stay—and the Sons of Gastarbeita are living proof of that.

In concert, Frederik, Germain, Mustafa, Bünyamin, and Gandy raised a ruckus. Their music combines elements of rap, funk, and noisy rock guitar sounds. Groovy basslines serve as backbone to the songs and force audience and band alike to jump up and down incessantly to the music. While a good part of their lyrics deal with racism, or criticize the coldness reigning in German society, the occasional love song is obligatory, as well as an anthem to their native region, the Ruhr district. Often, the Sons of Gastarbeita play with stereotypes, put on Arabian head garbs, sing about 1,001 nights, and toy around with the clichés Germans use when speaking about Turks, the Arab world, and Islam. The band is young, energetic, their music is a lot of fun; as is their stage show. On this particular night the group provoked chants by teenage girls in the audience demanding that the five guys immediately undress. As the artists pondered whether or not to give a third encore (clothed or unclothed), I left the concert and walked to my car.

Across the street, I passed a group of seven or eight Turkish boys, between sixteen and nineteen years old, who were standing and dancing around an automobile, the doors of which had been opened to let out the booming beats of black American music that played on the car stereo. The boys rapped along to the music. Or, to be precise: they made up their own lyrics in English, and rapped over the beat. In the dreariest part of a dreary city, in a parking lot situated between a rundown suburban train station and the monstrous highway structure of the A 40, these young men, also "sons of Gastarbeita," transformed public space. They staged their own party, performing for themselves and for any passersby their skillful rapping and their flowing dance moves. They weren't just consumers of music—their performance was a combination of listening, dancing, inventing lyrics, and rapping.

This night in the parking lot—and I remained there for a little while to watch—was, naturally, a wonderful experience for somebody who comes from a cultural studies background, and I have always believed that people who consume today's music, movies, TV shows are not merely passive recipients but produce their own meanings, as active participants in the process of shaping popular culture. These Turkish kids, I thought, tap the resources provided by global pop culture to find their own cultural idiom. MTV does not leave them stupid or mindless. Instead, via television, the music of one minority—African Americans—crosses the ocean and reaches another minority: the Sons of Gastarbeita both inside and outside the club. A medium to express hope, self-confidence, and the yearning for equality reaches across the Atlantic.

Does it really work this way? Why, then, did the German teenagers who looted a home for asylum-seekers in Rostock in 1992 wear baseball caps marked with an X, merchandise connected with Spike Lee's biopic *Malcolm X*, caps worn by many African American rap stars at the time? These teenagers clearly emulated black musicians and fashions, as the caps and other insignia of homeboyism and of ghetto culture show. However, though they admired the music of people of color, they saw no reason not to use violence against people of color in their own neighborhood. For some German cultural critics, these incidents proved that the "end of youth culture" had come. From now on the belief that youth subcultures were closely linked with a liberating, progressive, antiracist stance seemed absurd. Music, video clips, and politicized baseball caps alike were nothing but tacky fashion gimmicks.[3]

Music critic Günther Jacob accuses German rap enthusiasts of using the American ghetto as a Disneyland of sorts. He compares the fascination of young Germans with inner-city America to the 1920s exoticism that spawned the Josephine Baker craze. The fact that rap records sell so well in Germany is to him not a sign of a true interest in black culture. Instead, Jacob argues, it signifies how our consumer culture appropriates everything that seems new or thrilling, and turns it into a product.[4] This prompts a central question in any discussion of the German face of rap: Are we dealing with a mere merchandising article? Or has German rap become a legitimate form of cultural expression—and a medium of cultural contact between the American ghetto and the German suburb?

Excellent histories of rap have appeared in recent years, chronicling its development from the early days when young African Americans and Latinos developed the arts of DJing and MCing in the South Bronx of the 1970s.[5] The rappers, the Masters of Ceremony, delivered their spoken rhymes to music mixed by a disc jockey on two record players. Often, performances would take place on street corners. Rap music in its original sense is not performed with live instruments—it is a collage of existing records. Even in the early days of rap, the term "hip hop" was coined as an umbrella term for the new modes of cultural expression developed in urban America in these years: rapping, DJing, breakdancing, and graffiti. "Hip hop remains a never-ending battle for status, prestige, and group adoration," says Tricia Rose.[6] Indeed, individual skills are highly important in hip hop. Its participants strive for the smoothest, yet most intricate rap, the biggest graffiti tag on the subway train, the most daring breakdancing moves, the wildest mix of records by a DJ.

While the battles between the young artists are fought with great intensity, the most distinguishing feature of hip hop culture is community: the hip hop network and its position in black America. Chuck D. of rap group Public Enemy has coined the phrase that rap is "black CNN"—a medium for communication and information connecting the American inner cities. Rappers have taken up issues such as racism, urban poverty, police brutality. It would be a mistake, though, to believe that rap is a purely political medium. It can be ironic, comic, even grotesque. With stunning creativity, rappers brag about their talent, strength, and sexual prowess; some artists continually put down women as "bitches" and "ho's"; sometimes making money, getting paid seems the only aim worth achieving. One example of a hip hop community with social and political aims, however, is the Zulu Nation, which was founded by Africa Bambaata, an organization of rappers, DJs, graffiti artists, and breakdancers united in the fight against drugs and violence.[7]

Twenty-eight-year-old Cora E. has defined herself repeatedly as a member of the Zulu Nation. She started connecting to hip hop as a breakdancer, then changed disciplines and became a rapper. After more than a decade of rapping, she finally signed a contract with a major record label. Her "hip hop education" took place in Kiel on the Baltic; she now works as a nurse in Heidelberg and has become the grande dame of German hip hop. "At first," she says, "all we could do was copy what happened in the American ghettos. But things have changed. An independent hip hop culture has developed its own traditions, its own styles and themes."[8] Youth centers all over Germany were important institutions: more and more young Germans were drawn to hip hop jams staged there and participated as dancers, artists, and musicians. Cora E. demonstrates how an African American subculture has been "Germanized."[9]

Cora's 1996 single "Schlüsselkind" (Latch Key Kid) is an excellent example of the way she uses the American idiom, yet transforms it to suit her needs. There are no references to ghetto life in this rap, no attempts are made to "sound black," no traces of American English can be found. Cora tells her life story: growing up as the child of divorced, middle-class parents, raised by a working mother; the boredom and aimlessness of teenage life in a medium-sized German city; her career as a youthful outcast who was expelled from several schools. Hip hop opened new horizons for her. "I almost drowned," she raps, "but a wave from America washed me back ashore." Cora's rap starts with the line, "I come from the middle class," signifying to her listeners: this might be rap, but it's not from the ghetto, and it's not about the ghetto.[10] "I only rap about things I know something about. Racism is something I do not experience. So I don't make it a topic," Cora says.[11] However, she very consciously reflects hip hop's multicultural, antiracist philosophy.

The German hip hop scene is immensely attractive to the sons and daughters of Gastarbeita, to the second-generation immigrants, to Germans of Asian or African descent. In 1995, the Turkish group Cartel was extremely successful both in Germany and in Turkey, commenting aggressively and provocatively on the situation of young Turks living in German cities. Rap artists such as Islamic Force, Aziza A., or Erci E. blend Oriental and American musical traditions in their songs.[12] One of the early anthems of German rap, "Fremd im eigenen Land" (A foreigner in my own country) by Advanced Chemistry, expressed the feeling of estrangement and growing anger among young "foreigners" frustrated by German laws, xenophobia, and racist violence. Fresh Familee, a Turkish-German crew from Ratingen, tackled similar issues.[13] And of course the Sons of Gastarbeita deliver highly political, if sometimes overly didactic raps. Two of the Sons even work as rap educators, conducting workshops in youth centers all over the Ruhr area. Gandy Chahine and Bünyamin Aslan prerecord beats and basslines on tape and then work with Turkish-German and other teenagers who start to develop the skills of rhyming and rapping for themselves.

Often, Gandy and Bünyamin say, this is the first time ever that these teenagers reflect in writing about their experiences with racism, hostility, marginalization. Gandy Chahine recalls social workers who were absolutely baffled because teenagers who had never before been able to concentrate on anything sat and worked for hours on the lyrics of their raps. Frequently, rap crews will form in such workshops and then continue to work independently long after the workshop has ended. In fact, the rappers I had met in the parking lot in Bochum-Wattenscheid had been alerted to rap as an idiom in such a workshop.[14]

Why is rap so attractive to them? "Because it's so easy to do"—that's how every rapper I spoke to answered this question. You don't have to be able to play an instrument. You don't have to buy a guitar, nor a drum set, nor an amplifier. All you need is a record player or a tape recorder and the will to express yourself. This is exactly the reason why in the 1970s African Americans and Latinos in the Bronx turned to rapping. The tools they needed were cheap and easily accessible.[15]

Another reason for hip hop's multicultural appeal is its use of sampling. Since rap music is a montage of existing records and soundbites, American DJs have always used the art of sampling as a means to pay tribute to artists they admired: you can hear the screams of soul singer James Brown or the saxophone of Charlie Parker on hip hop records. Also, you will often hear segments of speeches by political leaders such as Malcolm X. Rap thus became an archive of African American culture, where the voices of the past could be heard in the music of the present. A similar strategy can be employed in multicultural Germany. Cribb 199, a hip hop band from Bremen, was formed by a Bosnian-German and two Turkish-German rappers. They combine the most up-to-date, 1990s beats with samples of Southeast European folklore, paying respect via sampling to two traditions that inform their lives: black American music and the music of their parents' or their own native countries.[16] For Turkish-German artist DJ Mahmut, Oriental samples also serve as a tool to confuse listeners, to toy with the stigmatizations of "foreignness."[17]

Is youth culture dead? Ever since the 1960s, ideas and images from across the Atlantic have stimulated the growth of emancipatory, liberating, countercultural movements in Western Europe. Can we now really view the transfer of American pop music to Germany as nothing more than a flow of fashion gimmicks, dollars, and deutschmarks? To many young second-generation Germans, rap, the latest form of African American music, seems very meaningful. Hip hop culture generated new modes of expression to be used by anyone—no matter how poor or how far away from the music education a middle-class upbringing might provide. An antiracist philosophy is organically connected to the new music. Rap, a vital, sometimes aggressive voice of the black minority in the United States, and, in variations, in the United Kingdom and in France, has also become one of the voices of the Turkish minority in Germany—an art form of the disenfranchised.

Ayse Caglar has commented on the complexities of this seemingly organic translation of a cultural idiom from the American to the German ghetto. Turkish rappers do define themselves frequently as "the blacks of Germany," using such band names as "White Nigger Posse." Yet it would be all too easy to label rap as an idiom created by those forever on the periphery, easily classifiable as cultural outsiders. In many cases, young Turkish-Germans create multicultural pop for the mainstream instead of politically alert hip hop for and from the margin.[18] And rap is not only used to negotiate ethnicity: gender also plays a role. To Cora E., even though she does not make much of it, hip hop was instrumental in asserting herself as a strong, outspoken, young woman in a male-dominated environment. In many German rap crews, though, male hip hoppers without immigrant backgrounds are rhyming to the beat. These are middle-class kids who are neither marginalized nor oppressed, neither poor nor victims of violence or racism. Do they, to quote Billie Holiday, have a "right to sing the blues?" Or do they mindlessly appropriate rap, doing injustice to the music of the ghetto?

Surprisingly, they ask themselves the same questions. One prime example is Kinderzimmer Productions, a band from whose first album I borrowed the Billie Holiday quote. "I represent the problems of the kids with rich parents," Henrik von Holtum raps in German, "nobody who turns off supplies, always somebody who's worse off."[19] Kinderzimmer Productions deliver a creative, highly sophisticated version of hip hop, making extensive use of jazz and soul samples. They speak about their predicament: the fact that their hip hop enthusiasm does not correspond with a marginalized minority status. They use their record to express their respect for African American culture. Yet their salute to the quiet city of Ulm, their hometown, "U-Stadt and You Don't Stop," sounds just as vital and energetic as any record about Brooklyn by American rappers.

Similar issues are raised by the members of a German rap group that in 1996 ranked among the most successful artists in the industry, with two top-ten singles in a row. Their group is called Fettes Brot, which translates as "fat bread." Its three young members come from sleepy small towns in the Hamburg area. Schiffmeister, one of the rappers, explains that he has always been conscious of the fact that the ghetto—the original home of rap music—was something he knew very little about, something he had no connections to. And even though he reads avidly about African American history, there are no traces of that in his lyrics.[20]

Rap as performed by Fettes Brot is a whimsical, self-ironic, groovy expression of middle-class kids, celebrating German and American popular culture alike, evading all clear messages. Appropriately, their biggest success so far was a single called "Jein"—the German combination of yes and no: "nyes."

One thing that Fettes Brot are quite serious about is the issue of masculinity. They evade the often homophobic rhymes and rituals used by many American rappers, who endlessly proclaim their toughness, sexual potency, and dominance over women. Fettes Brot are outspoken on the subject and unafraid of questioning and ridiculing their own manhood—as demonstrated in one of their latest videos, in which they cruise the streets on giant macho motorcycles while costumed as man-sized Easter bunnies. This approach to hip hop, however, was also made possible by American predecessors. De La Soul, a crew from Long Island, were among the first to add a softer, more self-ironic touch to the genre. "Their example opened rap for us," Schiffmeister explains.[21]

The intricate absurdities produced by Fettes Brot frequently give way to intelligent reflections on issues such as gender roles, family conflict, and indecision. Since, in rap, the voice is such an important instrument, words, rhymes, puns, jokes, and playing with clichés are much more important than in contemporary rock music. Some of the most talented young poets in Germany, I would suggest, are currently rapping over beats—the three word-wizards of Fettes Brot among them.

The cultural transfer taking place here is fascinating: art forms that originate in the American urban ghetto and have deep roots in African American history have become a central part of German popular culture. While breakdancing's heyday seems to have passed, DJing and rap music are more popular than ever. Graffiti art has transformed the face of German cities, and certainly of German commuter trains. Consider, for instance, the city of Dortmund, one of the "graffiti capitals" of Germany, where young rap aficionados take pride in using the spraycan and the microphone with equal excellence.[22] Underneath the mainstream current of globalized American pop culture runs the stream of hip hop and connects young Americans with young Germans.

In-depth research on German hip hop should examine more than just the lyrics of the rap songs and instead provide a comprehensive cultural analysis that also explores the beats, sounds, and samples of the records, the styles of the dancers, the colors and curves of the graffiti tags. Most importantly, such a study should focus on oral history interviews with German hip hop artists, activists, and spectators. Does their fascination for beats and rhymes go hand in hand with an interest in the social and political problems of African Americans? What do they know about the ghetto that figures so prominently in the records to which they listen? Does the multicultural, antiracist philosophy of rap have any lasting consequences on the thinking of these young Germans? And how do minority Germans relate their own situation to that of African Americans, whose dancing and rapping they find so attractive? These questions could yield some fascinating insights into today's German-American contact. As for the oral history project proposed here: rappers are among the most well-spoken youth around. They love to talk, they do it with a passion— that's what rap is all about. The opportunity to let them talk to us should not be missed.

This survey only scratched the surface of hip hop culture and rap music in Germany. Some 6,000 young Germans participate actively in the hip hop community as rappers, breakdancers, graffiti artists, as passionate spectators. At this moment, however, hip hop activists claim that the German rap scene is losing its vitality. Tight public budgets force many of the youth centers where the scene originated to cut down on programs.

Hip hop jams are taking place less and less frequently, and the use of drugs seems to have gone up again. Increasingly, gangs cause problems.[23] Yet hundreds of thousands of young Germans purchase records and visit concerts of German rap crews such as Die Fantastischen Vier and Rödelheim Hartreim Projekt. More and more German-language rap acts are signed by major record companies. Clever managers design synthetic groups such as Dortmund-based Tic Tac Toe that dominate the market without ever having had contact with the hip hop scene. Thus, German rap faces a test: Will it survive without the nourishing, state-financed network provided by youth centers? Will the truly gifted, funny, aggressive, sophisticated, street-smart rappers find means to counter the challenge posed by the shallow rhymes of these hip hop-clones? They probably will: not only do they have the "right to rap," they also have the skills.

Notes

1. On Madonna's appropriation of black styles, see Bell Hooks, *Black Looks. Race and Representation* (Boston: South End Press, 1992), 157–64.

2. The author wishes to thank all the hip hop artists and activists he interviewed in the course of this project, some of whom are not named in this article, for their time and their cooperation. Most of all, the author is grateful for their music.

3. Diedrich Diederichsen, *Freiheit macht arm. Das Leben nach Rock 'n' Roll* (Köln: Kiepenheuer & Witsch, 1993), 254.

4. Günter Jacob, "Differenz und Diskurs. Zum Umgang mit importiertem Hip Hop," *Rap*, ed. Wolfgang Karrer and Ingrid Kerkhoff (Hamburg: Argument, 1996), 170–72; Günter Jacob, *Agit-Pop. Schwarze Musik für weiße Hörer* (Berlin: Edition ID-Archiv, 1993), 193.

5. Wolfgang Karrer and Ingrid Kerkhoff, eds., *Rap* (Hamburg: Argument, 1996); Adam Sexton, ed., *Rap on Rap. Straight-Up Talk on Hip-Hop Culture* (New York: Delta, 1995); Tricia Rose, *Black Noise. Rap Music and Black Culture in Contemporary America* (Hanover, N. H.: Wesleyan University Press, 1994); Andrew Ross and Tricia Rose, eds., *Microphone Fiends. Youth Music and Youth Culture* (New York: Routledge, 1994); Tim Brennan, "Off the Gangsta Tip: A Rap Appreciation, or Forgetting about Los Angeles," *Critical Inquiry* 20 (1994): 663–93; David Toop, *Rap Attack 2. African Rap to Global Hip Hop*, 2nd ed. (London: Serpent's Tail, 1991).

6. Rose, 36

7. Toop, 57–60.

8. Cora E., personal interview, 8 February 1997.

9. Thomas Fuchs, "Hip Hop in Deutschland," *Rap*, ed. Karrer and Kerkhoff, 167; Christoph Ribbat, "Borrowed Beats and Native Tongues: Multicultural Rap in Germany," in *German-American Cultural Review* (spring 1997): 14–17.

10. Cora E., *Schlüsselkind*, EMI, 1996.

11. Cora E., personal interview, 8 February 1997.

12. Imran Ayata and Annette Weber, "Türkischsprachiger Hip Hop in Deutschland," *Spex* (August 1997): 32–35

13. Rolf Klose, "'Looking for the Perfect Beat'! Hip Hop als neue 'Jugendmusikbewegung' und die Möglichkeiten für die Jugendarbeit," Master's thesis, Fachhochschule Düsseldorf, 1993, 70.

14. Gandy Chahine and Bünyamin Aslan, personal interview, 28 January 1997.

15. Rose, 34–35.

16. Cribb 199, "No Panic, No Stress," EMI, 1996.

17. Ayata and Weber, 34.

18. Ayse Caglar, "Verordnete Rebellion: Deutsch-türkischer Rap und türkischer Pop in Berlin," *Globalkolorit: Multikulturalismus und Populärkultur*, ed. Ruth Mayer and Mark Terkessidis (St. Andrä: Hannibal, 1998) 41–56.

19. Kinderzimmer Productions, "I Got a Right to Sing the Blues," "U-Stadt and You Don't Stop," *Im Auftrag ewiger Jugend und Glückseligkeit*, EFA, 1996.

20. Schiffmeister, König Boris, Dr. Renz (Fettes Brot), personal interview, 10 February 1999.

21. Ibid.

22. Der Lange (rapper, Dortmund), personal interview, 15 July 1997.

23. Yan Mangels (MZEE hip hop agency, Cologne), personal interview, 12 February 1997.

IV   The Empire Strikes Back

Masako Notoji

Cultural Transformation of John Philip Sousa and Disneyland in Japan

American popular culture products, from music to fast food to theme parks, appear to standardize tastes and lifestyles around the world. But, in actuality, the values and meanings attached to such exports are often reconstructed and redefined within the contexts of the importing societies. As one of the world's most enthusiastic consumers of things American, Japan has digested and domesticated quintessentially American cultural symbols into powerful vehicles of its own social change. John Philip Sousa's marches, for example, have been incorporated into highly regimented athletic events in Japanese public schools to become a familiar part of the country's official educational culture. The Japanese have also accepted Disneyland, another key symbol of America's self-celebration, by stripping its ideological content and using the Japanese interpretations of globalization and individual happiness. Using these examples, this essay analyzes the forces that transform and repackage American cultural imports in foreign markets.

I became interested in John Philip Sousa some years ago while doing research on the World's Columbian Exposition of 1893. I was comparing American cultural nationalism as exercised through the Chicago fair, alongside the claims of modernity and the uniqueness of culture that the Japanese government attempted to make at the fair. By the opening of the Chicago fair, Sousa was already being referred to as the "March King" and was the most popular musical figure of his day. Born of immigrant parents (his father was Portuguese and his mother Bavarian), Sousa unified the previous musical traditions of unpretentious Irish bandmasters and disciplined German conductors. He became the fourteenth and the first American-born leader of the U.S. Marine Band but, in 1892, left his low-salaried government job to organize his own civilian band. The

219

Sousa Band conducted an enormously successful series of concerts at the Chicago fairground. If the Chicago Exposition of 1893 was the "first expression of American thought as a unity," as Henry Adams stated, Sousa's patriotic music heralded the glory of America's national destiny.

The Sousa legacy continues one century later, as witnessed by former president Reagan's signing of "The Stars and Stripes Forever" into America's official national march in 1987. Witness also the conspicuous use of Sousa in the Atlanta Olympic opening ceremony in 1996. This much is perhaps common knowledge for most Americans and those familiar with American culture. But how do we interpret the continuing popularity of Sousa in places outside the United States? Sousa's music is also widely known across the Pacific, with or without its Americanism.

The question of cultural nationalism struck me when I was discussing Sousa with my undergraduate students at the University of Tokyo. In my seminar on American popular culture, we read an article in which the historian Neil Harris stated that Sousa's marches "remain a major national treasure, disciplined statements of exuberance *as unmistakably American as the Strauss waltz is Viennese*" (emphasis mine). Then I played for the class a CD containing representative Sousa marches. As we listened to "Stars and Stripes Forever," "Washington Post March," "The Invincible Eagle," "Liberty Bell," and so on, my Japanese students said that they were familiar with every one of them and that these marches evoked not the patriotic images of America, but the fond memories of their own childhoods.

In Japan, Sousa's marches are widely associated with a major sports event in public schools, called "undokai." This athletic event is usually held annually or biannually in the primary and secondary schools for the purpose of building students' physical strength and to teach them the virtue of discipline and team spirit. It is a whole day event, involving the entire school, and parents and other adults in the community participate as enthusiastic spectators. The program usually contains individual and group competitions in footrace, tug-of-war and other games, group calisthenics and dances, and, yes, marches. Sousa's military marches provide essential background music for the excitement of the event. The Japanese are a people who believe in rehearsals, and the whole program of the sports day rituals is rehearsed for weeks. Having gone through the Japanese public educational system myself, I, too, connect Sousa with my personal memories of the school sports day. However, I also spent many years living in Los Angeles, where I saw how Americans react to Sousa's music played during July Fourth events in the Hollywood Bowl and other public parks. As a result, I have come to associate Sousa more with his native land. Thus, it was curious to discover that Sousa continues to symbolize the excitement of sports day for today's younger generation of Japanese.

Historically, the concept of the Japanese sports day came from both Great Britain and the United States. It was spread to public schools to inculcate in the minds of the very young patriotic sentiment and a realistic image of Japan as a newly born nation-state. Interestingly, this official system of modernizing and mobilizing youths was grafted onto the premodern, folk tradition of community festivals and resulted in a strange mixture of pseudo-military drill practice and outdoor, communal picnic. After the Second World War, sports events lost their militaristic components, but marches remained, with the dominant musical accompaniment still Sousa.

Exactly when the use of Sousa marches began is not clear. There is evidence, however, that Sousa's music was widely played by the Japanese Military and Navy Bands, as well as high school bands. The first time Sousa ever played in Japan was in 1905 at an outdoor concert in Tokyo's Hibiya Park, the first Western-style public park in Japan. Included in the program was "Stars and Stripes Forever," along with "Tales of the Vienna Woods" by Johann Strauss. It is intriguing to note that even at a 1908 concert celebrating the Japanese Emperor's birthday, Sousa's "Revival March" was the piece played for the grand finale.

The gradual worsening of Japanese-U.S. relations and the buildup of Japanese military power in the 1930s discouraged the public performance of American music, particularly jazz. But major record companies continued to produce records of Sousa marches until 1941. Between 1927 and 1941, as many as 53 Sousa records, 15 of which contained "Stars and Stripes Forever," were released, which suggests the presence of an enthusiastic listening audience. In 1932, Sousa died at the age of 78. Major Japanese newspapers and magazines mourned the passing of the "March King." One music critic wrote, "Sousa's music has a distinct personality. When you listen to a Sousa march, even if it's the first time you hear that particular piece, you immediately know it's Sousa. Cheerful and sweet while solid, it's a beautiful, exhilarating piece of music. If anyone dares criticize Sousa, I'll be ready to take up the fight at any time" (translated by the author). Considering the rise of anti-American sentiment in the 1930s, this kind of friendly reference to Sousa is surprising.

After Japan entered into the Pacific War, the performance of American marches was forbidden by the government, but young Japanese students continued to play Sousa in school bands. One student band member, Kiyoshi Oishi, remembers how, when he was drafted into the army in December 1943, his schoolmates sent him off by playing "Stars and Stripes Forever." While this may seem like the absolutely wrong piece of music with which to send off a Japanese soldier about to fight the United States, Oishi explained that it is only strange in retrospect. At the time, it seemed a completely appropriate tune for the occasion.

This episode and the association of Sousa with nostalgic memories of the school sports day lead us to the question of what it means to love Sousa without making any meaningful associations with the United States. The globalization of the "American Way of Life" and things American since the beginning of the twentieth century has alarmed intellectuals in the rest of the world, who worry about the "degradation" and "colonization" of traditional cultures by the all-powerful cultural imperialism of the United States. This line of argument, however, assumes the dominating and unilateral influence of the "sending culture" over the "receiving culture," and lacks an understanding of the dynamic process in which the meaning and function of the original culture is reconstructed in the new context of the receiver.

If culture is understood as a system of symbols and meanings, what a particular symbol means has to be learned. Symbols are also polysemic; there is no one-to-one relationship between symbolic signifiers and their objects. For example, the stars and stripes of the American flag stand for the United States of America only by an agreement between American citizens and their federal government. This conventional code has to be learned, since the connection between the flag and the country is arbitrary. By the same token, Sousa's musical piece "The Stars and Stripes Forever" for Americans represents patriotism, which is learned through the process of socialization and performative experience. But the same music may represent something entirely different for other groups of people.

For the Japanese mentioned in this paper, the identification of "Stars and Stripes Forever" with a sense of camaraderie with their old schoolmates eclipsed their knowledge of the foreign origin of the music. There is no doubt that the widespread popularity of Sousa in Japan was part of the Americanization of modern Japanese culture, but, at the same time, there was a "domesticating" and "Japanizing" process at work. To understand the transformation of Sousa in Japan, we need to analyze carefully the changing relationship between the music's composer and the music's interpreters within the context of ongoing social interaction. Through a long process of incorporation into the official school culture (endorsed by both the central bureaucracy of the Ministry of Education and local school boards) and with the particular association with a nationalistic sports event in public schools, Sousa has been transformed from America's national treasure into a symbol of Japan's self-celebration.

With this in mind, it is not surprising that the Japanese tour of the newly created Sousa Band enjoyed popular, nationwide acclaim in July

1996. I went to one of the concerts, which was attended by Japanese of all ages. After the more formal repertoire of classical music was over, Keith Brion and his New Sousa Band began to play the familiar Sousa marches. Suddenly, the whole place turned into something resembling a boisterous family reunion. The concert brochure made note of the Japan Sousa Society, a group founded by 18 Japanese Sousa fans on 6 November, 1993 to commemorate Sousa's 139th birthday. Many of the 18 became hooked on Sousa through playing in high school bands; the president of the society was the music director of the Tokyo Division of the Japanese Marine Band. Currently, the Japan Sousa Society has nearly 100 members, who meet monthly to listen to Sousa records, study Sousa's history, promote the performance of Sousa, and exchange information with Sousa-lovers overseas.

It was just one month after the overwhelming success of the New Sousa Band that I read a newspaper report that the Chinese state television officials had deleted Sousa's "Stars and Stripes Forever" from a televised concert program of American music. This gesture may or may not tell us anything about the popular attitudes of Chinese toward Sousa, but the newspaper article reminded me of the French intellectuals who denounced Euro-Disneyland as a "cultural-Chernobyl." Located in the suburbs of Paris, Euro-Disney is the fourth Disney theme park. Disneyland's Tokyo version has achieved even greater success than its predecessors in the United States, attracting more than 15 million visitors every year, and continues to thrive. If Sousa for the Chinese and Disney for the French meant American cultural invasion, these American imports were quickly absorbed into the indigenous system of values and practices in Japan.

If you live in Japan, hardly a day goes by without stumbling into something Disney. Disney merchandise is everywhere on the street and in people's homes. When I go to my branch of the Tokyo-Mitsubishi bank, I see the smiling Mickey Mouse soliciting customers to deposit their biannual bonus into the bank. At Japanese weddings, the newlywed couple very often dances to music from Disney's *Beauty and the Beast* or *Aladdin*. The most common gift for a newborn baby is a Disney product; a journalist friend told me that he and his wife were quite disturbed that the very first word their child uttered was "Mickey." I was also surprised when my aunt, who recently survived cancer surgery, told me that she will be able to die in peace if she can once visit Tokyo Disneyland with her granddaughter.

Of course, there are many Japanese who could not care less about Disney, but the Disney phenomenon has hit a large enough cross-section of Japanese age groups and social classes to warrant a serious anthropological inquiry. What is it about the magic of Disney that fascinates the

Japanese to such extremes? It may be that the coming of Disneyland to Japan was a natural evolution of the Americanization of postwar Japan. During this period of rapid economic growth, the idea of democracy was strategically tied to consumerism by both the government and corporate sectors, and America has played a significant role as a model of the good life and an equitable middle-class society. The buildup of a large-scale domestic market for household domestic appliances, for example, was supported by the gendered ideology that housewives were the central actors of the affluent, democratic family. Americanization of the Japanese lifestyle was thus rendered less threatening to Japanese cultural integrity by having women as the agent of social change. One might call this process a "female filter" through which a potentially dangerous foreign culture loses its hard edge. Incidentally, automobiles—another symbol of imported technology—were initially given feminine names such as Violet, Blue Bird, and Fair Lady, which is the Japanese name for the Nissan Z sports car.

By the early 1980s, when nearly 90 percent of Japanese felt that they had achieved middle-class status and found themselves surrounded by electronic gadgets and high-tech cars, consumer interest shifted from material things toward more intangible symbols of individual happiness. The opening of Tokyo Disneyland filled this cultural void as the Japanese were making the transition from work-oriented to leisure-oriented values. Again, it was women, young and old, who flooded the Disney park, and the Disney culture has in general assumed a more feminine image in Japan than in the United States.

However, to understand the success of Tokyo Disneyland within the framework of Americanization alone would only be answering the question halfway. For on the other side of the same coin is a display of Japanese cultural nationalism. After the initial shock phase passed, the Japanese began to see Tokyo Disneyland as their playground. It may have been made in America, but it was theirs nonetheless. The fact that this Disney park is fully owned and operated by a Japanese corporation has added to the feeling that it is a Japanese enterprise. Tokyo Disneyland is commonly referred to as larger and cleaner than the American original. Many older Japanese also say that Tokyo Disneyland helps them appreciate the peace and prosperity of Japan, that the Japanese have come a long way from the hardships of war to the age of affluence. There have also been efforts to feature traditional Japanese holidays and costumes in special Tokyo Disneyland events, so it is not uncommon to see Mickey and Minnie in kimonos.

For the younger generation of Japanese, Tokyo Disneyland is a stage on which to act out different identities. Taking the hodgepodge of fictionalized narratives from the medieval Cinderella castle to the pirates of the Caribbean to the dark thrills of space travel, young visitors to the park become playful actors of their own fantasies. After visiting the park enough times that there are no more new discoveries, Japanese visitors' reactions become theatrical; each has his/her own routine of exactly when to say "Wow!," when to scream, and when to sing along with Mickey Mouse. The Americanness of the place only adds to their feeling of freedom, loosening their inhibiting image of everyday life and their place in it.

This reflects the general inclination of the Japanese to use bits of American or any other foreign culture to recreate their own identities. In other words, the whole world has become a giant lifestyle catalog, and the America that young Japanese are especially likely to choose is that of the 1950s. Disneyland has freeze-dried the cultural vitality and dazzling youth imagery of fifties' America, and the Japanese can thus daydream their own eternal youth and prosperity.

We have seen that the process of Americanization in Japan has gone hand in hand with a careful safeguarding of the native culture. The strategy of feminization is one important method of domestication. Another is the sanction of official authorities, which gives prestige to and certifies the safety of foreign imports. Just as John Philip Sousa has become a familiar icon (and tune) in the official school rituals of Japan, so too has Tokyo Disneyland become a sanctioned place for school trips. The Japanese who grew up the 1950s remember being taken to see Disney movies as part of their school curricula. Present-day English-language textbooks contain biographical essays on Walt Disney and the lyrics of popular Disney songs. Japanese high school bands, which have long played the tunes of John Philip Sousa, now include Disney melodies on their program. Disney's "Fantillusion," the theme music to a new Disneyland nighttime parade, is part of almost every school band concert.

On the surface, the Japanese may appear to be tireless and indiscriminate cultural consumers. But the foreignness of imported culture, and particularly American culture, is filtered through the careful hands of cultural brokers. As we have seen in the cases of Sousa and Disney, American culture is deconstructed and recontextualized into the everyday experience of the people. American popular culture is not the monopoly of Americans; it is a medium through which people around the world constantly reorganize their individual and collective identities. We may perhaps better understand American culture if we see it as the totality of the ideas and practices that people everywhere project onto and perform around the symbols that originated in the United States.

While standing on the street corner in Lisbon, Portugal, the country of John Philip Sousa's ancestors, I witnessed people enjoying McDonald's and Pizza Hut and children wearing Disney clothes. They remind me not of some street scenes in America, but of my home in Tokyo. It's tempting simply to note that "it's a small world after all," but it is more complex than that. We must continue to explore the possibilities of every diversifying use and definition of "America."

Myles Dungan and David Gray

Consumption of American Pop Culture in Ireland and England

Introduction (Myles)

The globalization of American culture is not a victimless crime. We are its victims. We are not only students of American culture, but consumers. Therefore, we want to focus on some of the many ways in which non-Americans respond to what are often classified as American cultural products. (We speak as an Irish and an English person with a knowledge of what applies to those countries, a fair degree of knowledge of what applies to Britain, and much less of what goes on elsewhere in Europe.) But we will refer occasionally to "Europe," because much of what we discuss pertains also to Europe more broadly. So how do we "Europeans" deal with American influences? The answer is necessarily multifold:

1. *Disapproval and the cultural sunblock*: We censor in cultural terms or we impose tariffs and controls in economic terms. We know already about the different American cultural products that were censored for different reasons in a variety of different societies. For instance, *The Cosby Show* was banned in South Africa during the Apartheid era for portraying too positive an image of black people and for showing them competing, and relating on an equal footing with, whites; the film *Natural Born Killers* was rejected as too violent in Ireland and other countries (despite what valid points the film made about the culture of violence and the way that the media deals with it). We blockade economically by imposing tariffs and quotas, even (and post-GATT, especially) against cultural products.[1]
2. *Unqualified love and acceptance*: As in "Crack open another Miller's honey, *Cheers* will be on TV in a minute!" (self-explanatory).

3. *Blank incomprehension*: As in, "Nice T-shirt you're wearing. Ever *been* to Harvard?" "No, I bought it in the local department store because I liked the color. I just wish it didn't have this stupid writing on it."

We're not going to deal with the above in any more detail than that. Instead, we'll devote our attention to the remaining three categories. David and I take turns explaining our respective English and Irish viewpoints.

4. *Arm's-length admiration and ironic consumption*
5. *Bemused rejection*
6. *Incorporation and re-exportation*

Arm's-Length Admiration

David Levinthal's notion of "A past that never was and always will be" is particularly fitting here. The English and the Irish have both appropriated facets of America's frontier mythology, and thereby contributed in different ways to America's cultural mythmaking. The mythology of the West—the Wild West, the frontier—occupies a central place in the European psyche as a key American cultural motif. The West of the American (and others') imagination is one that, while never having actually existed, has become so firmly entrenched in America's mythology (among Americans and non-Americans alike) that it has effectively supplanted the real history of the West as historical truth. While we know that the American West is myth, we are often blissfully unaware of the *real* version, and are therefore complicit in America's ongoing reinvention of itself. The mythology of the West is familiar to all of us. It is the world of bedtime stories from our own society. It's Sherwood Forest, Camelot without the "noblesse," the Norse Sagas without the boats. It's *El Cid, Ben Hur*. It is not entirely myth, but it is hardly history either. We've seen it all before; the West is an American reworking of the myths and stories that are part of our humanity, our collective consciousness.

The American West in the Irish Subconscious (Myles)

The desire of non-American cultures to embrace American myth is evinced in its own cinema. The Irish film *Into the West* appropriates various elements of the mythology of the American West in its depiction of the rootless lives of a family of Irish travelers, or "tinkers." The life of the traveling community in the film is nomadic, and based on dealing (in scrap, furniture, or anything else). They have their own argot—Pavee.

The film is also about a horse, and here's where the Western resonances begin. But this is a white horse—which has entirely different mythic connotations—and its name is Tir an n-Og—which has Irish mythic connotations relating to the "Land of Youth."

In one scene (while sitting on Tir an n-Og in their council flat) protagonists and brothers Ossie and Teto reveal their identification with the West:

> Ossie (to his older brother, Teto): Was there a wild west in Ireland?
> Teto: There still is—on the other side of the mountains.
> Ossie: Then are we travelers the Indians?
> Teto: No, we're the cowboys.

Teto's identification with cowboys is interesting in a number of ways. The travelers have the rootlessness of cowboys, and the term "cowboy" is used in Ireland as an insult, one which is often appended to the mercantile pursuits of travelers, or "cowboy operators" who peddle questionable goods. However, they are actually much more akin to the Indians in that they have been systematically chased off "the road" (a term I use in a rock 'n' roll sense). Their culture has been denied and subjugated, as was that of Native Americans. And the stereotype they carry is of lazy, drunken, welfare cheats who mistreat their wives—attributes not uncommonly levied at Native Americans by the dominant culture. But the film is all about the escape to the West—the West of Ireland—a new frontier, a mystical, mythical place with resonances of the Wild West and the old Irish legends. It is about the escape from cramped urban spaces to the "other" space we are all supposed to cherish. It is also about the escape from rigid social controls, another key motif of the western. Because of the way in which a changing and modernizing society often rejects and turns away from many of its folk traditions and myths or legends (before ultimately turning back to many of them), the film might not have worked for an Irish audience without the secondary theme of the parallel escape into the west, the American West. The play on Celtic Mythology would not have been sufficient. The success of the film is also interesting in terms of the incorporation and re-exportation of American culture. Although it was a small budget film, which was only possible because Gabriel Byrne wanted to make it, and because he had his (now ex) wife, American actress Ellen Barkin, play a part, *Into the West* did quite nicely in the United States.

Down Our Noses: "Ironic" English Consumption of American Cultural Products (David)

While, as Myles points out, the Irish have a certain affinity with the mythology of the American West, the English also are not averse to enjoying and finding meaning in expressions of American popular mythology. We do so through American television, literature, music, and its cinema. And those of us who visit America can do so through our own experience. However, an enduring sense of lofty superiority among the English generally makes us more apprehensive about buying into America's more celebratory and self-affirming ideologies. (I am referring here to an attitude that is rather tritely expressed among the English generally, though by the British more broadly). That is, when we do consume and enjoy American popular culture, we often do so with a somewhat pompous sense of irony, embracing those American cultural products that confirm—warts and all—the popular view of American culture as unsophisticated and absurd. This allows us to enjoy American culture while mocking those aspects that our own culture rejects as tacky, superficial, or "typically American." This allows us to regard our consumption of American popular culture less as an expression of flattery, and more as an opportunity to revel in the belief that we were right about how unsophisticated and debased American culture was all along while also bolstering our sense of grandeur. Celebrating those cultural products (for example, television shows and cult literature) which astutely confirm these views allows us to tell ourselves that we're mocking America when, in fact, they allow us to participate in and enjoy a culture that we find perversely alluring. It seems that we want it both ways. We want to enjoy the vital, tuned-in side of American culture (through those cultural products which confirm the America of our imaginations) while maintaining the position of elevated, haughty voyeurs. A case of using America's insight into its own predicament to heighten our own cultural status.

The Simpsons: Confirming the America of Our Imaginations (David)

The paradoxical, love-hate regard for American culture and the necessity for American cultural products to mirror our preconceptions of America is witnessed in our love of The Simpsons. The show has climbed to its present cult status (it is watched by over three million British viewers every week) from mid-1980s relative obscurity as a filler on the Tracey Ullman Show (a rare case of a British television star being more enthusiastically embraced by an American audience than at home). While we love each of the Simpsons for their particular idiosyncrasies, it is primarily Homer's vacuousness and need for immediate gratification that we find so hilarious. These are the very characteristics of American culture that are so often ridiculed in common English parlance. Homer's sheer stupidity and his inability to grasp anything outside of his Duff-beer-TV mindset appeal to us because they mirror the popular English image of the American psyche. It is the intelligent and socially astute Lisa, how-ever, who provides the necessary balance, a glimmer of hope that, be-neath the veneer of vacuousness, more insightful Americans lurk. Our identification with Lisa's frustration with the absurdity of her family and the culture that surrounds them allows us to affirm our disapproval of similar traits, many of which are often blamed on American influence (game-show culture, junk food, advertising, corporatism—just look at our TV and media and witness the spread of American-style recreational complexes) creeping dangerously into our own culture. While we tend to laugh loudest at those observations which accentuate the cultural traits that we identify with Americans more broadly, there is an underlying sense that our own culture is increasingly resonant with the one satirized in *The Simpsons*. While ostensibly the English love *The Simpsons* be-cause it neatly confirms the America and Americans of our imaginations, privately, the show is pertinent because it chimes with our fears about the fate of our own culture. We might like to imagine ourselves as bookish observers, ruefully lamenting cultural debasement at home and farther afield, but actually, we enjoy junk culture just as much as anyone else. (In fact, the British eat more junk food than any other Europeans, watch more television than most, and also have particularly high alcohol con-sumption.) While we might take delight in reading *The Simpsons* as an allegory for the American psyche, the world that it parodies is one that is ominously familiar.

Enlisting "Insightful" Americans to Prove Us Right (David)

Homer et al. are not the only Americans that English enthusiasts of American culture have enlisted in enjoying the America of our imagina-tions. Some of the most useful allies in our mission to reveal America for what we believe (and want) it to be have been cult and popular American writers. There is a (condescending) tendency among some English ob-servers to regard astute American writers as "exceptions to the rule." The work of the beat poets, of acerbic writers like Hunter S. Thompson and Charles Bukowski, or of more widely read American writers who have dramatized the madness or absurdity of American life, such as Thomas Pynchon and Joseph Heller, has been read by English readers with a cer-tain sense of highbrow authority. While their work seems to confirm most readers' beliefs about the underlying perversity of modern Ameri-can culture, the impulse of the English to maintain cultural authority en-tails darker motives. Our admiration for such writers is often based on a feeling that they're exposing the "real" America, one that is somehow de-nied in "official" discourse. Whether it's Bukowski's autobiographical

Post Office in which Henry Chinaski negotiates a self-destructive struggle against the postal service, Yossarian's bizarre struggle against a bureaucratic military establishment during World War II in Heller's *Catch-22*, or Oedipa Mass's search for meaning in Pynchon's *The Crying of Lot 49*, when American writers expose their own culture for the fantastic dystopia that we like to think it is, we are much more likely to eulogize them. If we can enlist "insightful" Americans to our mission to bolster our own loftiness by proving that we were right all along, then all the better for our quest for cultural ascendancy.

This tendency is witnessed in the popularity in Britain of Michael Moore's explorations into the darker side of American corporatism in his documentary series *TV Nation* and film *The Big One*. Moore, an ex-General Motors worker at Flint, Michigan, was so incensed at losing his job that he embarked on a crusade to expose the injustices of American corporatism. Alongside a brigade of disenchanted workers or ex-workers, or alongside mascot Crackers, the Corporate Crime-Fighting Chicken, Moore confronts corporate directors who have abused their workforces (General Motors, Disney, Nike, for example). While English audiences tend to appreciate Moore's crusade, it is not so much the righteousness of his mission that we are gripped by as the absurdity of the society that he is exposing. At the end of the show, therefore, we are more likely to nod our heads knowingly, while proclaiming, "Only in America!" As our "other" space, Moore's America is a place that we dip into for a while in order to pick up some reference points for our stock view of America as the capital of corporate corruption. But this timeworn tendency of the English to embrace Americans who parody or criticize their own culture can become tiresome (and offensive) when overplayed. Indeed, we have an inclination to give such Americans positive reinforcement, implying that they are merely unfortunate (but "insightful") victims of a dysfunctional culture. (Moore has been referred to in this way).

The extremely popular American author and journalist Bill Bryson has received a similar reception in Britain in recent years. Anyone who has read *Lost Continent* (an account of his road trip through the United States) will be familiar with the way that Americans are often viewed from our side of the pond. In *Lost Continent*, Bryson (originally from Des Moines, Iowa, but now moving sporadically between America and the U.K.) paints a landscape inhabited by the very Americans that the English always liked to imagine it was. Bryson's travel journal depicts an America characterized by extremes. The gratuitous glitz and exhibitionism of burger-culture and twenty-four-hour shopping is contrasted with backwater small towns whose parochial inhabitants regard the traveling author with either suspicion or vapidity. In his search for the America of *his* imagination, Bryson gives us dense K-Mart shoppers ("Every woman in there has at least four children and they all look as if they have been fathered by a different man"); provincial Midwestern women with butterfly glasses and beehive hairdos (Gary Larson's *Far Side* cartoons brought to life), and Southern rednecks ("Backward undereducated shit-kickers"). Bryson's strategy relies on his shrewd awareness of just the kinds of stereotypes that the English love to hold about Americans. These are largely based on well-established English stereotypes of backwater Americans and American tourists. The main characteristics of the latter include:

- Loud, uninhibited voices in public places (always a cue for the English to roll their eyes and "tut" to each other).
- Fashion crimes: Baseball cap with team name, Hawaiian shirt, long socks, camera (the archetypal American tourist garb); sweatshirts adorned with university name splashed brazenly across the chest (the English/British are rarely as demonstrative of any pride they may have for their academic institution).
- Parochial worldview: Old adages such as, "Oh, you're English! Do you know the Queen?" Or, "Spain? Isn't that in Mexico?" (I did actually hear someone say this last one).

Taken together, these enduring English stereotypes boil down to the belief that Americans are vacuous, eternally unsophisticated, and have a distinct lack of social etiquette. The problem is that we have learned these stereotypes largely from English television portrayals of Americans and from American tourists themselves, who are after all not exactly representative of Americans more generally. (Our beer-swilling, loutish visitors to Spain give the English a similarly unfortunate reputation across Europe.) Furthermore, only about five percent of Americans have passports, and those who do travel outside the United States are obviously going to look and act like tourists. Nevertheless, these are some of the stereotypes that Bryson's somewhat contrived take on his own culture panders to.

Bryson's works are extremely palatable to English readers because they allow us to enjoy the America of our imaginations (what Myles and I call our "other" space). And, like Bryson, anyone who has enjoyed a road trip through America will know that this is probably the best way to experience the America of our imaginations, to live out the movie scenes that we were brought up on. I myself was confronted by the archetypal Rod Steigeresque Southern cop during my own road trip. Ironically enough for me, this was in a town called London in Kentucky. My (Minnesotan) girlfriend and I were driving through there during spring break

1998 in search of a motel but had jumped out of the car to take a photograph of a large sign that seemed to confirm our idea of Southern law enforcement perfectly. It read, in large red and blue letters: "Re-elect Ed Parsley: Jailer." Having had our fun for a couple of minutes, we gleefully hopped back into the car and drove away, only to see flashing police lights in the rear-view mirror. What followed was pure movie scene stuff. A rotund, crewcutted cop approached my window and, mopping his sweaty brow, chewing gum inside bloated cheeks, said in a Southern drawl, "Where ya from, Boy?" "England," I replied. "Yeah, well this here's a dry county . . . you been drinkin?" . . . "No." (He repeated this line of questioning several times during the conversation.) Then he spied the two empty 3.2 beer cans on the back seat that we had drank hours earlier, and, in no time, he had me out of the car and blowing into his face while he shone his big cop's torch into my face and sniffed my breath in a way that made me feel rather uncomfortable. "When did ya drink those beers?" he demanded. "This here's a dry county. Drinkin' alcohol's an arrestable offence!" I now had visions of waking up in a cell with a good ole' boy grinning and breathing into my face. He continued to sniff and added, "Ya been eatin' mints, aintcha, Boy?" . . . "Yes, but I haven't been drinking, I just like tic-tacs." Then it got a little weird. He asked me, "Do you know anyone from Ireland?" I thought of mentioning my Grandad but thought better of it. "No," I replied. "Do you know anyone called Waylon, boy?" I thought of mentioning Waylon Jennings, to break the tension, but again answered (wisely I am sure), that I didn't. "Well that's me, Boy!—Sheriff Waylon!—and I want ya to know my name cuz ahm-a cuttin' ya a deal today, and lettin' ya go! . . . But see, this here's a *drrrrrrrrrry* county . . . and there ain't no alcohol for another eighty miles, so if I was you, ahd jist keep drivin' on that-a-way." After rummaging through our ice-box and having one last sniff of my girlfriend's breath, he ambled back to his patrol car, and then shadowed us for a mile or two, gazing at us at three sets of traffic lights to be sure we weren't hanging around to bring further chaos to his orderly town.

So here was the South of our imaginations. One where menacing local cops hung around waiting to run college kids with out-of-state plates out of town. Rod Steiger's sheriff was alive and kicking in London, Kentucky, and it made our day, by allowing us to live that movie scene (and live to tell the tale over a pint of decent bitter in good old blighty, which is after all, the most important part for English voyeurs of American culture like me who are keen to experience and talk about the America of our imaginations). The English, like the Irish, also grew up on a diet of Hollywood films and therefore have similar investments in enjoying

American mythology, and such experiences as these allow us to experience a little piece of it (in this case, a slice of Southern hospitality in the mode of *In the Heat of the Night* without the racial intimidation, or, say, *Deliverance* without the actual physical abuse). Being run out of town by a Southern sheriff is probably the closest I am likely to get to a frontier experience. While the stereotypes do exist, they are just as much a part of our imaginations as of reality. Experiencing them, either directly or through movies and books, allows the English to revel in the certainty that America is indeed the very place, and is inhabited by the very people that we always claimed it was.

The "Sneaking Regarders" (Myles)

While the English adopt complicated systems in order to enjoy the parts of American culture that they either admire or find useful in reinforcing their self-esteem, in Ireland, the paradoxical regard for American culture is revealed in the existence of a race we call the "sneaking regarders." The Irish, of course, do not have the legacy of having been former "masters" as do the English, and therefore do not share the English urge to "save face" by having to employ such strategies as David has described. In Irish myth, the man who steps into the line of fire is very often a tragic figure, one whose bravery is admirable, but who is brushed aside and gives way to the less obviously courageous figure, or even to the villain.

America remains the world's "other space." We "play" at being Americans (just as Americans play at being Irish or English), but, ultimately, the mythical U.S. West is part of our "other space." This is not "our" space, however. American society, in theory, at any rate, prizes the individual and his or her rights. Other countries' cultures don't even pay lip service to the sort of attitude suggested by the "cult of the individual" inherent in the American Western. We may sneakingly admire the man who takes on the bad guys and does the job himself—the Gary Cooper figure who is let down by his peers and stands alone—but in Europe we don't expect that sort of social breakdown. We don't anticipate having to stand alone. Perhaps, in our own way, we are naive, just as Americans are naive in clinging to the belief that the individual can really perform such heroics and is really prized in American society to the extent that their Westerns would have us believe. So, ultimately, we Irish see the Western as something beguiling. We see in it some aspects of ourselves. We occasionally adapt it. We play around with it (literally, in the case of children). But, despite our sneaking regard for it, we ultimately keep it at arm's length as something emblematic of another culture.

Bemused Rejection

The Case of American Football (Myles)

Consider, now, how the mid-1980s rush of interest in American football has waned, and it is plain that American football does not have the same hold on the British popular imagination that it once did. First, we have to look at why this strange, hybrid game ever made any inroads in the first place. It did so at a time when *the* international sport, football—or soccer, as Americans prefer to call it (what has American football got to do with the feet when only two players on the team are allowed to kick the ball, and then only in certain situations?)—in Europe, was going through a crisis. This crisis culminated with the appalling Heysel Stadium tragedy in which English fans from Liverpool (actually one of the clubs with a more civilized following in the football league at the time) were responsible for the deaths of dozens of Italian supporters.

Many Europeans, especially mortified British people who felt that they could not take their children to soccer matches because of fear of terrace violence, went looking for something else. Along came a new TV channel, Britain's Channel 4. With all the main sports parceled out among the first three British channels, Channel 4 had to find some of its own. Purely as an experiment (it was, after all, an experimental station), it showed an hour of American Football on Sundays, a full week after the games were played. Much to the programmer's surprise, it caught on. Audiences grew from one to four million, a large audience for a minority channel. Then, the NFL discovered that the British had discovered them, as had many other European countries. Thus, they began to export teams for preseason American Bowl games. This was not out any of great desire to open up an NFL franchise in London or Frankfurt this side of the next millennium, mind you, but merely to enhance the international merchandising potential of their product. In other words, they wanted to sell more T-shirts, mugs, towels, and the like. In this endeavor, the NFL succeeded. In conjunction with Budweiser beer, which was attempting to break into European markets at the time, they projected an image of Americanism that was alluring, and that made no pretense to be anything other than outrageously American. But if you believe—as we do—that the product America sells most successfully is America itself, then the result was hardly surprising.

NFL merchandising is still reasonably successful, but the major soccer clubs caught on very quickly, and they have now asserted themselves in that particular marketplace. Manchester United make a tidy profit from merchandising ("Go to bed with Ryan Giggs" duvet covers, for example), while A. C. Milan made four times as much from their merchandising as from tickets. However, while we learned from Americans much about merchandising—though we overdid it to a ridiculously tacky extent—as a sport, American Football has long since peaked and begun to slide in terms of interest. This can be seen in Channel 4's figures. It is evident in terms of the various false starts at getting an NFL World League underway. And it is reflected in the dwindling numbers of Europeans actually playing the game. So, why the waning interest in American football? This is largely due to the game being so utterly alien. As alien as Sumo wrestling (which incidentally, Channel 4 also showed quite successfully) is to European and American audiences.[2]

In what way is it alien? The very nature of the game reflects contradictions inherent in the American myth. The society that is supposed to epitomize the cult of the individual is trying to propagate a sport that is one of the most rigidly schematized, planned, and structured team games ever devised (as well as being one of the most complicated in terms of its rules). It therefore suppresses the individuality that we love in soccer and covertly admire in the Western. Players don't just run, they run patterns. They don't just play, they run plays. Even the quarterback, the playmaker, in nine cases out of ten, is simply being called upon to execute someone else's plan. He's not like the play-making midfielder in soccer who may be following a general, rather than a specific, plan.

In short, in its trappings and philosophy, American football is all too nakedly, pitilessly, "in your face" American. The overt sexism revealed by the presence of cheerleaders is not necessarily American, and perhaps it is better than the old (and not entirely vanished) culture of soccer that looks askance at the very presence of women. The overt violence of the game is something many people find disturbing. The suspicion is that the wearing of all the padding is only a cover for the desire to go out and injure one's opponent. There is a perception that the right to make explosive physical contact with an opponent not in possession of the ball is unduly vicious. On the other hand, there is an entirely contradictory belief that American footballers are "soft" ("girl's blouses" is the Irish expression for their attire) because of all the padding they wear, which rugby players don't. The terminology of the game encourages the macho, violent image, however. The connotations of war abound (e.g., bomb trenches), and even the names of teams such as the "Raiders" and "Chargers" (and they are only in the weak, feminine, and submissive AFC, which has lost the last ten Superbowls) invite comparison to military campaigns and battles.

Then there is the very American philosophy of winning. Somebody has to win. The concept of the draw hardly exists. Even in a league format there has to be a winner and a loser. If not, teams are made to play another fifteen minutes on the clock (or forty-five minutes in real time). The fact that it takes three hours to play an hour-long game is of course another contributory factor to the decline of the game. In football—sorry, *soccer*—the concept of the draw is perfectly acceptable. Even in a knock-out situation, in most countries, there will be a replay of the entire match—sorry, game—before there is any form of "sudden death."

For all of these reasons, American football will always be *American* and will be admired and enjoyed in the way that the western is. But as for getting us to play it, no thanks. There is something vaguely risible about Europeans dressing up as gladiators and playing American football. "Way to go!" doesn't sound quite the same in a Dublin accent. "Jaysus, you made a right bollix of that!" doesn't sound quite the same as "You blew that assignment, kid." As for getting us to watch in the tens of millions, no way. The desire of big advertising spenders in that great transnational state *Corporatia* to have a small number of international icons around whom they can run ads will have to wait.[3] So we'll party on Superbowl night and play at being American, but we won't abandon soccer for American football. The English may have invented soccer, but it is no longer an English game (not since England got walloped by Hungary at Wembley forty years ago). It is also a game capable of reinterpretation in different countries: the Irish and English play it one way, the Dutch and Germans another, the Brazilians an entirely different way. One suspects that were American football ever played internationally at a high level, it would be done . . . the American way.

Incorporation and Re-exportation

It's Only Rock 'n' Roll and We Like It (And It's Ours Too) (Myles)

America gave the world popular music. Thanks! The world would be a poorer place without it. But it would be wrong to see the spread of popular music as an example of Americanization. For a start, so many of the inputs into American music are international anyway, and there have been so many attempts to control or censor its spread that its popularity cannot simply be accounted for by the fact of its Americanness.

I want to deal with one of the more subversive forms of popular music: rock 'n' roll. The attraction of rock 'n' roll lay in the taint of rebellion, and the modernity that was associated with it. Rock 'n' roll *was* an American Kingdom. Elvis was its king. Buddy Holly was its Prince Royal. (It is all documented musically by Don McLean in *American Pie*.) But somewhere around the beginning of the sixties, the scruffy proletariat from England, the "sans culottes" from Liverpool and London, stole the "thorny crown." Rock 'n' roll in the 1960s *was* the Beatles and the Rolling Stones. Europe, which during the dominance of jazz and the big band sound era had made virtually no major contribution to popular music, was now producing mainstream rock 'n' roll, of both an English and a hybrid variety (more English in the case of the Beatles, more hybrid in the case of the Stones); it was then re-exporting it to the United States, where it was lapped up by screaming fans aping *British* behavior and wearing *British* pop fashions culled from the pegs of Carnaby Street. Now how about that!

What was even worse from the point of view of mainstream American popular music was that many of the British groups (the Kinks and The Who were other fine exponents) had been influenced by more than just Elvis and Buddy Holly; that is, by more than the type of music that had been sanitized and "whitened" by the American music industry for home consumption and export. British groups also drew on the originals of the species. These groups were influenced by black artists such as Little Richard, Chuck Berry, and, going even further back, Leadbelly and Muddy Waters, without whom there would never have been an Elvis Presley.

In the 1970s, popular music went down a hole, becoming spoilt, rich, pompous and overbearing. Along came the punk movement, again from Britain, to give it a kick in the ass. To rock 'n' roll, punk was a catalyst rather than an aiding phenomenon in its own right, but it did the necessary deed in time. Out of that revitalization of rock 'n' roll came a new generation of people who had not known a time without the genre. It was *theirs*. America no longer had a monopoly on cool. It belonged to the world. If you played in a rock 'n' roll band in Ireland, England, or Austria, you weren't playing at being an American. You could walk around Dublin, Manchester, or Salzburg in your bondage pants and "Destroy" T-shirt and be cool. And although American punk purists will point out correctly that U.S. bands such as the New York Dolls, Television, the Ramones and Talking Heads predated the Sex Pistols and The Clash by several years . . . well, punk just never had the same impact there as it did in Britain. Interestingly, in the aftermath of punk, Dublin spawned what would eventually become one of the biggest bands in the world: U2. The band's unequaled success in America (with the possible exception of REM) to this day continues to re-export what has traditionally been seen as an American phenomenon: stadium rock.

America in Your Living Room: Consuming American Culture through TV (Myles)

The choice of American cultural products is often an economic rather than a cultural one. American TV is cheaper than European. It has already made back its investment costs in the United States and can be dumped cheaply on the European market. These offerings are hardly much of a threat to European culture except insofar as they prevent home-produced programs from getting to the small screen. Irish and English viewers much prefer their own programs and they usually occupy the top slots in the ratings but are far more expensive. With increasing leisure time (and unemployment—massive in Ireland) there is a demand for dawn-to-dusk TV. Those hours have to be filled with something. So we fill it with cheap material from the United States. We save our home-produced material (on which we spend most of our money) for prime time slots. This is the stuff people want to see, though they will often watch the imports that don't fall into the "must see" category.

Interestingly, now that the Australians have got into the production of cheap bi/tri-weekly soap operas, these have become far more alluring to Irish and English audiences than American soaps (which had their heyday with the weekly *Dallas* and *Dynasty*). Irish and English audiences go for British soaps first, followed by Australian ones (*Neighbours, Home and Away*). Australian soaps have a number of appealing similarities with American culture. English is the spoken language, they have a positive "party" image, and the mix of sun, sand, sea, and sex is as alluring as anything from the United States (where a lot of the material deals with ethnic and often dysfunctional families in a cringingly moralistic manner).

Conclusion: Consuming as Cultural Reconciliation (Myles and David)

When considering the real influence of American culture it is important to realize the impulses that created that culture. What is America? What are Americans? The dominant American language comes from England. Many of its exciting political and philosophical ideas about democracy come from the French enlightenment. It was populated by people who were running away from something, who were marginalized. They were modern in the sense that they brought with them ideas that were too "avant-garde" or revolutionary for the "ancien" societies they fled. Many also brought with them a distaste for the "high" cultures of the societies they left, whose cultural activity they associated with the elite, the ascendancy. In some cases, the distaste was puritanical; in some it was socialistic; in some (such as the Irish), it was an expression of nationalism. So many of the inputs into the American psyche, and thus into its myth creation were also European. It is little wonder, therefore, that somewhere along the line Europe would come to embrace the culture to which it gave birth. Call it a case of cultural reconciliation.

Neither is it surprising, however, that the Irish and the English would have reservations and develop defensive strategies when buying into American popular culture. Whether this takes the form of keeping America at arm's length or looking down our noses at it while enjoying it, this highlights our desire to try to have it both ways. While the Irish and the English each have a dogged determination to maintain the distinct character of their own cultures and are quick to reject (ostensibly at least) elements of American culture (burger culture, corporatism), both do have investments in buying into American popular culture, because as our "other" space, the America of our imaginations is a place where we can experience all the things that are either disapproved of or unavailable in our own cultures. But the "flip-side" of this "other" space is that we also use America as a kind of yardstick (it represents what we fear we might become) against which we gauge the perilous evolution of our own culture. As the Irish and the English have both had such significant inputs into American culture and its national character, and our two cultures seem increasingly resonant with American culture as a result, it is hardly surprising that we each see a little of ourselves in it, and find so many of its cultural products so appealing, even with our tongues firmly in our cheeks.

Notes

1. American film and TV products are made for the mass market, make money before they reach Europe, and can be sold there very cheaply. So, at the insistence of France (behind whose cloak other nations lurk), which wants to protect its film industry and its culture, film was excluded from GATT.

2. (Myles) Let me note that, criticisms aside, I love American football—I broadcast it on TV for six years; I've been to three Superbowls and numerous other games and I love the hype of it all. I just don't like the way that hype is aped in European soccer.

3. (Myles) Campaigns with increased economies of scale promise sports figures who will be as recognizable as Dan Marino in the United States, and Romario everywhere else. However, the closest Corporatia have come is Michael Jordan.

Gülriz Büken

Backlash

An Argument against the Spread of
American Popular Culture in Turkey

> Conventional warfare struck at the heart to kill and then conquer;
> Economic war struck at the belly to exploit and acquire riches;
> Cultural war strikes at the head to paralyze without killing, to
> conquer by slow rot, and to obtain wealth through the
> disintegration of cultures and peoples.
> —Henri Gobbard, *La Guerre Culturelle*

The intensification of the export of American popular culture was an indispensable facet of America's economic expansionist policy during the post–World War II years. America had ample opportunity to boost its market economy by disseminating consumerism by way of establishing the hegemony of its popular culture over many parts of the globe. This missionary undertaking was facilitated even more by the disintegration of the Soviet Block in the 1980s. In the 1990s, American consumer-sustained cultural hegemony, and the adaptation of the American lifestyle globally, is detectable not only in Western Europe but all over the world. As John Sullivan has observed:

One of the curiosities of travelling abroad is to be continually reminded of America. Button-down shirts, blue jeans, hamburgers (whether McDonald's or some local imitation like the oddly named Wimpy), jazz, Hollywood icons from John Wayne to Marilyn Monroe—the modern world has a sharply American look and a sometimes deafening American sound.[1]

Eastern Europe, as well as Turkey, also manifest the Americanizing trends creeping across the European continent. As with European societies infected by the lure of American culture, influential segments of Turkish society—especially the upper middle class and the rich—have adopted American consumer habits and cultural values, regardless of the serious social problems and cultural erosion this will inevitably create. The Americanization process, however, should not be interpreted as complete erosion of cultural identity or wholesale alteration of Turkish notions of national identity but as a serious threat to the retainment of cultural heritage by the younger generation. Similarly, modernization should be distinguished from blindfolded imitation of the American way of life and the adopting of cultural values that negate Turkish mores and moral values.

Americanization of Turkey was expedited during Turgut Özal's presidency[2] when private enterprise and consumerism were revitalized by state economic policies; nevertheless, Turkey was introduced to the American way of life as early as the mid-nineteenth-century. "It was a sensational event when *Missouri* anchored in Bosphorous: what it brought to Turkey was not only the coffin of the late Ambassador of the Turkish Republic to the United States but indeed a new way of life."[3] Several writers of the period drew attention to the potential of this encounter for social and cultural transformation;[4] nevertheless, consumer ideology and the American way of life were imported into Turkey with the first Frigidaire. "To become a small America" had become the core concept of Adnan Menderes' government in the 1950s and 60s;[5] economic aid under the Truman Doctrine coupled with admiration for the superpower of the world facilitated the internalization of American popular culture by the nouveau-riche that was created by the devaluation of 1946. During the Democrat Party period new economic policies foregrounding free enterprise and capitalism were adopted. While inflation soared on the one hand, free trade led to the exhaustion of foreign currency reserves on the other; these were spent on importing cars and household items. American-made consumer products, sold in small shops collectively called the American Bazaar, met the needs of the nouveaux-riches, who could afford to emulate the American way of life. Turkish magazines designed after American models such as *Bütün Dünya* (Whole World, 1948)—a direct translation of *Reader's Digest* into Turkish—played an important role in the diffusion of American popular culture.[6]

Nowadays, McDonald's, Pizza Hut, Kentucky Fried Chicken, Open Buffet, Supermarket, Hypermarket, Shopping Centre/Mall, Suburb, Townhouse, Sports Centre, Disneyland are names Turkish people recognize. According to some, these are signs of the annexation of Turkey to the global village; according to others, they are the milestones of American cultural and economic hegemony over the global village. For those surviving in the peripheries of the metropolitan centers or in underdeveloped hinterland Anatolia, they are the symbols of a virtual way of life beyond their reach.[7] Indeed, they are the milieu by which American popular culture is internalized, no matter how it is labeled—Americanization, cocacolonization, or mcdonaldization. Identifying McDonald's as the symbol of America and its coveted market economy, George Ritzer has introduced the concept of "McDonaldization," which he defines as a wideranging, "inexorable process," the impact of which is felt in "education, work, travel, leisure-time activities, dieting, politics, the family, and virtually every other aspect of society."[8] Indeed, in 1999, the McDonaldization of Turkey appears to be well and truly in motion. The metropolitan centers in Turkey, if not the whole country yet, have been transformed into a small-scale America where even the stable currency used in major transactions is the American dollar.

Nowadays, American popular culture is lived and consumed most of the time in Turkey, unconsciously and often quite naturally. Its consumption is facilitated by the variety and availability of consumer products, the growth of consumer credit, the accessibility of radio and TV to all corners of the country, the increase in the number and services of advertising agencies, and the rapid spread of communications technology. Under the direction of the leading class and the captains of industry, it is generated by the mass media promoting prescribed worldviews and ideologies that come as a package along with commercialism, capitalism, and consumerism.[9] However, the hidden cost of embracing American consumerism was that Turkey began to trade in its own authentic cultural traditions and autonomy for a disconcerting homogenization and standardization of its culture.

Mass media was the key force in cultivating the atmosphere in which American popular culture could flourish and exert its pervasive and corrosive effect on Turkish popular culture. American movies projected fake or idealized images of an affluent society, soap operas concentrated on image-making, entertainment programs promoting American values made their way into Turkish homes. A game show, significantly called The Wheel of Fortune, both commercializes entertainment by giving away consumer products as prizes and provokes the drive for competition. However, the lure of TV often alienates friends; it even divides family members, who sit glued to their seats and brainwashed into buying the latest products. In Turkey, as in the rest of the world, TV has also widened the gap between those who can afford to participate in commercial television's world of affluence and those who may only observe it from the outside.

Turkish food traditions are yielding to the competition of the major artifacts of contemporary global culture: McDonald's and Coca-Cola have caused drastic changes in Turkish eating and drinking habits. In recent years, the Turkish versions of McDonalds—"*Dürüm*land," or "*Kebap*House"—have served the traditional dishes of *shish kebab* and *döner kebab* (gyro), *lahmacun* (Turkish pizza), but have served them "American style." While they offer a clean, comfortably informal atmosphere, they also are characterized by a predictability and hyperefficiency that ultimately diminishes the pleasure of food by reducing it to "a factory assembly line product."[10] Lost is the warm, home-like atmosphere wherein carefully prepared traditional dishes are to be enjoyed in a relaxed setting. These fast food outlets are frequented by Turkish children and youngsters, who eagerly embrace Americanization of their diets. We are therefore bringing up a generation of hamburger and cola addicts with little or no interest in the traditional dishes of one of the richest cuisines of the world. Even more disturbing is Turkish youths' inclination toward American-style social behavior characterized by comfort-seeking, self-satisfaction, and mechanical homogeneity, dictated by what is in vogue. Such behavior thwarts Turkish norms and traditionally accepted social interaction based on decorum and austerity. Their parents, too, have developed the American habit of eating a large proportion of their meals outside their homes or serving frozen, microwavable, canned, or prepared foods at the family dinner table, regardless of their poor nutritional quality. Coca-Cola, beer, gin and tonic, whisky have already supplanted *ayran*, the traditional Turkish beverage, or *raki*, the traditional strong alcoholic drink.[11] Turkish coffee, meticulously prepared and served in demitasses, is nowadays regarded merely as a quaint delicacy to be consumed mainly by tourists. The elderly Turks who still sip it do so with nostalgia. Most Turkish homes and offices in cities now are stocked either with coffee machines that brew imported percolator coffee, or with hot pots for fixing Nescafé, which has come to be known as American coffee. The tea houses, where tea, the traditional Turkish drink, used to be served with samovars and special tea glasses, are also becoming tourist attractions. The coffee machines that have infiltrated the kitchens of almost all homes are symbolically hacking at the roots of tradition and threatening to contaminate Turkey's cultural heritage with an alien culture.

If American-style food consumption is merely one of many ways of internalizing American popular culture, the American way of combining shopping and entertainment in a hyperreality is another. Asserting their hegemony over the Turkish department stores modeled after Sears such as Vakko, Beymen, and Carsi, to name a few, the shopping centers and malls constructed mainly in the suburbs of metropolitan centers serve this purpose. Unlike the closed bazaar, a hallmark of Istanbul's rich historical background and traditional heritage, what is sold in the malls— Atakule and Karum in downtown Ankara, Galleria and Bilkent Center in suburban Ankara, or Akmerkez, Atrium, Migros Center, and Galleria in Istanbul—is not only luxury merchandise but also prescribed values and a way of life. Like fast food readily served or brought to your door, these fancy, glass-roofed, cloistered wonderlands unabashedly propagate commerciality: sheltered shops and megastores overflowing with confectionery, designer jewelery, exclusive designer clothing and shoes, the desirable brands of sporting goods, gifts, toys, computer games—mostly imported luxury items. For lower-middle-class families, these shopping complexes are places of frustration, resentment, and estrangement from the privileged few. Conversely, being able to shop at these stores has become a status symbol, thus increasing the rift between the classes. For those who could not afford to shop at these stores with hard cash, there is an insidious antidote: credit cards and instalment plans ensure that one will keep up with one's neighbors, friends, or workmates, even if one cannot keep up with the bills. Debt used to be a source of shame; nowadays spending —not thrift—is a virtue.

Shopping for new clothes and shoes before the two religious holidays used to be an important ritual. Now, clothes shopping during sales in the shopping complexes has replaced this ritual, stripping the religious holidays of their traditional significance. The malls, considered by teenagers as little heavens, pose a serious threat for Turkish youngsters, as they are places where they can pick up the habits of American "mall bunnies" and "mall rats": hanging out in the food court outlets until late at night and greeting each other using gestures and words they have picked up from American movies and soap operas. Moreover, the well-to-do upper middle-class youth, who too often are given more money than they need, can vent their lust for conspicuous consumption. Their disruptive impact on social and cultural permanence is felt more and more as "the old virtues of thrift and self-control are rapidly giving way to a culture of gratification."[12] This is quite apart from the role of the old markets which, as social centers, promoted social and cultural solidarity.

With the introduction of luxury hotels, health spas, holiday villages, and time-sharing in summer resorts—Petro Kent, Club Armoni, Club Flipper—not only were the traditional architectural designs abandoned, but people's leisure-time activities also changed dramatically. Upper middle-class Turks enjoy frequenting American-style bars, eating out in sumptuous restaurants, enjoying swimming pools and saunas, playing tennis and golf, and buying time-shares in exclusive clubs or even summer homes. When Conrad Hilton opened a hotel in Istanbul in 1955, proudly declaring that "Each of our hotels . . . is a Little America," he could hardly have foreseen that, eventually, all luxury hotels in Turkey would become "little Americas" replacing the traditional lifestyle with the art of living in the American way: sophisticated, splendorous, and dream-like. More and more Turkish families are buying package tours, even on instalment plans, to get away during religious or national holidays. This is a sobering change from the past, when they would instead join relatives or visit their neighbors and acquaintances to strengthen social solidarity.

Mastering the art of living in the American way could not be consummated without exchanging the traditional living quarters for new homes that look more like American homes. These homes are often located in suburban settlements that mushroomed throughout the 1970s and later. The demand for a car, and often a second car, has increased car sales as well as related automobile services such as roadside gas stations fully equipped with fast food restaurants and drugstores. National and international corporate institutions use these suburban settlements to exploit more fully Turkish fascination with American popular culture, with the promise of a novel lifestyle and culture. Among such other suburbias as Ataköy Marina, Bahçeşehir (Garden City) in Istanbul, Venetian Houses in Izmir, Mutluköy (Happy Village) in Ankara, Bilkent (City of Knowledge) is unique. This mind-numbingly monotonous suburban cityscape is crowned with Bilkent Plaza and Shopping Center and Sports International, offering prestige and a high standard of comfort combined with a unique aesthetic and efficient management. Major cities are rapidly expanding into sprawling suburbs, which seriously threaten social intercourse. When they are not out visiting shopping complexes, overworked family members remain within their homes, surrounded by remote-controlled TV sets and videos, or in their gardens where they fuss over barbeques and sip scotch or gin and tonic.

Affluent Turkish youth of the 1960s were already exposed to American popular culture when they were children through comic books and movies. Since their upper-middle-class parents could afford to send them to private schools, they learned English, danced to rock 'n' roll, listened to the Platters and Pat Boone, and wore bobby-sox, loafers, and sweaters. In the 1990s the younger members of this cohort, known as the TV generation, have grown up watching The Muppet Show or Disney cartoons and consuming the products of Walt Disney industries. Thus, at early ages, they are exposed to the mentality and way of life Disney's cartoons reflect: the reconstructions of world folklore and children's literature highlighted with American images and values. The older ones watch American-made movies or spend hours at home playing computer games such as Mortal Combat. It is not surprising that their constant exposure to American cultural icons has bred more familiarity with Pocahontas, Ninja Turtles, Batman, and Terminator than with Deli Dumrul, the Turkish Robin Hood of Dede Korkut Stories. Also underappreciated are Oğuz Khan, Keloğlan, and Hodja Nasrettin, the well-known folk heroes, and *Karagöz* and *Hacivat*, the two renowned characters of the traditional shadow theater. Their outdoor entertainments are provided with playgrounds within malls or miniature Disneylands such as Tatilya/Republic of Entertainment in Istanbul. Similarly, most of the children's magazines and literature are of American origin and accordingly mold the mentality of Turkish children so that they grow up Americanized. While being conditioned as potential consumers of American cultural products, they are estranged from their oral tradition and from their cultural heritage.

Ensnared by the allure of a remote-controlled lifestyle, Turkish youth are effectively turned into couch potatoes. This amounts to America enacting cultural imperialism via mass media, winning the hearts and minds of Turkish youths. Dressed in blue jeans and Caterpillar brand sport shoes, Turkish youths are indistinguishable from their American counterparts—both in their appearance and, to a large extent, in their collective mentality. In addition to changes in physical appearance, words and expressions such as "prestige," "image," "cool!" "take care," "what's up?" and "what's in it for me?" have seeped into common use among Turkish youth, who are fully aware of the social and economic currency such language implies. Even worse is the fervent desire for U.S. citizenship. Pressed by economic difficulties and influenced by the media, which presents the United States as a land of opportunity and affluence, a majority of high school and even university graduates apply for the lottery organized by the American Immigration Office.

The spread of American popular culture, primarily among the upper-middle-class and peripherally among the lower-class Turkish population has created in its wake an opposition to the ideology behind it. The resurgence of fundamentalism in recent years which poses a serious threat to secularism, is responsible for creating the rift that has opened up between the Americanized privileged class and the lower middle class and poor. The fundamentalist Welfare Party has increased its power by claiming to be able to procure equality, well-being, and prosperity for all, as opposed to the capitalistic system, which, according to them, caters to the ambitions for success and prosperity of the privileged few. After the demise of the Welfare Party in January 1998, the newly founded Virtue Party continued to preach "just order" over and against "imitative order." The major issue they have brought forward is the headscarf that all the Muslim women should wear in public according to the fundamentalists. Demonstrations by high school and university students who insisted on entering their classrooms wearing their headscarves culminated in an event that provoked a strong response in the Parliament as well as hot public debates: The Virtue Party candidate from Istanbul—Merve Kavakçi—came to the Parliament wearing her headscarf, in defiance of the Reforms of Atatürk and the Constitution. Ironically, it was soon discovered that she was an American citizen, which disqualified her for membership in the Turkish Parliament anyway. A similarly provocative stance was taken by the organizers of a fashion show in Adana, during which the models appeared on the podium wearing headscarves and carrying posters of Atatürk, shown with his mother and wife whose hair was covered.

Another significant reaction to American popular culture is the phenomenology of *kitsch* or *arabesque,* which emerged as a socioeconomic side effect of the Americanization process.[13] From 1975 and into the eighties, *arabesque* came to define a lifestyle, generally of people who emigrated from rural areas to urban centers and faced certain—primarily economic—problems of adapting to the new urban bourgeois lifestyle: they could neither conserve their own cultural values and systems in this setting nor melt into the upper-middle class.[14] Caught midway between, they developed their own version of popular culture. Certain kinds of objects, furniture, and costume became the signatures of their new way of life as, unable to afford the accoutrements of the upper middle class, they found refuge and cultural identification in reproductions of them.[15]

This, the internalization of American popular culture by the influential segment of the Turkish population has had some undesirable consequences: the dissolution of moral norms and social values, the disintegration of traditional lifestyles that define cultural identity, the creation of cultural discrepancy between the Americanized and the traditionally oriented groups/classes, and the drastic modification of the nature of Turkish popular culture. Traditional popular culture was a bulwark against the hegemony of pressure groups of wealth and power. It expresses the hopes of the oppressed for a better world and of their struggles to achieve it, as represented by *The Epic of Köroğlu, The Epic of Çakircali Mehmet Efe,* or the folk poetry of Yunus Emre. Now, however, the oppositional nature of Turkish popular culture has been corroded, and that culture has been transformed into an instrument of class hegemony. The United States, self-proclaimed champion of individualism, independence and democracy, has, through its spread of global consumerism, quite undemocratically contributed to the erosion of distinctive national cultures.

Notes

1. John O' Sullivan, *National Review* 44, no. 1 (1992):6.
2. Turgut Özal, who served as the prime minister of Turkey from 1983 to 1989, foregrounded "economic pragmatism" in his foreign policy. He was the eighth president of Turkey 1989–1993.
3. Ahmet Oktay, *Türkiyede Popüler Kültür* (Popular Culture in Turkey) (Istanbul: Yapi Kredi, 1994), 77.
4. Concern for the cultural ramifications of introducing the American way of life to Turkey was expressed by Naim Tirali in his short story collection *America for 25 Cents* (1948). Similarly, Cevat Fehmi Başkut's play *Paydos* (It Is Over), written and staged in the same year, "is the first play that criticizes the get-rich-quick mentality and the social status it can provide, which negate all traditional norms and cultural values." Addressing the wife of the idealist schoolteacher, the wife of the smart swindler summarizes the consumer mentality that will prevail in Turkey in the years to come: "How many refrigerators do you have at home? We have two!!" The playwright draws attention to social and cultural deterioration resulting from the towering importance of the pursuit of money and power as absolute values. See *Cumhuriyetin 75 Yıeı* (75 Years of the Republic), ed., Feridun Akin (Istanbul: Yapi Kredi, 1999), 1:313.
5. Adnan Menderes was among the four who founded the Democrat Party on 7 January 1946. He became prime minister when the Democrat Party won the elections in 1950 and was instrumental in the implementation of a liberal economic policy based on private enterprise and capital.
6. A detailed analysis of the introduction of Turkey to the American way of life is provided by Ahmet Oktay, 77–98.
7. Alemdar Korkmaz and İrfan Erdoğan, *Popüler Kültür ve Iletişim* (Popular Culture and Communication) (Ankara: Ümit, 1994), 9.
8. George Ritzer, *The McDonaldization of Society* (Thousand Oaks, Calif.: Pine Forge, 1993) 1.
9. According to the 1997 research conducted by Piar Gallup, 43.2 percent of the people are watching TV, 67.5 percent foreign soap operas, 78.6 percent American-made films, and 53.7 percent talk show/entertainment programs (Istanbul: Piar Gallup Research Co., 1997) 114, 116–17.
10. Susan Marling, *American Affair: The Americanization of Britain* (London: Boxtree, 1993) 87.
11. According to statistical data obtained in 1997, the percentage of the people who drink cola is 63.9, as opposed to those who drink ayran, 23.8. Similarly, the percentage of those who drink beer is 13.2, whereas those who drink *raki* is 9.1 (Istanbul: Piar Gallup Research Co., 1997) 192–94.
12. Michael Miller, *The Bon Marche* (Princeton: Princeton University Press, 1981), 206–7.
13. *Arabesque*, literally "of the lower class" or "unrefined taste," also refers to a kind of music that emerged in the 1960s, which has compositional patterns like those of Arabic music tones, utterly different from Turkish classical and folk music.
14. Filiz Yenişehirlioğlu, *"Kitsch, Arabesque, Popular Aesthetics . . .": Identity, Marginality, Space,* ed. Z. Aktüre and B. Junod (Ankara: Middle East Technical University, 1992), 81.
15. Hasan Bülent Kahraman, ibid., 84.

Michael Ermarth

German Unification as Self-Inflicted Americanization

Critical Views on the Course of Contemporary German Development

America does not exist. It is the un-thing-in-itself [das Unding an sich].
—Robert Müller, "Der Roman des Amerikanismus" (1913)

This melting down and stamping into uniformity—this
McDonaldization—all eating and drinking the same and everything
looking the same (oh, what a state of prosperity and welfare!)—this is
not the "multicultural society" but inhumanity itself, utterly desolate.
—Günter Nenning, *Die Nation kommt wieder* (1990)

When I wake up at night, I don't think about History but rather head
right for the refrigerator. When I am plundering it out,
History doesn't mean much to me.
—Chancellor Helmut Kohl (1995)[1]

In a recent work entitled *Little America: The Americanization of the German Republic* (1995), the journalist Rolf Winter has asserted: "On the path of Americanization, Germany has passed the point of no return, as they say in air-traffic control talk. . . . The Germans are discovering themselves all over again and finding that they are Americans." With bitter irony, Winter inverts the old nostrum "the world will heal itself by the German essence" into a prognostication of global gloom and doom. By

251

Winter's account, present-day postunification Germany portends little but mindless superficiality and soulless dehumanization, speeding along the media-paved superhighway to the "culture-death" of planetary Americanization. Winter's indictment against this process of cultural perdition damns his fellow-Germans as not only completely and cravenly Americanized but even "more American than the Americans" in the sense of debasement and alienation. The newly unified German Republic is presented as beyond any return to sanity and wholesome identity, while the rest of the world is portrayed as moving down the same disastrous course, without possible halting places, modifications, or mid-course corrections. Winter is adamant that Americanization, as a totalizing process, remains all or nothing: "As America goes, so goes the world—this is certainly true. But also, where America comes, it comes totally. A partial Americanization is impossible. A little Americanization is as impossible in the longer run as being a little bit pregnant."[2]

As former U.S. correspondent and chief editor of the raunchy popular weekly *Stern* and the more refined, glossy *Geo* magazine, Rolf Winter is hardly an obscure, ivory-tower recluse or hermit-oracle crying out from obscurity. As a seasoned culture critic, he seems to know intimately the Americanizing style of escalating "hype" whereof he speaks; moreover, he also seems to indulge in it quite freely himself. He appears to feel forced into combatting the vulgar "pop cult" images and mass buzzwords of Americanization with equally relentless catchwords and stereotypes. Indeed, his book itself stands as a stunning example of just what its author claims to be combatting—facile "pop" vulgarization, sensationalistic hype, and an overwrought rhetorical style. If inadvertently, Winter's book qualifies as the prime piece of evidence for his overall argument, as it shows by its cliché-mongering and hyperbole that even avowed enemies of Americanization seem to fall prey to co-optation.

Winter's diatribe on the alleged Americanization—and craven self-Americanization—of his country is merely the most recent scourge in a long tradition of German commentary on the subject. The topic has remained loaded for countless commentators for more than a century and a half, including the half-century of the Federal Republic and the near decade of the reunified Berlin Republic. In 1992 the neo-conservative historian Karlheinz Weissmann wrote:

Of course it cannot be denied that "Americanization" progresses ever onward, not just in the acceptance of modern technology, but above all in the system of popular images and trivial myths that originate in the USA. . . . Americanization can hardly be overestimated in its cultural effects. Since the turn of the century it has transpired as a global process, enveloping Europe first but sparing neither the old high cultures of Asia nor the hunter-gatherers of the Amazon basin, neither the bedouins of Arabia nor the postcommunist societies. Its easy accessibility and high entertainment value make possible the fullest penetration of this kind of civilization.[3]

Americanization as a sweeping planetary inundation has remained an indispensable conception for many serious writers and thinkers of diverse political stripes and cultural orientations. The idea of Americanization continues today more than ever to serve as a sort of talismanic epithet within the vast, unsettled realm of contemporary culture and identity.

Americanization continues to call forth visceral responses across the spectrum of German opinion. In the mid-1980s, the left-nationalist political scientist Kurt Tudyka observed that in order to reflect honestly upon themselves and to wrest any sense of sovereign selfhood from their troubled past, Germans had not only to "de-Americanize" themselves but to become outright anti-American:

From American diapers to American warheads, no one in this country can get away from the "American way of life and death"—a way of living and dying in the American style. America is inside us and the Americans are not just among us but rather "We have all become Americans," as the German Chancellor [then Helmut Schmidt] acknowledged in 1976.[4]

After the fall of the Wall in November 1989 and the onset of unification measures, the disgruntled and distinguished old-left intellectual, Erich Kuby insisted that "self-critical reflection by Germans upon their own history" must necessarily "at present contain the grounds for a certain anti-Americanism."[5] In 1994 Frank Schirrmacher, cultural editor of the conservative *Frankfurter Allgemeine Zeitung*, underscored the continuing centrality of the Americanization question to the identity of the new Germany.[6] In the wake of all the complex changes in Germany, Europe, and the world over the last decade, the refrain of Americanization continues today largely unabated.

In the twentieth century as a whole, German reflection upon both German identity and longterm sociocultural trajectory has been inextricably entwined with the notion of Americanization.[7] For those Germans prone to ponder questions of identity and direction, Americanization has served as the foremost orienting idea *of* modern times *in* modern times. That the United States has emerged over the last decade as the world's "sole remaining super-power" and as the supposed main motor of "globalization" has only added to this role. In a book published shortly before he was named German Foreign Minister in the new government of Gerhard Schröder, the pragmatic Green Joschka Fischer provided a rather mindboggling generalization: "Globalization in its present form is always also Americanization."[8]

As did once the idea (rather than the reality) of the Holy Roman Empire, so have the modern ideas of Americanization continued to summon forth visions of future development, whether as utopia or dystopia. This was especially true for the Weimar and Bonn Republics, which were characterized by supporters and detractors alike as outdoing themselves in emulation, in order to become "more American than the Americans."[9] Surprisingly, this same orienting function, but with radically antithetical values, could also be asserted for the Nazi Third Reich, as a self-styled version of a purified, ultra-German special pathway (*Sonderweg*) through and beyond Western modernity.[10] With very different intentions, the former German Democratic Republic, which tried to constitute its own antifascist national peoples' socialism, railed against the allegedly Americanized, monopoly-capitalist, and chauvinist West Germany.

Already before World War I, the insightful journalist Robert Müller called for a pan-Germanic and all-European counter-Americanism *(Konträr-Amerikanismus)* to save European culture from triviality.[11] The spread of the American way of life has continued to elicit not only wholesale critiques but also calls to counter-Americanism as the main thrust of a larger project of overcoming modernism with transmodernism. Today Müller's call for a concerted counter-Americanism finds a resonant echo in contemporary pleas for de-Americanization, renationalization, and transmodernization as preconditions for genuinely German and European cultural identities.

. . .

To establish some clear contours in a vast topic, I want to highlight three fundamental tendencies of thought that have appeared repeatedly in German attitudes toward Americanization in the twentieth century, especially among articulate opinion setters, public intellectuals, and culture critics. These three dispositions have largely constituted the German "modernity syndrome," which found its supreme shibboleth in the notion of Americanization.[12] These tendencies can be discerned in current critiques of postunification Germany, as well as in the more general discussion of the transition from a familiar modernity to postmodernity. Under the sway of these three tendencies of thought, the German case of (self-)Americanization is claimed to be emblematic of a larger global issue: for, as Winter insists, Germany will somehow continue to show the way to the world, even if that way is the "super-American" way.

With some feeble alliteration on my part, these intellectual tendencies may be defined schematically as: (1) *anticipatory anxiety* about the future, a sense of panic regarding the darker sides of "progress"—including overpopulation, the exhaustion and obliteration of nature, the poisoning of the environment, hypercommercialism and consumerism, and the homogenization of different cultures into stale uniformity; (2) *hermeneutical hybris* or *cultural clairvoyance,* taking the form of special claims to better-understanding *(Besser-Verstehen)* of foreign cultures; (3) the urge to create a German alternative to American-style model modernity.

Whether pursuing commercial markets, scientific research, technological development, military strategy, national unification (or reunification), or, more recently, combatting neo-Nazi recidivism, Germany has felt compelled to stay not just one but two jumps ahead. In times of perceived crisis, a ready strategy for the nation was the desperate venture into wars, which went awry and turned into catastrophic world wars.

Now facing global competition, postunification Germany still feels heavy handicaps, including proximity to volatile regions, demographic and budget deficits, along with the ever-present Nazi past, now compounded with the DDR past. Friedrich Nietzsche, a deeply German yet avowed anti-German thinker, underscored the transmodern tendencies of his fellow Germans: "they belong to the day-before-yesterday and the day-after-tomorrow—as yet they have no today."[13]

The time needed to assimilate the staggering losses and gains of Germany's modern development continues to remain elusive, especially in the face of the global technological changes ushering in the next century. What a century ago was rebuked as the hectic "American tempo" or "Jewish haste" has perforce become second nature to most contemporary Germans, but not without anxieties about the ever-accelerating pace of life. In a revealing book entitled *People Without Time: Essay on the Hurried Fatherland* (1990), the Green-oriented social thinker Lothar Baier applied the image to reunification itself, warning: "The speedy colonization of the DDR could under certain circumstances turn into a boomerang."[14]

Beyond fostering the idea of an exalted sphere of culture (*Kultur*) against profane, practical civilization (*Zivilisation*) identified with the West and especially America, the German urge to transcendental thinking encouraged the even bolder claim to better-understanding (*Besser-Verstehen*) of other cultures, worldviews, and mindsets. Such *Besser-Verstehen* claimed to understand others better than these others could understand themselves. This idea harks back to the philosopher Johann G. Fichte's injunction in the fourth of his famous "Addresses to the German Nation," delivered in 1807 amid the humiliation of Napoleonic occupation: "Hence the German, if only he makes use of all advantages, can always be superior to the foreigner and understand him fully, even better than the foreigner understands himself."[15]

Here at the intersection of self-identity and otherness, there emerged a pattern of swings between extremes of xenophilia and xenophobia; this pattern was often reflected upon by Germans themselves. It was Nietzsche who detected an undercurrent of *ressentiment* in German attitudes toward things foreign: "The Germans shift between a devotion to the foreign and a vengeful demand for originality."[16] Nietzsche insisted that to become a German in the truest sense, one had to become "un-German": "To be a good German means to de-Germanize oneself."[17] German writers often insisted that the only proper stance toward the modern world was the protestant posture of being *in* but not fully *of* the world. In an insightful summary of this temporal transcendentalism historian David King observes:

Modernity arrived late in Germany and was received ambivalently. . . . Modern German culture and society would become modern, but critically modern. Germany became early on and for a long time remained the great modern dissenter.[18]

For roughly the past century, Germany has distinguished itself as simultaneously trying to get the biggest jump on modern developments and venturing the most radical critiques of modernity.

In the turbulent wake of German reunification, a chorus of contemporary writers has, much in the manner of Rolf Winter, assailed recent trends in Germany as the final consummation of a longstanding pattern of self-alienation. Especially vehement has been the denunciation of German normalization as nothing other than Americanization. In the examples that follow, I will trace the views of some prominent writers, artists, and public thinkers concerning this most recent round of Americanization. As exponents of radical reflection, these writers are hardly representative of any common German *vox populi,* but I should add that neither are they isolated figures without any popular resonance. Their habit of adopting each other's images and metaphors bespeaks a community of elite discourse regarding Germany's recent development.

These critics interpret reunification as yet another German traumatic wound or amputation (under the general anesthesia of Americanization), leaving the spiritual phantom-limb of a "lost" or "other" Germany waiting still to be redeemed. These writers portray unification as a largely unrecognized cultural disaster (*Kulturkatastrophe*) that has further alienated Germans from themselves and each other. The sardonic slogan of neo-German identity, "We are the money" in Elfriede Müller's 1991 play *Goldener Oktober,* epitomizes both the inverted-world and boomerang interpretations of German unification.[19] Besides denouncing capitalist-consumerist excess, a minority of disabused "left people on the right" propagate a postmodern politics of cultural identity, proclaiming an authentically German Germany as the true cultural heartland in a renationalized European Europe.[20] They advocate a campaign of de-Americanization in order to secure a new Euro-German cultural identity appropriate to postmodern and post–Cold War conditions.

One voice among the deeply disillusioned is the well-known filmmaker Wim Wenders. In a 10 November 1991 address, marking the second anniversary of the fall of the Berlin Wall, Wenders characterized postunification Germany as a vacuum filled with native-born foreigners inhabiting their own country, which can be called Germany in name only: "It seems to me that we are all still foreigners and are trying to settle an unfamiliar land called Germany."[21] Wenders' ghostly figuration of self-foreigners corresponds to the proverbial image of Germany as wanderer between two worlds. But Wenders goes on to give a sharply barbed thrust to the image of Germans as aliens in their own land. He describes himself and his entire generation as ripe for colonization by American films and comics because such vibrant American fun contrasts starkly with German deadly seriousness and its deathly historical outcomes.[22] Wenders excoriates the German tendency to import its identity from abroad:

I know I am simplifying but I will say it anyway: once again as before, as during the postwar period and during the time of the economic miracle, things are being produced and cultivated in Germany for export all over the entire world, and in exchange we are importing foreign images and stories (*Geschichten*), that is myths, dreams, and our sense of life itself. And by the same token, as the American economy declines, it is American images that more and more exclusively nourish the imaginations of the peoples of this world.[23]

Germany, finally reunited in freedom, peace, and relative prosperity, remains for Wenders bereft of the inner spiritual power to generate its own genuine myths and stories. America's myth has become Germany's self-myth.

As a distinguished filmmaker with a complex love-hate relation with the United States and Hollywood images, Wenders devotes utmost attention to the invasiveness of the media. Germans have become habituated to living their lives vicariously.[24] Wenders reconsecrates the German language with a sacred mission, while at the same time finding scant hope for any real change of heart among his cohorts. His closing words carry the somber ring of the later Heidegger, with its apotheosizing of language as the sole spiritual refuge amid the universal depravity of the modern world:

Our balm (*Heil*) in this country without balm—some words one really has to dig out from under mountains of refuse—is our German language. It is refined, exact, subtle, loving, sharp, and at the same time sheltering. It is rich. It is in fact the only real richness in this country that thinks it is rich and really is not. Our language is all that which this country no longer is, is not yet again, and perhaps never again will be.[25]

Significantly, Wenders never actually uses the un-balmy, nettlesome word "Americanization" in his anniversary address, but even without the *word* itself, the *world* of Americanization is present in postwar Germany, for as a chief character in Wenders' film *Im Lauf der Zeit* says, "The Amis have colonized our unconscious." Although American official and military presence has scaled back significantly since unification, the contagion of American popular culture and images of its way of life remain unmitigated and indeed vastly enhanced in the view of many contemporary culture critics. In a 1987 *Spiegel* interview, Wenders projected his own ghastly vision of the looming, media-driven global "night of the living dead":

I am convinced that the most important industry of mankind—more even than the weapons industry—will sooner or later be the entertainment industry; and that every culture and every identity—every chance for self-determination—will be beaten down by this infernal sort of production. One can see this best in American towns where the people live a completely mindless existence [*völlig verblödetes Dasein*], as in a science fiction novel about people who are completely drugged and can be managed like zombies. But that is not just the case with Americans. It is spreading. One cannot stop it, either by warnings or by actions.[26]

For Wenders—as for Winter, Weissmann, and others—there no longer seems to be any German "special way" evading this Americanization. Wenders presents himself as a forlorn soothsayer in a cultural vacuum, a voice crying in the wilderness of Americanized postmodernity. But he is not as lonesome as he would have his listeners believe, for he has considerable distinguished company.

Wenders' generational cohort Alfred Mechtersheimer—an international security-affairs specialist and Bundestag Deputy from 1987 to 1990—has likewise spoken of the acute need for German healing, along with other far-reaching tasks for Germany. Mechtersheimer comes from the political rather than poetic sphere. Like the others, he finds in Americanization a lethal German sickness, which is metastasizing throughout the world:

It should be said that the all-pervading Americanization (*Durchamerikanisierung*) of the world is less assignable to the USA than to those on all continents who have not defended themselves against it; for example the Germans, who lacking their own political identity have not shown any resistance.

Having relocated the center of gravity of this creeping catastrophe, the author calls for an anti-American International to achieve the de-Americanization of the world:

It is only logical when the protest against war and an order of world-injustice brings the accusation of anti-Americanism. Then "anti-American" becomes a positive predicate and "American" a synonym for a worldwide, inhuman process of development. Anti-Americanism has a threefold direction: naturally, the policies of the USA, but also the Americanism of the non-Americans who accept and advance U.S. policies and values in their own countries, and finally the Americanism in ourselves. Therefore "anti-American" is not a nationalist but a humanitarian category.[27]

In his book *Peacemaker Germany: A Plea for New Patriotism* (1993), Mechtersheimer mixes left and right, populism and elitism, into a mélange of nationalism, socialism, environmentalism, pacificism, ancestral *Heimat* sentiment, regionalism, and robustly neo-nationalist Europeanism. In short, Mechtersheimer comes out in favor of everything that he thinks Americanization is eradicating. As a political prophet of the renationalization of Europe, he conjures up the most difficult and heroic German world-mission of all time: the de-Americanization of the world.

In its claim to global leadership, a country with such a culture of expansion and violence increases global problems and can contribute little to their solution. If it were possible to roll back American influence, this would contribute to the alleviation of global catastrophes. The de-Americanization of the whole world (*Entamerikanisierung der Welt*)—not just of international politics—would be a program of rescue (*Rettung*).[28]

Germany remains uniquely suited to transcend itself into becoming the paragon of de-Americanization. Mechtersheimer perceives genuine culture as the "magnetic force of the future," so that, properly purged of poisonous elements, it will once again become the primal source that it once was. Mechtersheimer exhorts:

The German cultural nation is today not a governmental institution, but rather a cultural community. It is beyond the bounds of any state, and is not defined by any political borders. It reaches from Central Europe to the smallest German-speaking minorities in all parts of the world. . . . Germany bears the main responsibility for the cultural unity of Europe and must work with cultural means to overcome the division of the continent.

This German duty remains, however, a Herculean task, because Westernization has sunk deep roots.

Europe must protect itself better against tendencies that destroy culture. Above all, smaller nations and regions are threatened with being overcome in alienation (*Ueberfremdung*) by an industrialized culture of artificiality (*eine industrielle Kunstkultur*), as exported above all by the USA.[29]

For Mechtersheimer, Americanization and its offshoot of Europeanization are both complicit in denationalization. Mechtersheimer claims to understand his fellow Germans better than they can understand themselves, given their zombie-like, "colonized" state of mind:

There is no enthusiasm in the German populace for this genuine European policy [ie. of neo-nationalist stripe—ME]. Instead, fears in the face of both the outside world and the German past lead Germans to a diffuse mode of behavior, in which Europeanization and creeping Americanization of all realms of life are accepted as the law of nature.[30]

A figure poised between Wenders and Mechtersheimer is the highly renowned East German dramatist Heiner Müller, who before his recent untimely death was called "Müller Deutschland" for his cross-cultural role of mediating between the two Germanys. Müller has reviled German reunification as an insidious double (or even triple and final) colonization. Following its earlier double-colonization by the United States and the Soviet Union, the newly united Germany has been colonizing itself internally into cultural oblivion. Müller diagnosed the frightful yet long-familiar pattern as early as 1990, right after the fall of the Wall:

We shall be submerged by American mass culture, and true culture will suffer. The DDR's old ideological kitsch, which people just ignored, will be replaced by commercial kitsch, which gets much larger and more eager audiences. That's dangerous.[31]

German unification thus remains much more dangerous to Germans than was the old Cold War division, since it annuls the creative dialectical tension between two Germanys into a uniform, mindless conformity. Müller expressly redeploys the hoary old German dichotomy between culture and civilization, daring to make reference to the Nazi past and Auschwitz, to drive his point home:

The economically overdeveloped but culturally underdeveloped civilization of West Germany is trying to extinguish by defamation and red-tape the culture of the former DDR, which grew up in opposition to Stalinist colonization. History will be rewritten by the victors a second time over. The repression of the Nazi period corresponds to and serves the demonization of DDR history. Forty years of Bautzen allows one to forget ten years of Auschwitz.[32]

For Müller, the sleek seven-league boots of capitalist "Wessis" (West Germans) are unmistakable American hand-me-downs, albeit with a new surface polish.[33] Referring to a West Berlin cultural functionary photographed in cowboy boots, Müller (who made a point of being photographed with Cuban cigars) remonstrates:

The victors do indeed write history, but I fear they are illiterate where it concerns any reading of the European heritage. With cowboy boots the cultural senator of Berlin strides through the cultural landscape of Berlin, the future (perhaps) metropolis. That corresponds to the trend of German unification.[34]

Oversized American boots—whether cowboy or combat—are culture-crushing, no matter who is wearing them. They can be filled best by super-Americanized, over-hyped media stars, some of whom still retain strong traces of original Germanic accents:

What causes me horror are such things as a *Spiegel* interview in which Arnold Schwarzenegger tells how he rose to be a megastar. "That, roughly, is our future." (Brecht, Fratzer-Fragments). I don't have anything against Schwarzenegger, but does he have to be the future?[35]

Müller remains pessimistic about not only Germany's contemporary sell-out but also Europe's identical fate of becoming a super-Americanized clone: "Without the DDR as grassroots-democratic alternative to the form of democracy of the BRD sustained by the Deutsche Bank—without this alternative, Europe will become a branch-company of the USA."[36] With hardly any intention to flatter New York, he also says with similar assurance: "New York is the future of Berlin."[37]

Müller is equally certain that high technology—somehow American in its Promethean hybris—means inevitably *low* (and eventually *no*) culture. Revising Napoleon's adage that "politics is destiny" in order to bring its outdated meaning into line with more modern/postmodern conditions, in which authentic political will counts for less and less, Müller echoes Heidegger, Adorno, the Jünger brothers, and countless other German culture critics in seeing technology as the motor amok in the inverted world: "Today technology is destiny. . . . To use technology is to be used by it."[38]

If Wenders grudgingly acknowledges a debt to America even while lamenting its further contagion, Hans-Jürgen Syberberg, another well-known German filmmaker and cultural commentator, shows no such tendencies toward self-recognition. Syberberg's polemic *On the Fortune and Misfortune of Art in Germany after the Last War* (1990) is so outrageously bilious that the uninstructed reader might think it a crude, if elaborate, parody of the whole school of cultural commentary examined in this essay. In quest of an authentic German art, Syberberg musters out Ernst Jünger, Martin Heidegger, Anselm Kiefer, along with other select seers to recover an authentic Germany of myth, fantasy, and unsullied utopia. Like Wenders and Müller, he finds that art must be rescued from the banality of modern normalcy. This task of redemption means that

Germany must be roused out of its stupor of Americanized (un)consciousness. Following upon the Western-style pseudo-liberations of 1945 and 1989, Syberberg proclaims a freedom in kingdom-come: "Our liberation is still ahead of us."[39] The authentic German forms of resistance, unity, and freedom remain unfulfilled tasks for the future.

According to Syberberg, "The prosperity of mass democracy means having the means to press buttons—of boom-boxes, video-machines, fast-food machines and automats, and the auto-joys (*Autofreuden*) of traffic jams."[40]

Postwar Germany for Syberberg has swung pendulum-like "from German misery to German mimicry."[41] Now Germany and Europe are both facing the ultimate moment of truth—the millennial decision between truth, homeland, place, and ancestral bonds on the one hand, and the counterfeit "boutique of the pluralist market society" on the other. Europe after 1989 must return to purified visions of both nature and history—in radically new and yet very ancient senses of both terms. If Europe can throw off what Syberberg calls the blasphemous trinity of "pop-neurosis, freak-decadence, and punk-triviality," it can transform itself into a "holy empire of European cultural nations, composed of individual national provinces."[42]

In Syberberg's account, the Germans have thrown out the holy infant of their own culture with two batches of polluted bathwater: not only the scalding Nazi purge but also the more comfortable American-style whirlpool bath of re-education, democratization, and ersatz pop culture. Syberberg is not averse to toying with the old slogans of the radical right, if such slogans can disrupt the automatic cycle of cultural decay and spiritual entropy: "The taboo against blood and soil has been really an attack on roots and vitality."[43] In the same vein of skirting on the edge of taboos, Syberberg claims that the systematic physical rape of German women in the East at the end of the war by Soviet troops was paralleled in the Western zones by the systematic American rape of the German landscape and culture: "The Russians raped the German women, the Americans gave them chocolate, whereupon they voluntarily spread their legs. Now these two peoples are meeting again, the raped and the seduced . . ."[44] Only if Germans can now awaken to overcome their multiple traumas—division, diaspora, loss of identity, cultural and environmental rape—only then will they become the truly fertile cultural womb of a new-yet-ancient West, purified of corrupting consumerism and the numbing effects of Americanized civilization.

Syberberg's extremist thinking revives dangerous anti-Semitic ideas. For Syberberg the end of the Cold War has brought not genuine peace and union, but only the Hollywood semblance of ersatz peace and phony happy endings. Syberberg diagnoses postmodernity as nothing other than perpetual, total war: "War dominates everywhere. The total war of mankind against plants, animals, and the elements." As many previous German seers who equated the United States and Soviet Union in their convergent forms of deadly materialism, Syberberg underscores what he calls the new "axis" stamping the postwar world—the axis between the United States and Israel: "We are living in the Jewish epoch of European cultural history, wherein we await—apocalyptically, at the high-point of technical power—the last judgment."[45] With the hegemony of Americanized modes of life, Syberberg claims to see an eastward displacement of the "cultural soul" of the Western heartland over to Israel: "The heart of [Western] Europe beats in Israel—this could be said of the Europe of the postwar period." In this topsy-turvy, everything-is-anything world, only the truly spiritual East can bring liberation from Europe's vacuity and loss of identity. Syberberg's mythical East promises a rejuvenating "new naiveté" that can liberate pent-up or atrophied ancestral forces and utopian energies:

The used-up life of the West has not yet reached the people of the East. The eastern system [i.e., the. former communist one—ME] has been thrown off to clear the way. For a moment we can reflect deeply. Pure, like the earth on the first day.[46]

With his vast anti-Semitic and Nazi visions of first and last days, Syberberg trots out and dabbles with every fatuous cliché in the long German discourse regarding Americanization, including its complicity with "Judaization" and "feminized" susceptibility to the blandishments of luxury consumption.

In similarly totalizing terms, Botho Strauss, who has been declared by many to be Germany's foremost contemporary writer, has presented a postmodern Germany of boundless profanation, defiling itself at every turn with "digitalization," "synchronization" and "asphaltization."[47] His notorious 1993 *Spiegel* essay "Anschwellender Bockgesang" (Swelling Tragic Threnody) is a cranky experiment in myth-mongering that has aptly been called the "Mein Krampf" ("My Cramp" as opposed to Hitler's "Mein Kampf," "My Battle") of postmodern German identity discourse. Like Wenders, Strauss is convinced that the modern media are totalitarian but still capable of becoming yet more so.

In *Beginnlosigkeit* (1992), Strauss claims that Germans have become better at impersonating Americans than at being themselves:

Today the German people no longer constitutes a secret treasure in the soul of the individual, from which he could draw strength. This people is nothing but a fickle, complacent potentate of the majority. An extinquisher of every real and ideal power. It speaks German only out of laziness; most of its interests and excitements are better expressed in American.[48]

After declaring that "History is open; myth is closed," Strauss predicts the imminent return of some postmodern form of mythic time. Here Strauss foresees the recurrence of what he calls the "fascist moment," which then may last eternally. Just as Syberberg is preoccupied with occupations, Strauss is unabashedly fascinated with fascism's power to fascinate:

Fascination with technological inventiveness combined with fascination for mythical roots and elemental feelings—that was a prime trait of European fascism. It was a premature, dangerous combination under naive, precybernetic conditions, so that one might like to claim—if it didn't sound so superficial—that the horrors and political gigantomachy arose from the incompatibility of these forces—the unbridged chasm between myth and technology. One was simply not at the technical level where one could smoothly synchronize these two forces. But this conjunction will certainly arise again—it will be perhaps the decisive attempt (*Versuch*) of the acrologue.[49]

In Strauss' far-seeing "tele-vision" into the future, super-computers do not so much annul the deep reflective power of human minds as rather "potentiate" it to unimaginable intensity, until human consciousness will finally turn into its own dread opposite. Human beings come to realize that they are nothing but a network of neurons within larger networks and internetworks.[50] The human life-world is hereby reduced to the lowest common denominator of binary codification in the galactic swirl of information bits: humankind has programmed itself out of its congenital anthropomorphism—along with its true historicity and humanity.

Strauss' postmodern imagery for contemporary Germany and the world at large conjures a vision as macabre as it is melancholy. The ongoing dual German unifications—with former East Germany and with Europe at large—portend not cooperative union but desolate ruination: "The rat-like scurrying of Germans away from the conflagrations of their own private house into the ruins of a common house."[51] Strauss resurrects the old German message of redemption from the East to counter the despiritualization from the West. The only conceivable way out, Strauss says boldly, is a kind of German about-face in its habit of self-estrangement; his prescription is for Germans "to become Russian" rather than "German-*heimatlich*," or Americanized. They must especially not become what Strauss coyly calls "*newyorkerisch*."[52]

The culture critics remain convinced that the myopic majority cannot really perceive or define what is befalling Germany and the world at large. Left-nationalists, combining neo-Marxist notions of hegemonic ideology with Heideggerian concepts of Being and language, argue that Germany's Americanization has advanced so totally that contemporaries no longer have a proper name for the process: it is simply normalcy or routine "life as usual." Fed up with this banal normalization, former DDR dramatist Frank Castorf has called for a "storm of steel" (in the vein of Ernst Jünger) to smash the cloying complacency of custom and of "banana-consumerism."

The astute *Spiegel* reporter Martin Doerry diagnoses the cryptic "new Fascho-sound" in contemporary Germany as stemming from the temptation of toying with deep-seated taboos: "Tormented by the boredom of the postmodern universe, they are looking for the ultimate kick, the truly shocking transgression against taboos."[53] In the current German semantic economy of cliché and taboo, Americanization, Auschwitz, and Nazism remain topics of nearly mythic proportions, often locked in a contorted and unlikely dialectical embrace.

. . .

Ironically, it is probably longterm economic trends rather than intellectual and cultural currents that could convert the prophecies of such critics into something more serious than "toying with taboos."[54] United Germany, like much of the rest of the world, is certain to go on struggling with multiple-identities. But it seems even more likely that Germany will no longer be able to carry on its identity struggles in the lap of economic luxury, with "economic miracle" as an assured way of life. Early hopes for strong economic growth after unification have in fact faltered and stalled upon serious structural problems, bringing sober declarations of the end of the postwar order of sustained economic prowess. The serious erosion of that very economic well-being which the culture critics lament as "luxury edition Americanization" could in fact propel questions of cultural identity to the level of acute political significance.

Since reunification in 1990, Germany has undergone the worst depression since the early 1930s. The painful restructuring of manufacturing sectors in both old and new Bundesländer has taken a great toll, with levels of unemployment in some eastern regions through the decade of the 1990s approximating those of the Great Depression. Amid serious concerns about meeting the competition of the next century, the head of Peugeot warned German auto executives in 1989 of a looming specter of "Nippon-Amerikanismus."[55] A short time later, Konrad Seitz argued in "The Japanese-American Challenge" that the sorry state of German research and development would allow it to become a "technological colony" of Japan and the United States.[56] The *Stuttgarter Nachrichten* observed in July 1992: "Even if we do not want to admit it: after unification we are no longer 'Superman.'" At this same time, under the headline "Angst about the D-Mark," the *Bildzeitung* noted the interlocking spirals of huge public debt, creeping inflation, and continuing high taxes and interest rates.[57] In this worsening economic setting, there have ensued ugly and even murderous instances of hatred against foreigners, along with signs of Germans' rancor against other Germans.

Ordinary Germans, whether Americanized or not, have found pride and self-esteem in remaining a rock-steady model of dynamic economic success. But over the last decade, amid the unsettling processes of globalization, Europeanization, and reunification, Germany is being compelled to revamp its social-market economy in very fundamental ways. Henry Kissinger's flippant characterization of the former West Germany as "an economy in search of an idea" now certainly needs to be amended to include the urgent search for both a new cultural idea *and* a new economic order for Germany within a new Europe. But so many tasks of structural innovation constitute an enormous strain on the social fabric, not to say budgets of all sorts.

The German uncertainty about the proper balance between the practical and the poetic in the higher realm of culture and spirit—this chronic German question reflects an eternal tension of mythic dimensions that has been richly creative but also at times woefully destructive. This balance is certainly *not* just a German question, even if it has been most contested in the German framework and idiom. The path of German normalization, as traversed alongside concomitant trends of Europeanization and globalization, will continue to be arduous.

Conclusion

After recognizing that Americanization can be equated with so many things, including everything and nothingness (and their reversal or inversion), perhaps it is high time for us to ask whether Americanization means anything at all. This question seems of immediate pertinence in view of the fact that Americanization has most often been characterized by German (and other European) critics as the advancing loss of human meaning altogether. Perhaps the actual process of Americanization fulfills itself in its own disappearance, as it blends into so many other things. As a suitably postmodern formula for the globalized consumer capitalism that he darkly calls the "next fascism," the old socialist (and now left-nationalist-socialist) Günter Nenning has coined a sound-bite full of derisory fury; his "world-in-a-word" catchword for the future is "Oneworld-unisexmediblödikonsumidummi . . . Mythos 2000."[58]

We might ask: is Americanization by any other name still the same? Will it continue to serve so mightily—so globally and so handily—as

"Mythos Twenty-First Century," as it did throughout the twentieth century for Germans and other peoples? In his 1992 work *Beginnlosigkeit,* Botho Strauss stresses how intellectual inertia conspire to make new beginnings impossible. He observes (presumably without reference to himself): "The clichés of knowledge with which so many scholars and intellectuals go about their business are downright embarrassing."[59] There is a real sense in which the culture critics' inveterate interpretation of modernity and modern life as Americanization remains downright embarrassing. It makes their business at once too easy and too predictable. On the other hand, it must be emphasized that, concerning the hyperbolic overinterpretation of the Americanization question, the Germans have been their own most clear-headed and unsparing critics.

Nearly a half-century ago Hannah Arendt made a telling observation that is just as pertinent today.

In reality, the process which Europeans dread as "Americanization" is the emergence of the modern world with all its perplexities and implications. It is probable that this process will be accelerated rather than hindered through the federation of Europe, which is also very likely a condition *sine qua non* for European survival. Whether or not European federation will be accompanied by the rise of anti-American pan-European nationalism, as one may sometimes fear today, unification of economic and demographic conditions is almost sure to create a state of affairs which will be very similar to that existing in the United States.[60]

In a similar vein but with diametrically opposite conclusions, Heiner Müller put his finger on the anxious pulse of modernity in saying: "The lack of orientation induces anxiety. And because of this anxiety, one reaches for simplifications."[61]

"Americanization" has been modernity's foremost simplification. Whether conceived as modern or postmodern, the world presently needs compassionate good will and tolerant, cross-cultural co-operation, not the totalizing sloganeering of "acrologues" and ideologues. Efforts at German-American understanding in the twentieth century—and at "German-German" understanding after reunification—show that it is often more difficult to understand the familiar and half-familiar than the altogether "Other."

Notes

1. Robert Müller, "Der Roman des Amerikanismus," *Saturn* 3, no. 9 (1913): 255; Günter Nenning, *Die Nation kommt wieder* (Osnabrück: Fromm, 1990), 54; Chancellor Helmut Kohl, quoted in *Die Zeit*, 16 Jan.1995: 2.

2. Rolf Winter, *Little America Die Amerikanisierung der deutschen Republik* (Hamburg: Rasch & Röhring, 1995), 186 and 190. See also Bernd Polster, ed.,

West Wind: Die Amerikansierung Europas (Cologne: DuMont, 1995). The totalizing view finds its proper corrective in Rob Kroes, who observes: "But even in the case of a clear and undeniable impact of American culture, the word 'Americanisation' is unduly alarmist. It reduces the complex processes of cultural influence, of borrowing, imitations and reception to the stark binary form of a zero-sum game. In a field of opposite alternatives, of a Europeanism as opposed to Americanism, any degree of Americanisation implies an equal degree of de-Europeanisation. To the extent that the word Americanisation can serve any useful analytical purpose at all, it should rather be taken as a short-hand reference to what is essentially a blackbox in the simple diagram of cultural reception and transmission." "Americanisation: What Are We Talking About," in R. Kroes, ed., *High Brow Meets Low Brow: American Culture as an Intellectual Concern* (Amsterdam: Free University Press, 1988), 303. See also Richard Pells, *Not Like US: How Europeans Have Loved, Hated, and Transformed American Culture Since World War II* (New York: Basic Books, 1997). It remains important, if also difficult, to distinguish between anti-Americanism and what might be called "anti-Americanization-ism." A more restricted and sectoral sense of Americanization is embodied in Hermann Fink, *Amerikanisierung in der deutschen Wirtschaft: Sprache, Handel, Güter und Dienstleistungen* (Frankfurt a. M.: Peter Lang, 1995); similarly, see also Volker Berghahn, *The Americanisation of West German Industry, 1945–1973* (Cambridge and New York: Cambridge University Press, 1986).

3. Karlheinz Weissmann, *Rückruf in die Geschichte: die deutsche Herausforderung* (Berlin: Ullstein, 1992), 69.

4. Kurt Tudyka, "Anti-Amerikanismus—was ist das?" in A. Guha and S. Papcke, eds., *Amerika—der riskante Partner* (Königstein: Athenäum, 1984), 117.

5. Erich Kuby, *Deutschland: Von verschuldeter Teilung zur unverdienten Einheit* (Munich: Moewig, 1990), 283.

6. Frank Schirrmacher, "'Hollywood Hegemony' at Issue as Germans Again Debate Identity" in *International Herald Tribune*, 30 May 1994.

7. See the collection Alf Lüdtke, Inge Marssolek, Adelheid von Saldern, eds, *Amerikanisierung: Traum und Alptraum im Deutschland des 20. Jahrhunderts* (Stuttgart: Steiner, 1996).

8. Joschka Fischer, *Für einen neuen Gesellschaftsvertrag: eine politische Antwort auf die globale Revolution* (Cologne: Kiepenheuer & Witsch, 1998), 7.

9. Thomas Schmid, *Staatsbegräbnis: Von ziviler Gesellschaft* (Berlin: Rotbuch, 1990), 92. For the early years of the Bonn Republic, see the slanted study by Ralph Willett, *The Americanisation of Germany, 1945–1949* (London and New York: Routledge, 1989).

10. See Philipp Gassert, *Amerika im dritten Reich: Ideologie, Propaganda und Volksmeinung 1933–1945* (Stuttgart: Steiner, 1997).

11. Robert Müller, *Gesammelte Essays* (Paderborn: Igel Verlag, 1995), 267.

12. The best brief interpretive summary with a pro-Western slant remains Arnold Bergstraesser, "Zum Problem der sogenannten Amerikanisierung Deutschlands," *Jahrbuch für Amerikastudien*, vol. 8, 1963, 13–23.

13. Nietzsche, *Sämtliche Werke* (Stuttgart: Kröner Verlag, 1953), 76:170.

14. Lothar Baier, *Volk ohne Zeit. Essay über das eilige Vaterland* (Berlin: Wagenbach, 1990), 111.

15. J G. Fichte, *Addresses to the German* (Fourth Address), ed. G. Kelly (New York: Harper and Row, 1968), 60.

16. Nietzsche, *Sämtliche Werke*, 83:410.

17. Ibid., 72/2:142.

18. David King, "Culture and Society in Modern Germany," in Gary Stark and Bede Karl Lackner, eds., *Essays on Culture and Society in Modern Germany* (Austin, Texas: Texas A&M University Press, 1982), 15. King (p.44) locates Hitler as follows: "Hitler was essentially an anti- and postmodern figure; that he was in fact premodern is less obvious." I suggest "transmodern" here, as it conveys the dialectical notion of "Konträr-Amerikanismus," of overcoming modernity with its own instrumentalities.

19. Elfriede Müller, *Die Arbeiterinnen. Goldener Oktober. Zwei Stücke* (Frankfurt a.M.: Verlag der Autoren, 1992), 159.

20. This strand and others have been lucidly analyzed in Hans-Georg Betz, *Postmodern Politics in Germany: The Politics of Resentment* (London: Macmillan, 1991).

21. Wim Wenders, "Reden über Deutschland," in *The Act of Seeing: Essays und Gespräche* (Frankfurt a. M.: Verlag der Autoren, 1993) 190.

22. Ibid.

23. Ibid., 194–95.

24. Ibid., 195.

25. Ibid., 198.

26. *Der Spiegel* 43 (1987): 235.

27. Alfred Mechtersheimer, "Antiamerikanisch—weshalb eigentlich nicht? Von der Pflicht, dem weltweit verheerenden Einfluss der USA zu widerstehen" in Helmut Thielen, ed., *Der Krieg der Köpfe. Von Golfkrieg zur Neuen Weltordnung* (Bad Honeff: Horlemann, 1991), 115, 118.

28. Alfred Mechtersheimer, *Friedensmacht Deutschland. Plädoyer für einen neuen Patriotismus* (Frankfurt a.M.: Ullstein, 1993), 61–62.

29. Ibid., 284–86.

30. Mechtersheimer, "Nation und Internationalismus," in H. Schwilk and U. Schmidt, eds., *Die selbstbewusste Nation* (Berlin: Ullstein, 1994), 351ff.

31. Quoted in John Ardagh, *Germany and the Germans: After Unification*, rev. ed. (London: Penguin, 1991), 482.

32. Heiner Mülller, "Was wird aus dem grösseren Deutschland?" in *Sinn und Form* 43, no.4 (1991), 667.

33. In the very same vein, essayist Joseph von Westphalen diagnoses German unification as a vast case of bulimia and feeding frenzy. Joseph von Westphalen, *Von deutscher Bulimie: Diagnose einer Fressgier. Vergebliche Streitschrift gegen die deutsche Einheit* (Munich: Knesebeck & Schuler, 1990).

34. Müller, "Was wird . . . ," 667.

35. Ibid., 669.

36. *Zur Lage der Nation: Heiner Müller im Interview mit Frank M. Raddatz* (Berlin: Rotbuch, 1990), 82.

37. Quoted in Stefan Ulbrich, ed, *Multikultopia* (Vilsburg: Arun, 1991), 97.

38. *Jenseits der Nation: Heiner Müller im Interview mit Frank M. Raddatz* (Berlin: Rotbuch, 1991), 18–19.

39. Hans Jürgen Syberberg, *Vom Unglück und Glück der Kunst in Deutschland nach dem letzten Kriege* (Munich: Mattes & Seitz, 1990), 151.

40. Ibid., 136.

41. Ibid., 154, 179.

42. Ibid., 169.

43. Ibid., 51. The right-nationalist Günter Maschke has claimed that this protracted "self-denial" has amounted to "psychic genocide, the German self-genocide." "Die Verschwörung der Flakhelfer," in *Inferiorität als Staatsräson* (Krefeld: Sinus, 1985), 105.

44. Ibid., 157.

45. Syberberg, *Vom Unglück*, 79.

46. Ibid, 23, 152, 193.

47. Botho Strauss, *Beginnlosigkeit: Reflexionen über Fleck und Linie* (Munich: Hanser, 1992), 131.

48. Ibid., 122.

49. Ibid., 118–19.

50. Ibid., 50.

51. Ibid., 120–21.

52. Ibid., 88.

53. Martin Doerry,"Wir brauchen Stahlgewitter" *Der Spiegel* 3 (1995):156–57.

54. Wolfgang Pohrdt, *Das Jahr danach* (Berlin: Edition Tiamat, 1992), 189, 310.

55. "Peugeot-Chef warnt vor "Nippon-Amerikanismus," *Süddeutsche Zeitung* 20 (20 Sept 1989), 33.

56. Konrad Seitz, *Die japanische-amerikanische Herausforderung: Deutschlands Hochtechnologie-Industrien kampfen ums Ueberleben* (Bonn: Verlag Bonn Aktuell, 1990).

57. Quoted in Pohrdt, *Das Jahr danach*, 219–20.

58. Günter Nenning, "Grenzenlos Deutsch," in Stefan Ulbrich, ed., *Gedanken zu Grossdeutschland* (Vilsbiburg: Arun, 1991), 53.

59. Botho Strauss, *Beginnlosigkeit*, 16.

60. Hannah Arendt, "The Threat of Conformism," in J. Kohn, ed., *Essays in Understanding 1930–1945* (New York: Harcourt Brace, 1994), 426–27. Decades ago Hannah Arendt compared American "barbarian philistinism" with "the equally annoying cultural and educated philistinism of European society, where culture has acquired snob-value, where it has become a matter of status to be educated enough to appreciate culture." Hannah Arendt, "The Crisis in Culture," *Between Past and Future* (New York: Penguin, 1977), 198.

61. Heiner Müller, *Jenseits*, 94. Another former East German writer, Jurek Becker, has offered a sobering proleptic judgment that combines all the German temporal "tenses" into an intimation of the "end of history" or at least the "end of modernity": "The most optimistic thing I can think to say is: perhaps we Germans will succeed in not arriving at the abyss sooner than most of the others." "My Father, the Germans, and Me," *Inter Nationes: German-American Cultural Review* (Winter 1994): 10. With droll Pomeranian patience, Bismarck once remarked that when the end of the world came, he would go to Mecklenburg, because everything happened a century later there! The "consumerist" Helmut Kohl simply goes to the refrigerator to calm his night thoughts.

V   Contemporary Issues

Rob Kroes

Advertising

The Commodification of American Icons of Freedom

A nation that stops representing itself in images stops being a nation. It is doomed to lead a life of derivation, vicariously enjoying worlds of imagery and imagination imported from abroad. Or so President Mitterrand reportedly mused. In a mood of cultural protectionism, against the backdrop of a seemingly unstoppable conquest of Europe's cultural space by American images, Mitterrand's France called for—but failed to get—a clause exempting cultural goods from the free-trade logic of GATT. The episode was reminiscent of earlier defensive ploys by France in the face of a threat of Americanization. More than one author has told the story of France's fight to keep Coca-Cola out of the country.[1] Coca-Cola became the symbol of everything that a certain intellectual discourse in Europe had always rejected in America, as the country that had succeeded in mass-marketing bad taste. If there was much to be envied in America as a model of modernity, it offered an example for the French to follow, but only selectively—under strict "parental guidance," so to speak. Yet the example as set by America was tempting, precisely because it undercut parental authority and cultural guardianship, promising the instant gratification of desire rather than its sublimation, consumption rather than consummation. Coca-Cola was the item that the French chose to symbolize this pernicious pleasure principle in the global transmission of American mass culture. The soft drink, in this French campaign, was turned into an icon of an alleged American strategy of cultural imperialism. It also gave the strategy a name: Coca-Colonization. *

More recently, another soft-drink commercial, for Seven-Up, illustrated the seductive semiotics that underlie so many of the messages that reach us from across the Atlantic Ocean. It did this without drawing on the repertoire of American icons. There was no Marlboro Man roaming the open space of an American West, no Castle Rock, no Statue of Liberty. Instead,

Seven-Up introduced a streetwise little brat, a cartoon character by the name of Fido Dido (If I do, they do?). Few among the European audience watching the commercial would have been aware of its American origins. As it happened, however, the cartoon character was American, and so was the commercial itself. Yet, for all intents and purposes, it could have been produced by advertising agencies anywhere. The only clearly American referent in the commercial was the product it tried to promote, a soft drink that saw its market share slipping and felt in need of a new image.

In the first installment of what evolved into a series of narratives centered on Fido Dido, we see Fido Dido meeting the hand of his maker. The breezy cartoon short is reminiscent of the Sistine Chapel imagery, in which a languid Adam, touching fingers with God, is brought to life. But Fido Dido's story has a special twist. His is not a passive encounter with a benevolent God, but a confrontation with parental authority, and with the commanding hand of social propriety. The hand of the maker, which appears not as a cartoon, but "in living color," holds a pencil and gets ready to retouch Fido Dido. When the hand smooths Fido Dido's unkempt hair, Fido Dido indignantly shakes it back into its previous state. Undeterred, the hand wields its pencil in continued attack, and dresses Fido Dido in jacket and tie. Next, the hand tries to erase Fido-Dido's can of Seven-Up, which also appears in full color. The hand is thwarted however, as the can is beyond such manipulation; the eraser is useless to delete it.

Fido Dido, meanwhile, has begun a full rebellion. Throwing off jacket and tie, he angrily kicks the pencil point. Its tip breaks and hangs limply—a fitting symbol of parental impotence. Victoriously, Fido Dido walks off the screen. As final retaliation, he uses his yo-yo to hit the pencil again, causing the broken point to fall off. His victory prize is a taste of the elixir of freedom: cool, sparkling Seven-Up. The semiotics all merge into one message: a simple soft drink has been turned into a symbol of freedom. Although the product, as well as the commercial and its cartoon star, may be American, the message is understood internationally.

We may see in this one example the end stage of a process of internationalization and generalization—decontextualization, if one wishes—of a sales pitch that was developed in America and, in its earlier stages, relied on much more explicit American iconography. We mentioned the Marlboro Man as a contemporary case of strong American symbolism. The West as open space, a realm of freedom, connects the sense of being one's own man to a simple commodity like a cigarette. Yet the Marlboro Man is only a recent example of the commodification of American symbols of freedom, a process that has gone on for over a century. America as empty space, the epic America of the frontier, and America's mythical West had served as a symbol of freedom long before the consumer revolution. The beckoning West had kept alive the dream, in far-away corners of Europe, of a life lived in freedom and independence. As the promise of a new world and a new era, it could vie with contemporary utopian, Marxist views, or similar emancipation movements. Posters for shipping lines, emigration societies, and land development agencies, contributed to the continuing construction of America as the very site of freedom and space. These posters marketed their services using imagery that represented the promise of freedom and escape America seemed to afford.

If such is the central appeal of "America" as an image, we need not be surprised at the craving for reproductions of this image. Chromo lithographs, photographs, and stereographs, with their suggestion of three-dimensionality, were often produced in response to this craving. They allowed people to move beyond the limited horizons of their daily lives and to enter into an imaginary space, a fantasy world. They simultaneously offered reality and escapist illusion.

Naturally, such pictures soon were turned into advertising tools. Depictions of the West, or rather of America as one huge space, could trigger fantasies of fulfillment and liberty, and common merchandise might hope to benefit by association with such images. The successful (if recently controversial) marriage of the Marlboro Man with the American West (or "Marlboro Country") had its forbears. As early as a century ago, advertisements tried to bring about this same union of product with concept. Consider, for instance, a colorful 1860 poster for the Virginia-based Christian and Lee Tobacco Company's Washoe Brand. There is no tobacco leaf, cigar, or pipe in sight; nor is there any visual reference to the tobacco's true geographical origins. What we see instead are images of the West—Western horsemen, far horizons—grouped around a medallion. The medallion is imprinted with a picture of the Goddess Columbia draped in the American flag, an eagle, a globe with the Western hemisphere turned forward, and a pot brimming with gold coins. Thus, the West appears as a vision of plenty . . . and, apparently, of tobacco.

Another poster, from the same period, advertises Westward Ho Smoking Tobacco. Its very name ties the tobacco to the beckoning call of the West. Yet the producer, G. W. Langhorne and Co., from Lynchburg, Virginia, did not leave it at that. The poster shows us an allegorical female figure, a version of Columbia with stark Indian features and with feathers in her hair. Her extended hand holds forth a calumet, her lower body is wrapped in the Stars and Stripes. This is not Europa abducted by Jupiter, this is America, impetuously galloping forth on elk-back: "Westward Ho!"

Apparently, well before the decade of the "roaring twenties," commerce had appropriated the allegorical repertoire of the American dream.

Thanks to new techniques of mechanical reproduction, images flooded the country and could be endlessly rearranged to render new symbolic messages. The West as a realm for the imagination could connect with the world of ordinary consumer goods, such as tobacco or cigarettes. Advertising developed into an art of symbolic alchemy that has continued to retain its potency. The symbolic connection that advertisers sought to establish hinged on the concept of "freedom." This linking of evocative images of American freedom and space tended to work best with leisure-time articles, such as cigarettes, beer, automobiles, or even blue jeans. Consumerism, leisure time, and "freedom" thus became inextricably interwoven.

Even today, "America" triggers an association with freedom. The iconography of America has become international. Italian jeans manufacturers now advertise their wares in Germany with posters depicting the United States' Monument Valley. The German cigarette brand West mounted an international advertising campaign with central metaphors revolving around the American West. The Dutch nonalcoholic beer Stender used the imaginary West of American road-movies for its television commercials. Stender's ads included tension-infused encounters between men and women at isolated gas stations in a seemingly empty West. These inevitably included a sly exchange of sidelong glances, the half-inviting, half-ironic sizing up, and the beginning of erotic tension. Surprisingly, the tension is only released when he or she, in gleaming black leather, exhibits the West's macho style and flips the top of a bottle of Stender. Then he or she mounts a gleaming motorbike and rides off into the empty desert land.

America's national symbols and myths have been translated into an international iconographic language, a visual lingua franca. They have been turned into free-floating signifiers, internationally understood, free for everyone to use. Yet it is only a replay, on an international scale, of what had previously occurred in the United States. Given the characteristic American bent for disassembling whatever presents itself as an organically coherent whole, only to reassemble it differently, America's leadership in the realm of symbols is not surprising. After all, the production of commercial messages utilizes this same cultural penchant for removing symbols from their historical context and rearranging them into novel configurations. The appropriate metaphor may be that of Lego-construction, which uses the individual pieces as just so many "empty signifiers," and combines them into ever-changing, meaningful structures. Commerce and advertising are but one area where we can see these rituals of cultural transformation at work. For indeed, consumer goods can freely change their meaning as well, appearing in ever-changing configurations, furnishing a realm of virtual reality, and serving as simulacra at the hands of the wizards of advertising. They become true phantasmas set free by the human imagination.

No bastion of conventional order is immune to this erosive freedom. In the area of advertising, as well as in other areas of cultural production, we can discern a moving American frontier, affecting an ever-increasing number of social conventions with its "deconstructing" logic. Recent shifts in this frontier have affected the established constructions of gender, rearranging at will reigning views of what constitutes the typically male and female, the masculine and feminine. "Genderbending" is the word that American English has invented for describing this process. Pop culture heroes such as Michael Jackson, Grace Jones, or Madonna project invented personae that are strangely androgynous. Hollywood has bent gender in films like *Alien II*, where the enemy computer is called "Mother" and the heroine copes in ways that are traditionally associated with a masculine protagonist.

Commercials like those for Stender also play on the repertoire of accepted gender definitions. The best recent example is a television commercial for Levi's 501, broadcast in The Netherlands. A young, chocolate-skinned woman, with bare midriff, is shown riding in a New York cab. While the driver ogles her in his rear-view mirror, his lips move a toothpick suggestively back and forth. She coolly adds a few final touches to her makeup. But then the tables are turned. The driver starts and abruptly slams on his brakes at the sound of an electric razor and the sight of his passenger shaving. The last shot is of the passenger walking away, the victor in another battle of the sexes, her Levi's as snug and inviting as ever, as the text reminds us that these Levi's were "Cut for Men Since 1850." In this advertisement, as in others like it, an entire new area has opened up for fantasies of freedom to roam.

There may be a cultural "deep structure" underlying such developments that is characteristically American, yet the appeal of such cultural *bricolage* is international. Even in the absence of clearly "American" markers, as in the case of our Fido Dido commercial, the underlying logic of recombination, or of tying "freedom" to a soft drink, is American. The appeal, though, is worldwide. In that sense, we have all become Americanized. We have grown accustomed to a specific American mode of cultural production, or rather to the ways in which American culture reproduces itself through endless variation and recombination. Not only have we cracked American cultural codes and come to read them flawlessly, we have also appropriated these codes. They have become part of our collective imaginary repertoire.

In the spring of 1994, walls all over Italy bore magnificent Levi's posters displaying a scene taken from the history of the conquest of the West. These sepia-tinted posters featured a covered wagon in what is clearly a dry and desolate Western landscape. A few men were shown gathered, in postures of relaxation, in front of the wagon. Clearly, the day's work has been done. The posters' legend informed readers that *Vendiamo un'autentica leggenda*—We sell an authentic legend. Clearly, this was a variation on Coca-Cola's claim of being "the real thing." Less clear was what the heck the authentic legend might be. Is it the Levi's blue jeans? The answer must be yes. Is it the American West? Again, the answer is yes. A commodity, a piece of merchandise as down-to-earth as a pair of workingman's trousers, has become a myth, while the West as a myth has become commodified. And Levi's, as the poster tells us, sells it.

Yet there is more to this poster. There is an ironic *sous-entendu*, an implied wink to the audience. After all, the audience has long since received the message. They *know* that Levi's is a myth and they *know* what the myth represents. It represents more than the West. It also represents their own collective memory of growing up in a Europe filled with American ingredients. Generation upon generation of Europeans, growing up after the war, can all tell their own story of a mythical America as they constructed it, drawing on American advertisements, songs, films, and so on. Ironically, these collective memories—these imagined Americas where people actually spent part of their pasts growing up—are now being commodified. To all those who, thanks to Jack Kerouac and a pop song, remember *Route 66* without ever having crossed the Atlantic, a Dutch travel agency now offers nostalgic trips down that artery. The road may no longer exist, but it reappears as a replica of itself, a simulacrum in the great Disney tradition.

This much is clear: generation upon generation of Europeans has grown up constructing meaningful worlds that they shared with their peers and that crucially drew on American ingredients. Mythical "Americas" have become part and parcel of the collective memory of Europeans. This takes us back to Mitterrand's musings. It seems as if he has fallen victim to a misreading of the way the collective memory of Europeans was built in the postwar period. Why indeed must a collective memory be a matter of, as Mitterrand has it, a country depicting itself in images? Why not admit that the collective memory of national populations is crucially a matter of the appropriation and digestion of foreign influences? One could ignore these only at the peril of centrally imposing definitions of what constitutes the nation. And, in fact, many of the arguments in favor of the cultural exemption clause, and of protecting national cultural identities, seem to betray this narrow paternalist view of the nation and its identity.

The Freedom of Choice

Commercial messages have been only one of the transmission belts of American culture abroad. Modern media of mass reproduction and mass distribution, like film, photography, the press, radio, television, sound recordings, have filled the semiotic space of people everywhere with messages made in America. Americans themselves, through their physical presence abroad, in the form of expatriate colonies, of armies, of businessmen, have equally contributed to the worldwide dissemination of their culture. Yet commercial messages, in the way they transmit American culture, are a particular case. They are not simply neutral carriers, conveying American culture for others to consume and enjoy; in fact, they give a particular twist to whatever ingredients of the American imagination they employ. A recent illustration of this process can be seen in a commercial message broadcast by CNN, the worldwide cable news network, and paid for by the "Advertising Council" in London. In what is in fact an advertisement for advertising, it is suggested that without advertising we all would be worse off, getting less information through the media. Advertising is presented as a necessary prop for the continued existence of a well-informed public in a functioning democracy. The little civics lesson offered by this commercial ends with the slogan: "Advertising—The Right to Choose."

This blending of the rationale of capitalism and democratic theory is not new. It is reminiscent of what happened in the early 1940s in America. Then, on the eve of America's participation in World War II, President Franklin Delano Roosevelt made his powerful contribution to American public discourse in his "Four Freedoms Speech," a rallying cry in which he called on his countrymen to fulfill an American world mission as he saw it. In all likelihood, Roosevelt had picked up the four freedoms as a rhetorical figure in the public domain. The Four Freedoms, as a group of four statues erected along the main concourse of the New York World Fair of 1939–40, had already left their imprint on the millions of visitors to the fair.

Working on his final draft of the State of the Union Address, Roosevelt briefly toyed with the idea of five freedoms, but clearly he did not want to move away from the popular foursome at the fair. If he wished his words to reverberate among the larger public, he needed to draw on a popular repertoire that was already established. The link with political views among the larger public was further reinforced through Norman Rockwell's series of four oil paintings, which were modeled after Roosevelt's speech, and which represented each of the four freedoms.

Using his appeal as an artist who had succeeded in rendering a romantic, small-town view of life cherished by millions of Americans, Rockwell managed to give an extra endearing touch to Roosevelt's message. Through the mass distribution of reproductions, Rockwell's paintings of the Four Freedoms facilitated the translation and transfer of Roosevelt's high-minded call to a mass audience.

If this is an illustration of American political culture as an element of American mass culture, of political rhetoric as it emanates from the public domain and returns to it, it was unaffected by the rationale of business. If anything had to be sold at all, it was a matter of political ideas; if a sales pitch was called for, it was a matter of public suasion, explaining the world to the larger democratic public and calling upon it to take appropriate action. Yet it was not long before Roosevelt's four freedoms would be joined by a fifth, in a 1944 advertisement by the Hoover Vacuum Cleaner Company in the *Saturday Evening Post*. Illustrated in the style of Norman Rockwell, the ad provides a familiar setting, as well as familiar faces: an old woman, a middle-aged man, and a young girl— "people from the neighborhood." They look upward toward a beam of light; providence, if not the good provider, is smiling upon them. In their arms they hold an abundance of packages, all of them gift-wrapped. This is Norman Rockwell country, but with a crucial difference: Rockwell's mythical small-town people, carriers of democratic virtue, now appear in the guise of Americans as consumers. Three years after Roosevelt decided that there were four, not five, freedoms, the Hoover advertisement reminded Americans that "the Fifth Freedom is Freedom of Choice." If America had joined the struggle to safeguard democratic values, this implied safeguarding the freedom of choice. By semantic sleight of hand, the (con)text of the advertisement shifted the meaning of freedom of choice: the "signified" was no longer the realm of politics, but the freedom of choice of the citizen in his role as consumer. Thus, spheres of freedom smoothly folded into one another.

And they still do. The Hoover Company chose to use language popular at the time, and to speak of a Freedom. The CNN message is also cast in the language of rights, reminding us of our Right to Choose. In either case, what we witness is the commodification of political discourse. The language of political ideals, of rights and freedoms, is being highjacked so that purposeful commercial action might be dressed in stolen clothes. Whether dressed as a freedom or a right, the commodifying logic appears again and again; it is not specific to any particular product. It is a logic we met before in those advertisements that tied the promise of freedom to cigarettes or soft drinks. It is a logic that commodifies and pedestrianizes political ideals by putting them in the service of commercial salesmanship. In that sense, we seem to have struck upon just another instance of the vulgarizing impact of American culture, one that corroborates a point made by so many European critics of American mass culture. Yet this is not the whole story. The very slogans chosen by sales departments, affirming our "Freedom of Choice," or our "Right to Choose," are semantically unstable and may well convey a message different from that the salesmen had in mind. A word like choice, when left unspecified, sits uneasily astride the divide between the political and the economic spheres. "Freedom of Choice" in particular may well read as the "Choice of Freedom," a simple inversion that may well put political ideas into the heads of an audience that is addressed in its role as consumers. Paradoxically, then, advertising stratagems cooked up by commercial sponsors may well have the effect of a civics lesson, if not of a subversive and anti-authoritarian call. Precisely there, it seems, lie the secrets of the appeal that so many American commercial messages have had, domestically as well as abroad.

Exploring frontiers of freedom—of children rebelling against parental authority, of sexual freedom, of freedom in matters of taste and in styles of behavior—the marketing of American consumer goods has been an instrument of political and cultural education, if not of emancipation. Generations of youngsters, growing up in a variety of settings in Europe, both east and west of the Iron Curtain, have vicariously enjoyed the pleasures of cultural alternatives conjured up in commercial vignettes. Simple items like a pair of blue jeans, Coca-Cola, a cigarette brand thus acquired an added value that helped these younger generations to give expression to an identity all their own. They have used American cultural language and have made American cultural codes their own. To this extent they have become Americanized. To the extent, however, that they have "done their own thing" while drawing on American cultural repertoires, Americanization is no longer the proper word for describing what has gone on. If anything, those at the receiving end of American mass culture have adapted it to make it serve their own ends. They have woven it into a cultural language, whose grammar, syntax, and semantics—metaphorically speaking—would still recognizably be French, Italian, or Czech. All that the recipients have done is make new statements in such a language.

There are more instances of such recontextualization. Surrounded as we are by jingles, posters, neon signs, and billboards, all trying to convey their commercial exhortations, we all at one point or another ironically recycle their repertoires; we quote slogans while bending their meaning; we mimic voices and faces familiar from radio and television. We weave them into our conversations, precisely because they are shared repertoires. Used in this way, two things happen. International repertoires become national, in the sense that they are given a particular twist in conversations, acquiring their new meanings only in particular national and linguistic settings. Secondly, commercial messages stop being commercial. A decommodification takes place in the sense that the point of the conversation is no longer a piece of merchandise or a specific economic transaction. In this ironic recycling of our commercial culture we become its masters rather than its slaves.

The Freedom of Reception

Many things have happened along the way since American mass culture started traveling abroad. American icons may have become the staple of a visual *lingua franca* that is understood anywhere in the world, yet their use can no longer be dictated solely from America.

For one thing, as we saw before, it is clear that European commercials made for European products may draw on semiotic repertoires initially developed in and transmitted from America. Yet, in a creolizing freedom not unlike America's modularizing cast of mind, Europeans in their turn now freely re-arrange and recombine the bits and pieces of American culture. They care little about authenticity. T-shirts produced in Europe are as likely to say "New York Lions" as they are to say "New York Giants."[2] What is more, American brand names, as free-floating signifiers, may even be decommodified and turned into carriers of a message that is no longer commercial at all.

Admittedly, the T-shirts, leather jackets, and baseball caps, sporting the hallowed names of Harley Davidson, Nike, or Coca-Cola, still have to be bought. Yet what one pays is the price of admission into a world of symbols shared by an international youth culture. Boys or girls with the word Coca-Cola on their T-shirts are not the unpaid peddlers of American merchandise. Quite the contrary. They have transcended such trite connotations and restored American icons to their pure semiotic state of messages of pleasure and freedom. Within this global youth culture, the icons youngsters carry are like the symbol of the fish that early Christians drew in the sand as a code of recognition. They are the members of a new International, geared to a postmodern world of consumerism rather than an early modern one centered on values of production.

There are many ironies here. What is often held against the emerging international mass, or pop culture, is precisely its international, if not cosmopolitan character. Clearly, this is a case of double standards. At the level of high culture, most clearly in its modernist phase, there has always been the dream of transcending the local, the provincial, the national, or, in social terms, of transgressing the narrow bounds of the bourgeois world and entering a realm that was nothing if not international: the transcendence lay in being truly "European," or "cosmopolitan." But clearly what is good at the level of high culture is seen as a threat when a similar process of internationalization occurs at the level of mass culture. Then, all of a sudden, the defense is not in terms of high versus low, as one might have expected, but in terms of national cultures and national identities imperiled by an emerging international mass culture. There is a further irony in this construction of the conflict, contrasting an emerging global culture seen as homogenizing to national cultures seen as havens of cultural diversity.

In the real world, of course, things are different. There may be a hierarchy of taste cultures, yet it is not a matter of higher taste cultures being the more national in orientation. It seems that this hierarchy of taste cultures is itself transnational, that indeed there are international audiences who at the high end all appreciate Beethoven and Bartok, or at the low end all fancy Madonna or Prince. Yet, in a replay of much older elitist tirades against low culture, advocates of high art see only endless diversity where their own taste is concerned, and sheer vulgar homogeneity at the level of mass culture. They have no sense of the variety of tastes and styles, of endless change and renewal in mass culture, simply because it all occurs far beyond their ken.

Finally, from the point of view of American mass culture traveling abroad, in many cases the exploration of cultural frontiers is taken to more radical lengths than anything one might see in America. Whereas sexual joy and freedom are merely hinted at in American commercials, European posters and TV commercials often are more explicit. Consider, for instance, the Italian wallposter of a brooding, erotic, barechested man standing astride a scantily clad, sexually aroused young woman crouched between his legs. She wears a crown reminiscent of the Statue of Liberty, and there is an American flag in the background. The commercial is for the one piece of clothing on the man's body: his blue jeans.

Similarly, in the Netherlands, a government-sponsored poster and TV campaign depicts a young couple making love. Both partners are naked; she sits on his lap, curving backwards in rapture. The text, in large print, reads: "Give your heart a new lease on life." Only the small print reveals the ad's true purpose: to invite people to become organ donors and to wear a donor codicil. Pasted across the country, on railway platforms, and on bus stops, this poster must have made visiting Americans bashfully turn their heads. Probably these visitors would not consider the campaign the outcome of a process of Americanization taken a few daring steps further. And how much more shocked would they be by another poster campaign, again sponsored by the Dutch government, on behalf of safe sex. This campaign graphically displays couples taking showers together, or engaged in similar forms of foreplay. In this instance, yet another frontier is being explored, if not crossed, for the Dutch safe sex campaigns includes depictions of gay couples, as well as heterosexual couples.

Admittedly, the poster campaigns described above do not convey commercial messages, although the Dutch government, in order to get its messages across, has adopted commercial advertising techniques by using advertising billboards, rented, one assumes, at the going market rate. So, in a sense, we have come full circle. Where the Hoover Company advertisement drew on republican language to claim the freedom of the advertiser, we now see advertising space being reclaimed for statements *pro bono publico*. If democracy is a marketplace, it has become inseparable from the economic market. It is in fact one indivisible and noisy place in which a jumble of cries and calls vie for the public's attention, echoing back and forth.

The perfect illustration of this was being pasted all across the Netherlands precisely at the time this article was being written. A huge poster advertises Levi's 508 jeans and playfully draws on American political language for its commercial message. What we see is the lower part of a half-nude male body, covered from the waist down by a pair of jeans. The slogan plays on the classic version of the Four Freedoms, citing: freedom of expression, freedom of thought, freedom of choice, and—Levi's 508— freedom of movement. The third freedom, as we have seen, already makes the transition from the political to the commercial; the fourth, political though it may sound, is meant to convey the greater room for movement provided by the baggier cut of the 508. The picture illustrates the point by showing the unmistakable bulge of a male member in full erection, casually touched by the hand of its owner. Clearly, the semiotics of American commercial strategies have been taken to greater lengths, so to speak, than would be conceivable in America. America may have been less embarrassed in exploring the continuities between the political and the commercial. Europe, of late, may have been more daring in its pursuit of happiness, graphically advertising it all across Europe's public space.[3]

For indeed, as European examples from the political and the economic marketplace serve to illustrate, the logic of a choice of freedom knows no bounds, once set free from controlling American standards of taste and decency. As is a *lingua franca*'s wont, it moves in a realm of free creolization, where the controlling authority of a mother culture no longer holds. Americanization, then, should be the story of the travels of an American cultural language and of other people acquiring that language. What they actually say with that language, however, is a different story altogether.

The Pleasures of Cultural Resistance

On the Op-Ed page of the New York *Times* of 11 December 1996, Thomas L. Friedman addressed the role of McDonald's in the current globalization of culture. He began by recounting a story popular among "the folks at McDonald's" about a young Japanese girl arriving in Los Angeles. Looking around, the young girl comments to her mother: "Look, mom, they have McDonald's here too."

What this illustrates in the eyes of people at McDonald's International—and Friedman goes on to elaborate this point—is the success of their strategy of multilocalism. By insisting on a high degree of local ownership, and by tailoring its products just enough to blend into local cultures, McDonald's counts on avoiding the worst cultural backlashes that some other U.S. companies have encountered. Part of the stake localities and nations now feel they have in McDonald's is therefore economic, through local sourcing, through ownership, and through employment.

But clearly, another part of the strategy is cultural, staving off a perception of the company as just another Trojan horse for a cultural imperialism under American auspices. Thus, in Japan, McDonald's renamed Ronald McDonald "Donald McDonald" because there is no "R" sound in Japanese. (That there is also no "L" in Japanese apparently did not worry them as much.) As Friedman quotes James Cantalupo, head of McDonald's International, "McDonald's stands for a lot more than just hamburgers and American fast food. Cultural sensitivity is part of it too. There is no 'Euroburger.' . . . We have a different chicken sandwich in England than we do in Germany. We are trying not to think as a cookie cutter."[4] Well, I'm not so sure. If this is what cultural sensitivity to local settings is all about, the strategy looks rather thin. Any student of popular culture in a context of globalization could come up with a number of illustrations belying Mr. Cantalupo's self-congratulatory statements.

Ironically, not even in the United States does McDonald's always have the rapport with local feelings one might expect of a company priding itself on its "cultural sensitivity." In 1994, the company closed one of its earliest restaurants, in Downey, California. It was an example of the early McDonald's style that was replicated time and again on roadsides across the country for the growing car culture of the 1950s. Surprisingly, in view of the fact that so many communities, in the United States and elsewhere, fight to keep fast-food chains off their main streets and away from their city centers, a groundswell occurred in Downey to save the restaurant. "We don't only want to save the pretty past, but the significant past," said Linda Dishman, executive director of the Los Angeles

Conservancy, a nonprofit group dedicated to preserving Southern California architecture.[5]

If this case illustrates McDonald's relative insensitivity to local publics, other examples would rather illustrate its cultural sensitivity approach to be ineffective. Two years ago, in the Italian industrial town of Turin, I witnessed a protest march organized by a local anarchist group. Their leaflets promoted "Anarchists against McDonald's, for the revolution." As they saw it, "McDonald's is above all an image, a symbol of the exploitation of man by man, of the environment by man, of animals by man. McDonald's is the nauseating odor spreading from its kitchen across the Piazza Castello."

Using the language of images and symbols, the group may unwittingly have drawn on repertoires developed by American critics of culture in the 1950s; yet the anarchists were using these repertoires to convict McDonald's for representing precisely the forces of exploitation, of mendacious publicity, of "enslavement, misery, and squalor," despite the company's attempts at being unobtrusive. The anarchists dismissed McDonald's response to environmental and dietary concerns; the company's attempts at recycling, or at offering "pathetic hamburgers for vegetarians," were in the eyes of the protest group nothing if not hypocritical.

On a nearby square I saw more signs of cultural resistance. An equestrian statue irresistibly drew the gaze of passers-by. That, one assumes, is precisely the point of this sculptural genre. Yet, what held my gaze was something different: spray-can graffiti on the four sides of the statue's base, all playing on one theme. "McDonald's merda," "Boycotta McDonald's," "McDonald's bastardi." I couldn't fail to notice the postmodernist jumble of meanings: here someone had been at work in angered protest against the Americanization of Italy, someone who at the same time had not shrunk from defacing the very heritage that his audience might see as threatened by American culture. The message of protest used an historic statue as a mere blackboard to write on; the writing itself was done with the tools of an international subculture that had its roots in America: the spray-can muralism of hip hop. Thus, the message managed to affirm the force of Americanization while trying to fend it off.

The Italian anarchist group's resistance against McDonald's as a symbol of capitalist exploitation may strike us as slightly old hat. Yet the connection they make may well translate into more contemporary language, conceiving of cultural globalization as concomitant to economic and technological globalization, such as the integration of markets, trade, finance, information, and corporate ownership. Many of these processes have their nodal points in America. Any graphical representation of

Internet exchanges, for example, would show the greatest density of traffic in the United States, connected to nodal knots elsewhere, each of lesser density. If America is still the hub of all these connections, it need not surprise us when cultural globalization as well appears as a very American phenomenon. It comes to the rest of the world in the image of American icons, dreams, metaphors, adding an aura of "Americanness" to much of contemporary popular culture, thus enhancing rather than diminishing its worldwide appeal. In the process, as our Turin example shows, the very forms of protest against America's alleged cultural imperialism may have become tinged by the very Americanization that protesters are busy trying to exorcise.

Notes

1. See R. Kuisel, *Seducing the French: The Dilemma of Americanization.* (Berkeley: University of California Press, 1993); and M. Pendergrast, *For God, Country and Coca-Cola: The Unauthorized History of the Great American Soft Drink and the Company That Makes It* (London: Weidenfeld and Nicolson, 1993).

2. As pointed out in a piece on U.S. Pop Culture in Europe, by Elizabeth Neuffer, in the Boston Sunday *Globe,* 9 October 1994, 22.

3. In this connection it is of interest to point out that the campaign for the Levi's 508 was produced by a Dutch advertising agency solely for the Dutch market. The video for the 501 that I referred to earlier was made by a British agency for the European market.

4. Thomas L. Friedman, "Big Mac II," New York *Times,* 11 Dec 1996, A27.

5. Verne G. Kopytoff, "It's Back: The Burger Stand From the Dawn of McCivilization," New York *Times,* 18 Dec. 1996, C3.

J. Michael Jaffe and Gabriel Weimann

New Lords of the Global Village?
Theories of Media Domination in the Internet Era

Control over the flow of information has been the focus of many human communication theories. Various critical perspectives view control over mass communication channels as a means of promoting dominant interests, usually to the exclusion of other interests perceived as irreconcilable, competing, or merely inconvenient. Included in this range of scholarship are theories of cultural imperialism, which describe nationalist and ethnocentric motivations of dominance, and theories of political economy, which describe media dominance as stemming from financial and economic imperatives. In this chapter, we propose to update media domination theories in the face of an emerging era of transnational communication corporations and decentralized communication networks.

The Early Notion of Cultural Imperialism

Many communication scholars, including Thomas Guback, Herbert Schiller, and Alan Wells, have ascribed an importance to the impact of Western media, particularly American and British media, throughout the world.[1] The great expansion of American television into the world around 1960 and the American dominance in exporting equipment, programming, and advertising, are seen by Schiller as part of a general effort of the American military-industrial complex to subject the world to American control and homogenized American commercial culture. As Jeremy Tunstall summarizes, "So powerful is the thrust of American commercial television that few nations can resist. Even nations that deliberately choose not to have commercial broadcasting find their policies being reversed by American advertising agencies."[2]

During the 1960s, Schiller argued, American policy seemed to focus even more strongly on subjugating and pacifying the poor nations.[3] Space satellites were to play a key part in this strategy. The U.S. government placed its telecommunications satellite policy in the hands of the giant electronics companies (AT&T, ITT, RCA) and then negotiated INTEL-SAT arrangements with the Western nations, giving the United States dominance over world communications. Ultimately, the policy was to beam American network television, complete with commercials, straight into household television sets around the world. The homogenization of world culture would then be complete. False consciousness and commercial popular culture would be plugged via satellite into every home.

In a similar vein, Alan Wells described how American television imperialism works in South America.[4] Since its birth, Latin American television has been dominated by U.S. financial institutions, companies, technologies, programming, and, above all, New York advertising agencies and practices. American advertising agencies not only produced most of the commercial breaks, but also sponsored, shaped, and determined the whole pattern of programming and importing from the United States. Tapio Varis produced the first reasonably comprehensive mapping of worldwide television import patterns, documenting American television programming exports around the world.[5]

A later study by Katz, Wedell, Pilsworth, and Shinar traces the history of both radio and television in ten Latin American, Asian, and African countries, as well as Cyprus.[6] This study suggests that the television imperialism thesis takes too little account of radio and of differences both within and between nations. It also strongly confirms that there was a high point of American influence on world television at some point in the 1960s. While Katz et al. reject any strong television imperialism thesis, they acknowledge the importance of production (transmission and studio) technology and provide much descriptive material that fits the thesis quite well. Like other students of television exports, they look with horror on the weight of commercial advertising, the predominance of American entertainment series, and the relative absence in most countries of high-quality educational or cultural television programming.

If we look beyond the American conspiracy argument, we can find powerful cultural, economic, and political factors that combine to promote American culture worldwide. Likewise, Stevenson argues that neither U.S. foreign policy nor British colonialism explains why U.S. media are growing in influence at the end of the twentieth century and are the model for media in most other countries.[7] Several other factors to be considered include:

1. Perceptions of American cultural values: Through its mythic narratives and celebrity icons, exported American pop culture encourages

initiative, ambition, and creativity while it tolerates, and often cele-
brates, individual eccentricity. Combined with the lure of financial
and popular success in the global market, these values are powerful,
attractive features of Western, and especially American, cultural
products.

2. The economy of the global media market: A publication in English
has, in theory, a potential audience of up to one-quarter of the
world's population. A similar advantage accrues to broadcast and
film, which can be shipped around the world without dubbing or
subtitling. This situation provides U.S. media organizations with a
significant advantage in accessing audiences and consumers of information worldwide. Furthermore, even with the costs of translation, purchasing Western media "products" is less expensive for
many localities than producing comparable fare.

3. The competitive, market-oriented structure of most American media:
Regardless of its artistic and cultural merits, a TV series that sur-
vives the ratings gauntlet of American networks has already been
tested for its popular appeal. With few exceptions, these American
hits become hits in other countries as well.

4. Western dominance in other areas of global communication: Hegemonic Western media organizations, with subsidiaries involved in
numerous communication media formats, enjoy a "synergy" or
mutually supporting embrace of all aspects of global communication. Dominance in news supports dominance in popular culture,
which supports dominance in technology, which supports dominance in journalistic style, which supports dominance in the English
language, and so on.

Political Economy and the New Lords of the Global Village

While one may argue that forces of cultural imperialism influence the distribution of news, entertainment, and other media artifacts, the notion
that these are specifically nationalist or ethnocentric imperatives fails to
account for a number of "facts on the ground." The developments we describe in the following paragraphs are better explained through a model
of political economy. Political economic theories analyze the economic
constraints that limit or bias the forms of mass culture distributed by
media elites, whom many label the "media lords."[8]

The world has changed since the notion of cultural imperialism was
first introduced. New communication organizations, new patterns of
ownership and flow of communication, and new media technologies
have emerged. Much of the emerging global culture is a product of

multinational corporate enterprise. The new media moguls, who do exist in large part as individuals rather than as anonymous corporate boards, are virtually unknown to the public, sometimes even in their own countries. They seem to form almost a global interlocking directorate with vertical and horizontal integration of the means of production and distribution. Consider, for example, one of the most powerful lords of the global village, the Australian-born Rupert Murdoch. His empire stretches from the South Pacific, across Europe and Britain, to North America. He owns fifty newspapers in Britain, the United States, Australia, and other countries. His assets include a Hollywood film studio, a TV network (Fox), fifteen cable TV stations in the United States, the European Sky TV satellite broadcasting system, over thirty magazines in the United States, Canada, Australia, and Europe, and publishing houses all over the world. His company controls music production companies, the Hong Kong satellite TV company (Star TV) and, of course, the *Sun*, the sleaziest national paper in London. Murdoch's holdings also include the *Times* of London, small dailies in Fiji and Papua New Guinea, a major daily in Hong Kong, and even a magazine in Hungary.

In recent years, the world witnessed the growth of several international media corporations. As Bagdikian observed:

A handful of mammoth private organizations have begun to dominate the world's mass media. Most of them confidently announce that by the 1990s they will control most of the world's important newspapers, magazines, books, broadcast stations, movies, recordings and videocassettes. Moreover, each of these planetary corporations plans to gather under its control every step in the information process, from creation of "the product" to all the various means by which modern technology delivers media messages to the public. "The product" is news, information, ideas, entertainment and popular culture; the public is the whole world.[9]

The American dominance in the global communication flow is less powerful than it was in the past. On the contrary, a growing concern is not the old complaint of excessive American cultural influence around the world, but the astonishing speed with which the United States is selling off its popular culture industries to foreign buyers. As Stevenson notes, "In every one of the popular media—books, magazines, music, movies, even newspapers—foreign buyers are snapping up U.S. properties with a speed and enthusiasm never seen before."[10] One of the largest chains of daily newspapers in the United States is the Canadian Thompson group, which owns 120 dailies. Among the French Hachette properties is the *Encyclopedia Americana,* and it should also be noted that the prestigious *Encyclopedia Britannica,* an American household fixture since 1902, headquartered in Chicago, was purchased in 1996 by Swiss-based financier Jacob Safra. In the United States, only television is protected by law from foreign ownership (which presumably is why Murdoch was so anxious to become a U.S. citizen). The prohibition is not really important, however, because the global system of production and distribution provides access to the U.S. market through joint productions, direct sales, and indirect ownership. New developments like fiber optics and satellites, computer networks and Internet, make it possible to publish and broadcast across the world at ever greater speeds and lower costs. National boundaries grow increasingly meaningless. In many countries, particularly those in Western Europe, government broadcasting monopolies are giving way to commercial operations with advertising increasingly aimed at megamarkets that stretch across continents. It is no accident that media consolidation has paralleled a similar trend among advertising agencies. The world's largest agency, Saatchi & Saatchi of London, has offices in eighty countries and buys 20 percent of the world's broadcast commercials.

This scenario does not match McLuhan's "universal understanding" or the original claims against American cultural imperialism. The driving force for these media giants is profits. Unlike the political-ideological motives behind the alleged media imperialism of the early sixties and seventies, the new lords of the media village are more business-oriented, though ideological motives should not be overlooked. Moreover, while Murdoch is relatively well known, many of the other modern moguls are not. Silvio Berlusconi in Italy, the late Robert Maxwell in Britain, the Japanese Sony Corporation, the Hachette organization in France, and Bertelsmann in Germany have played down their dominance of multinational multimedia ownership. All are taking advantage of new technology, global management strategies, and a tide of hands-off government policies to extend their operations and influence beyond national and regional borders. Despite the wide array of national memberships they represent, the new lords of the village do have political and cultural impact, as noted by Bagdikian:

The lords of the global village have their own political agenda. All resist economic changes that do not support their own financial interests. Together, they exert a homogenizing power over ideas, culture and commerce that affects populations larger than any in history. Neither Caesar nor Hitler, Franklin Roosevelt nor any Pope, has commanded as much power to shape the Information on which so many people depend to make decisions about everything from whom to vote for to what to eat.[11]

As the world heads into the twenty-first century, the notion of media domination assumes new dimensions and new meanings. In order to understand how the functions and goals of the media lords are evolving, we need to address the social and political contexts in which they operate.

The Global Village Redefined

A contemporary evaluation of McLuhan's vision of the global village reveals both confirmations and refutations. Our global communication networks are, at the very least, sending the same or similar messages to people around the globe, as exemplified by superchannels like CNN and MTV. To the degree that we can see our global neighbors and understand their values and concerns better, as they understand ours, we likely share at least complementary, if not identical, global awarenesses. A political economic perspective would explain that these shared awarenesses are filtered through lenses and blinders set in place by the media barons. Media imperialism arguments would point out that the sensibilities and viewpoints expressed are exclusively American or, more generally, Western.

While our awarenesses might be shared along certain conceptual dimensions, a realization of McLuhan's prediction of "a general cosmic consciousness" appears nowhere on the horizon. Though capitalist domination of communication channels actually supports the development of shared values, other physical, geopolitical realities and perceptions have a way of separating our globe into local spheres and alliances of interest. Knowing what the neighbors in our village are feeling, however, is quite different from sharing those feelings. We believe it likely that the evolution of global communication networks has served to sharpen our awareness of both intercultural differences and similarities.

To portray the influence of the media barons as absolute and monolithic is, in our view, simplistic. The collective experience of both academia and industry in the field of mass communication supports the idea that audiences are quite selective in what they watch and what they take away from media messages.[12] The media barons cannot ignore popular trends that reflect phenomena and influences beyond their control; hence, the ascension of the royal court oracles, the Gallup and Nielsen viewer rating and polling companies. We do not doubt that media organizations attempt to monopolize the collective attention of their audiences, which, after all, is a zero-sum-gain, prized commodity. That is, an audience member attends to one message source only by ignoring another. While one can certainly isolate similarities and patterns in the mediated content released to overseas markets, the notion that these patterns have a "homogenizing" effect is difficult to demonstrate in light of complex social, political, cultural, and intercultural processes.

Trends in the technological development of public media, and the response of media conglomerates to these trends, seem to support the thesis that the media lords are becoming increasingly involved in the distribution of more diverse varieties of messages to more narrowly segmented audiences. As such, the idea of a homogenizing process seems especially anachronistic.

Technological Developments

Technological developments of our communication networks are introducing new social dynamics at all levels of communication, from the intrapersonal to the macro levels. These new dynamics affect the development and distribution of information on a wide scale and therefore operate within the systemic "territory" of the media barons.

One hundred and fifty years ago, with the invention of the telegraph, humankind took the first step into the age of electronic communication. Ironically, the format of the telegraph, morse code, was a forerunner of digital binary, the basis of modern computer-mediated communication, or "CMC." The telegraph eliminated barriers of time and distance, marking the first major change in the physical transfer of information in five thousand years. About thirty years later, the development of circuit-switching technology ushered in the telephone, a one-to-one multipoint network. After another twenty years, the elements of audio were borne on radio waves and introduced the concept of massively replicable messages or "broadcasts."

In telephone systems, circuit-switching connects point A to point B along a series of paths that are physically switched together to form a temporary circuit or electronic communication channel. The "caller," in effect, rents the circuit for the duration of the call. Until 1990, with the exception of ham radio and telegraphy, circuit-switching technology represented the only practical, universally accepted means for the ordinary citizen to communicate with other citizens electronically. In other words, the distribution control resided in centrally controlled hardware configured independently of the message.

Popular use of the Internet as a public communication resource began in 1992. A descendant of a military communication network intended to withstand nuclear war, Internet communication is based on digital "packet-switching." Packet-switching starts with a document, text, image, video, or audio, that has been encoded digitally, and divides the document into smaller segments or "packets." Tacked on to each packet is its Internet destination, as well as information regarding its orientation within the document. The sending computer then sends the packets out, one by one, as Internet circuits to waypoints on the way to the final destination become available. Much like a railway cargo car, each packet travels from midpoint to midpoint, changing connections, until it arrives at its destination, where the original document is "reassembled" from its component packets.

A protocol known as "store and forward" represents a tacit agreement between Internet servers that any packets received for other destinations will be stored and forwarded as soon as room is available for the next leg of the packet's journey. In this system, control over distribution resides not in some centralized entity, but rather in the message itself.

The reliability of packet-switching networks is much greater than circuit-switching networks insofar as the digital message can be re-sent until the destination confirms its receipt. Since no physical alteration of a circuit is executed, and no single entity ties up any connection, costs incurred by individual messages, including e-mail messages and other file transfers, are relatively low or even negligible. Computer-mediated data files consist not of atoms, but of massless electronic bits, easily stored and transferred. Therefore, they can be copied ad infinitum and routed to multiple destinations, also at negligible cost compared with paper mail; hence, the proliferation of mailing lists and electronic bulletin board conferences.

Presently, any configuration of point-to-point communication is feasible on the Internet. One person can send messages to literally millions of others, or smaller subgroups of users, who have Internet addresses. Through information transfer protocols of FTP, Gopher, and the WWW, individuals can download (i.e., receive via automated links) and effectively share the same messages. Furthermore, individual users can conduct specific content searches, thereby realizing the concept of "on demand" media reception.

The hardware and software technology required for sampling and transferring audio and video on the Internet is, depending upon the desired quality of information resolution, within the financial reach of most middle-class individuals in the West. Furthermore, software that enables full duplex (simultaneous two-way) communication across the Internet is available and inexpensive. In other words, the equivalent of free telephone and videophone service is available on the Internet. While there are still factors that favor circuit-switched over packet-switched nontextual communication, it is still not known how or if regional and national telephone service providers will react to this financially attractive potential competitor.

There are compelling indications that the Internet is diffusing worldwide as a popular public media cluster. Demographic analysis of Internet adoption trends indicate that in the United States the technology is diffusing into a wide segment of society. A Nielsen Media Research (1996) survey estimated 63.8 million users, or about 24 percent of the American population as being online. A market research study conducted by O'Reilly and Associates[13] revealed that roughly two-thirds of American users are male while Nielsen[14] and Georgia Tech's Eighth Graphics, Visualization, and Usability (GVU) Center Survey[15] found that 40 percent of American Internet users are female. This indicates a rapid gender equalization trend considering that four years earlier 90 percent of surveyed American Internet users were male. The gender bias in Europe, however, is greater, with 85 percent of its users being male. The average age of the American Internet user is between thirty-five and forty, although a disproportionately large number of users are older than sixty-five. Trends in the Georgia Tech GVU's Fifth Survey,[16] coupled with those in the Nielsen study, indicate that the adoption of Internet technology is spreading into the lower socioeconomic strata of society.

The interconnective nature of Internet communication can serve to either promote or hinder the ideals of the global village. On the one hand, any individual can be attended to by a great many people, provided there is a widely-held interest in the topic or source. The Internet was instrumental in distributing information from sources in Tianamen Square, SCUD-bombed Tel-Aviv, and war-torn Bosnia at a time when these sources were not given airtime by the major global news organizations. One-to-one and multi-user CMC can help geographically distant individuals from different cultures to clarify their intercultural understandings and to identify their common concerns and interests.

On the other hand, while the limited channels of broadcast media effectively unify their geographically defined audiences, the Internet's unconstrained interconnectivity seems better suited for hosting many small, nongeographic communities based on shared interest. Individuals who do not share the same interest or points of view might never receive the same information. The current popular maxim of progressive citizenship, "Think Globally, Act Locally," might prove meaningless if too many of us find relatively little to discuss with our geographic neighbors.

While the development of personal computer-mediated communication has presented new opportunities for individuals to communicate within extended social networks, prior to the last five years it did not appear to be a significant concern to media giants. This situation has changed at least partly as a result of the process of convergence.

Convergence refers to a process of redefinition and combination of computer, mass media, and personal media technologies within all-purpose data networks.[17] "Personal media" refers to media technologies, including telephone, videorecording, and letter-writing, which handle messages intended for individuals.[18] Computers are acquiring display characteristics associated with broadcast radio and television as a result of their increasing capabilities of displaying and processing digital audio, visual, and text information. It is now quite common for personal computers, labeled as "multimedia systems" by their vendors and intended for homes and educational institutions, to include stereo speakers and full analog video playback capability. Some even have TV and radio reception tuners built in. A complementary convergence process has resulted in technology that makes a television set "Internet-ready." Some major electronics manufacturers have begun to market hardware dedicated solely to user-friendly Internet communication, including electronic mail and WWW content, to be displayed through a television set. Whichever technological route becomes more successfully diffused, these accessories enable individual, private users to consume an ever-growing variety of multimedia content from both radio-wave broadcast and Internet sources. One consequence of the greater degree of interactivity and control over the way in which information is accessed and presented is the increased blurring of the boundary between personal and mass media into "public media."

Decentralization and Control

While convergence might make parts of the Internet look, sound, and read a lot like television, radio, and the press, it is not a part of the exclusive domain of the media lords—at least not yet. Each computer directly connected to the Internet controls the data flow that courses through it, whether it is receiving or sending files, or whether it is serving as a way-station for information "just passing through." Overall coordination of Internet technical standards is undertaken by the Internet Society (ISOC), an eighteen-member board of Internet experts that comments on technical policies and oversees other boards and task forces dealing with network policy. Aside from this body, however, no central authority "runs" the Internet. The costs of the physical maintenance of communication through local PTTs are largely borne by these server operators individually and collectively.

Decisions regarding "socially acceptable" usage of the network would have to be negotiated on the basis of common motivations and values of the operators of tens of thousands of Internet-connected computers. As these universal values are few and far between among such a diverse collection of entities, from Greenpeace to General Motors, from Oxford University to the U.S. military, and from the National Organization of Women to the American Civil Liberties Union to the Christian Coalition, a universal or comprehensive set of guidelines is unlikely. Furthermore, different countries, and in America, even different states, have different local criteria for acceptable expression.

There are other systemic problems with imposing wide-reaching censorship measures while simultaneously expecting to reap the progressive benefits associated with decentralized communication. Censorship is anathema in academic and scientific realms that are often engaged in a continuous testing and challenging of assumptions. Technologically speaking, since the Internet's decentralized control was designed to overcome interference from nuclear weapons, it is not difficult to see that interference from censorship is at least as easy to bypass. Attempts to impose censorship restrictions through parts of the Internet result in a rerouting of information paths and formats such that the information eventually gets through.

The social evolution of the Internet has, since its inception, exhibited a strong current of libertarianism. Its transition from a major military initiative to a self-proclaimed progressive tool of intellectual cooperation has led many to believe that it is an example of humanity at its best—without influences of central control or constraint. The pervasive culture of "cyberpunk," the mischievous, pseudonymous role-playing in the virtual world of cyberspace, tends to challenge sacred cows, to push the envelope of acceptable discourse within the environment of a simulated, virtual world. From a socially progressive perspective, it is difficult to imagine how social groups with diverse agendas might find common ground on the Internet if one or both sets of values might be barred from free expression.

The lack of universal standards of acceptable communication content on the Internet, however, has not prevented Internet access providers from imposing constraints within their own domains. Few Internet users actually have direct Internet connections from their own computers. Internet users are either members or clients of organizations that provide Internet access via one or more central or "server" computers, connected to users' computers through either modem or local, institutional network connections. As such, some users are constrained by "acceptable use policies" that reflect specific organizational values and serve as conditions for network access demanded by the host institution. The nature and extent of these policies, and their manner of enforcement, can be viewed as different degrees of localized censorship.

Despite the decentralization of the Internet, and perhaps because of the anarchic subculture that characterizes it, many countries, practicing different levels of civil liberty and totalitarianism, have attempted to place various restrictions upon communication that exhibits elements of locally defined indecency and political dissent. Methods of control used in Singapore and China have included denying Internet access, routing all national incoming Internet traffic to centralized servers and either sampling or monitoring data transfer. Countries that try to "black out" certain paths or sites on the Internet might suffer from losing access to the beneficial commercial and other information ties resident in or routed through them. Effective censorship requires monitoring of communication channels, a situation that would pose significant problems for business confidentiality. Furthermore, Microsoft CEO Bill Gates equated Singapore's attempt to benefit economically from the Internet, while preventing certain forms of political and aesthetic expression, with trying to "have their cake and eat it too."[19] As the czar of Microsoft's digital information empire, Bill Gates' personal stake in the international free flow of information, however, should not be overlooked.

In 1995, the Clinton administration supported the Communication Decency Act, which held Internet users liable for sending or merely making available information, in any format, that might be conceptually included within an undefined range of "indecent" or "obscene" content. During the same period, the Clinton administration failed to achieve its stated aim of installing the Clipper chip in every modem and fax machine in America as well as in many markets abroad. While providing encryption for individuals and businesses, the chip would have enabled government agencies to monitor and decode Clipper-encoded information. The legal basis for the chip's function was a federal equation of encryption with defense technology and the threat that private computer communication might pose to national defense. Justice Department officials claimed that the surveillance potential was necessary in order to apprehend criminals, especially drug dealers, who might be using the Internet to conduct their business. A virulent, well-organized backlash on the part of Internet users contributed to the abandonment of the Clipper chip and underscored the determination of "netizens" to keep the network uncensored.

A major conceptual stumbling block for those who set Internet policy is the difficulty of classifying the Internet within the known parameters of previous communication technologies. On the one hand, e-mail (asynchronous one-to-one) and "talk" (synchronous one-to-one) facilities are most closely associated with private communication. Electronic mail messages, however, can also be sent to an unlimited but specified number of recipients. A worldwide-web (WWW) page, which can be made available by its host for public accessibility, can be received by any Internet user who knows the address or activates an associated link—whether or not the web page's author or owner so desires. Therefore, it might be considered as a potential publication or, if it is universally popular, as a mass media artifact. There have been ongoing and numerous calls by jurists, ethicists, and advocates to redefine and re-evaluate long-held norms regarding intellectual property and free speech as they affect cyberspace.

For the media lords, the Internet poses new and uncertain challenges. Their power in global media derives from their disproportionate, central control over an information distribution system with limited transmission control and expensive capital investment. The decentralized Internet is a network that can sustain, at least theoretically, a relatively unlimited number of message transmitters, and that requires relatively negligible capital investment. The media lords cannot "acquire" the Internet in the same way they might buy affiliate television stations or newspapers; this would mean purchasing, on a continuous basis, any and all computers that hook up to the network. It is even more unlikely that the collection of private corporations, public interest groups, and academic institutions that communicate over the Internet would agree to be bought out.

Economically speaking, digital, decentralized media present a curious conundrum. Most economic theory is based upon the presumption of control over limited resources and zero-sum-gain. That is, if someone controls a resource, then someone else cannot. Distribution costs associated with broadcast technologies, labor and materials costs of paper publishing, and organizational costs of content development limit the number of contestants on the playing field and therefore restrict the range of competition. Cable television, for example, relies on the limited availability of satellite transponders. The same parallel routing capabilities that made the United States C^3 (command, control, communication) system so robust also reduces the limitations to a larger volume of traffic. For the time being, while some internal networks, or "intranets," have experienced traffic overloads requiring upgrades to their internal capabilities, there seem to be no distribution resource limitations on the Internet.

The reaction of the media lords to the new decentralized media will depend on several factors influenced by the interplay of public, mass, and personal communication on the Internet. The relative freedom of expression presents both advantages and disadvantages to those who would be gatekeepers, opinion-leaders, and impressarios. It is clear that the flood of additional information available to consumers will cause many, if not most, to seek out information filters. Whereas the media lords previously ruled by capitalist decree, they will retain their eminence in the future only by default—that is, by virtue of consumers' cognitive overload.

The Adaptation of the Media Giants

The early nineties ushered in a great increase in popular attention to computer-mediated communication (CMC). Whereas e-mail and bulletin board systems had been growing in popularity since the mid-eighties, a critical mass of public and private interest groups became more vocal in their demands for either public or universal access to CMC capabilities and resources. There was clearly no shortage of advocates for popular CMC, whose pitch ranged from the pragmatic to the utopian. In 1991, American vice-president (then Tennessee senator) Albert Gore, Jr., shared his own vision of an information superhighway to advance American education and commerce.[20]

Initially, the mass media seemed to respond with tempered indifference and amused curiosity toward the early, task-oriented, text-only Internet. However, the subsequent critical mass of popular acceptance, coupled with new systems and software that made multimedia content transfer "user-friendly," coincided with a much less friendly treatment from the mass media. Magazine articles, news stories, and television reports portrayed the user-friendly, multimedia Internet as a haven for pedophiles, pornographers, software bootleggers, and malicious hackers. *Time* Magazine, the flagship of the Time/Warner media empire, figuratively tripped over itself to publicize the assertions of a Carnegie-Mellon undergraduate, Marty Rimm, that a great majority of Internet traffic was devoted to pornography.[21] Almost immediately, Rimm's study and claims were widely discredited by academic, legal, and journalistic Internet experts,[22] as well as by individuals whom Rimm cited as "contributors" to his research, for conceptual and methodological shortcomings amounting to gross exaggerations and misleading conclusions regarding the extent of pornographic traffic on the Internet.

The reactions of the media lords in the electronic mass media could be interpreted as defense responses to a significant threat to their dominance. After all, the Internet was, and still is, rife with flagrant copyright violations concerning materials owned by major media corporations. The values associated with intellectual property are not lost on creative individuals either. An almost cost-free distribution channel has opened up to media content consumers, who can download CD quality music as well as digital images and video, making copies that are of no lesser aesthetic quality than the original. News-gathering, the most expensive aspect of a media entity, might be bypassed by alternative providers, or the content may be stolen and redistributed by information pirates. Last but not least, the Internet was home to a set of media unconstrained by censorship. In short, the initial fear was that the public media of the Internet would become a mass media eclipsing centralized broadcast media.

Now, three years after the opening salvos by the broadcast and cable networks against the Internet, a new equilibrium seems to be emerging.

Rather than depict the Internet as an antisocial set of social communication formats, major media organizations have actually established their own presences on the Internet, specifically on the multimedia World Wide Web (WWW). An increasing number of television programs, newspapers, and magazines are publicizing their "http" addresses. This turn of events is likely the result of a reconceptualization of the Internet on the part of the lords. Rather than view the Internet as a competitive agent that cannot be "bought out," the media giants are likely considering potential benefits of maintaining an involved presence on the Internet.

Commercial media organizations attach a great deal of importance to being perceived as industry leaders. Publicizing a WWW address evokes an association with the leading edge of communication technology. As such, an association with the Internet helps traditional media entities maintain images of both present and future industry viability.

There are very compelling reasons to believe that media giants will garner a great amount of influence on the Internet as non-exclusive information filters. The volume of content on the Internet is so staggeringly large that trying to find specific information can be daunting, and more data is being added every day by individuals, businesses, academic institutions, and other organizations. The Internet's growth has been accompanied by the development of search engines, such as Digital Equipment's AltaVista and Yahoo, to help in the location of topic-relevant information. Many people will likely limit their information searching efforts to sources recognized from more traditional, ubiquitous, and passive media formats, such as television or print. The popular recognition of media organizations like CNN and the New York *Times* gives their WWW sites a distinct advantage over other Internet-based news information sources. Likewise, Internet "surfers" looking for popular culture content might well be attracted to the "brand recognition" of WWW sites maintained by the likes of Time/Warner or Paramount.

Internet-based WWW sites can collect fees for advertisements, usually with links to the advertiser's own set of Web pages. Advertisements on the Web can appear in many forms and can remain onscreen as part of a web page's content. Compared with the costs of maintaining bandwidth on the radio broadcast spectrum, Internet-based information distribution is relatively cost-free. A fast, well-equipped Internet server presently costs far less than a television advertisement, and WWW sites are accessible on a continuous basis. With regard to marketing, it should be noted that WWW-site managers have the capability of tracking exactly who accesses their sites, unlike broadcast communication professionals, who must rely on the system of ratings to intrusively monitor a small sample of the broadcast information consumer population.

Most or all of the content presented on the media lords' WWW pages has been or will be repurposed, that is, recycled, for use in other media formats. CNN's web pages contain links to both recent and archived stories covered in their cable broadcasts. While they might be obsolete for broadcast purposes, they might be quite useful for a WWW information consumer seeking more details about a past event. In addition, the information intended for broadcast consumers in one local area can be archived and made available for other information consumers. Also, in line with Bagdikian's concept of synergy, the WWW is an ideal venue for presenting associative links among the various information offerings under the umbrella of a media conglomerate. When one accesses the web pages of Warner Brothers, one is immediately presented with an impressive graphic interface with hypermedia links to lavishly designed sites that publicize newly released motion pictures, home video products, upcoming television shows, and souvenir paraphernalia marketing outlets. In short, a virtual information mall steers the visitor exclusively to Warner Bros. offerings.

As more and more consumers use the WWW to download video clips, sound bites, and text segments, our expectations for "on-demand" content acquisition will likely become more routinized. It is not hard to imagine that as video quality and transmission speeds rise, "on-demand" information might become "pay-per" information, that is, information for which the source charges according to a per-access tariff.[23] By participating in the "grand experiment" of multimedia information-sharing on the WWW, the media lords, who control the lion's share of popular cultural property, are positioning themselves quite effectively for the possibility of such a crossover.

Perhaps, though, the most compelling reason for the media lords to foray into the Internet is that it provides an inroad into both personal and public media. Personal media refer to communication channels whose technologies are geared toward individual communication. Public media pertain to channels that involve large groups of individuals at some level of interactive communication. The Roman forum is the archetype of public space, a commons of many-to-many information exchange. The Internet itself can be characterized as a set of both personal and public media formats because its flow of information involves continuous information choices of individual users as they interact individually or as part of larger groups. Through e-mail and Usenet discussion groups, dyads and larger groups often present direct links to WWW sites as part of their discourse. Not only, therefore, do the media lords become referents in a conversation, but their messages and cultural symbols are directly a part of Internet discourse.

By maintaining a presence in the public space, the media conglomerates can interact with and monitor other participants. While the media lords might wield some influence in the development of popular culture, the substance of that culture is often discovered or developed outside the domain of the lords and subsequently acquired. New rock 'n' roll bands, new authors, and new trends, to name some examples, are sought by mass media purveyors who benefit with increased mass patronage if their instincts prove correct. The Internet provides the opportunity for creative individuals and groups, of far less stature than the media giants, to present their creations to others who want to experience them. Numerous discussion groups on the Internet, which focus on politics, music, fiction, and other subjects, discuss new ideas and trends and often provide direct, Internet-based links to sites that present the innovations. If one assumes that the proportion of Internet users within society at large will increase, then the existence of the Internet can help the media lords in their manufacturing of popular culture. They can sample cultural concepts and popular reaction to those concepts through the same decentralized network.

Presently, on the basis of the generally positive tone the media lords use in dealing with the Internet, they seem content to be big fish swimming in a very big Internet pond, and they seem to be willing to live and let live. In other words, they seem willing to accept a status quo in which the Internet's facilities of receiving and disseminating information are free to individual users, the "little fish," as well. Technological utopians would state that the low-cost, decentralized communication technology, combined with low-cost digital content generation and libertarian CMC activism, presents this as a fait accompli to the media lords. However, it should be remembered, as seen in the cases of Singapore and China, that the initiatives of powerful centralized entities can act, with varying degrees of effectiveness, to limit both freedom and popular involvement within their domains.

The Future of the Oligarchy

The development and progress of decentralized networks hardly seem to pose a threat to the popularity of the traditional, passive media or, therefore, to the dominance of the media lords. While interactive public media formats provide attractions and capabilities unmet by previous media formats, Nicholas Negroponte predicts a popular coexistence of passive mass media with the more interactive personal and public media, citing the relative simplicity and frugality of the former.[24] The nature of this coexistence will, to some degree, define the future of the relationship between the information-rich and the information-poor, as well as social perceptions of status based on the possession of information. The recent appearance of advertisements on mass media news and entertainment programs for their WWW counterparts enhances the status of these shows and of their host corporations, while it points the way to an implied future or, at the very least, to the forum of the socioeconomic information elite who are both savvy and wealthy enough to afford access.

The coexistence of the Internet "forum" and the "court" of the media lords, however, is still an uncertain one, dependent upon the processes of public policy and the political and economic initiatives of mass media power brokers. If the lords' priority is to serve their stockholders, and the symbiosis of court and forum is divined as the most profitable path, then this situation might constitute a new norm of media industry–public interaction.

On the other hand, if Bagdikian's view of the media lords as jealous guardians of political economic ideology, or Tunstall's thesis of cultural imperialism, holds true, we should see increasing pressure exerted by media conglomerates to limit access and/or content on the Internet in order to eliminate the competition for the attention of information consumers. In any event, the presence of the lords on the Internet will most probably increase as the network's popularity increases and as the technology for information transfer improves.

The media lords will likely continue to function as keepers of the archives of shared culture as well as agenda-setting focal points of social surveillance. As such, a defining characteristic of media dominance will continue to be the ownership and acquisition of popular cultural properties as well as the development of cultural trends. What remains to be seen is how new artifacts and trends enter the pantheon of shared culture and how social processes in the public realm influence the selection. To a limited degree, the development of an electronic commons, in the present incarnation of the Internet, provides an unprecedented opportunity to observe some of the processes of cultural negotiation at work.

New alliances between computer and media companies, exemplified by NBC's recent joint WWW project with Microsoft and other partnerships between software firms and Hollywood studios, reflect the trend of media convergence and a shift toward public and interactive media. In parallel, the media lords and the captains of computer media technology are jockeying for position in order to set standards. In the case of the media lords, these are cultural and aesthetic standards. The captains of computer media technology, including Microsoft's Bill Gates, are competing with one another to provide the hardware and software technology standards that determine how the messages will reach us and what they will look and sound like. The setting of technical and aesthetic standards, especially in a public medium, helps the media giants to distinguish their content as it provides information consumers with new criteria of Internet-based information quality. Thus, while the media lords might not be able to maintain dominance in a decentralized network through controlling and restricting the vast majority of information traffic, they will certainly take steps to distinguish themselves from the Internet's more common folk.

Conclusion: The Rise of the Global City

In conclusion, with the development of decentralized communication networks, the global village has become a global city, a virtual megalopolis with countless parallel interactions, transactions, and concentrations of interests. This reflects a movement away from the global village model of broadcast television, which has been guided by central, cross-cultural denominators of human values. While there are certainly cultural universals and values of human interest that are shared globally, people need to affiliate with other people who share more individuating interests. It is likely that the perspectives presented by the media lords for global consumption will further diversify in the future. To ascend as an influential communicating entity in such a complex scenario will involve a complex multiplicity of interests and values within the media conglomerate itself.

While the idea of a global city might seem a bit less sanguine than the idyllic vision of a close-knit global village, it better accounts for the complex lines of competition and cooperation among actors in the social communication network. The model itself does not abolish inequity between the media elites and those who are informationally disadvantaged for political or economic reasons. It does, however, propose a theoretically systemic potential for the kind of social organization that can provide (a) alternatives to the media conglomerates on the public turf and (b) private and shared space for both acknowledging and resolving social differences, so as to negotiate different contexts of shared culture. Theories of media dominance require updating to reflect significant changes and new observations in the field. These changes include a redefinition of the relationship and communication power balance between the traditional mass media industry and its consumers. The rise of decentralized networks, with an unlimited potential for interconnectivity among individuals and groups, presents both new challenges and opportunities for locating and presenting meaningful cultural information. As a result, the mass media dominance based on ideological imperialism is shifting in favor of an information market dominance based on cultural recruitment and segmentation.

Notes

1. See Thomas Guback, *The International Film Industry* (Bloomington: Indiana University Press, 1969); Herbert I. Schiller, *Mass Communications and American Empire* (Boston: Beacon, 1971); Alan Wells, *Picture Tube Imperialism? The Impact of US TV in Latin America* (New York: Orbis, 1972).

2. Jeremy Tunstall, *The Media Are American: Anglo-American Media in the World* (New York: Columbia University Press, 1977), 38.

3. See Schiller, *Mass Communications*. Also, see Herbert I. Schiller, "Information: America's Global Empire," *Channels* (September–October, 1981): 33.

4. See Wells, *Picture Tube Imperialism?*

5. Tapio Varis, "Global traffic in television," *Journal of Communication* 24 (1974): 107.

6. See Elihu Katz, E. G. Wedell, M. J. Pilsworth, and D. Shinar, *Broadcasting in the Third World* (Cambridge, Mass.: Harvard University Press, 1977).

7. Robert L. Stevenson, *Global Communication in the Twenty-first Century* (New York: Longman, 1994).

8. Stanley J. Baran and Dennis K. Davis, *Mass Communication Theory: Foundations, Ferment, and Future* (Belmont, California: Wadsworth, 1995), 324.

9. Ben Bagdikian, "The Lords of the Global Village," *The Nation* 248, no. 23 (1989): 805.

10. Stevenson, *Global Communication in the Twenty-first Century,* 12.

11. Bagdikian, "The Lords of the Global Village," 807.

12. See Baran and Davis, *Mass Communication Theory,* 139–43; Joseph T. Klapper, *The Effects of Mass Communication* (New York: Free Press, 1960); Everett M. Rogers, *Diffusion of Innovations,* 3rd ed. (New York: Free Press, 1983).

13. O'Reilly and Associates, *Internet User Study* (1995), available from World Wide Web at http://www.ora.com/www/research/users/index.html.

14. Nielsen Media Research, *The Internet Demographics Recontact Study* (1996), available from World Wide Web at http://www.nielsenmedia.com/cnet-pres/omenu.htm.

15. Georgia Tech. (Georgia Institute of Technology) Graphics, Visualization, and Usability (GVU) Center, *Eighth User Survey* (1997), available from World Wide Web at http://www.cc.gatech.edu/gvu/user_surveys/.

16. Georgia Tech. GVU Center, *Fifth User Survey* (1996).

17. Joseph Straubhaar and Robert LaRose, *Communications Media in the Information Society* (Belmont, California: Wadsworth, 1996), 20.

18. Gladys Ganley, *The Exploding Political Power of Personal Media* (Norwood, N.J.: Ablex, 1992).

19. *The Straits Times* (13 February, 1995), "Cyberspace Revolution Will Transform Global Culture—Bill Gates," 27.

20. Howard Rheingold, *The Virtual Community* (New York: Harper Perennial, 1993).

21. See Philip Elmer-Dewitt, "On a Screen Near You: Cyberporn," *Time* Magazine (3 July 1995): 38–45 For the findings of the study itself, see Martin Rimm, "Marketing Pornography on the Information Superhighway," *Georgetown Law Journal* 83 (June 1995), 1849–1934.

22. For a meticulous guide to the drawbacks of the Rimm study, see Donna L. Hoffman and Thomas P. Novak, "A Detailed Analysis of the Conceptual, Logi-

cal, and Methodological Flaws in the Article: 'Marketing Pornography on the Information Superhighway'" (2 July 1995), available from World Wide Web at http://www2000.ogsm.vanderbilt.edu/rimm.cgi.

David G. Post, Visiting Associate Professor of Law at Georgetown University, whose *Law Journal* published Rimm's findings, discusses the lack of peer review and other methodological problems in Rimm's article in "A Preliminary Discussion of Methodological Peculiarities in the Rimm Study of Pornography on the 'Information Superhighway'" (28 June 1995), available from World Wide Web at http://www2000.ogsm.vanderbilt.edu/novak/david.post.html.

David Touretzky, a Senior Research Scientist of the Computer Science Department at Carnegie-Mellon University, Rimm's academic institution, labeled Rimm's study "a mixture of interesting anecdotes, unsupported assertions, shoddy statistics, and trashy sensationalism," in a letter (3 July 1995) submitted to the New York *Times*; available from World Wide Web at http://www2000.ogsm.vanderbilt.edu/novak/dave.touretzky.html.

23. Vincent Mosco, *The Pay-Per Society* (Norwood, N.J.: Ablex, 1989).

24. Nicholas Negroponte, *Being Digital* (New York: Vintage, 1995).

Reinhold Wagnleitner

Encartafication or Emancipation

The Internet as the New American Frontier?

> Capital burns off the nuance in a culture. Foreign investment, global
> markets, corporate acquisitions, the flow of information through
> transnational media, the attenuating influence of money that's
> electronic and sex that's cyberspaced, untouched money and computer-
> safe sex, the convergence of consumer desire—not that people want the
> same things, necessarily, but they want the same range of choices.
> —Don DeLillo, *Underworld* (New York: Simon and Schuster, 1997)

Trying to find some relief from the glittering computer screen, the British-
mystery-buff tries to unwind with one of Colin Dexter's Inspector Morse
novels, *Death Is Now My Neighbour.*[1] Small is the solace for the
computer-weary reader when (s)he finds the following quotation from
Terence Benczik's *A Possible Future for Computer Technology*: "A recent
survey has revealed that 80.5 percent of Oxford dons seek out the likely
pornographic potential on the Internet before making use of that facility
for purposes connected with their own disciplines or research. The figure
for students, in the same university, is 2 percent lower." While these numbers surely indicate that there is progress, what constitutes pornography
remains in the eyes of the beholder. I always have sympathized with Albert Einstein, who once asked what was pornographic about a naked
woman's breasts compared to the decorated breast of a general.

Suppose we call it sex. Between sex and the military, we have two of
the most important facets of the ubiquitous virtual reality of the Internet.
The former, however, is the Internet's hottest item, which draws by far
the most users globally, the latter having disappeared from the open net

to build its own virtual military world. Practically all surveys conclude that sex is the most searched for subject on the Internet. Seven of the top ten search words typed into search engines by British users in late 1997 were sex related. According to this study, in October 1997 alone, the word *sex* was typed in 1.5 million times.

Only in the spring of 1999, sex for the first time was overtaken by a new search term: mp3, a technology used for downloading high quality sound and video files. But rest assured, the top hundred sites of www.searchterms.com at the end of the twentieth century still count thirty-seven sexual terms, with a concentration on "illegal" sexual activities—probably one of the explanations for the U.S. domination of the web—while a large proportion of the rest are names of actresses and models. These lists function like a cultural barometer of the Internet, they are "windows to the soul of the Net-searching world."[2] While many observers find the present situation quite unnerving, future developments may even be less attractive. "Sex will always be a part of the Internet, but its importance will be significantly reduced over the next couple of years," *Web* assures us. "Shopping will be far more popular than sex on the Internet by 2000."[3] Isn't that just wonderful and utterly reassuring?

Less reassuring is the impression of the relative strength of European vs. American popular culture on the Internet: my search attempts on one of the leading Internet consultancies and developers, NUA, about Entertainment in Europe came up with the following, rather depressing, result:

Search results based on the following information:
Subject: Entertainment
Geographic reference: Europe
"No matching records found"

To suggest this zero result presents the whole story of a European presence on the Internet is far too pessimistic. Still, as the research of Erwin Giedenbacher and Christian Gruber has shown, the proportion of U.S. movies and soap operas relative to their European counterparts on websites is not only about ten to one, but there are also considerably more references to American films and TV products on German and other European websites than to locally produced entertainment products.[4]

We get quite different but similarly shocking results when we try cross-referencing the subject "entertainment" with another geographic reference: North America. This search uncovered two especially revealing bits of information. *Newsbytes* (6 October 1997) informs us that 25 percent of office computers in the United States contain pornography of various genres including child pornography. This study was carried out over an eleven-month period by Digital Detective Services, Inc. (DDS), a detective agency that specializes in investigating computer-based crimes and activities. DDS is often employed to investigate employees suspected of giving away company trade secrets or of misusing their company computers in any other way.[5] Upsetting news indeed: child pornography *and* digital detective services!

Of course, digital big brothers lurk not only on the work front, as is demonstrated by a study of Blacksburg, Virginia. Blacksburg, a small city of 34,000, currently has 24,000 inhabitants online, thanks to a four-year experiment by Virginia that made the little town the most densely wired place on the whole globe. Hopes for an improved digital democracy and business so far have not been fulfilled, although 24,000 people online are writing 250,000 e-mail messages a day. On average, the Blacksburgers are online seventy-eight minutes a day, and, quite surprisingly, senior citizens have become the number one users. The most prevalent topic of conversation online (aside from old jokes and complaints about broken hips and prostate problems) is "how can I upgrade my computer to make it faster?" While the town hall's digital address on 300 South Main (http://www.bev.net) holds little attraction, the Blacksburgers overran sex and gay websites so much that the local webmaster forgot everything he had heard about freedom of speech from Thomas Jefferson and shut down his neighbors' access. No one dared to protest publicly; after all Blacksburg counts forty-eight churches within its city limits.[6]

My web search of North American entertainment also uncovered a *Philadelphia Online* report (25 September 1997) claiming that American teenagers converge online, and more often use the Internet to communicate with each other more often than for Web browsing. More and more teens are finding that what is lacking in an e-mail friendship—namely physical contact—is easily compensated for by the ability to experiment with multiple online identities and by the ability to avoid the trauma of meeting peers face to face. According to *Philadelphia Online*, teens are turning their backs on traditional dating methods and converging online in teen chat rooms in search of members of the opposite (or same) sex. Chat rooms offer teenagers chances to try on new identities, experiment with their developing personalities, and generally avoid a lot of the unpleasant social awkwardness associated with being a teenager. Parents are warned to become concerned only when teenagers are using cyberspace as an alternative to their own reality.[7]

But concerned mothers and fathers have already been alerted to the perils of their younger children's "interactivity," because the future of the Internet is already largely happening in the market for children. Disney (Disney.com—The Web Site for Families), Viacom (Nickelodeon—entertainment and games, just for kids!), and many others are vying for the attention (and brand loyalty) of this most promising social segment. In the United States alone, almost 10 million children were already online in late 1997—a number that is expected to swell to 45 million by the year 2002. A FIND/SVP report, *Children on the Internet* (24 October 1997), has shown that 14 percent of people under eighteen were online then. Children, therefore, are probably the fastest growing section of Internet users.[8]

The massive increase in the number of children online, an increase of 444 percent since 1995, is paralleled only by the impressive explosion of the Internet's volume, which is doubling every ninety days.[9] According to official estimates, about 19 million U.S. kids under age eighteen have access to home computers, and while the online children's market is still (pardon the pun) young, tremendous possibilities loom on the horizon: by the end of 2002, child-generated revenues will grow from just over $306 million in 1996 to nearly $1.8 billion.[10] In the study "Kids Online" (spring 1999), NFO *Interactive* reported that the average online child [*sic*] spends five to seven hours per week online although their parents estimate they spend only 4.2. One in six is allowed to make online purchases. Almost three-quarters are doing homework online (so they say) and 70 percent are playing games.[11] Kids and teens are the two largest growth sectors on the Internet. According to Jupiter Communications, approximately 8.6 million kids and 8.4 million teens were online in the United States in 1998. By 2002, there will be 21.9 million kids and 16.6 million teens. By 2002, Jupiter predicts teens will account for $1.2 billion and kids will account for $100 million of the e-commerce dollars spent.[12]

Here it is time to raise my first caveat. When talking about American popular culture, many self-proclaimed experts usually refer to products and trends that were popular novelties when they were young, which in all practicality means that, by the time it is written about (in scholarly fashion, anyway), the parade of popular culture has already passed by its consumers, if it has not already *passed away* itself.[13] Fashion cycles have become fast-paced whirlwinds. For example, most of the cultural products that originated in real ghettos have been fractured, diluted, and reconfigured in a plethora of reimagined ghetto styles. Therefore, most theoretical approaches often prove eerily anachronistic. That is why it is useful to keep the following test results in mind. A few years ago, an American college professor asked second- and third-graders in a Jasper, Tennessee, public school to identify Elvis Presley. Below are a few representative responses:

"He was a great big man and he invented rock and roll."
"He lives in a big house in Memphis and he only comes out at night."
"He's this big, black guy who invented the electric guitar."

And, my favorite:

"He was an old guy who was a king somewhere."

The most important message of this test is, of course, that none of the above is true, and that what seems an enduring cultural icon is, in fact, already in the process of being forgotten. So the question is not whether Elvis is dead but when the dead Elvis will be.[14]

However virtual the children's realms in Cyberspace may be, gender differences remain real. While boys continue to enjoy ever more violent games, this is not true for girls. Forty-nine percent of female users fall in the two to twelve age group, and that market alone is valued at $60 million. However, the female demographic drops to only 37 percent once the girls become thirteen. "Purple Moon," a research company that specializes in girls-only games, has come to the not-so-new conclusion that girls prefer subtle competition as opposed to in-your-face violence; that girls like to form relationships as opposed to killing everything in sight; and that girls like to make up their own stories rather than being bombarded with tightly structured narratives.[15] In 1998–1999 the increase in Internet adoption by consumers has been driven by women and it is only a question of time before the number of women on the net will surpass that of men. Already by 2001, Computer Economics predicts, women will account for 45 percent of the world's Internet users.[16]

One cannot help but wonder why we assume—as a fact of nature regardless of nurture—that boys will not also be opposed to in-your-face violence or to killing everything in sight. But the Internet in this context is not different from other forms of modern popular entertainment. Nor, sadly, is it much different from popular education methods. We should remind ourselves that many earlier forms of traditional (American and European) popular culture were anything but quaint and also contained violence, crudeness, and transgressions of social rules. That said, any analysis of late twentieth-century American mass entertainment will surely conclude that, confronted with an ever increasing and unprecedented growth of displays of violence, we had reached a new level of excess.

While we may disagree about the particular "Americanness" of these exploding signs of violence in popular culture products, violence in the realm of popular culture surely has acquired a specifically American look. The American-dominated infotainment industries have become the really heavy industries of the twentieth and, most probably, of the twenty-first century, whether in the areas of production, distribution, marketability, sales, or consumption. "Hollywood," therefore, has become the biggest educational institution on planet earth. Why should the Internet be any different, when its commercial entertainment packages are dominated by the same or at least by similar companies to those that created these products for the greatest possible variety of channels, and profit(ed) from their global popularity in the first place?[17]

As Reuters noted on 20 August 1997: "Sex Drives the Internet's Technological Developments: Adult entertainment is the number one income generator on the Internet according to a recent study. The study showed that globally sex related queries are the most frequently entered criteria in search engines despite the relatively small amount of domains providing adult entertainment." The problem isn't sex, however, but rather the lack of it. The problem is sex that, by definition, avoids physical contact. Sex rules the Internet, cry the critics, but the real problem, as I see it, isn't sex alone, but sex—and virtual sex at that—in combination with violence, power, business, and exploitation. Cybersex, then, tells us more about a strange new world of sexual angst than about supposedly never-before-heard-of perversities! Virtual affairs present an easy beginning, an easy end, and no problems the next morning. Quipped Dinty W. Moore in *The Emperor's Virtual Clothes: The Naked Truth about Internet Culture*, "I have seen the future. And already miss the past."[18]

O ie of the side effects of America's global liberating mission is that no more emperors are left, naked or dressed. Yet at the end of the American Century, quite a few Americans acted surprised when they discovered that "Sex, Lies, and Videotape" signified an American president and not some far away decadent aristocrat. Ironically, the outcome of the immense push for the promotion of the "Information Superhighway" by the White House and Vice-President Al Gore could hardly have foreseen that the Web would pass its major test exactly in the moment when it survived the millions of curious websurfers who all wanted to access the Starr report simultaneously. Still, there are always winners within the system of capitalism. Witness the 25 September 1998 headline of the *Computer News Daily*: "Clinton Causes Internet Share Prices to Surge." The Clinton sex scandal heralded unprecedented interest in shares in Internet companies and the acceptance of the Web as a mass media outlet by speculators. The Starr report and the testimony video brought record numbers of consumers online. As a result, the share price of a number of major Internet companies rose dramatically during the week of the report's release. Online bookseller Amazon.com and the search engine Yahoo saw the highest increases, with share prices rising by 19 percent and 15 percent respectively.[19]

In 1997, the American Psychological Association remarked that "Internet sex offers information and education while being the perfect medium for human interaction for the socially challenged."[20] Am I socially challenged or just simply puzzled by the euphemism *adult* entertainment?

Nevertheless, the American Psychological Convention reported—surprise, surprise—that Internet addicts are not looking for information but entertainment. The report "Internet Addiction" also revealed that pathological Internet users are logging on in a bid to create another persona.[21]

That bid to create another persona has been an important part of the allure of American popular culture not only both within the United States and abroad, but also for the leading computer wizards, the avant-garde of cyberspace PR, and the sharpest business tycoons. For it is one of the most interesting facets of the Internet that, while its image is one of freedom and *private* genius, its real—and mostly hidden—background is actually one of massive *public* funding—and *military* funding at that. So let us turn, for a moment, to the ancient history of cyberspace.[22]

The Internet seems so futuristic, the information age so devoid of any history (and, thereby, so typically American), that its devotees and propagandists find the circumstances of its birth difficult to grasp. But the fact remains that the computer network connecting more than 170 millions of users (in May 1999) stands as a monument to military plans for fighting the Second World War, the Cold War, and the avoided final conflagration with the Soviet Union. And, it could be further argued, the spectacular advances of computer sciences in the West did more to bring down the empire of the Soviet Union than any other individual development—with the possible exception of the allure of American popular culture.

This military background is not a lineage the cyber-enthusiasts want to dwell on. It is no wonder that the Pentagon is not too enthusiastic about these facts. Still, nearly all of the popular accounts on the Internet entirely skip the circumstances of cyber-paternity of the U.S. Air Force, Army, Navy and secret services. Perhaps these strange and revealing omissions are understandable. Internet boosters have created an instant mythology, featuring a fiercely libertarian "Hackers' ethic" and the "freewheeling, untamable soul" of cyberspace. In an analogy to the road, the electronic autobahn has been written all across the watchtower, and the Internet has been instantaneously absorbed into the myths of popular culture. The information superhighway, therefore, is not only on the road again on Route 66 but by definition has become the new frontier, seemingly without frontiers. The computer kids now are the real new Lone Rangers and Cyberspace the prairie of the twenty-first century. The "netizens" admiringly look up at their new stars, computer nerds and hackers, whiz-kids and brainstorm troopers while one of the central popular myths of the United States—from dishwasher to millionaire—has been supplanted by the nerdy garage-inventor to billionaire myth. But cyberspace has a cyberpast and we will write cyberhistory.

No doubt, the GI stamp—the government issue stamp—cools a lot of the hot air of the hyped victory of the free market. The contributions of individual inventors, technicians, businesspeople, and "imagineers" remain undisputed, as unquestioned as the massive cooperation of government, universities, and industry—in short, the military-industrial establishment. American popular culture and the computer technology for a long time now have been inseparable. But it seems hard to swallow the triad of pop culture, internet, and military. Still, there's no Top Gun without Top Computers—and vice versa. The Internet, therefore, is not only the largest machine "man" has ever created, but also the largest *military* machine ever constructed.

As with most great advances in the history of ideas, there was not one single defining Internet event. No eureka-fruit fell on a cyber–Isaac Newton.[23] Nor did any visionary set out to build a new communications medium, though Vannevar Bush's deliberations in his July 1945 essay "As We May Think" come pretty close.[24] After all, in 1944, the chairmen of IBM still thought that the world would need only five computers, maximum. The prehistory of the Internet started in the mists of the "rationalization" of warfare by the Allies in the Second World War and the creation of the first analytical system, designed to increase U-boat sinking rates and coordinate radar-operated aircraft batteries. During the early Cold War, the ancient period of the Internet, no cost seemed too high for the struggle against communism, and the three U.S. military services massively contracted out research to universities and nonprofit organizations.

The World Wide Web (W3) was preceded by the military C3—command, control, and communication. The Sputnik shock and the vision of breakdown of all communications after a nuclear Armageddon ("nuclear survivability") lay behind the Pentagon's creation of the Advanced Research Projects Agency (ARPA), which initiated the medieval phase of the Internet in 1957. Packet-switching computers were the answer for creating a grid that could survive, and now the war-planning needs of the military and the research interests of computer scientists converged even more. The Pentagon throughout the 1960s and 1970s was the near exclusive financier of artificial intelligence research. ARPA acted as the patron of computer research, a Medici to the mathematical Michelangelos, as Edwin Diamond and Stephen Bates have noted.

Many researchers repressed the thought of their proximity to the military during the Vietnam War. They insisted that Pentagon funding did not make them part of the military-industrial complex, despite the fact that ARPA had added the letter D to its name, which made things pretty clear: DARPA now stood for Defense Advanced Research Projects Agency, and up to 95 percent of digital research budgets continued to come from the military during the following decade, the early modern phase of the Internet Age. But the net took on a life of its own, and while DARPA was not amused to discover a pop culture network and a score of other mailing lists, the military brass who wanted to clamp down on such frivolities could be convinced that these lists were beneficial, serving the vital purpose of testing the network's capacity.

Yet another shock was to come in the age of the Internet's modern history. The idea of the Internet being solely American was challenged by the fact that the World Wide Web was invented at the European Laboratory for Particle Physics, CERN, in Geneva, by a British scientist. By the late 1980s CERN had become the largest Internet site in Europe, and this fact influenced positively the acceptance and spread of Internet techniques both in Europe and elsewhere—and helped the American military to hasten the decision that the common (military and civilian) Internet days would be over rather sooner than later. A key result of all these happenings was that by 1989 CERN's Internet facility was ready to become the medium within which the British scientist Tim Berners-Lee would create the World Wide Web with a truly visionary idea.[25]

It is rather ironic that the Web was invented as a side effect of forty years of particle physics experiments. It has happened many times during the history of science that the most impressive results of large-scale scientific achievements showed up far away from the main directions of those efforts. Only when the DARPA net shut down in 1990 did the Internet (at least the one we know about) lose its direct connection to the military and thereby the taxpayer's money. That is, only since the beginning of the 1990s have the most heavily traveled routes of the information superhighway been in private hands, and when Marc Andreessen invented the Netscape Navigator in 1993 the cyberspace world entered contemporary history.

You may now ask what a British mystery, sex, violence, and the military have to do with American popular culture, and you would be quite right to pose that question. Of course, sex is no more American than it is Albanian and it could be argued that quite important segments of U.S. culture even show the strongest traces of Puritanism and prudishness imaginable. Yes, true, but then prudishness and pornography usually go together. And, even more important, in the realm of popular culture the image is decisive, and in the world of images sex *is* American. Just as in the genre of science fiction, the geographic space connotating sex in pornographic writing had been predominantly European—in Paris, London, Berlin, Vienna—up to the First World War. After that, its imaginary geographic location moved westward. Power made the same shift—and power, after all, is very sexy. How else could we explain the fact that a very recent poll, which was carried through in more than one hundred countries, revealed that the favorite sexual dream partners for men *worldwide* are Demi Moore, Sharon Stone, and Madonna, whereas women prefer Tom Cruise.[26]

No doubt, recent technological developments and, not to forget, neo-liberal politics of privatization have changed the interior workings of the infotainment business quite considerably over the last two decades. Just as we have seen the democratic public potential of radio and television blocked by an institutional framework of free enterprise—a U.S. model that has been followed nearly everywhere throughout the 1990s—the Internet most probably also will fall into the same pattern and private corporate control of the infrastructure will become a nonnegotiable, quasi-natural condition. Reaganomics and Thatcherism have had a tremendous impact on the media world, and deregulation—the code word for corporate nonaccountability—has been made the global standard by the transnational corporate economy.[27]

The 1990s, therefore, constitute an extremely important watershed in the era of global media. Despite the power of American media after the Second World War, most media systems had been predominantly national before the 1990s. The creation of a really global commercial market will have many consequences. "The rise to dominance of the global commercial media system is more than an economic matter; it also has clear implications of media content, politics, and culture."[28] This system is controlled by fewer than ten global transnational corporations, thus narrowing down a traditionally oligopolistic market even further. The dawn of the twenty-first century is experiencing an unprecedented struggle among media, software, and telephone companies for control over electronic shopping, television cables, new digital telephones, and satellite technology. Whether television, video, or Internet, no stone will remain unturned. Those companies that control the data networks will also control the flow of monies and goods of the next century.

At least partially, this globalization of the U.S. model is a result of the enormous power of the U.S. government, economy, and media policies. After the breakdown of the Soviet Union, this pattern of globalization of the U.S. model seems to have been adopted nearly everywhere as the exclusive archetype for the organization of worldwide communication industries. For many years, U.S. governments, in cooperation with some of their allies, have pushed privately structured, open, neo-liberal economies and market-based media systems, while destabilizing anti-free-market systems on a global basis. Based on the comforting hegemonic position of American popular culture industries, their undisputed competitiveness in all areas of communication, and the attractiveness of the entertainment product, the United States since World War II has consistently insisted on the opening of all communication markets and their privatization—resulting in a global erosion of the public space.[29]

At the same time, J. Michael Jaffe and Gabriel Weimann have noted the astonishing speed with which quite a few of the gems of American popular culture industries have been sold to foreign buyers over the last years. Rupert Murdoch's News Corporation, the late Robert Maxwell, the Japanese Sony and Matsushita Corporations, the Hachette organization in France, Bertelsmann and Kirch in Germany—these are some of the new lords of the global village, together with the American giants Time/Warner, Disney, and Viacom. But even if the hardware may not be exclusively American anymore, and even if the software is originally European (like Bambi, The Hunchback of Notre Dame and Hercules) or universal (like sex), these popular culture products still will register most certainly as American in the mental maps of their predominantly young consumers on and off the Internet.

Whatever the actual nationality of the owners and shareholders of the media industries may be, their common interests are clear, despite all competition. They follow American business beliefs and practices and they have only two real enemies: public media and all kinds of state interventions that cut profits. The political agenda of the lords of the global village, therefore, is more or less the same, whether they are Australian or Italian, U.S.-American or French, German or British.

The popularity of American popular culture and its immense money-making potential have not only a variety of sources and advantages, they also have a lot in common. The business of America has become show business, and the global market reach of the English language, which goes back to the British Empire, gives it tremendous advantages over all competitors. Jaffe and Weimann see those hegemonic Western media organizations, whose subsidiaries are involved in all communication media formats to create mutual support, as having a synergy that means nothing less than this: "dominance in politics supports dominance in news, which supports dominance in popular culture, which supports dominance in technology, which supports dominance in journalistic style, which supports dominance in the English language, and so on."[30]

The Internet as real structure and as hype so far has been a mostly not-so-new extension of earlier forms of dependencies and exclusions. According to the latest NUA statistics, the world total online was 171.25 million in May 1999. Of those, only 1.14 million lived in Africa, 5.29 million in Latin America, 0.88 in the Middle East, 26.97 million in Asia and the Pacific area, 40.09 million in Europe, and 97.03 in Canada and the United States of America. At the end of the twentieth century most netizens will still live in North America.[31] And by 2005 the total number of netizens is expected to have doubled.

The latest comparative user data of May 1998 and May 1999 published by Media Matrix are quite impressive: globally the number of users grew by 15 percent in that period, in Japan alone by 50 percent. Twenty-eight billion websites were visited in May 1999 alone, 70 percent more than a year before. The average user spent 7.6 hours online in 1999, compared to 5.3 in 1998. The ten most visited websites were the AOL Network, Microsoft, Yahoo, Lycos, Go Network, GeoCities, The Exite Network, Time Warner Online, Amazon, and AltaVista. By the end of 1999, e-commerce or e-business is estimated to be more than $15 billion, with an expected raise to $1.1 trillion by 2002. But the differences between the United States and the rest of the world have been staggering. The United States alone is expected to generate $842 billion, while all the other regions together will generate only about $300 billion.[32] Total internet business in Western Europe, according to International Data Corp., in 1998 amounted to only 0.1 percent of total domestic expenditure. In the United States the figure was 0.5, and while 10 percent of Americans were buying online, the European number was a mere 1.5 percent.[33] The demand for high-tech workers has been so enormous in North America that more than 140,000 highly paid foreign experts have found jobs in the United States alone, while the European Internet skills gap has already resulted in the inability to fill hundreds of thousands of highly skilled positions.[34]

The Internet has become the most important (cyber)space for economic, cultural, and political (and military?) competition, thereby raising the stakes for future cooperation between the United States and her allies and foes alike. While the Computer Industry Almanac[35] predicts that 327 million people will be online—82 percent in the 15 countries leading in Internet density—by the year 2000, Al Gore, who was the first candidate to open his presidential campaign on the Internet, prognosticates that by 2007 nearly half of the U.S. workforce will work either in industries that produce or in businesses that heavily use information technologies. Of course, the involvement of the Internet in U.S. presidential elections isn't really conducive to understatement. Still, by the end of 1998, almost 99 percent of the 13 million servers working for the Internet were concentrated in North America, Western Europe, and Japan. The "rest" of the world, a negligible 5 billion people, was represented by 1 percent of the hosts.[36] Furthermore, the power struggle over who will control the allocation of Internet domains has become one of the pressing economic issues between the United States and the European Union. The Green Paper of the Clinton administration has completely ignored the wishes of other countries and, as matters stand in 1999, the American government continues to insist on having the final say. A virtual "the buck stops here," indeed.[37]

If it is so exciting that 171 million people have gone online by May 1999, then it may be wise to sober up—because those 171 million people constitute less than 3 percent of the population of the world. In reality, the haves and the have-nots are being divided even more (and not only virtually) by the Internet, which to the great majority may for a long time remain an *Extra*-Net. And while the "emerging" nations, from China to Brazil, Indonesia to Pakistan, and India to Malaysia, may well change the outlook of the Internet completely, the question remains whether even in that scenario it will not be dominated by members of their most "Westernized" elite. Experiences with older channels of communication have shown that the global attraction of the products of American popular culture and their hybrid forms is nearly endless, because they consistently prove so profitable.[38]

Some (mostly) American companies experienced another tremendous boost in 1997 by sharing some common interests and real U.S. business acumen: the major U.S. television companies received the broadcast spectrum for a second channel for every TV station in the nation. These new digital broadcasts will immensely increase the programming power of the companies to broadcast everything from TV programs to new pay-per-view services like stock quotes, paging, software distribution, and subscription programs. The value of these new slices of airwaves, if they had been auctioned off by the government, was estimated at $70 billion by the Federal Communications Commission. But there was no auction and the new airwaves were given away absolutely for free to some of the world's most powerful media corporations: Rupert Murdoch's News Corporation (Fox TV), General Electric Co. (NBC), Walt Disney Co. (ABC), and Westinghouse Electric Corp. (CBS).[39] The "market economy" is alive and well.

The globalization of culture therefore first and foremost means the globalization of the cultural influence of a few transnational corporations, which control much of what the global audience becomes aware of in the first place, from the beginning phases of production, through distribution and consumption. And, it is safe to say, the cultural outlook of this "globalization" is predominantly informed by cultural practices of the "West." "West," of course, is as inappropriate a term as "the First World," but, whatever this sphere of influence is called, it retains its links to earlier forms of colonialism.

If Americanization, always a rather shady concept, is no longer the question, then is globalization the new question? Globalization of what?

Do I see more Indian or Mexican films in our cinemas? Do I hear more Chinese or Japanese music on our radios? The fact that the public is the whole world does not necessarily mean that the cultures of the whole world are available to the public. Actually, the domination of American stars and products on the Internet is even more impressive (and potentially oppressive), if that is possible, than in all other older fields of infotainment. The most recent Hollywood power list—in personnel if not in companies—is almost exclusively American, and in the list of the top one hundred stars on the Internet non-Americans can be counted on the fingers of one hand, if we include in that group Princess Diana, who held the number one position in the end of 1997, the year of her death. By the end of 1998, Diana had dropped to number 12 and by June 1999 to number 17—a good indicator of the half-life on the Internet. In the same period, President Clinton dropped three notches from 1 to 3 while Monica Lewinsky ascended from 8 to 6. Otherwise the hit parade showed the usual suspects—with one exception: Pamela Anderson 1, Madonna 2, Demi Moore 3, Cindy Crawford 5, and Gillian Anderson 7—the exception being Hillary Clinton, who came in fourth.[40] But if the globalization of culture means two billion people watching the funeral of the Princess of Wales, then that term conceptually stands for a rather meaningless void. No doubt, the globalization of profits is a one-way street, but that is quite another story. Or is it?

Still, despite all attempts at monopolization of audience attention by these global media players, their power is not *yet* absolute and the Internet is not *yet* controlled from their switchboards. Umberto Eco interprets this as "one of the upsides of the anti-monopolistic nature of the Net: controlling the technology does not mean controlling the flow of information."[41] It is true that the image of the Internet underwent a dramatic transformation: from a communication channel controlled by the military to a supposedly progressive, libertarian, and empowering channel of intellectual cooperation. This development has converted many to assume that it characterizes "progress" at its best—unadulterated by censorship and political interference.

But is that the image or the reality of the Internet? Only very naive disciples could ever come up with such a daydream, and these people needed only the Starr report to prove those hopes as part of the hype generated around the Net. The real struggle for power has been fought for quite a while and surfaced during the Microsoft antitrust case, which may prove as important as the case against Standard Oil a century earlier. No other industry ever was as tightly controlled by one company as the computer industries by Microsoft. One of Bill Gates' major opponents, Larry Ellison, the founder of Microsoft's biggest competitor, Oracle, has accused

Microsoft of exerting about the same control and function as the central committee of the former Soviet Union.[42] Whatever the outcome of that lawsuit, Bill Gates has become the richest person on earth, with Microsoft co-founder Paul Allen coming in third, and Microsoft president Steven Ballmer fourth.[43] We will see whether "Disneyfication" or diversification, "Encartafication"[44] or emancipation, imperialism or pluralism will win the day. The CD-rom encyclopaedia Encarta,[45] which was bought by Microsoft in 1994, already has become the globally most widely distributed repository of human knowledge, and Microsoft's photography agency, Corbis Corporation,[46] which swallowed Sigma in early 1999, has become the dominating digital picture gallery of all time. The Internet as gateway or Gates' way, that is the question. Judging from historical precedence, any optimism must be highly guarded. But then not all may be lost when the Internet is getting its own patron saint: St. Isidor, San Pedro Regalado (Patrón de los Internautas), and Santa Tecla are in the final running in the Vatican.[47]

In *From Internet to Information Superhighway*, Howard Besser looks through the hyperbole about the democratic possibilities of the new wonders of cyberspace and draws a more realistic conclusion, one that categorizes the Internet with older channels of one-way communication rather than as a new global network of democratic consumers. For Besser, the information superhighway may just turn out to be a "ten-lane highway coming into the home, with only a tiny path leading back out—just wide enough to take a credit card number or to answer multiple-choice questions."[48]

Already, there seems little reason for any of the hype and euphoria spread by the Ayathollas of the Internet. Neither the "speed" of the "World Wide Wait," nor the potential for worldwide information *exchange* is really convincing. The more companies go online, the more the Net assumes the look of a giant public relations highway—with a few unconnected information sidewalks for cultural pedestrians here and there. In the long run, the tyranny of information waste may only create mostly meaningless trash devoid of any messages: speed talk but no thought (Arthur Kroker). And democratization and freedom? As software agents track the Internet choices of unsuspecting surfers, even a new "class war"—between those who have digital access and savvy and those who don't—a struggle for power that is anything but virtual, may be possible. The information elite will be online (and some of them in power); what the offline multitudes will be is not so difficult to imagine.

Not surprisingly, Noam Chomsky's prediction is that there will be an eventual corporate takeover of the Internet because "the Pentagon is not going to give people as a gift a technique for free communication which undermines the major media; if it's going to take out that way it will be because of a struggle like any other victory for freedom."[49] Without doubt, the image of the Trojan horse has become quite inflated. Still we may ask ourselves whether this "free" gift isn't any Big Brother's dream come true: all digital communications, whether telephones, e-mails, faxes, or pagers, have been completely open to the U.S. National Security Agency and other secret services for years, more open than any open book ever was. Needless to say, Europe can't wait to join the club. The plans of the European Union to finalize a global telecommunications surveillance system with the FBI's help were put only temporarily on the back burner just before the E.U. elections of June 1999.[50]

In the long run, the advantages of the *relative* freedom of the Internet for transnational media corporations may outweigh the disadvantages. While they may not be able to buy the Internet altogether, as they can other media products, they may still come out on top in the end.[51] One thing seems to be clear: "Whereas the media lords previously ruled by capitalist decree, they will retain their eminence in the future only by default—that is by virtue of consumers' cognitive overload."[52] So the major companies are swamping the Internet, getting more PR, setting industry standards, and strengthening their presence in a public space, which allows them not only to interact with and monitor other participants but also cheaply to sample new artistic trends and cultural concepts and test popular reaction to them. Synergy is becoming the synonym, if not the code word, for exploding profits from original (?) product to gift shop.

Indeed, over the last twenty years, the major Hollywood companies have been turned into image empires with tentacles reaching down, not only to movies and TV programs, but also to books, records, theme parks, toys, clothes, kitchen utensils, travel agencies, and even hardware. The feature film business no longer exists in its own right, but is increasingly becoming part of an integrated, global image business, central to the broader media strategies of entertainment companies and conglomerates. However, the major studios are the fundamental building blocks of the emerging entertainment blockbuster companies.[53] And they will remain so in the Internet age, which will see a growing struggle for control over access. The biggest economic battles over the last decades have nearly all been fought over infotainment companies, and that struggle is continuing. The new alliances between media, software, and telephone companies abound and experience tells us . . .

What does experience tell us? For anyone who thinks the Gutenberg Galaxy has come to an end there may still lie some surprises ahead, which are, if anything, rather ironic.[54] The virtual bookstore www.Amazon.com has established itself not only as the largest bookstore on the globe, but also as the leading Internet retailer. It was the first Internet company ever to have one million customers in many different countries. Up to this point www.amazon.com has kept its lead, followed by Blue Mountain Arts' Electronic Greeting Cards, eBay, ONSALE.com, and Ticketmaster.[55] Already in 1997, www.Amazon.com was number 25 of all web sites accessed in the United States—immediately after *USA Today* and *The Weather Channel*.[56] From sex and drugs and rock 'n' roll to sex and books and fun on the beach. Back to the future, indeed.

Notes

1. Colin Dexter, *Death Is Now My Neighbour* (London: Macmillan, 1996).
2. Matthew McAllester, "Soul searching: Our most popular search engine requests offer revelations to philosophers and advertisers alike," in http://www. newsday.com/plugin/ccovo812.htm (accessed 14 May 1999).
3. *Nando Times* in http://www. nua.org/surveys/index.cgi (accessed 7 November 1998).
4. See http://www.sbg.ac.at/gesc/people/eg/vortrag/film1.htm (accessed 7 May 1999). The author thanks Erwin Giedenbacher, Christian Gruber, and Johann Fröhlich for their untiring support (and patience) in all questions concerning computers and the Internet.
5. *Newsbytes* in http://www. nua.org/surveys/index.cgi (accessed 7 November 1997).
6. "Das Blacksburg-Experiment," *Der Spiegel* 46 (1997): 146–48; http:// www.bev.net/ (accessed 7 November 1998).
7. *Philadelphia Online* in http://www. nua.org/surveys/index.cgi (accessed 7 November 1997).
8. *FIND/SVP*, in http://www. nua.org/surveys/index.cgi (accessed 9 November 1997).
9. *FIND/SVP, Children on the Internet* (August 1997) in http://www.find-svp.com/cgi-bin/RetrieveiItem-cgi?pub=ET013 (accessed 7 November 1997).
10. *Jupiter Communications*, 14 March 1997, in http://www.nua.org/surveys/index.cgi (accessed 4 May 1997).
11. *Delivering the World Online*, http://www.nfoi.com/nfointeractive/Default.asp (accessed 4 May 1999).
12. *Kids and Teens to Spend More Online*, http://www.cyberatlas.com/big_picture/demographics/teens.html (accessed 7 May 1999).
13. Richard Maltby, *Passing Parade: A History of Popular Culture in the Twentieth Century* (Oxford and New York: Oxford University Press, 1989).
14. Greil Marcus, *Dead Elvis: A Chronicle of a Cultural Obsession* (Cambridge: Harvard University Press, 1992).
15. *Jupiter Communications*, 18 August 1997, in http://www.nua.org/surveys/index.cgi?blocknumer=11 (accessed 13 November 1997).
16. http://www.cyberatlas.com/big_picture/demographics/gender.html (accessed 3 May 1999).
17. Reinhold Wagnleitner, "Die Marilyn-Monroe-Doktrin oder das Streben nach GlŸck durch Konsum," *IWM Working Papers,* no. 5, 1997, http://www.univie.ac.at/iwm/workpap/wagnleit.htm (accessed 8 November 1999).

18. Dinty W. Moore, *The Emperor's Virtual Clothes: The Naked Truth about Internet Culture* (Chapel Hill: Algonquin Books, 1995).

19. NUA Internet Surveys: http://www.nua.ie/surveys/ (accessed 3 October 1998).

20. Reuters quoted in http://www.nua.org/surveys/index.cgi (accessed 3 October 1998).

21. Nando Techserver, "Internet Addicts Are Not Looking for Information," quoted in http://www.nua.org/surveys/index.cgi (accessed 3 October 1997).

22. Edwin Diamond and Stephen Bates, "The Ancient History of the Internet," *American Studies Journal* 39 (November 1996): 1–4; Katie Hafner and Matthew Lyon, *Where Wizards Stay Up Late: The Origins of the Internet* (New York: Simon & Schuster, 1997).

23. Ibid.

24. Vannevar Bush, "As We May Think," *Atlantic Monthly* 176 (July 1945): 101–8.

25. "The Man Who Invented the Web," *Time* Magazine 149, no. 20 (19 May 1997), http://cgi.pathfinder.com/time/magazine/1997/dom/970519/tech.the_man_who_i.html (accessed 1 June 1999).

26. Reinhold Wagnleitner, "The Empire of the Fun or Talkin' Soviet Union Blues: The Sound of Freedom and U.S. Cultural Hegemony in Europe," *Diplomatic History* 23, no. 3 (summer 1999): 499–524.

27. Herbert Schiller, *Information Inequality* (New York: Routledge, 1996).

28. Robert W. McChesney, "Corporate Concentration: A Threat to the Right to Communicate?" http://commposite.uqam.ca/videaz/docs/romcen.html (accessed 23 June 1999).

29. Edward S. Herman and Noam Chomsky, *Manufacturing Consent: The Political Economy of the Mass Media* (New York: Pantheon Books, 1988); Edward S. Herman, *The Global Media: The New Missionaries of Corporate Capitalism* (London: Cassell, 1997).

30. J. Michael Jaffe and Gabriel Weimann, "New Lords of the Global Village? Reconsidering Theories of Media Domination," p. 290 in this volume.

31. *NUA Internet Surveys,* http://www.nua.net/surveys/how_many_online/index.html (accessed 22 June 1999).

32. Deloitte Consulting, "Ecommerce to Top USD 1.1 Trillion by 2002," http://www.nua.ie/surveys/?f=VS&art_id=905354980&rel=true (accessed 24 June 1999).

33. See "Europe's Handicap" in *Time digital,* 28 June 1999, http://www.timedigital.com (accessed 3 July 1999).

34. "Internet ist Massenarbeitgeber der Zukunft Vize Präsident Al Gore," 24 June 1999, http://futurezone.orf.at/futurezone.orf?read=detail&id=2048&tmp=45864 (accessed 25 June 1999).

35. Computer Industry Almanac, http://www.c-i-a.com/ (accessed 24 June 1999).

36. "The Emerging 20 Nations," in http://www.cyberatlas.com/market/geographics/index.html (accessed 18 September 1998).

37. "Frankreich kritisiert US-Peäne," http://www.intern.de/98/06/04.shtml (accessed 14 May 1999).

38. Reinhold Wagnleitner, *Coca-Colonization and the Cold War: The Cultural Mission of the United States in Austria after the Second World War* (Chapel Hill, London: University of North Carolina Press, 1994).

39. Sam Vincent Meddis, "Washington's $70 billion high-tech giveaway," in http://www.usatoday.com/life/cyber/ccarch/cco217.a.htm (accessed 11 November 1997).

40. However inaccurate website statistics may be and although they are slightly changing week by week, the listings certainly do show important trends—especially the lack of European "stars," with the exception of some models. Even princes Charles and Edwards have dropped rock bottom during 1999. *100 Hot Search—100 Hot Stars,* http://www.100hot.com/star/(accessed 11 June 1999).

41. "The World According to Eco," in *Wired* 5.03 (March 1997).

42. Interview with Larry Ellison in *Der Spiegel,* 26 September 1998, 134–36.

43. "Billionaires Club Booms," 21 June 1999, http://bizyahoo.com/apf/990621/forbes_bil_2.html (accessed 3 July 1999).

44. Encarta refers to Microsoft's CD-ROM encyclopedia, which is "bundled" (or automatically provided) with Microsoft computers. Competitors such as Oracle have argued that this "freebie" constitutes an industry monopoly and should be discontinued. This allegation was upheld by U.S. District Judge Thomas Penfield Jackson in his findings of fact of 5 November 1999, in which he held Microsoft responsible for violating legitimate business practices, harming the interests of consumers, and distorting competition with its Internet Explorer. The Microsoft Trial, Findings of Fact, http://www.seattletimes.com/microsoft/ruling.html (accessed 5 January 2000).

45. Sylvia Carr, "'Microsoft Encarta 98 Encyclopedia Deluxe Edition' (almost) everything from A to Z," CNET Reviews, 29 October 1997, http://www.cnet.com/Content/Reviews/JustIn/Items/0,118,260,00.html (accessed 29 October 1997).

46. Corbis: The Place for Pictures on the Internet, http://www.corbis.com/ (accessed 8 October 1999).

47. *Wired,* 14 June 1999, http://www.wired.com/news/news/culture/story/20202.html (accessed 17 June 1999).

48. Howard Besser, "From Internet to Information Highway," in James Brook and Iain A. Boal, eds., *Resisting the Virtual Life: The Culture and Politics of Information* (San Francisco: City Lights, 1995), 59–70, 63.

49. Noam Chomsky interviewed by Rosie X and Chris Mountford in *geek girl—the world's first cyberfeminist magazine,* http://www.geekgirl.com.au/geekgirl/002manga/chomsky.html (accessed 14 September 1998).

50. ENFOPOL Timeline 1991–1999. Compiled by Duncan Campbell, Erich Moechel, and Christiane Schulzki-Haddouti. Additional data provided by Statewatch, http://www.heise.de/tp/english/special/enfo/6382/1.html (accessed 14 May 1999); "An Appraisal of the Technologies of Political Control," *Scientific and Technological Options Assessment (STOA) Interim Study Executive Summary,* September 1998, http://www.europarl.eu.int/dg4/stoa/en/publi/166499/execsum.htm (accessed 14 October 1998); "EU-FBI telecommunications surveillance system moves two steps closer," http://www.statewatch.org/news2.htm (accessed 23 June 1999); *Global Surveillance System Launched by FBI and European Union: A Statewatch Report,* http://www.can-offshore.com/global_surveillance_FBI.htm (accessed 23 June 1999).

51. Dean Alger, *MEGAMEDIA: How Giant Corporations Dominate Mass Media, Distort Competition, and Endanger Democracy* (Lanham, Boulder, New York, Oxford: Rowman & Littlefield, 1998).

52. Jaffe and Weimann, "New Lords of the Global Village," p. 300 in this volume.

53. Janet Wasko, *Hollywood in the Information Age* (Oxford: Polity Press, 1994).

54. See, for example, Project Gutenberg, a huge library of electronically stored books: http://www.gutenberg.net/.

55. The Web's Most Popular Shopping Sites, 2 June 1999, http://www.100hot.com/shopping/ (accessed 2 June 1999).

56. *Gina,* 15 October 1997, in http://www.nua.org/surveys/index.cgi?/blocknumber=1 (accessed 2 June 1999).

Contributors

John G. Blair has served as the University of Geneva's Professor of American Literature and Civilization since 1970. His three books are entitled *The Poetic Art of W. H. Auden* (1965), *The Confidence Man in Modern Fiction* (1979), and *Modular America: Cross-Cultural Perspectives on the Emergence of the American Way* (1988). The latter was awarded the American Studies Association's Ralph Henry Gabriel Prize for outstanding interdisciplinary contributions to the field. He has served as Visiting Professor of American Studies in France (University of Strasbourg, 1967–1968) and China (Beijing Foreign Studies University, 1988–1989). His current research emphasizes culture studies including stage entertainments, immigrant writing, and comparative studies of civilizations (China, India, and the West).

Aurora Bosch is a senior tenured lecturer at the University of Valencia, Spain, where she teaches history. She wrote her doctoral thesis on the agrarian labor movement during the Spanish Republic and the Civil War, and has written *Ugetistas y libertarios* (1983) and collaborated on *Estudios sobre la Segunda Republica* (1993). Her current interests include comparative history, especially in relation to the American labor movement and that of other "new" countries. Her essay "Why Is There No Labor Party in the US? A Comparative Case Study: Australia and the United States, 1783–1914" was nominated for the *Journal of American History*'s annual prize for best foreign essay on U.S. history. She is currently writing a book on American history commissioned by a Spanish publisher.

Gülriz Büken is Associate Professor of American Literature and American Studies at Bilkent University, Ankara, Turkey. She has received numerous fellowships for international study, including the British Council Fellowship for English Studies at Cambridge, the USIS Fellowship for the Salzburg Seminar in American Studies in Salzburg, the Berlin Free University Grant for research at the John F. Kennedy Institute in Berlin, and a Fulbright Grant for research at the University of Texas at Austin. Her publications include "Macdonaldization of Britain: The Impact of American Consumer Culture on Britain," in *Crossing the Boundaries: Cultural Studies in U.K. and the U.S., Proceedings of Cultural Studies Seminar*, 1996.

James T. Campbell is Associate Professor of American Civilization and Afro-American Studies at Brown University. From 1996 to 1998, he was Senior Research Officer at the Institute for Advanced Social Research at Johannesburg's University of the Witwatersrand. In 1996, he was awarded both the Organization of American Historians' Frederick Jackson Turner Prize and the Carl Sandburg Literary Award for Non-Fiction. He has published numerous articles on the politics of South Africa; his book is entitled *Songs of Zion: The African Methodist Episcopal Church in the United States and South Africa* (1995).

329

Myles Dungan received his M.A. in history from University College Dublin in 1977. He is a presenter for the "Five/Seven Live" daily radio program on RTE (Irish National Radio) as well as for "Divided World," a televised current affairs program on development and conflict issues in the developing world. His books include *Distant Drums: Irish Veterans of Foreign Armies* (1993); *Irish Voices from the Great War* (1995), and *They Shall Grow Not Old: Irish Soldiers and the Great War* (1997).

Michael Ermarth is a professor of history at Dartmouth College, specializing in German intellectual history. His publications include *Wilhelm Dilthey: The Critique of Historical Reason* (1978); *Kurt Wolff: A Portrait of Life and Letters* (1992); *America and the Shaping of German Society, 1945–1955* (1993); *Karl Jaspers: The Great Philosophers*, vols. 3 and 4 (1993, 1995). He is currently finishing a major study entitled *Germany's Inner America: Americanization, "Counter-Americanism" and Transmodernity in the Twentieth Century*.

Thomas Fuchs is an assistant professor of American cultural studies and American literature at the Institut fuer Fremdsprachliche Philologien, Otto-von-Guericke Universitaet Magdeburg. His article entitled "USA-Populaerkultur in der DDR: Bewertung und Interpretation in den Medien und in der Amerikanistik" will appear in a forthcoming anthology tentatively entitled *Amerikastudien in der DDR*.

David Gray, a native of England, is a graduate of Lancaster University and is currently a Ph.D. student in the American Studies Program at the University of Minnesota. His study of political cartoon images of Irish and Italian immigrants won the Mulford Sibley Prize for the best senior thesis at the University of Minnesota in 1998. He served as editorial assistant for *Here, There and Everywhere* in the summer of 1998.

J. Michael Jaffe researches and lectures on computer-mediated communication, health communication, and communication-related cognition at the University of Haifa, Israel. He joined the faculty in 1995, upon completion of his Ph.D. in Mass Communication Research at the University of Michigan, where his dissertation focused on affective effects of interactive, computer-aided first-aid instruction. Before undertaking his doctoral studies, he worked as an electrical engineer. His current interests include the exploration of possible cultural factors in reducing tobacco use and the potential for persuasion in interactive media. His work has been published in journals such as the *Information Society* and the *Journal of Health Communication*.

Rob Kroes is Professor of American Studies and Director of the American Institute of the University of Amsterdam, and past president of the European Association of American Studies. His most recent book is *If You've Seen One, You've Seen the Mall: Europeans and American Mass Culture* (1996). He is also editor and co-author of several works, including *Living With America, 1946–1996* (1997).

Elaine Tyler May is Professor of American Studies and History at the University of Minnesota. She recently served as president of the American Studies Association of the United States, and as Fulbright Distinguished Professor of American History at University College, Dublin, Ireland. She is the author of several books and articles on American domestic and political culture, including *Great Expectations:*

Marriage and Divorce in Post-Victorian America (1980), *Homeward Bound: American Families in the Cold War Era* (1988), and *Barren in the Promised Land: Childless Americans and the Pursuit of Happiness (1995)*. She has twice served as a faculty member at the Salzburg Seminar for American Studies.

Michael May holds a B.A. in history from Grinnell College and is a former intern at the Salzburg Seminar. He is former editor of *Responsive Philanthropy*, the quarterly of the National Committee for Responsive Philanthropy, and has written widely on public policy issues pertaining to the nonprofit sector. The essay included in this volume is drawn from research he conducted recently in Russia for a radio documentary he produced on Russian jazz during the Cold War.

Giuliana Muscio is Associate Professor of Cinema at the University of Padua, Italy. She is author of *Hollywood's New Deal* (Temple University Press, 1996) and of works in Italian on screenwriting, the Hollywood blacklist, and the relation between Hollywood and Washington in the 1930s and in the 1950s.

Masako Notoji is Professor at the Graduate School of Arts and Sciences of the University of Tokyo. She has written widely on American popular culture in Japan, including essays in Japanese and English on Tokyo Disneyland and its impact and reception in Japan. She is active in the Japanese Association of American Studies and has taught and lectured widely in Japan, the United States, and Europe.

Nosa Owens-Ibie is a lecturer in the Department of Mass Communications at the University of Lagos, Nigeria. His articles on various aspects of the Nigerian media have been published in numerous journals and anthologies. His two most recent articles, "How Video Films Developed in Nigeria" (1998) and "Communication Dilemmas in Traditional African Society"(1997), both appeared in the *Journal of Media Development*.

Christoph Ribbat is an assistant professor of American studies at Ruhr University in Bochum, Germany, where he also took his Ph.D. in history in 1995. From September 1997 to February 1998, he was a Visiting Fulbright Scholar at Cooper Union, New York City. His first book, *Religiöse Erregung,* published in 1996, explored religious fanaticism in working-class Germany around 1900. He is currently conducting research for a book on American photographs from Germany since 1945.

M. Fernanda del Rincón is librarian in the Valencian Regional Parliament. She wrote her M.A. thesis, titled "Mujeres Azules. La Sección Femenina 1939– 1945" (1986), on the Falangist women's organization, and subsequently has written several articles about feminist organization at the beginning of the Franco regime. She is now working on the role of women in the transition to democracy in Spain.

Oliver M. A. Schmidt studied modern history, political science, and American studies at the University of Erlangen, Ohio University in Athens, the University of Munich, and the European University Institute in Florence (Italy). In 1999 he received his Ph.D. from Harvard University for his doctoral dissertation on U.S. cultural diplomacy and the formation of Atlanticist elites in Western Germany after 1945.

Elizabeth Vihlen is currently completing her Ph.D. at the State University of New York, Stonybrook, where she also received her M.A. in 1994. She has presented numerous papers related to her dissertation on "Sounding French: Jazz in Postwar France." She is both an instructor of history and a curriculum consultant at the United States Merchant Marine Academy in Kings Point, New York.

Penny M. Von Eschen (Ph.D., Columbia University, 1994) is an associate professor of history at the University of Michigan. Her book, *Race Against Empire: Black Americans and Anticolonialism, 1937–1957* (1997), was winner of the 1998 Stuart L. Bernath book prize of the Society of Historians of Foreign Relations. She is co-editor of a forthcoming volume entitled *Re-thinking Black Radicalism.*

Reinhold Wagnleitner is Associate Professor of Modern History at the University of Salzburg, Austria. He also played and sang in Austrian pop, rock, and jazz bands. He has lectured and taught extensively in Europe and the United States, including serving as a Fulbright Scholar twice, at the University of Minnesota, Minneapolis, and as a Fellow of the American Council of Learned Societies affiliated to the School of Foreign Service, Georgetown University, in Washington, D.C. He has served as a member of the faculty of the Salzburg Seminar several times, and in 1995–1996 he was president of the Austrian Association for American Studies. The English translation of his book, *Coca-Colonization and the Cold War: The Cultural Mission of the United States in Austria after the Second World War* (1994), was awarded the 1995 Stuart L. Bernath Prize by the Society of Historians of American Foreign Relations. He is author and editor of several other books and articles and is co-editor, with John G. Blair, of *Empire: American Studies* (1997).

Gabriel Weimann is Professor of Communication at Haifa University, Israel. His research interests include the study of media effects, personal influence, modern terrorism and the media, and public opinion. He has three books: *The Influentials: People Who Influence People* (1995); *The Theater of Terror* (1994), and *Hate on Trial* (1986). He has another book in press, entitled *Communicating Unreality: Modern Media and the Reconstruction of Reality.* His numerous research reports have been published in journals such as the *Journal of Communication, Public Opinion Quarterly, Communication Research, Journal of Broadcasting and Electronic Media,* and *American Sociological Review.*

Theodore Wilson is Professor of History at the University of Kansas, where he recently received the Wilson T. Kemper Fellowship for teaching excellence. In 1995–1996, he was the Fulbright Distinguished Professor in American History at University College, Dublin. He is the author of many books and articles on American foreign relations, most recently *The First Summit: Roosevelt and Churchill at Placentia Bay, 1941* (1991).

Index

Aaron, Daniel, 76n.27, 77n.33
Abada, Tom, 137
ABC (American Broadcasting
 Company), 321
Abiola, Moshood, 138
Abusch, Alexander, 203
Accra (Ghana), 163
Acheson, Dean, 53
A. C. Milan, 237
Adams, Henry, 220
"Addresses to the German Nation"
 (Fichte), 255
Adenauer, Konrad, 194, 199
Adorno, Theodor, 261
Adult entertainment, 314
Advanced Chemistry (rap group), 211
Advanced Research Projects Agency
 (ARPA), 316
Adventure in Iraq (film), 88
Advertising, 273–87; for advertising,
 279; American West in, 275–76, 278;
 emerging as professional industry, 42;
 European-made for European prod-
 ucts, 282; and freedom, 276; and free-
 dom of choice, 279–82; free-floating
 signifiers in, 276–77; genderbending
 in, 277; for Hoover Vacuum Cleaner
 Company, 280, 284; Levi's ads in the
 Netherlands, 277, 284, 287n.2; Levi's
 poster in Italy, 277–78; Marlboro
 Man, 273, 274, 275; New York agencies' domination, 289; public service
 advertising in the Netherlands, 283–
 84; Saatchi & Saatchi, 292; for Seven-
 Up, 273–74, 277; in South Africa, 43;
 for the World Wide Web, 305; on the
 World Wide Web, 302

Africa: Louis Armstrong's Accra concert,
 163; Louis Armstrong's tour of, 169–
 70; and *Présence Africaine*, 162n.48;
 Rhodesia, 54; total online in, 319. *See
 also* Nigeria; South Africa
Africa Bambata, 210
African Americans: African Methodist
 Episcopal Church, 40; civil rights
 gains after World War II, 49–50; East
 German attitude toward, 193–94;
 economic conditions of jazz musicians, 156; French critics distinguishing white and black jazz, 151, 152–
 53, 161nn. 18, 23; French reception
 of culture of, 160n.12; and German
 rap music, 207, 209, 212, 214; in
 Hollywood movies, 93, 98n.45; in
 Liverpool during World War II, 1; in
 minstrel shows, 31n.1; music in South
 Africa, 46; on Nigerian television,
 136; and *Présence Africaine*,
 162n.48; and right-wing criticism of
 American popular culture, 5; segregation, 36, 155; situation comedies on
 South African television, 57; and
 State Department jazz tours, 8, 167,
 170–74; *Umteteli wa Bantu* maga-
 zine on, 44
African Broadcasting Corporation, 47–
 48
African Film Productions, 48
African Independent Television (AIT),
 135
African Methodist Episcopal Church, 40
African Realty Trust, 47
Afrikaners, 36, 44–45, 49, 50, 55
Agee, James, 90, 98nn. 40, 44

Ailey, Alvin, 163
"Ain't That a Shame" (Domino), 197
Alabama (ship), 36
Algeria, 172
Alien II (film), 277
Allen, Paul, 323
Alpbach, 74n.6
AltaVista, 302, 320
Amazon.com, 314, 320, 324–25
America for 25 Cents (Tirali), 250n.4
American Bazaar (Turkey), 241
American Broadcasting Company (ABC), 321
American Decca record company, 196
American football, 236–38
American Institute (Oslo), 72, 74n.5
Americano a Roma, Un (film), 130n.10
American Pie (McLean), 205n.15, 239
American popular culture: as all over the world, 1; appeal of, 289–90; as changing its meaning when it crosses borders, 10; Cold War and the spread of, 6; debates over, 4–6; as disruptive and centrifugal, 1; East German fear of, 192, 193, 201–2; how American is it, 2; international sources of, 240; in Ireland and England, 227–41; in Japan, 219, 225; left-wing criticism of, 5–6; money-making potential of, 319; nineteenth-century exports of, 17–33; right-wing criticism of, 5, 6; scholarly attention to influence of, 4; selling off to foreign buyers, 291, 319; in South Africa, 34–63; in Turkey, 242–50; as unifying and centripetal, 1; violence in, 313; World War I and spread of, 5; World War II in spread of, 6. *See also* American television; Blackface minstrel shows; Hollywood movies; Internet; Music; Wild West shows
American Romance, An (film), 89
American studies: American Institute in Oslo, 72, 74n.5; the Cold War in entrenchment of, 2; European Association for American Studies, 66, 72; in Europe in 1940s, 74n.5; Salzburg Seminar and, 64–75; support increasing after World War II, 68

American television: as all over the world, 1; children's broadcasting, 138; as cultural imperialism, 288–90; in England and Ireland, 240; and escapism, 141; foreign ownership prohibited, 291–92; MTV, 26–27, 293; Murdoch holdings, 291; new airwaves given to, 321; in Nigeria, 132–46; as recouping its costs locally, 56, 240; satellite transmission of, 289; in South Africa, 34, 55–56, 57; in Turkey, 244. *See also programs by name*
Amerikanismus, 9, 254, 269n.18
"Ami Go Home!" (Busch), 200–1
Amo, Antonio del, 106
Anderson, Pamela, 322
Andreessen, Marc, 317
Andreotti, Giulio, 120
Angeli, Pier, 125, 128
Anglo-American Corporation, 40
Anini, Lawrence, 145n.1
Ankara (Turkey), 246, 247
Another Life (television program), 138
Antimiscegenation laws, 36
Anti-Semitism, 5, 262–63
Antonioni, Michelangelo, 127
AOL Network, 320
Apartheid: and American segregation, 36; and the Cold War, 49–55; intensifying opposition to, 55
Aptheker, Herbert, 199
Arabesque, 249, 250n.13
Arch of Triumph (film), 108
Arelu (television program), 137
Arendt, Hannah, 267, 270n.60
Argentina, 27
Armstrong, Louis: African tour of, 163, 169–70, 173; criticized as an Uncle Tom, 168; as cultural ambassador, 165; Eisenhower criticized by, 154, 168, 181–82; French interest in, 151; Hamburg concert of 1955, 197; in New Orleans revival, 152; in *The Real Ambassadors* revue, 168; recordings in South Africa, 46
ARPA (Advanced Research Projects Agency), 316

Asia: cultural programs in Vietnam, 172; Dizzy Gillespie concert in Pakistan, 170; Hong Kong, 27; jazz tours to Thailand, 172; Singapore, 299; total online in, 319. *See also* China; India; Japan
Aslan, Bünyamin, 208, 211
Asriel, Andre, 193–94, 203
AT&T, 289
Atlantic record company, 151
Australia: blackface minstrel shows in, 17, 21; television soap opera production in, 240; Wild West shows in, 18
Austria: Alpbach symposium, 74n.6; Indianer clubs, 26. *See also* Salzburg Seminar
Automobile industry, in South Africa, 41, 42, 43, 52, 55
Averty, Jean-Christophe, 153
Awful Truth, The (film), 103
Aziza E., 211

Bacall, Lauren, 104
Bagdikian, Ben, 291, 292, 303, 305
Baghdad Pact, 169
Baier, Lothar, 255
Baker, Josephine, 209
Ballantine, Christopher, 47
Ballmer, Steven, 323
Barefoot Contessa, The (film), 111
Barkin, Ellen, 229
Barney (television program), 138
Barnum, P. T., 24
Barzman, Ben, 121
Basketball, 139
Başkut, Cevat Fehmi, 250n.4
Bates, Stephen, 316
Bayles, Martha, 198
BDR. *See* Federal Republic of Germany
Beamlink Network, 137
Beatles, the, 1–2, 205n.15, 239
Bebop, 151–52, 160n.8
Bechet, Sidney, 151
Becker, George, 39
Becker, Jurek, 270n.61
Belair, Felix, 165
Bell, Ulrich, 89
Bell for Adano, A (film), 92

Benczik, Terence, 309
Benny Goodman Story, The (film), 151
Benson, T. O. S., 133
Berghahn, Volker, 75n.13
Bergman, Ingrid, 108, 125
Berlin, 197
Berlin-Ecke Schönhauser (film), 203
Berlusconi, Silvio, 292
Berners-Lee, Tim, 317
Berry, Chuck, 194, 206n.30, 239
Berry, John, 121
Bertelsmann, 292, 319
Besser, Howard, 323
Besser-Verstehen, 255
Best Years of Our Lives, The (film), 93–94, 99n.50
Big One, The (Moore), 232
Bilkent (Turkey), 247
"Bioskoopbeskawing," 45, 49
Birdseye Corporation, 52
Black, Gregory, 87, 89
"Black-and-White Minstrel Show" (BBC television), 31n.2
Blackboard Jungle (film), 197, 202
Black Elk, 24
Blackface minstrel shows, 18–23; American audience for, 19, 21; in Australia, 17, 21; black companies in, 31n.1; in Britain, 19–22; British and American troupes diverging, 21; burnt cork makeup for, 31n.3; Christy's Minstrels' skit, 27–29; in continental Europe, 17, 22; in English-language world, 17; as exemplary case of cultural exportation, 22–23; in France, 22; in Germany, 22; heyday of American, 18; in Holland, 32n.11; in India, 22; Irish-American performers in, 18; local imitators of, 26; losing its identifiable Americanness, 23; origins of, 17, 18; race as represented in, 7, 18–19; in South Africa, 17, 21, 22, 46; wordplay as central to, 22
Blacklisting, 121–22, 199
Blacksburg (Virginia), 311
Blair, John, 7
Blue jeans. *See* Levi's jeans
Blum-Byrnes agreement of 1946, 159n.2

Bogart, Humphrey, 110, 124
Bold and the Beautiful, The (television
  program), 140
Boleslawski, Richard, 109
Bonomi, Ivanoe, 130n.8
Boone, Pat, 196, 197, 247
Boorstin, Daniel, 72
Borstelmann, Tim, 164
Bosch, Aurora, 7, 118
Boucicault, Dion, 31n.8
Bower, Roger, 133–34
"Bowery Boys" (South Africa), 39
Bowery theater (New York City), 21
Boxer Rebellion, 18, 25
Bravo (magazine), 196, 197
Brazil: MTV imitators in, 27; South
  African city planning influence by, 34;
  telenovelas shown in Nigeria, 136
Brazzi, Rossano, 128
Brecht, Bertolt, 195
Breen, Joseph I., 93, 94, 99n.50
Breidenbach, Joana, 9
Brenan, Gerald, 101
Brezhnev, Leonid, 188
Bril, Igor, Quartet, 190
Bringing Up Baby (film), 103
Brion, Keith, 223
Britain: American football in, 236–38;
  American popular culture in Ireland
  and England, 227–41; American tele-
  vision in, 240; Australian soap operas
  in, 240; "Black-and-White Minstrel
  Show," 31n.2; blackface minstrel
  shows in, 19–22; Channel 4, 236,
  237; exports to South Africa, 39–40;
  foreign programming on Nigerian
  television, 142–44; Free Cinema,
  122; on "insightful" Americans, 231–
  35; investment in South Africa, 40,
  42; ironic consumption of American
  cultural products in, 229–30; Liverpool, 1, 236, 239; punk movement in,
  239; in rock 'n' roll's development,
  238–39; *The Simpsons* in, 230–31;
  South Africa asserting its autonomy
  from, 51; stereotypes of Americans in,
  233–34; Thatcherism, 318. *See also*
  London

Brooks, Jeffrey, 187
Broonzy, Big Bill, 153
Brown, James, 212
Brubeck, Dave, 163, 167–68, 169,
  176n.27
Brubeck, Iola, 167–68, 169, 176n.27
Bryson, Bill, 232–33
Bryson, Lyman, 76n.26
Budweiser beer, 236
Buffalo Bill's Wild West, 23–25;
  bonafide Indians in, 24, 25; Boxer
  Rebellion acted out by, 18, 25; command performance for Queen Victoria, 25; exported to Western world in
  its entirety, 18; first European tour of,
  24–25; imitators of, 26; as immedi-
  ately accessible, 23, 25; in London,
  23, 25; marketing of, 25; program for
  1901 season, 29–31; Sioux made
  prototypical Indian by, 32n.23; spec-
  tatorship of, 23; as supranational, 23;
  triumph of the Western over the
  "primitive" in, 18, 23; verbalization
  as minimal in, 25, 32n.21
Büken, Gülriz, 9
Bukowski, Charles, 231–32
Bulletin board systems, 300–1
Bulletin du Hot Club de France, Le
  (magazine), 159n.3
Bureau of Motion Pictures (Office of
  War Information), 87
Busch, Ernst, 195, 200–1
Bush, Vannevar, 316
Bütün Dünya (magazine), 243
Byrne, Gabriel, 229

Cabero, Juan Antonio, 107
Cable News Network (CNN), 137, 279,
  280, 293, 302, 303
Caglar, Ayse, 212
Cahiers du jazz, Les (magazine), 160n.3
Callari, Francesco, 123
Campbell, James T., 7
Campbell, Richard, 67
Camus, Albert, 162n.48
Canada: in Ford, South Africa, 41;
  Thompson group of newspapers, 291;
  total online in, 319

Cantalupo, James, 285
Cape Town (South Africa), 37
Capital (television program), 136
Capitol record company, 151
Capra, Frank, 94, 103
Carmen Merino, María del, 106
Carnaby Street, 239
Cartel (rap group), 211
Casablanca (film), 110
Castorf, Frank, 265
Catch-22 (Heller), 232
Catholic Church. *See* Roman Catholic Church
CBN (Christian Broadcasting Network), 137, 138
CBS (Columbia Broadcasting System), 133, 321
Censorship: in Franco's Spain, 108–11; Hollywood self-censorship during World War II, 87–89; of the Internet, 298; in South Africa, 49
CERN, 317
Chahine, Gandy, 208, 211
Chamoun, Camille, 169
Chaplin, Charlie, 103
Charlie Chan movies, 88, 96n.17
Chat rooms, 311
Checkmate (television program), 140
Cheerleaders, 237
Cherrington, Ben M., 68
Chiari, Walter, 125
Chica "Topolino," Una (Puente), 113
Child pornography, 310–11
Children on the Internet (FIND/SVP report), 312
Children's broadcasting, 138
China: Boxer Rebellion, 18, 25; Internet control in, 299; as represented in Hollywood movies, 88, 96n.17; "Stars and Stripes Forever" deleted from concert in, 223
China Seas (film), 109
Chomsky, Noam, 323–24
Christian, Linda, 125
Christian Broadcasting Network (CBN), 137, 138
Christy's Minstrels, 27–29
Chuck D., 210

Cinecittà: in fascist Italy's motion picture policy, 106; Hollywood movies made at, 120–22, 123–24; leftist American cinema artists seeking refuge in, 7–8, 121–22; as refugee camp after the war, 117
Cinema. *See* Motion pictures
Cinema Law (Italy), 120
Cinema nuovo (magazine), 121, 131n.16
Circuit-switching technology, 294, 295
Clancy Street Kids (film), 89
Clapperboard Television, Lagos (Nigeria), 136
Clash, The, 239
Clinton, Bill, 58, 299, 314, 322
Clinton, Hillary, 322
Clipper chip, 299
Club Saint-Germain (Paris), 151
CMC (computer-mediated communication), 294–97, 300–1
CNN (Cable News Network), 137, 279, 280, 293, 302, 303
Coca-Cola: French campaign against, 273; in South Africa, 42, 55; in Turkey, 245; as youth culture icon, 282
Coca-Colonization, 273
Cockrell, Dale, 22
Cody, William F. "Buffalo Bill": arranging buffalo hunt for Grand Duke of Russia, 23; stage melodramas of 1870s, 24. *See also* Buffalo Bill's Wild West
Cold War: and American popular culture's spread, 6; apartheid and, 49–55; blacklisting, 121–22, 199; in France, 149–50, 161n.34; Hollywood movies in, 118; in the Internet's origins, 315–17; Italian popular film magazines during, 119–20; jazz as propaganda in, 157–58, 163–79; mass media in, 118; Matthiessen as victim of, 77n.33; rock 'n' roll in the German Democratic Republic during, 192–206; Russian jazz during, 179, 182; and the Salzburg Seminar, 68, 69–70; Spanish-American rapprochement during, 105

Columbia Broadcasting System (CBS), 133, 321
Commonwealth Fund, 76n.28
Communication, mass. *See* Mass media
Communication Decency Act of 1995, 299
Computer-mediated communication (CMC), 294–97, 300–1
Conant, James B., 67
Conformity, 5, 155
Congo, 169–70
Conover, Willis, 157, 163, 167, 176n.18, 189
Consolidated Gold Fields, 39
Consumerism: in Americanization of postwar Japan, 224; French jazz fans criticizing, 149, 155–56; German anxiety about, 255; and leisure time and freedom, 276; Russian conspicuous consumption, 191; South African consumer society created, 41–45; in Spain, 114; in Turkey, 241, 244; U.S. boosting its economy by disseminating, 242; of youth culture, 282
Convergence, 296–97, 305
Cooper, Gary, 235
Copans, Sim, 153
Coppola, Francis, 117
Cora E., 210–11, 212
Corbis Corporation, 323
Cortese, Valentina, 128
Cosby Show, The (television program), 35, 56, 227
Courtois, A., 151
Cousins, Norman, 95
Cowboy in Manhattan (film), 89
Crain, Jeanne, 93
Crawford, Cindy, 322
Crawford, Joan, 93, 104
Credit cards, 246
Creel Commission, 7
Creolization, 10, 282, 284
Cribb (rap group), 212
Crowther, Bosley, 91
Cruise, Tom, 318
Crying of Lot 49, The (Pynchon), 232
Cukor, George, 103
Cultural diplomacy: Louis Armstrong as ambassador of American culture, 165; purpose of American, 84; Salzburg Seminar and, 65, 66, 68, 69, 73–74
Cultural exchange: the Cold War and, 70; jazz tours, 164, 167, 169, 171, 174; Smith-Mundt Act and, 68, 76n.29
"Cultural Exchange" (song), 168, 176n.27
Cultural imperialism: and American media dominance, 288–90; American popular culture seen as, 6, 193, 222; Coca-Cola as icon of, 273; Hollywood movies as, 123; of McDonald's, 285, 287; Salzburg Seminar as, 65; as simplification, 35; in Turkey, 248
Cultural presentation programs, 164–65, 166
Culture. *See* American popular culture; High culture; Mass culture
Cumings, Bruce, 164
Cuyler, Jacob, 36
Cyberpunk, 298
Czerny, Peter, 203

"Daar Kom Die Alabama" (folk song), 36
Dallas (television program), 55, 240
Dambe (television program), 137
Dances, 111, 113, 203
Danelin, Vladimir, 191
DARPA (Defense Advanced Research Projects Agency), 316–17
Dassin, Jules, 121
Davies, Elspeth, 76n.26
Davis, Miles, 151, 152, 154, 167
Dawson, Claude I., 101–2
DBN (Degue Broadcasting Network), 135, 140
DDR. *See* German Democratic Republic
Dean, James, 125
DeBeers Company, 39
Debt, 246
Defense Advanced Research Projects Agency (DARPA), 316–17
De Gaulle, Charles, 161n.34

Degue Broadcasting Network (DBN), 135, 140
De La Soul, 213
Delaunay, Charles, 153, 159n.3, 161n.18, 162n.48
DeLillo, Don, 309
Deliverance (film), 235
Democracy in America (Toqueville), 153
Democratic Christian Party (Italy), 116, 124, 129n.2
Democrat Party (Turkey), 241, 250n.5
Den Hollander, Arie N. D., 68
Department of State. *See* U.S. State Department
Depression, the, 103, 104
Deregulation, 318
De Santis, Giuseppe, 129n.3
De Sica, Vittorio, 126, 129n.3, 131n.16
Desmins Broadcast (Nigeria) Limited, Kaduna, 136
Desmond, Paul, 169
Destino (weekly), 104–5
Detour (film), 92
Diamond, Edwin, 316
Diana, Princess, 322
Diddley, Bo, 194, 206n.30
Digital Detective Services, Inc., 310–11
Diplomacy, cultural. *See* Cultural diplomacy
Dishman, Linda, 285–86
Disney cartoons, 247
Disney company, 311, 319, 321
Disneyland: Euro-Disneyland, 223; Tokyo Disneyland, 219, 223–26
Divorce, 124
DJ Mahmut, 212
Dmytryk, Edward, 131n.16
Doerry, Martin, 265
Dolce vita, La (film), 126, 128
Domino, Fats, 197
Dortmund (Germany), 214
Double Indemnity (film), 110
Down Beat (magazine), 151, 165
Downey (California), 285–86
"Draft Outline of a Directive on Projection of America" (Wilson), 83–85, 95
Dragon Seed (film), 88
Dragosei, Italo, 127

Drum (magazine), 163
Dublin, 239
Duck Soup (film), 102
Duhamel, Georges, 150
Dulles, John Foster, 169
Dungan, Myles, 9
Dunne, Irene, 124
Dvoskin, Victor, 188–89, 190
Dynasty (television program), 55, 240

East Germany. *See* German Democratic Republic
EBay, 325
Eco, Umberto, 322
E-commerce (electronic shopping), 318, 320
Edelhagen, Kurt, 197
Edutainment, 139
Edward VII, 25
Einstein, Albert, 309
Eisenhower, Dwight, 105, 154, 165, 168, 182
Eisler, Hanns, 195, 206n.29
Ekberg, Anita, 126
Electronic Greeting Cards, 325
Electronic shopping (e-commerce), 318, 320
Elledge, Scott, 67
Ellender, Allen, 165
Ellington, Duke, 151, 163, 167, 171–72, 180, 184
Ellison, Larry, 322
Ellwood, David, 122, 131n.18
E-mail, 299, 300–1, 303
Encarta encyclopedia, 323, 327n.44
Encryption, 299
Encyclopedia Americana, 291
Encyclopedia Britannica, 291
Endflied, Cy, 121
Engelhard, Charles, 54
England. *See* Britain
English language, 290, 319
Entertainment: adult entertainment, 314; dances, 111, 113, 203; edutainment, 139; infotainment, 139, 313, 318, 322; on Nigerian television, 138–40; in South Africa, 46–49; vaudeville, 46. *See also* Blackface minstrel shows;

Entertainment (*continued*)
  Motion pictures; Music; Sports; Television; Wild West shows
Erci E., 211
Ermarth, Michael, 9
Ethiopian Serenaders, 20
Ethnocentrism, 10
Ethnological exhibits, 26
Euro-Disneyland, 223
Europe: Internet presence of, 310; total
  online in, 319; World Wide Web as
  invention of, 317. *See also* Austria;
  Britain; France; Germany; Holland;
  Ireland; Italy; Spain
European Association for American
  Studies (EAAS), 66, 72
European Union, 324
Exceptionalism, 72
Exchange, cultural. *See* Cultural
  exchange
Exite Network, 320
Export-Import Bank, 54, 105

Fantastischen Vier, Die, 215
"Fantillusion" (Disney theme), 225
Fast, Howard, 199
Fast food outlets: Pizza Hut, 226; in
  Turkey, 245. *See also* McDonald's
FDJ (Free German Youth), 194, 201, 203
Feather, Leonard, 152–53, 176n.18
Federal Republic of Germany (BDR):
  American popular culture in, 192;
  and "Ami Go Home!" movement,
  201; attitudes toward the United
  States in, 196–97; continuity with
  Nazi cultural policies, 193; East Germany
  as competing with, 192–93; as
  economically overdeveloped and culturally
  underdeveloped, 260; as an
  economy in search of an idea, 266; as
  more American than the Americans,
  254; rock 'n' roll in, 196–98; WDR
  radio, 196
Fellini, Federico, 127
Ferrara, Abel, 117
Festival (magazine), 123
Fettes Brot, 213–14
Fichte, Johann G., 255

Fields, W. C., 46
Filipacchi, Daniel, 160n.3
Film. *See* Motion pictures
Film noir, 150
Firestone, 42, 50
Fischer, Joschka, 253
Food: frozen food in South Africa, 52;
  Turkish food traditions and Americanization,
  245. *See also* Fast food
  outlets
Football, 236–38
Ford, John, 103, 119
Ford, South Africa, 41
Fortune (magazine), 50–51
"Four Freedoms Speech" (Roosevelt),
  279–80
Fox network, 291, 321
France: African American and white jazz
  distinguished in, 151, 152–53,
  161nn. 18, 23; on African American
  culture, 160n.12; Americanization in
  postwar, 149; blackface minstrel
  shows in, 22; Coca-Cola opposed by,
  273; Cold War's effect on, 149–50,
  161n.34; consumerism criticized by
  jazz fans in, 149, 155–56; cultural
  identity and jazz in, 149, 158–59;
  Euro-Disneyland, 223; as European
  jazz capital, 158; Hachette, 291, 292,
  319; Hollywood movies in, 150,
  159n.2; International Salons of Jazz,
  158; jazz in the 1950s, 149–62; jazz
  magazines in, 151, 159n.3; Ministry
  of Culture established, 150; Mitterrand,
  273, 278; Paris, 151, 158; on
  propagandistic use of jazz, 157–58;
  racism criticized by jazz fans in, 149,
  153–55; racism in, 154–55; social
  characteristics of jazz fans in, 150
Francis, André, 153
Franco, Francisco: censorship of Hollywood
  movies under, 108–11; cinematographic
  policy of, 105–8;
  dictatorship of, 100–1; passion for
  the cinema, 100; rapprochement with
  U.S. during Cold War, 105; script for
  La Raza written by, 100, 114n.2;
  women's equality abolished by, 112

Franco, Ramón, 100
Franklin, Aretha, 207
Fraser-Chalmers, 39
Freedom: and advertising, 276; advertising and freedom of choice, 279–82; American West associated with, 274–75; Roosevelt's "Four Freedoms Speech," 279–80
Free German Youth (FDJ), 194, 201, 203
Free speech, 300
Free trade, 273
Frelinghuysen, Kelly and Peter, 166
"Fremd im eigenen Land" (Advanced Chemistry), 211
Fresh Familee, 211
Friedman, Thomas L., 285
From Here to Eternity (film), 111
From the Heart of Europe (Matthiessen), 69
Frontier mythology, 228
Frozen food, 52, 245
FTP, 295
Fuchs, Thomas, 8
Fulbright Act of 1946, 68, 76n.29

Gable, Clark, 109
Galaxy Television (Ibadan), 135
Gallup company, 293
Gangster movies, 84, 89, 92–93
Gardner, Ava, 104, 125
Garnett, Tay, 109
Gassman, Vittorio, 125, 128
Gastarbeiter, 208, 211
Gates, Bill, 299, 305, 322–23, 327n.44
GATT, 273
GDR. *See* German Democratic Republic
Genderbending, 277
Gendizer, Irene, 164
General Electric, 39, 321
General Motors, 42, 43, 52, 55
General Tire, 50
Generations (television program), 136
Geneva, 26
Gentleman's Agreement (film), 93
Geo (magazine), 252
GeoCities, 320
German Democratic Republic (DDR;

GDR): on African American culture, 193–94; Americanization of West Germany opposed by, 254; anti-Americanism of, 200–1; continuity with Nazi cultural policies, 193; Federal Republic of Germany as competitor of, 192–93; Free German Youth, 194, 201, 203; jazz in, 203, 206n.30; Mielke's campaign against punks, 205n.7; national German dance culture in, 203; popular music played on the radio in, 202; on Paul Robeson, 194, 199–200; rock 'n' roll in, 192–206; 60/40 rule, 202, 203; Ulbricht, 203, 206n.29; unified Germany handicapped by, 255, 260; as young country, 194
German language, 257
Germany: Bertelsmann, 292, 319; blackface minstrel shows in, 22; dual unifications of, 264; economic difficulties in, 265–66; foreign programming on Nigerian television, 142–44; *Gastarbeiter,* 208, 211; graffiti art in, 214; Graham's performance of *Phaedras* in, 166; handicaps in face of global competition, 255; Indianer clubs, 26; and modernity, 256; as more American than the Americans, 252; MTV imitators in, 27; multiple identities in, 265; Nazism, 254, 265; neo-Nazism, 255; rap music in, 8–9, 207–16; transcendental thinking in, 255; twentieth-century attitudes toward Americanization, 254–55; unification as self-inflicted Americanization, 251–70; Weimar Republic, 194–95, 254. *See also* Federal Republic of Germany; German Democratic Republic
Germi, Pietro, 118–19
Getz, Stan, 152, 172
Gide, André, 162n.48
Gilda (film), 92, 104, 110
Gillespie, Dizzy, 151, 157, 163, 165, 170, 175n.11
Ginsberg, Vida, 76n.26

Globalization: as always also Americanization, 253; cultural, economic, and
technological as concomitant, 286–
87; and German normalization, 266;
and localization, 9–10, 22, 219, 222;
McDonald's in, 285; in nineteenth
century, 17–33; as not a victimless
crime, 227; as temporary phenomenon, 27; transnational corporations
in, 318, 321; U.S. as main motor of,
253; U.S. free enterprise model in,
318–19
"Globalization of American Popular
Culture, The" (Salzburg Seminar session), 2–3
Global village: contemporary evaluation
of, 293–94; as a global city, 306; In-
ternet and the, 296; media domina-
tion of, 288–308; media lords in,
290–92
Globocentrism, 10
Gobbard, Henri, 242
Goldener Oktober (Müller), 256
Go Network, 320
Gone with the Wind (film), 110
Goodman, Benny, 151, 157, 163, 167,
172
Goodyear Tire, 50
Gopher (information transfer protocol),
295
Gore, Albert, Jr., 58, 301, 314, 320
"Government Information Manual for
the Motion Picture Industry," 87
Graffiti art, 210, 214
Graham, Martha, 163, 166, 172
Gramsci, Antonio, 116
Grant, Cary, 89
Granz, Norman, 156–57
Grapes of Wrath (film), 108
Gray, David, 9
Great Britain. *See* Britain
Great Dictator, The (film), 108
Greenberg, Stanley, 58
Gruber, Christian, 310
Gruber, Karl, 71
Guback, Thomas, 288

Hachette, 291, 292, 319

Haley, Bill, 197, 202, 204, 206n.30
Hamm, Charles, 22
Hammond, John Hays, 39
Hampton, Lionel, 157
Hardy Family series of films, 104
Harlem Swingsters, 46
Harris, Neil, 220
Harvard Student Council, 67
Harvard Summer School. *See* Salzburg
Seminar
Hawks, Howard, 103
Hays Code, 104
Hays Office, 87, 93, 94
Hayworth, Rita, 104, 110
Heidegger, Martin, 257, 261, 264
Heller, Clemens, 66–67, 69, 70, 76n.21,
77nn. 31, 32
Heller, Joseph, 231, 232
Henderson, Joe, 190
Hepburn, Katharine, 104
Hersey, John, 92
Herz, Martin, 69–70, 78n.35
Hess, Jacques, 161n.23
Heysel Stadium tragedy, 236
Hibiya Park (Tokyo), 221
High culture: American immigrants hav-
ing distaste for, 240–41; Germans on
U.S. lack of, 196; international aspi-
rations of, 282–83; mass culture as
replacing, 4–5; at Salzburg Seminar,
71
High technology, 261
Hilton, Conrad, 247
Hines, Earl, 167
Hip hop: defined, 209–10. *See also* Rap
music
Hitchcock, Alfred, 128
Hitler, Adolf, 269n.18
Hixson, Walter, 164, 167
Hodeir, André, 152, 157, 160n.11,
161n.18, 162n.48
Hoffmann, Stanley, 71
Hofmeyr, Isabel, 44, 45
Hogan, Hulk, 139
Holiday (film), 103
Holiday, Billie, 213
Holland (The Netherlands): blackface
minstrel shows in, 32n.11; explicit

sexuality in public service advertising in, 283–84; Levi's advertising, 277, 284, 287n.2; Stender nonalcoholic beer advertising, 276

Holly, Buddy, 238, 239

Hollywood (magazine), 122–23, 124, 127–28, 131n.16

Hollywood movies, 81–131; as all over the world, 1; blacklisting of filmmakers, 121–22; Charlie Chan movies, 88, 96n.17; Cinecittà production of, 120–22, 123–24; in the Cold War, 118; collaboration between Washington and Hollywood, 7; in England and Ireland, 234–35; English language in, 290; as escapist, 126; fascist Italy's quota system for, 106; in France, 150, 159n.2; gangster movies, 84, 89, 92–93; *Hardy Family* series, 104; Hays Code, 104; Hays Office, 87, 93, 94; in immediate postwar years, 91–94; Italian film personalities in, 128; Italian neorealist influence on, 117, 121; in Italy in the postwar period, 116–31; major complexities of life ignored in, 91; as mass culture not popular culture, 119; negative image of America created by, 84–87; on Nigerian television, 138; of 1930s and 1940s, 103; projecting American culture abroad, 1942–1947, 83–99; and racism, 93, 98n.45; self-censorship during World War II, 87–89; in South Africa, 35, 48–49, 57; in Spain under Franco, 7, 100–15; stars on the Internet, 322; in Turkey, 244; war films, 90, 97n.32; Web sites for, 310; women in postwar, 104; during World War II, 83–91; World War II legitimating, 117. See also *titles, studios, directors, and actors by name*

"Hollywood Ten," 121

Holmes, G. S., Company, 37

Home and Away (television program), 240

Home of the Brave (film), 93

Hong Kong, 27

Hoover, Herbert, 40

Hoover Vacuum Cleaner Company, 280, 284

Hot Club de France, 160n.10

Houston, Whitney, 207

How Green Was My Valley (film), 108

Huisgenoot, Die (newspaper), 45

Hull, Richard, 41

Huston, John, 98n.44, 121

Hutcherson, Bobby, 190

Hypermedia links, 303

IBM, 52, 316

Ibrahim, Mallam Mohammed, 137

Im Lauf der Zeit (film), 258

Imperialism, cultural. *See* Cultural imperialism

India: blackface minstrel shows in, 22; movies shown on Nigerian television, 136; State Department jazz tours skipping, 170

Indianer clubs, 26

Individual, cult of the, 235

"Information Superhighway," 314, 323

Information transfer protocols, 295

Infotainment, 139, 313, 318, 322

Ingersoll Company, 39

In nome della legge (film), 118–19

Intellectual property, 300

"Interlude" (Lundstrem), 182

Internationalen Hochschulwochen (Alpbach), 74n.6

International Salons of Jazz, 158

Internet, 309–27; America as at the hub of, 287; American stars and products dominating, 322; anti-monopolistic nature of, 322; censorship of, 298; children online, 311–13; coexistence with media lords, 305; Cold War origins of, 315–17; control of, 297–300; copyright violations on, 301; corporate takeover of, 323–24; creating another persona on, 315; as decentralized, 298, 300; demographic analysis of users, 295–96; encryption, 299; European presence on, 310; gender bias in use of, 296, 313; and the global village, 296; haves and

Internet (*continued*)
  have-nots divided by, 321; interconnective nature of, 296; libertarian
  ethos of, 298, 315; media giants'
  adaptation to, 300–4, 324; packet-
  switching in, 294–95; pornography
  on, 301, 309–10; search engines,
  302; servers in U.S., 320; sex on,
  309–10, 314; social evolution of,
  298; software agents tracking use of,
  323; teenagers online, 311; unconstrained interconnectivity of, 296;
  Westernized elite dominating, 321;
  women online, 296, 313; world total
  online, 319–20; worldwide dialogue
  on, 9. *See also* World Wide Web
  (WWW)
"Internet Addiction" (report), 315
Internet Society (ISOC), 297
In the Heat of the Night (film), 235
Into the West (film), 228–29
"Invincible Eagle, The" (Sousa), 220
Iran, 169
Iraq, 88, 169, 172
Ireland: American popular culture in,
  227–41; American television in, 240;
  American West in subconscious of,
  228–29; Australian soap operas in,
  240; "sneaking regarders" of Ameri-
  can culture in, 235
Islamic Force (rapper), 211
Israel, 263
Istanbul, 246, 247, 248
Italian comedy, 126, 128
Italy: and American film stars, 124–25;
  Americanization in, 116–17, 127; as
  best market for Hollywood movies in
  Europe, 118; capping Hollywood
  movie imports, 120; Cinema Law,
  120; Democratic Christian Party, 116,
  124, 129n.2; evolution of film production from 1945, 127–28; explicit
  sexuality in advertising in, 283; fascist
  motion picture policy, 105–6, 117;
  fashion and crafts, 124–25; Hollywood losing control over, 127–28;
  Hollywood movies in the postwar
  period, 116–31; Hollywood movie

techniques adopted by, 125–26; illiteracy in nineteenth-century, 32n.21;
  Italian comedy, 126, 128; Levi's jeans
  poster, 277–78; "maggiorate," 125;
  modernization and American films in
  the 1950s, 122–27; MTV imitators
  in, 27; Mussolini, 105, 107; national
  identity in, 116, 122, 129n.2; popular
  film magazines, 119–20, 122–24,
  126, 130n.11; *sandaloni*, 125;
  spaghetti westerns, 128; Turin
  protests against McDonald's, 286. *See
  also* Cinecittà
It Happened in Springfield (film), 93
It's a Wonderful Life (film), 93–94
ITT, 289
It Takes a Thief (television program),
  132, 145n.1
Izvestia (newspaper), 181

Jackson, Michael, 207, 277
Jacob, Günther, 209
Jaffe, J. Michael, 9, 319
Japan: American cultural symbols domesticated in, 219, 225; Americanization of postwar, 224; Disney
  merchandise in, 223; Internet growth
  in, 320; McDonald's in, 285; MTV
  imitators in, 27; New Sousa Band
  tour of, 222–23; Sony Corporation,
  292, 319; John Philip Sousa in, 219–
  23; Tokyo Disneyland, 219, 223–26;
  undokai, 220–21
Japan Sousa Society, 223
Jazz: as anticommercial, 155, 157; appeal throughout the world, 165;
  bebop, 151–52, 160n.8; as a black
  music, 155; Dave Brubeck, 163, 167–
  68, 169, 176n.27; as Cold War propaganda, 157–58, 163–79; Miles
  Davis, 151, 152, 154, 167; Duke
  Ellington, 151, 163, 167, 171–72,
  180, 184; in France in the 1950s,
  149–62; French critics distinguishing
  African American and white, 151,
  152–53, 161nn. 18, 23; in German
  Democratic Republic, 203, 206n.30;
  Stan Getz, 152, 172; Dizzy Gillespie,

151, 157, 163, 165, 170, 175n.11;
Benny Goodman, 151, 157, 163, 167,
172; Earl Hines, 167; Stan Kenton,
152; Thelonious Monk, 151; New
Orleans jazz, 151, 152, 160n.8; Char-
lie Parker, 151, 156, 212; race in
French attitude toward, 8; in Shang-
hai, 180, 182, 185; South African
mbaqanga, 46; in the Soviet Union,
166–67, 179–91; State Department
tours, 8, 157, 163–79; as uniquely
American, 166; West Coast jazz, 151,
152, 160n.8
Jazz Art Club (Moscow), 190
Jazz at the Philharmonic (J.A.T.P.) con-
certs, 156–57
Jazz Hot (magazine), 151, 153, 154,
157, 158, 159n.3
Jazz: Its Evolution and Its Essence
(Hodeir), 152
Jazz Magazine, 151, 154, 159n.3
Jazz Maniacs, 46
Jeans. *See* Levi's jeans
Jefferson, Thomas, 37
Jeffries, Jim, 49
"Jein" (Fettes Brot), 213
"Jim Crow," 19
"Jim Dandy," 21
Jim Lehrer Newshour (television pro-
gram), 137
Johannesburg: American influence in, 35;
Americans in development of, 39; the
"Bowery Boys," 39; Commissioner
Street, 48; The Empire theater, 48;
Killarney suburb, 47
Johnson, Jack, 49
Johnson, Lyndon B., 172
Jones, Dorothy, 90–91, 94, 97n.32
Jones, Grace, 277
Jordan, Michael, 139
Jowett, Garth, 93–94
Juan Carlos (king of Spain), 105
Jünger, Ernst, 261, 265
Junge Welt (newspaper), 201, 206n.29

Karachi (Pakistan), 170
Kassim, Abdel Karim, 169
Katz, Elihu, 289

Kavakçi, Merve, 249
Kaye, Danny, 88
Kazan, Elia, 93, 131n.16
Kazin, Alfred, 68
Kelly, Edna F., 166
Kelly, Grace, 108–9
Kennedy, David, 41
Kennedy, Stetson, 153
Kenton, Stan, 152
Kerr, Deborah, 111
Keyes, Geoffrey, 77n.32
Khrushchev, Nikita, 184
"Kids Online" (study), 312
Kiefer, Anselm, 261
Killer, The (film), 92
Kimberley (South Africa), 38–39
Kinderzimmer Productions, 213
King, David, 269n.18
King, Henry, 111
Kinks, the, 239
Kissinger, Henry, 266
Kitsch, 249
Kohl, Helmut, 251, 270n.61
Konträr-Amerikanismus, 254, 269n.18
Koppes, Clayton, 87, 89
"Koreasong" (Busch), 201
Kroes, Rob, 9, 268n.2
Kroker, Arthur, 323
Kuby, Erich, 253
Kultur, 255

Ladd, Alan, 89
Lady from Shanghai, The (film), 104,
109
Lafitte, Guy, 151
Lagos (Nigeria), 133, 134
Lancaster, Burt, 111
Lang, Fritz, 103
Larkey, Edward, 206nn. 30, 36
Latin America: Mexico, 136, 142–44;
television in, 289; total online in, 319.
See also Brazil
Lattuada, Alberto, 119
Laughton, Charles, 109
Leadbelly, 239
Leave Her to Heaven (film), 110
Lebanon, 169
Lee, Spike, 209

Legrand, Michel, 151
Lehmann, Theo, 203
Lehrer, Jim, 137
Leirus, Michel, 162n.48
Leisure time, 276
Lennon, John, 205n.15
Leontief, Wassily, 68
Let There Be Light (film), 98n.44
Levinthal, David, 228
Levi's jeans: the Cold War as won by,
    164; Dutch advertising for, 277, 284,
    287n.2; in France, 150; Italian poster
    for, 277–78
Lewinsky, Monica, 322
Lewis, R. J. B., 76n.27
"Liberty Bell" (Sousa), 220
Lied der Zeit record company, 195
Lifeboat (film), 93
Lindley, Daniel, 36
Lipsi (dance), 203
Liston, Melba, 165
Little Colonel, The (film), 102
Little Richard, 194, 239
Liverpool, 1, 236, 239
Lloyd, Frank, 109
Lollobrigida, Gina, 125, 126, 128
London: blackface minstrel shows in, 17,
    20, 31n.7; Boucicault's *The Octoroon*
    in, 31n.8; Buffalo Bill's Wild West in,
    23, 25; Carnaby Street, 239; Kalahari
    Bushmen exhibit of 1847, 26; in rock
    'n' roll development, 239
Loren, Sophia, 125, 126
Lorenz, Konrad, 71
Losey, Joseph, 121
Lost Continent (Bryson), 232
Lost Weekend, The (film), 93
Lott, Eric, 19
Lucky Jordan (film), 89
Lundstrem, Oleg: band as longest-run-
    ning swing band, 179; as grandfather
    of Russian jazz, 179; on jazz as inter-
    national, 179, 184; jazz discovered
    by, 180; on jazz during Stalin years,
    185; in Kazan, 182, 185–86; in late
    Soviet era, 186; post-Soviet transition
    to capitalism of, 186; returning to
    Russia in 1947, 182; in Shanghai,

180; after Stalin's death, 184; Starr's
    account of, 185–86; Tatar music
    arranged by, 183–84
Luxardo, 126
Lycos, 320

Maase, Kaspar, 196–97
Madonna, 207, 277, 283, 318, 322
Madrid, 101, 102
"Maggiorate," 125
Malan, Daniel, 45, 50, 51
Malcolm X, 212
Malcolm X (film), 209
"Mall rats," 246
Malls: in South Africa, 34, 35, 56; in
    Turkey, 245–46
Malraux, André, 150
Malson, Lucien, 154, 155, 161n.23
Maltz, Albert, 199
Manchester United, 236–37
Mandela, Nelson, 58
Mankiewicz, Joseph L., 111, 121
Mann, Klaus, 129n.3
Marlboro Man, 273, 274, 275
Marshall Plan, 149, 182, 200
Marx, Groucho, 102
Marx Brothers, 102, 103
Maschke, Günter, 270n.43
Mass culture: Americans seen as robotic
    consumers of, 85; high culture
    replaced by, 4–5; internationalization
    of, 282–83; as *lingua franca,* 282;
    political culture as element of Ameri-
    can, 280; popular culture contrasted
    with, 119; recontextualizing of Amer-
    ican, 281–82; Soviet attempt at creat-
    ing, 186–87
Mass marketing: in South Africa, 43–
    45. *See also* Advertising
Mass media: adaptation to the Internet,
    300–4, 324; American messages in,
    279; audiences as selective, 293; in
    the Cold War, 118; convergence,
    296–97, 305; diversity of messages
    in, 293–94; media lords, 290–92,
    319, 324; the oligarchy's future, 304–
    6; as so "American" as to constitute a
    cultural Trojan horse, 17; in South

Africa, 45–49; technological develop-
ments in, 294–97; theories of global
domination of, 288–308; in Turkey,
244; U.S. free enterprise model in,
318. *See also* Internet; Motion pic-
tures; Television
Materialism, 156
Matsushita Corporation, 319
Matthiessen, Francis O., 64, 65, 68, 69,
74nn. 2, 5, 77n.33
Maxwell, Robert, 292, 319
May, Elaine Tyler, 4
May, Michael, 8
Maydieu, P., 162n.48
Mbaqanga, 46
Mbeki, Thabo, 58
McAdoo, Orpheus Myron, 22, 46, 57
McCarey, Leo, 103, 109
McDonald, Neil, 76n.26
McDonaldization, 244
McDonald's: as all over the world, 1;
cultural sensitivity of, 285; Downey,
California, restaurant closing, 285–
86; in globalization of culture, 285; in
Japan, 285; multilocalism strategy of,
285; as reminding people of home,
226; in South Africa, 57–58; Turin,
Italy, protests against, 286; in Turkey,
245
McLean, Don, 239
McLuhan, Marshall, 292, 293
Mead, Margaret, 68, 70, 73
Mead, Robert O., 72
Mechtersheimer, Alfred, 258–60
Media, mass. *See* Mass media
Mee and You (television program), 138–
39
Menderes, Adnan, 241, 250n.5
Merchandising, sports, 236–37
Mexico, 136, 142–44
MGM, 104, 130n.12
Miami Vice (television program), 56
Microsoft, 299, 305, 320, 322–23,
327n.44
Middle East: *Adventure in Iraq,* 88;
Brubeck tour of, 169; Israel, 263;
total online in, 319. *See also* Turkey
Midwest Television (Nigeria), 132

Mielke, Erich, 205n.7
Mildred Pierce (film), 92–93
Milliken, Carl, 130n.8
Milner, Lord, 40
Minaj Systems Television (MSTV)
Obosi, 135–36
Mining engineering, 38–39
Minstrel shows. *See* Blackface minstrel
shows
Miracle, The (film), 117
Mission to Moscow (film), 90
Missouri (ship), 241
Mitterrand, François, 273, 278
Mixed Marriages Commission (South
Africa), 36
Mobil Oil, 52
Modernization, 241
Mofe-Damijo, Mee, 139
Mogambo (film), 109
Mohr, Kurt, 157
Molden, Fritz, 71–72, 78n.43
Molden, Otto, 74n.6
Monk, Thelonious, 151
Monod, Théodore, 162n.48
Moore, Demi, 318, 322
Moore, Dinty W., 314
Moore, George Washington, 20
Moore, Michael, 232
Morgan, J. P., 40
Morse code, 294
Moser, Simon, 74n.6
Motion pictures: "bioskoopbeskawing"
concept, 45, 49; evolution of Italian
film production from 1945, 127–28;
fascist Italy's policy on, 105–6, 117;
film noir, 150; Franco's cinemato-
graphic policy, 105–8; Italian com-
edy, 126, 128; Italian *sandaloni,* 125;
the "New Spanish Cinema," 108; in
South Africa, 47–49; spaghetti westerns, 128; Spanish industry before
civil war, 106, 115n.10; Spanish popularity of, 101; World War II attendance boom, 117. *See also* Hollywood movies; Neorealism; *and titles,
studios, directors, and actors by name*
Motion Pictures Producers Distributors
Association (MPPDA), 118

Mounier, Emmanuel, 162n.48
Movies. *See* Motion pictures
Mp3, 310
Mr. Lucky (film), 89
MTV, 26–27, 293
Müller, Elfriede, 256
Müller, Heiner, 260–61, 267
Müller, Robert, 251, 254
Mulligan, Gerry, 152
Multimedia systems, 297
Multinational (transnational) corpora-
 tions, 291, 318, 321, 324
Murdoch, Rupert, 291, 292, 319, 321
Murhi International Television (MITV),
 135
Muscio, Giuliana, 7
Music, 147–216; MTV, 26–27, 293;
 rhythm & blues, 1, 193–94, 197,
 198, 206n.30; John Philip Sousa in
 Japan, 219–23; in South Africa, 46–
 47. *See also* Blackface minstrel shows;
 Jazz; Rap music; Recording industry;
 Rock 'n' roll
Music und Gesellschaft (monthly), 204n
Music USA (Voice of America program),
 157, 163, 167, 176n.18, 189
Mussolini, Benito, 105, 107
Mutiny on the Bounty (film), 109–10
Myrdal, Gunnar, 174, 178n.45

Nash, Philleo, 99n.45
Nathan, Hans, 19
National Broadcasting Company (NBC),
 133, 305, 321
National Broadcasting Company Inter-
 national Limited (NBI), 133
National Football League (NFL), 236–
 38
National Party (South Africa), 45, 50,
 51, 53, 55, 56
National Party of Nigeria (NPN), 135
National Theater Academy, 165
Natives' (Urban Areas) Act of 1923
 (South Africa), 44
Natural Born Killers (film), 227
Nazism, 254, 265
NBC (National Broadcasting Company),
 133, 305, 321

NBC (Nigerian Broadcasting Corporation), 133, 137, 140
Ndiolo, Ifeoma, 139
Negroponte, Nicholas, 304
Neighbours (television program), 240
Nenning, Günter, 251, 266
Neo-liberalism, 318
Neo-Nazism, 255
Neorealism, 129n.3; Americanized ver-
 sion of, 127; as born outside the stu-
 dios, 117–18; communist intellectuals
 and, 118; Hollywood influence on,
 118–19; Hollywood movies influ-
 enced by, 117, 121; Hollywood
 movies strangling, 126, 127; and Ital-
 ian national identity, 116; leftist
 American filmmakers in, 121,
 131n.16; left-wing associations of,
 120; pink neorealist comedies, 126
Nescafé, 245
Netherlands, The. *See* Holland
Netscape Navigator, 317
New Orleans jazz, 151, 152, 160n.8
Newport Jazz Festival, 204
News, television. *See* Television news
News Corporation, 291, 292, 319, 321
New Sousa Band, 222–23
"New Spanish Cinema," 108
New York City: advertising agencies,
 289; blackface minstrel shows in, 17,
 18; Boucicault's *The Octoroon* in,
 31n.8; four freedoms at 1939 World
 Fair, 279
New York Dolls, 239
Nichols, Red, 156
Nickelodeon, 311
Nielsen company, 293
Nietzsche, Friedrich, 255, 256
Nigeria: American-style Nigerian televi-
 sion shows, 140; American television
 in, 132–46; Lawrence Anini, 145n.1;
 Broadcasting Code of 1993, 140;
 controls on television in, 140–41;
 cultural context of television in, 136–
 37; Decree 24 of 1977, 134; Decree
 25 of 1988, 135; economics of television in, 135–36; entertainment programming in, 138–40; foreign

television programming by country of origin, 141–44; genres and trends in television in, 137–40; *It Takes a Thief* in, 132, 145n.1; Lagos, 133, 134; Midwest Television, 132; origins of television in, 133–34; political context of television in, 135; private television, 135–36; public service television, 135; structure and organization of television in, 134–35; Technical Committee on Privatization and Commercialization, 135; television news, 135, 137

Nigerian Broadcasting Corporation (NBC), 133, 137, 140

Nigerian Television Authority (NTA), 134, 135, 137, 138, 140

Nigerian Television Service (NTS) Channel 10, 133–34

Ninkovich, Frank, 4

Nixon, Rob, 55

"No Susanna" (Busch), 201

Notoji, Masako, 9

NTA (Nigerian Television Authority), 134, 135, 137, 138, 140

NTS (Nigerian Television Service) Channel 10, 133–34

NUA, 310, 319

Nuestra Natacha (film), 106

Objecktiv (magazine), 204

Octoroon, The (Boucicault), 31n.8

Office of War Information (OWI), 83–90, 95, 98n.45, 117

Oil, 38, 52, 169

Oishi, Kiyoshi, 221

Olajuwon, Hakeem, 139

Old Dominion Foundation, 76n.28

Olusola, S., 134

ONSALE.com, 325

Open City (film), 129n.3

Oppenheimer, Ernest, 40

Oprah Winfrey Show (television program), 138

Oracle, 322

Otis Elevator Company, 39

Outspan (magazine), 43–44, 46, 60n.19

Owens-Ibie, Nosa, 8

OWI (Office of War Information), 83–90, 95, 98n.45, 117

Özal, Turgut, 241

Packet-switching, 294–95

Painted Veil, The (film), 109

Pakistan, 170

Palm Beach Story (film), 89

Panassié, Hugues, 152, 153, 159n.3, 160n.10, 162n.48

Pane amore e fantasia (film), 126

Paradise Case, The (film), 128

Paramount, 89

Paris, 151, 158

Parker, Charlie, 151, 156, 212

Parker, "Colonel" Tom, 198–99, 205n.15

Patrick, Deval, 58

Paydos (Başkut), 250n.4

Pell, Richard, 91

Perkins, Dexter, 77nn. 32, 33

Perojo, Benito, 106

Personal media, 296–97, 303

Pete Kelly's Blues (film), 151

Phaedras (dance), 166

Phillips, Flip, 157

Phonograph, 46

Pilsworth, M. J., 289

Pinky (film), 93

Pizza Hut, 226

Plateau Radio Television, Jos (Nigeria), 136

Plateau State (Nigeria), 137

Platters, The, 247

Playboy Magazine, 165

Popular culture. *See* American popular culture

Pornography: and American popular culture, 317–18; on the Internet, 301, 309–10; on office computers, 310–11

Port Elizabeth (South Africa), 41, 42, 47, 50

Post, David G., 308n.22

Postman Always Rings Twice, The (film), 104

Post Office (Bukowski), 232

Powell, Bud, 151

Power, Tyrone, 125
Pravda (newspaper), 181
Praz, Mario, 76n.26
Présence Africaine (journal), 162n.48
President's Emergency Fund, 165
Presley, Elvis: and British rock 'n' roll, 238, 239; contemporary children's knowledge of, 312–13; East German authorities on, 203, 204, 206n.30; joins the Army, 198–99, 205n.15; West German popularity of, 196, 197
Prince, 207, 283
Privatization, 135, 318, 319
Processed food, 52, 245
Progress, darker sides of, 254–55
Public Enemy (film), 89
Public Enemy (rap group), 210
Puente, José Vicente, 113
Punk movement, 205n.7, 239
Pyle, Ernie, 92
Pynchon, Thomas, 231, 232

Quo vadis? (film), 120, 130n.12

Race: blackface minstrel shows' depiction of, 7, 18–19; in Johnson-Jeffries fight, 49; and R&B, 198; in South African Americanization, 35. *See also* African Americans; Racism
Racism: East German attacks on American, 193, 199; in France, 154–55; French jazz fans criticizing, 149, 153–55; and Hollywood movies, 93, 98n.45; rap music on, 208; segregation, 36, 155; and State Department jazz tours, 170–74
Radio Corporation of America (RCA), 133, 289
Rambo (film), 138
Ramones, 239
R&B (rhythm & blues), 1, 193–94, 197, 198, 206n.30
Rap music: as consciously black, 207; in Germany, 8–9, 207–16; hip hop culture, 209–10; individual skills as important in, 210; origins of, 209–10; sampling in, 212; in South Africa, 57; on women, 210; word play in, 214

Rauhut, Michael, 202
Ray, Johnny, 204
Raza, La (film), 100, 114n.2
RCA (Radio Corporation of America), 133, 289
Reader's Digest (magazine), 243
Reagan, Ronald, 186, 220
Reaganomics, 318
Real Ambassadors, The (revue), 168, 176n.27
Recording industry: advertising jazz records in France, 151; in "clean-up drives," 198; Japanese Sousa recordings, 221; and rock 'n' roll in Germany, 196; in South Africa, 46; Soviet jazz records, 189, 190
Red and Hot (Starr), 182–83, 185–86
Reinhardt, Max, 2, 67, 75n.17
REM (band), 239
"Revival March" (Sousa), 221
Reynolds, Harry, 21
Rhodes, Cecil, 39
Rhodesia, 54
Rhythm & blues (R&B), 1, 193–94, 197, 198, 206n.30
RIAS (Radio in the American Sector Berlin), 202
Ribbat, Christoph, 8
Rice, Thomas Dartmouth, 19, 31n.7
Rimm, Marty, 301, 307n.22
Rincón, M. Fernanda del, 7, 118
Risi, Dino, 126
Ritzer, George, 244
Rivet, Paul, 162n.48
RKO, 89
Robertson, Pat, 137
Robeson, Paul, 194, 199–200
Robinson, Earl, 199
"Rock around the Clock" (Haley), 196, 202
Rockefeller Foundation, 76n.28
Rock 'n' roll: the Beatles, 1–2, 205n.15, 239; Chuck Berry, 194, 206n.30, 239; British role in, 238–39; Bo Diddley, 194, 206n.30; domestication of, 199, 205n.15; Fats Domino, 197; as escapism, 206n.36; German capitalists and communists opposed to, 8; in

German Democratic Republic, 192–206; Bill Haley, 197, 202, 204, 206n.30; Buddy Holly, 238, 239; Little Richard, 194, 239; punk movement, 205n.7, 239; rap music contrasted with, 207; reception in the United States, 198–99; the Rolling Stones, 239; stadium rock, 239; in West Germany, 196–98. *See also* Presley, Elvis

Rockwell, Norman, 279–80

Rödelheim Hartreim Projekt, 215

Rodgers, Jimmie, 46

Rogers, Will, 46

Rolling Stones, 239

Roman Catholic Church: and Franco's dictatorship, 100–1; and Hollywood movies in Italy, 118, 126–27; moral repression in Franco's Spain, 111; on *La Raza,* 100; Spanish film imports defending values of, 107, 108; in Spanish motion picture censorship, 109, 110; Vatican II, 114; on women's dress and behavior in Spain, 112

Rooney, John, 165

Roosevelt, Franklin D., 92, 98n.37, 279–80

Roots (television program), 136, 138, 146n.26

Rose, Tricia, 210

Rosner, Eddie, 181, 182, 184

Rossellini, Roberto, 125, 129n.3

Rossen, Robert, 121

Rostock (Germany), 209

Rostotsky, Alex, 188

Rostow, Walt, 68, 76n.26

"Roter Wedding" (Busch), 195

Rudolf, Reginald, 203

Ruggles of Red Gap (film), 109

Ruhrgebiet, 208

Russia. *See* Soviet Union

Ryabov, Eugene, 188, 190

Saatchi & Saatchi, 292

Safra, Jacob, 291

Sahara (film), 89, 97n.25

Saigon, 172

St. James Theater (London), 21

Salle Pleyel (Paris), 151, 158

Salvemini, Gretna, 68

Salzburg Seminar: and American studies, 64–75; and the Cold War, 7, 68, 69–70; communist activity alleged at, 69, 77n.30; as East-West exchange station, 73, 79n.50; Europeans as receptive to, 71; European tastes catered to, 71; first seminar of 1947, 67–68, 76n.24; four factors in emergence of, 65–66; "The Globalization of American Popular Culture" session, 2–3; incorporation of, 66, 76n.24; literature on, 75n.16; origins of, 2, 66–67; shortcomings of, 73; tensions among Americans at, 70; and the U.S. State Department, 68, 69

Sampling, 212

Sampson, Edith, 174

Sandaloni, 125

Sartre, Jean-Paul, 158, 162n.48

Saturday Evening Post (magazine), 43

Saxophone, 182, 184

Scarface (film), 86

Scarlet Pimpernel, The (film), 109

Schiffmeister, 213

Schiller, Herbert, 288–89

Schirrmacher, Frank, 253

Schlatter, Richard, 76n.26

Schlesinger, Isadore W., 47–48

Schlesinger Organisation, 47

"Schlüsselkind" (Cora E.), 210

Schmidt, Oliver, 2, 7

Scientific management, 42

Scorsese, Martin, 117

Scott, Tony, 157

Search engines, 302

Sección Femenina (Spain), 112, 113

Second International Festival of Youth and Students (1950), 201

Second Language Movement (South Africa), 44–45

Secret Six (film), 89

Seeger, Gisela, 195

Segregation, 36, 155

Seitz, Konrad, 265

Selznick, David O., 89, 90, 97n.28

Senghor, Léopold, 162n.48

Senza pietà (film), 119
Sesame Street (television program), 138
Seven-Up, 273–74, 277
Sex on the Internet, 309–10, 314
Sex Pistols, 239
Shanghai, 180, 182, 185
Sharpeville massacre, 54
Sheridan, Philip, 23
Shinar, D., 289
Shopping malls: in South Africa, 34, 35, 56; in Turkey, 245–46
Shostakovich, Dmitri, 184
Shuster, George N., 68
Simons, Thomas W., 171
Simpsons, The (television program), 230–31
Sims, Zoot, 152
Since You Went Away (film), 89–90, 97n.28
Sinden, Donald, 109
Singapore, 299
Singer sewing machine, 59n.5
Sioux, 32n.23
Sitting Bull, 24, 32n.18
60/40 rule (East Germany), 202, 203
Skard, Sigmund, 72–73, 74n.5, 79nn. 49, 51
Sky TV, 291
Slagtersnek uprising, 36
Smith, Hamilton, 39
Smith, Henry Nash, 76n.27
Smith-Mundt Act of 1948, 68, 76n.29
Smuts, Jan, 51
Snake Pit, The (film), 93
Snows of Kilimanjaro, The (film), 111
Soap operas, 138, 140, 240, 244, 310
Soccer, 236, 237, 238
"Solidaritätslied, das" (Busch), 195
Some Like It Hot (film), 111
Sons of Gastarbeita (rap group), 208, 211
Sony Corporation, 292, 319
So Proudly We Hail (film), 89
Sorpasso, Il (film), 126
Sousa, John Philip, 219–23
South Africa: advertising industry in, 43; African Broadcasting Corporation, 47–48; Afrikaners, 36, 44–45,

49, 50, 55; Americanization of, 34–63; American television in, 34, 55–56, 57; antecedents of Americanization, 36–38; apartheid, 36, 49–55; automobile industry in, 43; autonomy from Britain, 51; Birdseye frozen-food in, 52; blackface minstrel shows in, 17, 21, 22, 46; borrowing from U.S. banks, 56–57, 63n.42; Britain's political role usurped by U.S., 34; British exports to, 39–40; Cape Town, 37; censorship in, 49; citrus industry, 48; consumer society created, 1919–38, 41–45; *The Cosby Show* in, 35, 56, 227; direct American investment in, 41, 50; entertainment in, 46–49; Export-Import Bank loans to, 54; farm implements imported from U.S., 38; Ford, South Africa, 41; fuel oils imported from U.S., 38; generational differences in Americanization, 35; Hollywood movies in, 35, 48–49, 57; *Die Huisgenoot* newspaper, 45; IBM in, 52; imperial preference policy, 40; infrastructure financed by U.S., 54; Kimberley, 38–39; management consultants in, 58; as market for American goods, 38; mass marketing in, 43–45; mass media in, 45–49; McDonald's in, 57–58; the mineral revolution, 38–40; Mixed Marriages Commission of 1939, 36; Mobil Oil refinery, 52; motion pictures in, 47–50; music in, 46–47; Nationalist-Labour Pact, 41, 43, 51; National Party, 45, 50, 51, 53, 55, 56; Natives' (Urban Areas) Act of 1923, 44; *Outspan* magazine, 43–44, 46, 60n.19; permit system, 40; pharmaceutical companies in, 52; phonograph sales in, 46; Port Elizabeth, 41, 42, 47, 50; postapartheid U.S. relations, 57–58; processed food in, 52; racial differences in Americanization, 35; rap music in, 57; rate of return on investment in, 52–53; recording industry in, 46; scientific management in, 42;

Sharpeville massacre, 54; shopping malls in, 34, 35, 56; as a special case, 36; subsidiaries of American companies in, 41–42, 51–52; Tariff Act of 1925, 41; television in, 48, 55–56, 57; *Umteteli wa Bantu* magazine, 44, 46; United Party, 51; uranium agreement with U.S., 53–54; U.S. as largest trading partner of, 41, 50; U.S. relations in 1970s and 1980s, 55–57; U.S. shoe industry importing skins from, 37; and U.S. strategic stockpiling program, 53; vaudeville in, 46; Wild West shows in, 46; Witwatersrand, 38, 39–40, 46; World Bank loans to, 54. *See also* Johannesburg

South African Broadcasting Corporation, 48, 55, 57

South African Business Efficiency (journal), 43

South African War of 1899–1902, 40

Soviet Union: American jazz competing with folk art and ballet of, 166; attempt to create mass culture, 186–87; Benny Goodman tour of, 167; jazz in, 166–67, 179–91; jazz tours of, 167; saxophone banned in, 182, 184; State Jazz Orchestra, 181, 182; *Stiliagi,* 184; U.S. cultural exchange program with, 167

Spaghetti westerns, 128

Spain: American film distributors boycotting, 108; censorship of Hollywood movies in, 108–11; cinemas per capita in 1947, 101; Classification Commission, 106; consumer society in, 114; *Destino* on Hollywood movies, 104–5; dubbing of Hollywood movies in, 106, 108; Eisenhower's 1959 visit to, 105; Franco's cinematographic policy, 105–8; Hollywood movies in Franco's, 7, 100–15; isolation from international community, 105; motion picture classification system, 109; motion picture industry before civil war, 106, 115n.10; the "New

Spanish Cinema," 108; radio soap operas in, 115n.4; Sección Femenina, 112, 113; Superior Censorship Committee, 109; topolino subculture, 102–3, 112–13; Vice-Secretariat of Popular Education, 109; women in Franco's, 102–3, 104, 111–13

Spellbound (film), 93

Sports: American football in Britain, 236–38; basketball, 139; Johnson-Jeffries fight, 49; merchandising, 236–37; on Nigerian television, 139; soccer, 236, 237, 238; wrestling, 139

Stadium rock, 239

Stahl, John M., 110

Standard Oil, 38

Stanwyck, Barbara, 104

Starr, Frederick, 182–83, 185–86

Starr report, 314, 322

"Stars and Stripes Forever" (Sousa), 220, 221–22, 223

Star TV, 291

State Department. *See* U.S. State Department

State Jazz Orchestra (Soviet Union), 181, 182

Steiger, Rod, 233, 234

Stender nonalcoholic beer, 276

Stern (magazine), 252

Sterns, Marshall, 176n.17

Stevenson, Robert L., 289, 291

Stiliagi, 184

Stites, Richard, 186

Stokvis, Pieter R. D., 32n.11

Stone, Sharon, 318

"Store and forward" protocol, 295

Story of GI Joe, The (film), 92, 98n.40

Strand, Paul, 131n.16

Strauss, Botho, 263–64, 267

Strauss, Franz-Josef, 203

Strauss, Johann, 221

Streetcar Named Desire (film), 131n.16

Sturges, Preston, 89

Sturmthal, Adolf, 71

Sullivan, John, 242

Sun (newspaper), 291

Sweeney, James, 76n.26

Syberberg, Hans-Jürgen, 261–63

Synergy, 290, 303, 324

"Tales of the Vienna Woods" (Strauss), 221
Talking Heads, 239
Tariff Act of 1925 (South Africa), 41
Tatum, Art, 151
Technical Committee on Privatization and Commercialization (TCPC) (Nigeria), 135
Teldec, 196
Telecommunications satellites, 289
Telefunken company, 196
Telegraph, 294
Telenovelas, 136
Telephone, 294, 295
Television: Britain's Channel 4, 236, 237; children's broadcasting, 138; free enterprise and public potential of, 318; Internet-ready television sets, 297; in Latin America, 289; Murdoch holdings, 291; in Nigeria, 132–46; soap operas, 138, 140, 240, 244, 310; in South Africa, 48, 55–56, 57. *See also* American television; Television news
Television (band), 239
Television news: CNN, 137, 279, 280, 293, 302, 303; *Jim Lehrer Newshour*, 137; in Nigeria, 135, 137
Temple, Shirley, 102
Ténot, Frank, 160n.3, 161n.23
Texas Jack, 24, 46
Thailand, 172
Thatcherism, 318
Théâtre des Champs-Elysées (Paris), 151
Thimig, Helene, 2, 67
Thistlewaite, Frank, 68
Thomas, Hugh, 102
Thompson, Hunter S., 231
Thompson group of newspapers, 291
Through Every Conceivable Variation (television program), 134
Ticketmaster, 325
Tic Tac Toe (rap group), 215
Time (magazine), 301
Times of London (newspaper), 291
Time/Warner, 301, 319, 320

Tirali, Naim, 250n.4
To Be Or Not To Be (film), 108
Tocqueville, Alexis de, 153
Tokyo, 221
Tokyo Disneyland, 219, 223–26
Tokyo-Mitsubishi bank, 223
Topolino subculture, 102–3, 112–13
To Secure These Rights (U.S. government document), 50
Touretzky, David, 308n.22
Transnational (multinational) corporations, 291, 318, 321, 324
Triumphalism, 91, 92, 164
Truman, Harry, 49–50, 53, 105, 199, 201
Truman Doctrine, 241
Tudyka, Kurt, 253
Tunstall, Jeremy, 288, 305
Turin (Italy), 286
Turkey: American popular culture in, 242–50; Ankara, 246, 247; *arabesque*, 249, 250n.13; consumerism in, 241, 244; Democrat Party, 241, 250n.5; the dollar used in, 244; folk heroes displaced by American cultural icons, 248; food traditions yielding to global culture, 245; fundamentalism in, 248–49; German *Gastarbeiter* and rap music, 208, 211; Istanbul, 246, 247, 248; mass media promoting Americanization in, 244; new homes looking American, 247; shopping malls in, 245–46; sprawling suburbs in, 247; Virtue Party, 248, 249; Welfare Party, 248; youth of the 1960s exposed to American culture, 247
Turkish coffee, 245
Turner, Lana, 104
TV Nation (Moore), 232
Twain, Mark, 39
Twentieth Century–Fox, 87–88

Ulbricht, Walter, 203, 206n.29
Ullman, Tracey, 230
Umteteli wa Bantu (magazine), 44, 46
Undokai, 220–21
United Kingdom. *See* Britain

United Party (South Africa), 51
Universalism, 72
Up in Arms (film), 88
Uranium, 53–54, 169
USA Today (newspaper), 325
Usenet discussion groups, 303
U.S. State Department: and Hollywood movies after World War II, 87; jazz tours sponsored by, 8, 157, 163–79; and the Salzburg Seminar, 68, 69; strategy for dealing with racism, 174, 178n.45
U2 (band), 239

Valli, Alida, 128
Varis, Tapio, 289
Vaudeville, 46
Viacom, 311, 319
Victoria, Queen, 25
Video clips, 303
Vidor, Charles, 110
Vietnam, 172
Vihlen, Elizabeth, 8
Villers, Michel de, 151, 157
Violence, 313
Virginia Jubilee Singers, 46, 57
Virginian, The (Wister), 24
Virginia Serenaders, 19–20
Virtue Party (Turkey), 248, 249
Visconti, Luchino, 127, 129n.3, 131n.16
Vizcaino Casas, F., 107
Voice of America, 157, 163, 167, 176n.18, 189
Von Eschen, Penny M., 8, 157
Von Holtum, Henrik, 213
Von Westphalen, Joseph, 269n.33
Voortrekkers, 36
Vorhaus, Bernard, 121

Wagnleitner, Reinhold, 3–4, 9, 164
Wallace, Henry A., 91, 95
War films, 90, 97n.32
Warner Brothers, 88, 93, 303
Warren, Robert Penn, 153
"Washington Post March" (Sousa), 220
Washington Review Board, 83
Washoe Brand tobacco, 275
Waterloo Bridge (film), 108

Waters, Muddy, 239
Wattenscheid (Germany), 208
WDR radio station (West Germany), 196
Weather Channel, The, 325
Wedell, E. G., 289
Weill, Kurt, 195
Weimann, Gabriel, 9, 319
Weimar Republic, 194–95, 254
Weinert, Erich, 195
Weissmann, Karlheinz, 252–53
Welfare Party (Turkey), 248
Welles, Orson, 103, 109, 121
Wells, Alan, 288, 289
Wenders, Wim, 257–58
West, American: in advertising, 275–76, 278; freedom associated with, 274–75; and Ireland, 235
West cigarettes, 276
West Coast jazz, 151, 152, 160n.8
Western Nigeria Government Broadcasting Corporation, 133
Western Nigeria Television (WNTV), 133, 135, 145n.2
West Germany. *See* Federal Republic of Germany
Westinghouse Electric Corp., 321
Weston, Randy, 163, 173
Westward Ho Smoking Tobacco, 275
Wheel of Fortune, The (television program), 244
Whiteman, Paul, 156
White Nigger Posse (rap group), 212
Who, The, 239
"Why We Fight" series of films, 87
Wilder, Billy, 93, 110, 111
Wild West shows: in Australia, 18; racial stereotypes in, 7; in South Africa, 46; Texas Jack, 24, 46; triumph of the Western over the "primitive" in, 18. *See also* Buffalo Bill's Wild West
Williams, Gardner, 38
Williams, Samuel F., 69, 71, 77n.30
Wilson (film), 90, 97n.30
Wilson, David, 83–85, 95
Wilson, John, 176n.17
Wilson, Michael, 121
Wilson, Theodore A., 7, 117, 123

Wilson, Woodrow, 92, 98n.37
Windmoeller, Eva, 196
Winfrey, Oprah, 138
Winning, 237–38
Winter, Rolf, 251–52, 254, 256
Winters, Shelley, 125
Wister, Owen, 24
Witwatersrand, 38, 39–40, 46
WNTV (Western Nigeria Television), 133, 135, 145n.2
Women: in Americanization of postwar Japan, 224; cheerleaders, 237; Depression and World War II changing role of, 104; in Franco's Spain, 102–3, 104, 111–13; Internet use by, 296, 313; in jazz, 165; in *Mildred Pierce*, 93; in postwar Hollywood movies, 104; in rap music, 210; and Turkish fundamentalism, 248–49
World Bank, 54
World's Columbian Exposition (1893), 219, 220
World Student Relief (WSR), 67, 76n.23
World War I, 5, 41
World War II: and American popular culture's spread, 6; Hollywood movies during, 83–91; motion picture attendance boom during, 117; Russian jazz during, 181; U.S.–South African trade increasing during, 50;

war films, 90, 97n.32; women's role changed by, 104
World Wide Web (WWW): advertising for, 305; advertising on, 302; associative links on, 303; children's sites, 312–13; control of, 299; as European invention, 317; as information transfer protocol, 295; media organizations on, 302–4; movie and soap opera sites, 310; NBC–Microsoft project, 305; Netscape Navigator, 317; Starr report on, 314, 322; on television, 297; video clips on, 303
Wrestling, 139
Wright, Benjamin, 76n.26

X symbol, 208

Yahoo, 302, 314, 320
You Can't Take It With You (film), 103
Young, Harold, 109
Youth culture, 282

Zanuck, Darryl F., 90, 97n.30
Zavattini, Cesare, 131n.16
Zinnemann, Fred, 111
"Zip Coon," 21
Zivilisation, 255
Zukrigl, Ina, 9
Zulu Nation (rap organization), 210